THE EVOLUTION OF THE JUVENILE COURT

YOUTH, CRIME, AND JUSTICE SERIES

General Editors: Franklin E. Zimring and David S. Tanenhaus

Homeroom Security: School Discipline in an Age of Fear
Aaron Kupchik

Kids, Cops, and Confessions: Inside the Interrogation Room
Barry C. Feld

Choosing the Future for American Juvenile Justice
Edited by Franklin E. Zimring and David S. Tanenhaus

Juvenile Justice in Global Perspective
Edited by Franklin E. Zimring, Máximo Langer, and David S. Tanenhaus

The Evolution of the Juvenile Court: Race, Politics, and the Criminalizing of Juvenile Justice
Barry C. Feld

The Evolution of the Juvenile Court

Race, Politics, and the Criminalizing of Juvenile Justice

Barry C. Feld

NEW YORK UNIVERSITY PRESS

New York

NEW YORK UNIVERSITY PRESS
New York
www.nyupress.org

First published in paperback in 2019

References to Internet websites (URLs) were accurate at the time of writing. Neither the author nor New York University Press is responsible for URLs that may have expired or changed since the manuscript was prepared.

Library of Congress Cataloging-in-Publication Data
Names: Feld, Barry C., author.
Title: The evolution of the juvenile court : race, politics, and the criminalizing of juvenile justice / Barry C. Feld.
Other titles: Youth, crime, and justice series.
Description: New York : New York University Press, [2017] | Series: Youth, crime, and justice series | "Also available as an ebook." | Includes bibliographical references and index.
Identifiers: LCCN 2017003870| ISBN 978-1-4798-9569-4 (cl. ; alk. paper) | ISBN 978-1-4798-7129-2 (pb. ; alk. paper)
Subjects: LCSH: Juvenile courts—United States—History. | Juvenile justice, Administration of—United States—History. | Juvenile delinquency—United States—History. | Discrimination in juvenile justice administration—United States—History. | Sex discrimination in justice administration—United States—History. | Juvenile delinquents—United States.
Classification: LCC KF9794 .F45 2017 | DDC 345.73/08109—dc23
LC record available at https://lccn.loc.gov/2017003870

New York University Press books are printed on acid-free paper, and their binding materials are chosen for strength and durability. We strive to use environmentally responsible suppliers and materials to the greatest extent possible in publishing our books.

Manufactured in the United States of America

10 9 8 7 6 5 4 3 2 1

Also available as an ebook

For Patricia, love of my life

CONTENTS

ACKNOWLEDGMENTS

I received institutional and personal assistance from many people to write this book. For more than four decades, the University of Minnesota Law School has been my intellectual home, a marvelous place to work, and strongly supportive of scholarly endeavors. I cannot adequately describe my gratitude to Dean David Wippman for his help to me and encouragement of this project. Three research assistants—Alicia Paller, Class of 2015; Carolyn Isaac, Class of 2016; Nadia Anguiano-Wehde, Class of 2017—provided exceptional help during the writing of this book and for which I am very grateful. The University of Minnesota Law School Library provides extraordinary backing for faculty. David Zopfi-Jordan and Connie Lenz retrieved resources with speed and efficiency. I am indebted to all these kind and generous people.

The Robina Institute of Criminal Law and Criminal Justice sponsored a conference at the University of Minnesota Law School in May 2016 to review an earlier draft of this book. I am grateful to its co-directors, Richard Frase and Kevin Reitz, for enabling this conclave. Richard Frase, Herbert Kritzer, Aaron Kupchik, Kate Kruse, Kelly Mitchell, Perry Moriearty, Ashley Nellis, Myron Orfield, Shelly Schaefer, Francis Shen, Michael Smith, David Tanenhaus, Michael Tonry, and Geoff Ward attended the conference, read the entire manuscript, provided detailed critiques, and suggested many ways to improve the book. Donna Bishop, Dan Mears, Simon Singer, and Franklin Zimring read the manuscript and provided additional guidance to help me find the through-line. Although I have tried to respond to their invaluable reviews, I alone am responsible for the final iteration of this book.

This book culminates several decades of research and writing about juvenile justice. I have published earlier versions of parts of several chapters in criminology journals, law reviews, books, and book chapters, although all have been substantially revised, rewritten, and changed beyond recognition. I am grateful to the following who have kindly allowed me to use my previous works: University of Minnesota Law Review for "Criminalizing Juvenile Justice: Rules of Procedure for the Juvenile Court," 69 *Minnesota Law Review* 141 (1984); Boston University Law School for "The Juvenile Court Meets the Principle of Offense," 68 *Boston University Law Review* 821 (1988); Oxford University Press for *Bad Kids: Race and the Transformation of the Juvenile Court* (1999); Wake Forest Law School for "The Constitutional Tension between *Apprendi* and *McKeiver*: Sentence Enhancements Based on Delinquency Convictions and the Quality of Justice in Juvenile Courts," 38 *Wake Forest Law Review* 1111 (2003); University of Minnesota Law Review for "Race, Politics, and Juvenile Justice: The Warren Court and the Conservative Backlash," 87 *Minnesota Law Review* 1447 (2003); Sage Publications for "Violent Girls or Relabeled Status Offenders? An Alternative Interpretation of the Data," 55 *Crime & Delinquency* 241 (2009); University of Mississippi Law School for "*T.L.O.* and *Redding*'s Unanswered (Misanswered) Fourth Amendment Questions: Few Rights and Fewer Remedies," 80 *Mississippi Law Journal* 847 (2011); Oxford University Press for "Procedural Rights in Juvenile Courts: Competence and Consequences," in Barry C. Feld and Donna Bishop, co-editors, *Oxford Handbook on Juvenile Crime and Juvenile Justice* (2012); Oxford University Press for "Transfer of Juveniles to Criminal Court," in Barry C. Feld and Donna Bishop, co-editors, *Oxford Handbook on Juvenile Crime and Juvenile Justice* (2012); University of Minnesota Law School for "Adolescent Criminal Responsibility, Proportionality, and Sentencing Policy: *Roper, Graham, Miller/Jackson*, and the Youth Discount," 31 *Journal of Law & Inequality* 263 (Spring 2013); Ohio State Law School for "The Youth Discount: Old Enough to Do the Crime, Too Young to Do the Time," 11 *Ohio State Journal of Criminal Law* 107 (2014).

I have dedicated this book to my wife, Patricia Feld. She has been the love of my life since fortune/fate/karma brought us together on a bridge. Her unconditional love and unstinting support have enabled me to grow personally and professionally. As parents, we have watched our children, Ari Daniel and Julia Elise, grow into spectacular adults. There are no words adequate to express my gratitude to Patty for the life we share. I promise that with the completion of this book, I will be a better and more attentive partner.

Barry C. Feld
Effie, MN

Introduction

The juvenile court lies at the intersection of two domains—youth policy and crime policy. How should the legal system respond when the kid is a criminal and the criminal is a kid? This raises another question: how and why do we think about children and criminals as we do? To further complicate these questions, how do race, ethnicity, and gender affect the ways we think about children and crime control? Moreover, how and why have these ideas changed over the past century and affected juvenile and criminal justice policies? Finally, how should the lessons of the recent past affect the justice system we design for youth going forward?

Since the juvenile court's creation more than a century ago, it has evolved though four periods—the Progressive Era, the Due Process Era, the Get Tough Era, and the contemporary Kids Are Different Era. These historical periods reflect larger social processes, do not divide neatly, and features from one era continue into and overlap with those of the next. But in each period, juvenile justice policies have reflected different views about children, crime control, race and gender, and appropriate ways to address youths' misconduct. In the midst of the current era in which we recognize again that children are not miniature adults, we have an opportunity to reimagine a policy and legal foundation for a more effective justice system for youth. This book examines the relationship between social structural factors and changes in juvenile justice policy, especially the complex changes that have occurred over the past half century.

Ideas about childhood, crime control, race, and gender are socially constructed. Social constructions assign meaning to objects or events and to people's relationships or understanding of them. Although these ideas appear natural or obvious to the people within a society who accept and internalize them, they are cultural artifacts and change with social conditions. In this analysis, I treat the juvenile court as the dependent variable—an institution whose meaning and practices change in response to other factors. Our ideas about children and crime control are intervening variables that influence the structure and function of juvenile courts. Changes in the economy, cities, families, and racial and ethnic demography affect our ideas about youth, crime, and the juvenile court. These societal factors operate through political processes in which legislators enact and courts apply laws that shape juvenile justice. Juvenile courts are statutory entities and state legislatures have considerable latitude to define their jurisdiction, procedures, and jurisprudence.

Over the past century, two competing social constructions or visions of adolescents have influenced policies toward young offenders. On the one hand, judges and law makers may characterize them as children—immature, vulnerable, and dependent. In this view, the state would take a protectionist stance to nurture and promote their welfare. On the other hand, law makers may characterize young people as quasi-adults—mature and responsible. In this view, the state would endorse a liberationist perspective, emphasize their autonomy and self-determination, and hold them accountable for their misbehavior. Despite the seeming contradiction between these characterizations, I argue that judges and legislators selectively choose between the two constructs—immature versus responsible—to maximize social control of young people. States treat juveniles like adults when formal equality results in practical inequality and use special juvenile court procedures that prove an advantage to the state.

Strategies of crime control mark the second idea shaping juvenile justice. When people violate the criminal law, legal scholars and criminologists typically differentiate between retributivist and utilitarian sanctions—deterrence, incapacitation, or rehabilitation. Theories of punishment reflect assumptions about whether peoples' behavior is deliberately chosen or the product of antecedent forces—free will versus determinism. Juvenile courts' historic claims to rehabilitate young offenders elicit the traditional dichotomy between treatment and punishment. Treatment focuses on offenders—what antecedent forces caused them to act as they did and how can we reform them and improve their life chances. Punishment focuses on the offense committed and imposes sanctions to denounce the act, alter the offender's calculus, or prevent its reoccurrence. Juvenile courts' founders believed that children were not autonomous, more dependent than adults on their families and communities, their behavior more determined than chosen, and that they should be treated rather than punished.

Although Progressive reformers proffered rehabilitation as the main justification for a separate juvenile court, diversion from criminal courts provided a second rationale at its inception and remains its primary virtue today. Regardless of juvenile courts' ability to rehabilitate children, simply deflecting them from criminal courts avoids their destructive consequences. Diversion constitutes a passive alternative that does less harm. Although juvenile courts then and now seldom achieve their rehabilitative goals, they shield youths from far worse life-altering punishment and collateral consequences.

The competing conceptions of childhood—immaturity and incompetence versus maturity and competence—and differing strategies of crime control—treatment or diversion versus punishment—affect the substantive goals and procedural means that juvenile courts use. Substantive law defines rights, obligations and duties, and how members of society are to behave. Procedural law defines the process for making, administering, and enforcing substantive law. Juvenile courts' ends and means— substance and procedure—represent the purposes of intervention and the process to achieve them when children break the law. How has the child become what he is, what can be done to change him, and how and who makes these determinations? These questions involve judgments about adolescents' culpability and competence. Culpability focuses on youths' mental state at the time of the crime and criminal responsibility. To what extent is a youth responsible for his actions and his conduct blameworthy? Substantive goals raise issues of treatment and punishment, diminished responsibility, and deserved consequences. Substantive questions—such as what should be done with this youth—arise when juvenile courts detain and sentence delinquents, transfer them to criminal court, and sentence them as adults. Competence involves the ability to do something successfully or efficiently. It focuses on youths' capacity to employ rights and ability to understand and participate in the legal process. Procedural issues involve youths' competence to stand trial, ability to exercise *Miranda* rights, right to counsel, and right to a jury trial.

Historical variations in juvenile courts' substantive goals— delinquency dispositions, transfer, and criminal sentencing—reflect lawmakers' and judges' ambivalent assessments of youths' culpability, criminal responsibility, and treatment or punishment. Juvenile courts' procedural means reflect conflicted appraisals of their developmental characteristics, decision-making capacities, and ability to exercise legal rights. Competing characterizations of youths' culpability and competence—immature or responsible, treatment/diversion or punishment, capable or inept—influenced juvenile courts' procedure and substance from their inception.

What independent factors account for changes in ideas about youth, crime control, and juvenile courts? Figure I.1 depicts some structural factors—economy, urbanization, family, ethnicity/race, and politics— that shape ideas and epochs of juvenile justice. These, as well as other, independent factors interact with and influence each other. Figure I.1 represents a generic way to think about these associations rather than a causal model. In each era, changes in economy affected the organization of cities, for example, during the transition from a rural agricultural to an urban industrial society or more recently from an industrial to an information/service economy. In each period, structural changes affected the configuration of cities, the structure and function of families, and how the state and parents socialized and controlled children, for example, earlier through integration into the work force versus current prolonged dependency. Structural economic changes contributed to urban demographic transformations as earlier waves of European immigrants and subsequently internal African American migrants flooded into and altered cities, and posed different problems of assimilation and integration. Finally, juvenile courts are legislative creations and political processes determine their institutional contours. Policy makers— legislators, judges, youth advocates, and others—contest ideas about children and crime control in the guise of debates about juvenile courts' age of jurisdiction, transfer methods, delinquency, and criminal sanctions. These debates change in response to social and political forces that affect youth and crime policy.

Youths' ethnicity, race, and gender mark another social construction around which juvenile justice policies have changed over the past century. In the early twentieth century, waves of immigrants from Southern and Eastern Europe entered the United States. Juvenile courts were one of several institutions Progressive reformers created to assimilate, accul-

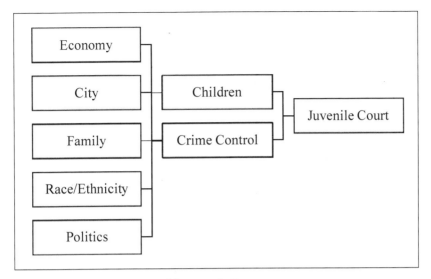

Figure I.1. Social Construction of the Juvenile Court

turate, and prepare them for citizenship. A half century later, the Great Migration of African Americans from Southern farms to Northern and Western cities posed challenges of integration in a society deeply divided by race.

The legal and political responses to African Americans during the second half of the twentieth century have had two distinct manifestations. During the 1950s and 1960s, the Supreme Court imposed equality norms on Southern states that embraced a segregated Jim Crow legal system and sought to bring Blacks into full participation as citizens. The decisions reflected a shift in constitutional jurisprudence to protect individual and civil rights. The Great Migration of African Americans in the decades before and after World War II increased their urbanization, placed racial equality and civil rights on the national political agenda, and motivated the Court to address racial discrimination and criminal and juvenile justice administration. The Court's desegregation decisions in *Brown v. Board of Education*, criminal procedure decisions like *Mapp v. Ohio* and *Miranda v. Arizona*, and juvenile court opinions like *In re Gault* share the common but unstated goals of protecting minority rights, limiting states' coercive powers, and bringing Blacks into the legal and cultural mainstream.

An almost immediate backlash to Blacks' civil rights gains began in the 1960s as Republican politicians pursued a Southern strategy, used crime and welfare as wedge issues to appeal to white voters' racial animus, and advocated get tough policies that affected juvenile and criminal justice administration. These repressive strategies had a disparate impact and disproportionately excluded Blacks from civil society. For adult offenders, it led to the era of mass incarceration. For younger offenders, get tough policies exacerbated racial differences in juvenile justice administration.

I focus primarily on the experience of African American children in the juvenile justice system. The justice system's response to various groups—African Americans, Latinos, Native Americans, Asians, ethnic Europeans, and others—unfolds against the centrality of whiteness in defining race relations. But all racial and ethnic groups did not share the same history or face equally destructive discrimination. The legacy of American racism is rooted in the original constitutional compromise that allowed slave-holding Southern states to count Blacks as "three fifths of all other persons" for legislative apportionment purposes, to increase their representation in the House and electoral votes and to enable them to exercise disproportional political power until the Civil War. Despite some racial progress, the integration and inclusion of Blacks remains what Gunnar Myrdal described three-quarters of a century ago as the unresolved *American Dilemma: The Negro Problem and Modern Democracy*. The Supreme Court's civil rights and due process decisions explicitly or implicitly addressed issues of inequality and injustice toward Blacks. The Get Tough Era of juvenile justice unfolded against the backdrop of the deindustrialization of urban America, the emergence of a Black underclass living in concentrated poverty, and the confluence of crack cocaine and gun violence.

Because of the unique experience of African Americans, there is more extensive research on Black children in the juvenile justice system than of young Hispanics, Native Americans, Asians, or members of other ethnic groups. Some analysts have examined other groups' encounters with systems of social control. David Adams's *Education for Extinction: American Indians and the Boarding School Experience* describes the boarding schools for Native American youth designed to acculturate and "civilize" them. Miroslava Chávez-García's *States of Delinquency:*

Race and Science in the Making of California's Juvenile Justice System examines the experiences of Hispanic youth in California. Other scholars can, should, and will write books about other racial and ethnic groups' encounters with juvenile justice. But that is not my goal in this book. No other group bears the legacy of slavery and the savage dominion of Jim Crow. No other group has been the direct target of criminal justice policies with deliberate disparate impact. Moreover, the political and legal responses to African Americans provide the connection between the Warren Court's emphases on civil rights and procedural justice and subsequent efforts to get tough on youth crime. Only the unique social and political status of African Americans can account for Republicans' Southern strategy to exploit urban crime and politicize juvenile and criminal justice policy.

Historically, juvenile courts' responses to girls have differed from the ones to boys. Industrialization brought young women to cities and exposed them to the hazards of prostitution and sexual exploitation. During the Progressive Era, Victorian sensibilities and concerns about female sexuality encouraged regulation of teenage girls for waywardness, incorrigibility, and sexual precocity. More recently, policy makers have recast girls' acting-out behavior as violent misconduct. Despite changes in practices, juvenile courts' responses to girls continue to differ from those to boys and reflect differences in the social construction of gender.

I divide this book into four parts corresponding with the four eras of juvenile justice—the Progressive Era, the Due Process Era, the Get Tough Era, and the Kids Are Different Era. Part I (Chapter 1) provides an overview of the early juvenile court—its structural origins, philosophical underpinnings, historic mission, and discriminatory practices. Part II (Chapter 2) examines the Warren Court's due process revolution of the 1960s—its response to racial inequality, its decisions to grant delinquents some procedural safeguards, and its intended and unintended consequences. Part III examines some causes and consequences of the Get Tough Era. Chapters 3 and 4 examine why and how perceptions of youth and crime changed during the Get Tough Era of the 1980s and 1990s. Chapter 3 examines macro-structural forces and political processes that created segregated areas of concentrated poverty. In the 1970s, factory closures produced massive layoffs that disproportionally affected minority workers. In the 1980s, crack cocaine and gun violence devastated inner cities reeling from deindustrialization and led to an increase in Black youth homicide. Chapter 4 examines the politics of race and crime. Conservative politicians used racial appeals, manipulated and exploited public fears, and waged a succession of wars on crime, drugs, and youth that disproportionately affected Black residents of inner cities. Chapter 5 examines punitive shifts in juvenile justice policies—transfer, detention, and sentencing—during the 1980s and 1990s that produced substantial racial disparities. Chapter 6 focuses on changing responses to females that reframed status offenders as violent girls. Chapter 7 examines the school-to-prison pipeline that paralleled punitive changes in juvenile justice and had a disproportionate impact on minority students. Part IV examines adolescent culpability and competence through the lens of Supreme Court decisions reaffirming that "children are different." Chapter 8 reviews the trilogy of Court decisions—*Roper*, *Graham*, and *Miller*—that emphasized youths' diminished responsibility. The Court relied on developmental psychology and neuroscience research to limit the most severe sentences states inflict on youths. Recognizing that children are different also implicates juveniles' competence to exercise rights and the quality of justice in juvenile courts. Chapter 9 examines research on adolescents' compromised competence, legal standards that treat juveniles like adults, juvenile courts' procedural deficiencies, and the heightened risks of wrongful convictions. The Epilogue draws on contemporary understanding of adolescent culpability and competence to envision a justice system for children. But juvenile courts do not directly cause delinquency and can do little to ameliorate its root causes— child poverty—which require more fundamental change.

CHAPTER 1. THE PROGRESSIVE JUVENILE COURT. At the end of the nineteenth century, the transition from an agrarian to a manufacturing economy increased immigration and fostered rapid urbanization.[1] Industrialization attracted massive waves of European immigrants who crowded into urban ghettos and altered the structure of cities. Assimilating and acculturating people who differed in language, religion, and culture posed challenges for the Anglo-Protestant Americans who had preceded them. The shift from family farms and shops to factories altered the roles of women and children. During this period, upper- and middle-class child-savers promoted a social construction of children as vulnerable, immature, and dependent, who required protection and supervision.[2] Positivist criminology attributed criminal behavior to external antecedent forces and reformers adopted discretionary policies to rehabilitate offenders—probation, parole, indeterminate sentences, and juvenile courts.[3] They created a separate justice system to shield children from criminal courts, jails, and prisons. Two goals animated juvenile courts' creators: an interventionist rationale and a diversionary one. The more expansive interventionist vision expected juvenile courts to identify causes of youths' misbehavior, to intervene, and to promote their development into responsible adults. Juvenile courts' less articulated diversionary purpose was to minimize the harms the criminal justice system inflicted on young people. They could accomplish their diversionary goal simply by providing an alternative to criminal courts even if their rehabilitative goal proved more elusive. Juvenile courts melded the new ideology of childhood with the new theory of crime control, introduced a judicial-welfare alternative to remove children from the criminal justice system, and promised individualized treatment in a nonpunitive child welfare system. Juvenile courts' rehabilitative mission envisioned a specialized judge trained in social work and child development whose empathy and insight would enable him to make dispositions in a child's best interests.[4] Progressives defined the court's jurisdiction broadly to include youths accused of crimes, noncriminal-status offenders at risk to become delinquents, and abused and neglected children. Juvenile courts' rehabilitative dispositions focused on youths' future welfare rather than their past offenses and could continue for the duration of minority. The courts' founders conceived of children as immature and irresponsible and opposed procedural safeguards that could impede open communication between judge and child.[5] Progressive reformers intended juvenile courts to discriminate: to control poor and immigrant children, to assimilate and Americanize them, and to distinguish between their own children and other people's children.[6] They exhibited less solicitude toward Black youngsters, most of whom remained in the South. While probation was the disposition of first resort, the institutions to which judges disproportionately committed poor and immigrant children more closely resembled youth prisons than clinics. Reformers exhibited special concern about females exposed to the corrupting influences of a rapidly industrializing society. Juvenile courts' status jurisdiction enabled them to intervene and regulate girls' noncriminal behavior such as sexual activity and immorality.[7]

CHAPTER 2. THE DUE PROCESS REVOLUTION AND THE JU-VENILE COURT. In the decades prior to and after World War II, the Great Migration from the rural South to the industrial North and West increased the urbanization of Blacks, placed issues of racial equality and civil rights on the national political agenda, and provided impetus for constitutional and legislative reforms.[8] The outbreak of World War I in 1914 curtailed European immigration and created a demand for southern Black laborers to work in northern factories. When Blacks left rural farms, they almost always moved to cities. In the post–World War II era, public policies and private practices forced them to live primarily in racially segregated ghettoes. With the urban influx, whites moved from cities to suburbs in ever larger numbers. In the 1950s and 1960s, a more assertive civil rights movement initially challenged segregation in the South and emerged as a social movement against racism throughout the country. In the decade between *Brown v. Board of Education* in 1954 and the passage of the Civil Rights Act in 1964, the Court and Congress adopted norms of racial equality and eliminated the legal foundations of segregation. Youth crime increased in the 1960s as baby boom children reached adolescence. The increased urbanization of Blacks led to higher crime rates in minority areas. Race riots rocked many American cities between 1964 and 1968. These broader structural and demographic changes and their effects provided the backdrop for the Warren Court's civil rights decisions, criminal procedure rulings, and juvenile court opinions. Its criminal procedure decisions reflected an attempt to protect minority citizens and to limit states' authority. The 1967 President's Crime Commission *Task Force Report on Juvenile Delinquency and Youth Crime* revealed juvenile courts' procedural deficiencies, inadequate correctional institutions, and racial disparities. Drawing on its critique, *In re Gault* highlighted the disjunction between juvenile courts' rehabilitative rhetoric—long used to justify the dearth of procedural safeguards—and the reality of court and correctional practices. Mandating procedural safeguards, the Court envisioned youths as competent to exercise legal rights and to participate in an adversarial system. Subsequent decisions further criminalized delinquency proceedings. *In re Winship* required states to prove delinquents' guilt by the criminal law standard of proof beyond a reasonable doubt. *Breed v. Jones* applied the ban on double jeopardy based on the functional equivalence of criminal trials and delinquency proceedings. However, *McKeiver v. Pennsylvania* denied delinquents the constitutional right to a jury trial available to criminal defendants because it might adversely affect juvenile courts' informality, flexibility, and confidentiality. Although granting delinquents some procedural rights might impair juvenile courts' ability to intervene in children's lives, safeguards would not impede their ability to divert youths and avoid the harms of the criminal justice system. But granting delinquents some safeguards legitimated increasingly punitive penalties that fell most heavily on minority offenders. The Court's due process revolution coincided with a synergy of campus disorders, escalating crime rates, urban racial rebellions, dissatisfaction with the treatment model, and emerging politics of crime that prompted calls for a return to classical criminal law and paved the way for get tough policies.[9]

CHAPTER 3. THE GET TOUGH ERA I: STRUCTURAL CHANGE AND YOUTH CRIME. Structural, economic, and racial demographic changes in American cities during the 1970s and 1980s contributed to escalating Black youth homicide rates at the end of the 1980s and provided the context within which states adopted get tough policies.[10] The Great Migration increased the concentration of impoverished African Americans consigned to inner-city ghettoes. Federal housing, highway, and mortgage policies combined with bank redlining and real estate blockbusting and related sales practices to create increasingly poor minority urban cores surrounded by predominantly white affluent suburbs. Unlike earlier European immigrants who provided valuable labor during the period of rapid industrialization, Black internal migrants arrived to face a shrinking manufacturing sector. Beginning in the early 1970s, the United States began to shift from a manufacturing to an information and service economy. The globalization of manufacturing and technological innovations eliminated many jobs of less skilled workers and produced a bifurcation of economic opportunities based on education and technical skills. The economic changes adversely affected Blacks more deeply than other groups because of their more recent entry into the manufacturing economy, their vulnerability in the social stratification system, their lower average educational attainment, and their spatial isolation from sectors of job growth. In the 1980s, deindustrialization and white flight left an impoverished Black underclass trapped in urban ghettos.[11] The introduction of crack cocaine and proliferation of guns sparked turf wars over control of drug markets. Black youth homicide rates sharply escalated and gun violence provided political impetus to transform juvenile justice policies.[12]

CHAPTER 4. THE GET TOUGH ERA II: POLITICS OF RACE AND CRIME. Following *Brown v. Board of Education*, civil rights activists responded to Southern whites' "massive resistance" to integration with direct action and civil disobedience. Southern politicians and law enforcement responded violently to disruptive strategies, described activists as "outside agitators," and conflated civil rights protests with crime. In the 1960s, the baby boom rise in youth crime and urban racial disorders evoked fear of crime in the streets. National Republican politicians decried a crisis of law and order, pursued a Southern strategy to appeal to white Southern voters' racial antipathy and resistance to school integration, and engineered a conservative backlash to foster a political realignment around race and public policy issues.[13] Conservatives rejected structural root-cause explanations of crime and poverty and instead attributed them to individuals' bad choices, personal character failings, and cultural shortcomings. Republicans' Southern strategy appealed to various constituencies—white Southerners, suburbanites, socially conservative ethnic Catholics and blue-collar workers—by using coded anti-Black rhetoric. Political divisions about race and social policy enabled conservative politicians to advocate punitive crime and welfare policies for electoral advantage. In the 1980s and 1990s, those policies produced mass incarceration for adult offenders, fostered changes in juvenile courts' transfer and sentencing laws, altered responses to female offenders, and fueled a school-to-prison pipeline.

CHAPTER 5. THE KID IS A CRIMINAL: TRANSFER AND DELINQUENCY SANCTIONS. Progressive reformers created juvenile courts to divert youths from the criminal justice system and to provide an alternative rehabilitative welfare system. During the Get Tough Era, changes in state laws challenged both their diversionary and interventionist goals. Retribution, deterrence, and selective incapacitation displaced rehabilitation as sentencing policy rationales and states replaced indeterminate delinquency sentences with determinate ones. States passed laws to transfer more and younger juveniles to criminal court for prosecution as adults.[14] They emphasized offenses rather than offenders and shifted discretion from judges to prosecutors to decide youth's juvenile or criminal status. Blended sentences further eroded the formal demarcation between juvenile and criminal courts. Studies consistently reported racial disparities in waiver decisions and get tough reforms exacerbated inequalities.[15] Once transferred, criminal court judges often imposed harsher sentences on youths than on comparable young adult defendants.[16] Transfer laws reflected legislators' expressive condemnation of crime without regard to its instrumental impact on offending or appreciation of youthful mitigation.

Get tough policies affected juvenile courts' detention and sentencing practices and eroded the always tenuous distinctions between treatment and punishment. Reflecting the politics of race and crime, juvenile courts detained minority youths at higher rates than white youths. States made delinquency sanctions tougher as well. They amended juvenile codes' purpose clauses to endorse punishment and adopted offense-based sentencing guidelines or mandatory minimum sentences.[17] Juvenile court judges' sentencing practices increasingly resembled those of criminal courts. Institutional conditions of confinement often precluded effective treatment. Juvenile courts' harsher sentences fell disproportionately heavily on minority youths.[18] While these changes undermined juvenile courts' traditional rehabilitative claims, delinquency sanctions were less harsh or life-course altering than those imposed in criminal courts. Juvenile courts fulfilled their diversionary mission—protecting youths from criminal punishment—even as their failure to achieve their rehabilitative goals became more evident.

CHAPTER 6. THE GIRL IS A CRIMINAL: THE IMPACT OF GET TOUGH POLICIES ON GIRLS. Historically, juvenile courts dealt with girls primarily for status offenses, often a euphemism for sexual activity or incipient prostitution. Federal and state policy changes in the 1970s limited judges' authority to commit noncriminal girls to delinquency institutions. During the Get Tough Era, justice system personnel perceived a frightening upsurge in violence by girls. Police arrests of female juveniles for offenses such as simple and aggravated assault increased more or decreased less than those of their male counterparts and augured a closing of the offending gender gap. However, comparing boys' and girls' official arrest data with self-report and victimization surveys suggests that the perceived increase in girl violence is a social construction rather than empirical reality. Changes in girls' arrests likely reflect a greater propensity to charge less serious conduct as assaults, changing police responses to domestic violence, and parents' diminished tolerance of females' acting out. Policies to divert status offenders from secure confinement provided an impetus for court personnel to relabel girls as delinquents to place them in institutions and reflect historic paternalistic efforts to control young women.

CHAPTER 7. THE STUDENT IS A CRIMINAL: GET TOUGH POLICIES AND THE SCHOOL-TO-PRISON PIPELINE. From their inception, public schools served important social control and acculturation functions. Progressives' passage of compulsory attendance and truancy laws enforceable by juvenile courts reflect schools' roles as agencies of social control, assimilation, and acculturation of immigrant children. A century later, school disciplinary practices changed in tandem with get tough juvenile justice policies. The Court in *T.L.O. vs. New Jersey* authorized school officials to search students under a lower Fourth Amendment standard than that required to search adults—reasonable suspicion rather than probable cause. Since the 1990s, the presence of police in schools—school resource officers—has increased greatly and they search students under the lower Fourth Amendment standard. Schools rely increasingly on technology—metal detectors, cameras, and drug canines—and heightened surveillance increases the likelihood of detecting wrong doing. Schools have adopted zero-tolerance policies toward misconduct and respond to student deviance with punitive and exclusionary sanctions. High-stakes testing give schools financial incentives to exclude low-performing students. The confluence of laws and policies have fostered a school-to-prison-pipeline that disproportionately affects urban Black males.

CHAPTER 8. THE CRIMINAL IS A KID: ADOLESCENTS' DIMINISHED CULPABILITY. During the Get Tough Era, states transferred more and younger juveniles for prosecution as adults without consideration of their criminal responsibility. In response to counterproductive punitiveness, the MacArthur Foundation sponsored a research network on developmental psychology and neuroscience that focused on adolescents' judgment and self-control and provided a rationale for youths' diminished criminal responsibility.[19] In 2005, the Court in *Roper v. Simmons* categorically barred states from executing youths for crimes committed prior to eighteen years of age. *Roper* offered three reasons—immature judgment, susceptibility to negative peer influences, and transitional personalities—to find that juveniles are categorically less criminally responsible than adults. Developmental psychological and neuroscience research supports the Court's conclusion that juveniles' immature decision making, impulsivity, and limited self-control reduced their culpability. *Graham v. Florida* applied *Roper*'s diminished responsibility rationale to youths convicted of non-homicide crimes and categorically prohibited judges from imposing life without parole sentences. *Miller v. Alabama* prohibited states from imposing *mandatory* life without parole sentences on juveniles convicted of murder and required individualized culpability assessments. Despite *Roper*, *Graham*, and *Miller*'s affirmation of adolescents' reduced culpability, the Court provided the affected juveniles with limited relief and legislators with little guidance to implement its constitutional conclusion that "children are different." State lawmakers and courts have adopted grudging and inconsistent responses to those opinions. I propose a categorical Youth Discount—shorter sentences for reduced culpability—as a straightforward approach to formally recognize youthfulness as a mitigating factor.

CHAPTER 9. THE DEFENDANT IS A KID: ADOLESCENTS' COMPETENCE TO EXERCISE PROCEDURAL RIGHTS. Delinquency proceedings are much more formal than those envisioned a century ago. Their increased complexity makes greater demands on children's ability to make legal decisions. Developmental psychologists have examined adolescents' capacity to participate in legal proceedings, their ability to exercise *Miranda* rights, and their competence to waive counsel. The research questions whether adolescents possess the cognitive ability, maturity, and judgment necessary to exercise legal rights. Many of the developmental features on which *Roper*, *Graham*, and *Miller* relied—impaired judgment and self-control, impulsivity, short-sightedness, and susceptibility to social influences—contribute to their reduced competence to exercise rights. Despite developmental differences, most states do not provide additional safeguards to protect juveniles from their own immaturity and instead use adult legal standards that put them at a disadvantage. Despite juvenile courts' increased punitiveness, the vast majority of states deny delinquents the right to a jury trial. As a result, states convict them more easily than similarly situated adults. Collateral consequences of delinquency convictions amplify juvenile courts' procedural deficiencies. States use prior delinquency convictions to transfer youths to criminal court and to enhance their sentences.[20] Delinquency convictions may provide the predicate for sex offender registration, while drug convictions may bar youths and their families from public housing, and the like.

EPILOGUE: OPPORTUNITIES AND OBSTACLES. There is a window of opportunity to pursue juvenile justice reforms. The crime drop reduces public anxiety and its political salience. Advances in developmental psychology and neuroscience heighten understanding of children's behavior and increase prospects to change it. Youth advocacy groups pressure courts and legislatures to implement reforms. The conclusion describes a justice system that reflects the founding principles of juvenile courts and increased appreciation that kids are different.

No justice system reforms can address the root causes of most delinquency—child poverty and its attendant consequences. Child poverty in the United States is two to five times higher than that of other Western democracies; poverty rates for children of color are quadruple those of white children. Other Western democracies successfully have adopted social policies—a children's allowance, paid parental leave, and subsidized child care—to alleviate child poverty. The United States' failure to reduce child poverty is rooted in political economy, racial and economic inequality, and a lack of political leadership or willingness to care for other people's children.

PART I

The Progressive Era

1

The Progressive Juvenile Court

Progressive reformers who created juvenile courts at the end of the nineteenth century culminated an ideological and legal differentiation of youths from adults that began centuries earlier.[1] Urban upper- and middle-class child-savers embraced an ideal of children's innocence and vulnerability that emerged during America's transition from an agricultural to an industrial economy. Because children lacked adult reason or legal capacity, their parents and the state had to educate them and prepare them for citizenship. Progressive reformers adopted a more modern and scientific conception of crime control—positivist criminology—that sought to identify the causes of criminality and to treat rather than punish offenders. Juvenile courts combined the new vision of children with new strategies of crime control to remove children from the criminal justice system—a diversionary rationale—to provide a rehabilitative alternative to criminal punishment—an interventionist rationale—and to enforce the newer conception of childhood.

This separate system simultaneously affirmed families' role in raising their children in conformity with the new ideas of childhood and expanded the state's prerogative to act as *parens patriae*—super-parent—and to control those who failed to do so. Because some parents did not subscribe to Progressives' views of child rearing, one of juvenile courts' functions was to control and regulate poor and immigrant families and youths. At their inception, reformers intended juvenile courts to assimilate and Americanize children of the Southern and Eastern European immigrants pouring into Eastern and Midwestern cities. At that time, they did not view Black children—most of whom still lived in the rural South—with the same solicitude accorded white ethnic youths in the North.[2]

This chapter first examines how modernization and industrialization attracted immigrants and altered the organization of cities. It then assays how modernization affected families and changed the social construction of childhood. The Progressive movement arose to control and administer social change associated with modernization and to assimilate and acculturate immigrants flooding into industrial cities. Progressive reformers drew on new ideologies of crime control—positivist criminology—to divert children from the criminal justice and to create a judicial-welfare hybrid to rehabilitate and control them. Juvenile courts rejected the trappings of criminal courts and used informal processes to identify children's needs. They created a two-track system of probation and institutional confinement that discriminated between "our children" and "other people's children."

Modernization: Industrialization, Immigration, and Urbanization

In the decades after the Civil War, economic modernization transformed America from a rural, agrarian, Anglo-Protestant society into a more ethnically diverse, urban, and industrial one.[3] Between 1870 and World War I, a national network of railroads fostered economic growth, changed manufacturing processes, and stimulated rapid development. Railroads connected and created national markets and expanded opportunities for large-scale manufacturing, mining, construction, trade, finance, and transportation.[4] Techniques of mass production enabled unskilled workers on assembly lines to boost industrial output. As industries grew, corporations increasingly dominated the economy. A new, better-educated class of managers, professionals, and engineers staffed burgeoning industries, worked within bureaucratic settings, and developed technocratic solutions to economic problems.

Expanded manufacturing and economic opportunities attracted new immigrants. Between 1890 and 1910, the numbers and countries of origin of European immigrants changed significantly. A trickle became a flood as more than one million immigrants per year entered the country between the 1890s and the outbreak of World War I. America's population nearly doubled between 1885 and 1915 and by 1920, immigrants or their children comprised about half the residents of the larger cities.[5] The populations of many cities doubled from one decade to the next, accompanied by sharp social dislocations, poverty, inequality, and increased crime.[6] The language, religion, and culture of the new immigrants from Southern and Eastern Europe differed from those of the Anglo-Protestant settlers who had preceded them.[7] They crowded into ethnic enclaves and slums around industrial centers. They threatened America's linguistic, cultural, and ethnic homogeneity and posed challenges of assimilation and acculturation for those whose forebears had arrived a few generations earlier.[8]

Industrialization, internal migration from the countryside, and European immigration altered the structure of cities. Previously, residential areas remained socially and economically heterogeneous. Most people lived within walking distance of their work, and social, economic, and ethnic residential segregation did not separate well-to-do people from poor ones.[9] With industrialization, urban density increased as new immigrants packed into ethnic ghettos and middle-class and wealthier peopled moved to emerging suburbs.[10] The overwhelming numbers, spatial segregation, and linguistic and cultural differences of the newer immigrants hindered their assimilation.[11] Many came from rural backgrounds and subscribed to traditional ideas of childhood in which children worked and participated in adult activities. Progressive child-savers' cultural construction of childhood clashed with that of immigrant parents who could not afford prolonged child dependency.[12]

Modern Family and Childhood

The transition from an agricultural to an industrial society shifted work from household-based economies to industries, contributed to a privatizing of family life, and modified the roles of women and children.[13] Children have less economic value in an industrial society than in an agricultural one in which they can work as farm hands. The shift from family farms or shops to factories affected the number and spacing of children.[14] The idea of childhood is socially constructed, specifies the social, emotional, and intellectual properties that people believe distinguish children from adults, and changes in response to other social forces.[15]

Until relatively recently, people viewed children as small adults who should be quickly integrated into grownup economic and social roles.[16] Only within the past two or three centuries did Western societies begin to distinguish the ages between infancy and adulthood as separate developmental periods.[17] In the more modern view, children are not miniature adults, childhood and adolescence represent separate developmental stages, and parents invest greater resources in rearing children.[18] Philippe Aries traced the modernizing conception of childhood to the upper bourgeoisie and nobility in sixteenth- and seventeenth-century Europe, whose views gradually diffused downward through the social classes.[19] Historians associate changes in attitudes toward children to a decline in infant mortality, increased literacy, and economic shifts from farm and home-shops to other work environments.[20]

By the early nineteenth century, the newer view of childhood began to alter child-rearing practices in America.[21] By the end of the century, urban upper- and middle-class parents invested greater efforts to prepare their children for adulthood and to restrict their autonomous departures from home. They envisioned children as vulnerable, dependent, and innocent, who required special protection and supervision.[22] Decreased fertility, increased life expectancy, and expanded educational opportunities enabled more privileged women to assume greater roles in improving the social, developmental, and material conditions under which their own and other people's children grew up.[23] They expanded their domestic roles as raisers of children and caretakers into the public realm. Child-saving women supported social and legal reforms to promote children's development and welfare—juvenile courts, child welfare, child labor, compulsory school attendance, kindergarten, and other endeavors.[24] They imposed their vision of childhood innocence and vulnerability on those who did not share it.[25]

Progressives, the State, and the Child

Progressive movements emerged at the end of the nineteenth century in response to the structural changes and dislocations associated with urbanization and industrialization. Progressive reformers shared middle- to upper-class backgrounds, higher levels of education, belief in the use of science and knowledge to manage change, and confidence in the social order within which they flourished. Progressives included diverse ideologies and political affiliations, reflected different temperaments and styles, and addressed myriad social problems associated with the industrial city: poverty, population density, disorder and crime, public health, and inadequate social services. The growing cities proved especially conducive to juvenile mischief and crime.[26] Progressives responded to monopoly economic power with corporate regulation and anti-trust laws; to political corruption with good government, civil service, and electoral reforms; to inadequate sanitation, poor housing, and tainted food with public health efforts, building codes, and food and drug regulation; and to crime and disorder with criminal and juvenile justice reforms.[27]

Progressive reformers embraced many child-saving programs to address threats to children's development: inadequate housing, dysfunctional and broken families, dependency and neglect, poverty, crime and delinquency, and economic exploitation. The emergence of new disciplines and professions like medicine, psychology, and social work at the end of the nineteenth century enabled Progressives to invoke science, rationality, and technical expertise to legitimate their agenda and expand their authority.[28] They believed that experts and professionals could and should solve social problems.[29]

Progressives used the state to inculcate their values through a process of democratization and citizen building. They believed that "[t]he state was to be an agent of reform as well as of repression, of care as well as control, of welfare as well as punishment."[30] They believed that children were more malleable than adults and would internalize their norms and expectations.[31] "The most distinguishing characteristic of Progressivism was its fundamental trust in the power of the state to do good. The state was not the enemy of liberty, but the friend of equality and to expand its domain and increase its power was to be in harmony with the spirit of the age. . . . The state was not a behemoth to be chained and fettered, but an agent capable of fulfilling an ambitious program."[32] Progressives viewed individual and societal welfare as co-extensive and saw no need to protect individuals from state benevolence.[33] Successful child development promoted social welfare and the family and the parental state shared joint responsibility.

Progressives sought to acculturate and Americanize the recent European immigrants to become middle-class Americans like themselves. Social Darwinism—"the survival of the fittest"—provided a comforting rationale for inequality and elite domination of those of inferior races.

But within the ethnic and racial hierarchies, reformers viewed European immigrants as indigenous whites, albeit of lower orders, and ultimately culturally, economically, and biologically assimilable, unlike members of the "colored" races.[34] In *A Piece of the Pie*, Stanley Lieberson emphasizes that Progressives' agenda to assimilate European immigrants differed sharply from the exclusionary and segregationist treatment of Blacks in the rural South.[35] When Blacks moved north during the Great Migration, these differences in policies of inclusion versus exclusion shaped their experiences very differently than those of the white European immigrants, differences that resonate into the twenty-first century.

The Progressives combined their belief in state power and professional expertise with the modern concept of childhood. The doctrine of *parens patriae*—the state as parent-surrogate—provided the legal foundation for intervention into family privacy and domestic arrangements.[36] Although *parens patriae* doctrine originated in medieval English law to assure property interests and feudal succession, the American colonies invoked it to protect children from destitute or neglectful parents.[37]

Progressives' child-saving mission embodied contradictory assumptions. On the one hand, they embraced an idealized vision of childhood that provided a standard against which to measure parents' success and children's deviance. While affirming parents' responsibility to raise their children, they simultaneously expanded the state's role to oversee their child-rearing practices and to intervene when they failed.[38] *Parens patriae* legitimated Progressives' programs to structure child development, to control and mold them, to protect them from parental maltreatment and economic exploitation, and to promote their growth for citizenship.[39] "The child was the carrier of tomorrow's hope whose innocence and freedom made him singularly receptive to education in rational, humane behavior. Protect him, nurture him, and in his manhood he would create the bright new world of the Progressives' vision."[40] Progressives equated adolescents with younger children to differentiate them from adults and to deny them access to grownups' roles and responsibilities.[41] One goal of the parental-state was citizen building to prepare young people for self-governance and participation in civil affairs.[42]

To prepare youths for citizenship, Progressives enacted a host of child-centered reforms—juvenile court, child labor, social welfare, and compulsory school attendance laws—that reflected and advanced their changing idea of childhood.[43] They intended these reforms to protect working-class and immigrant youths during the transition from childhood to adulthood and to prevent them from assuming adult economic and social roles prematurely.[44]

Progressives expanded public schools as one of several age-segregated institutions with which to acculturate and control young people. The Common School movement began in New England in the 1830s and 1840s and antedated the juvenile court by about half a century. It shared similar goals to assimilate foreigners, inculcate common language and values among all citizens, and provide a form of social control to prevent crime.[45] By the end of the nineteenth century, literacy became a prerequisite to functioning in an industrial economy and formal education became one of children's primary developmental tasks.[46] School officials adopted the bureaucratic structure of factories and corporations and applied techniques of mass production in the educational context.[47] Age-graded schools enabled reformers to classify youths by age, supervise and control them, and inculcate the dominant culture's values. To prepare children as future workers, schools demanded discipline, punctuality, and the ability to perform repetitive tasks and to adhere to schedules.[48] Schools structured the power relationships between administrators and teachers and between teachers and students to replicate divisions of labor and to socialize young people for domination and subordination in the industrial economy.[49] "The emphasis on the orderly movement of students and their obedience to strict codes of conduct is important both to schools' operational functioning and to their societal functions. . . . [S]trict disciplinary regimens in working class schools help to promote smooth and voluntary transitions into an industrial workplace that tightly regulates and subordinates laborers."[50] By emphasizing certain cognitive skills and rewarding students who, by virtue of their class position, came to school best equipped to exhibit those behaviors, schools reinforced and replicated social inequality.[51] I argue in Chapter 7 that the contemporary school-to-prison pipeline reflects schools' historic role of maintaining social control and reinforcing race and class inequality.

Criminal Responsibility and the Juvenile Court

Before Progressives created juvenile courts, the criminal law's infancy defense provided the only substantive legal doctrine that recognized children's diminished responsibility.[52] Criminal law assumed that people exercised free will, chose to engage in blameworthy conduct, and deserved punishment for the harms they caused. It recognized that those who did not know right from wrong—severely mentally ill adults and very young children—could not be blamed for making bad choices or be deterred by threat of legal sanctions. Insanity and infancy provided narrow exceptions to the presumption of criminal responsibility. The infancy defense presumed that children younger than seven years of age lacked criminal responsibility, viewed those fourteen years of age or older as fully responsible, and rebuttably presumed that those between seven and thirteen years of age lacked criminal capacity.[53]

At the beginning of the nineteenth century, the modernizing view of childhood and the differentiation of youths from adults led to the creation of separate institutions for youth. Jackson-era reformers feared that judges might dismiss cases against or jurors might acquit young offenders to avoid imposing harsh sentences for minor crimes.[54] In East Coast cities in the early to mid-nineteenth century, they created Houses of Refuge—age-segregated correctional institutions—to avoid jury nullification and increase control of youths.[55] Refuges were specialized institutions in which to shelter miscreant youth from the perceived corrupting influences of social change.[56] Refuge legislation distinguished between juvenile and adults, provided separate institutions for children, authorized indeterminate commitments to those sanctuaries, and broadened state authority to regulate a miscellany of youths—criminal offenders; wayward and disobedient children; and orphaned, dependent, or neglected youngsters.[57] In 1838, the Pennsylvania Supreme Court in *Ex parte Crouse* invoked the *parens patriae* doctrine to uphold confinement of troublesome youths.

> [M]ay not the natural parents, when unequal to the task of education, or unworthy of it, be superseded by the *parens patriae*, or common guardian of the community? It is to be remembered that the public has a paramount interest in the virtue and knowledge of its members, and that, of

strict right, the business of education belongs to it. . . . The infant has been snatched from a course which must have ended in confirmed depravity; and not only is the restraint of her person lawful, but it would be an act of extreme cruelty to release her from it.[58]

Refuges' proactive intervention with minor, noncriminal, and unsupervised youth provided an antecedent to juvenile courts' status jurisdiction.

The first Houses of Refuge in Northern cities initially served only white males, but soon admitted white girls as well. Refuge managers originally excluded Black youths, whom they relegated to the criminal justice system because they doubted their potential for rehabilitation and feared racial commingling.[59] When they later admitted Black youths, they housed them in separate or segregated facilities. Black children typically remained in institutions longer than their white counterparts because white employers and families considered them less desirable candidates for apprenticeships or placing-out.[60]

By mid-century, reformers created separate reformatories to which to commit vagrant and criminal youths.[61] The building of reformatories coincided with increased immigration of Irish and other ethnic groups and provided a strategy to control them. Reformatory founders organized institutions on a cottage plan to replicate a family setting and located them in rural locales to insulate children from corrupting urban environments.[62] "Those who sought to reform juvenile delinquents in mid-19th century America spoke the lofty language of nurture and environmentalism. Reform schools, they claimed, were not prisons but home-like institutions, veritable founts of generous sentiment. In fact, they were prisons, often brutal and disorderly ones."[63] Despite the deficiencies of Northern reformatories, the experiences of Black youths in the South were far worse. Southern states convicted, incarcerated, leased out, or consigned them to labor on chain gangs and sometimes executed them like their adult counterparts.[64]

By the end of the nineteenth century, the changing ideas of childhood and newer explanations of criminality led to the creation of a separate juvenile court in Cook County, Illinois, in 1899. The juvenile court engrafted a separate judiciary and courtroom onto earlier generations' reforms—refuges and reformatories, separation of youths from adults, expansive authority over offenders and noncriminal youths, and minimal procedural safeguards.[65] The juvenile court culminated the century-long process of differentiating adolescents from adults and coordinated previously distinct process—investigation, detention, hearing, disposition, and correctional institutions—under one agency.[66]

Criminal justice policies reflect underlying ideological assumptions about the causes of and responses to crime.[67] Ideologies of crime "structure the ways in which we think about criminals, providing the intellectual frameworks (whether scientific or religious or commonsensical) through which we see these individuals, understand their motivations, and dispose of their cases. Cultural patterns also structure the ways in which we feel about offenders."[68] At the end of the nineteenth century, positivist criminology supplanted classical formulation of crime as the product of free-will choices, attempted to identify antecedent forces that caused criminality, and provided a more modern and scientific conception of social control.[69] The classical criminal law assumed free-willed actors made blameworthy choices and deserved punishment for their crimes. Positivist criminology asserted that antecedent forces—biological, psychological, social, or environmental—caused criminal behavior.[70] It attributed crime to deterministic forces that constrained a person to act as he did rather than to a deliberate exercise of free will. Adherents of this perspective sought to scientifically identify those deterministic forces and develop ameliorative responses.[71]

Progressives believed that social disorganization associated with urban growth caused delinquency and required interventions to reform rather than to punish errant youths.[72] Katherine Beckett describes the underlying ideological foundation for both criminal justice and social welfare practices. "[D]eviant behavior is at least partially caused (rather than freely chosen). Progressive reformers therefore identified rehabilitation—operationally defined as the use of 'individualized corrective measures adapted to the specific case or the particular problem'—as the appropriate response to deviant behavior."[73] Elizabeth Scott and Laurence Steinberg describe juvenile courts' rehabilitative premise even more strongly—"the *sole* purpose of state intervention in delinquency cases was to promote the welfare of delinquent youths through rehabilitative interventions."[74]

Attributing criminal behavior to deterministic forces rather than to evil choices, Progressives downplayed actors' moral responsibility and focused on reform rather than punishment.[75] Positivism—the scientific search for causes and cures of crime—was one example of intellectual modernization—which emphasized the values of rationality, professionalism, and expertise—and drew support from other contemporaneous developments.[76] Darwin's theory of evolution provided a rationale for inherited or biological determinants of criminal behavior.[77] Germ theory provided medical practitioners with a scientific understanding of the causes of diseases and strategies with which to treat or prevent them.[78] Criminal justice personnel analogized their practices to the medical profession and purported to treat offenders. In contrast with criminal law's emphasis on blameworthy choices, the new criminology and justice system professionals borrowed medical methodology and vocabulary to enhance legitimacy and used metaphors like "pathology" and "infection" to diagnose and treat offenders.

The rehabilitative ideal rests on ideological assumptions about human malleability, the ability to effect reform, and agreement about the goals of change. Francis Allen describes its central assumptions:

> The rehabilitative ideal . . . assumed, first, that human behavior is the product of antecedent causes. These causes can be identified. . . . Knowledge of the antecedents of human behavior makes possible an approach to the scientific control of human behavior. . . . [I]it is assumed that measures employed to treat the convicted offender should serve a therapeutic function; that such measures should be designed to effect changes in the behavior of the convicted person in the interest of his own happiness, health, and satisfaction and in the interest of social defense.[79]

According to Allen, shared beliefs about ends and means—the goals of change and strategies to achieve them—sustain the rehabilitative ideal. Progressives believed that the new behavioral sciences provided the tools with which to change immigrants' and poor peoples' personality, character, and morals and lead them to adopt their middle-class values.[80]

The rehabilitative project also affirmed democratic ideals. For Progressives, urban slums and ethnic ghettos prevented development of self-governance and participatory citizenship.[81] Even though it took the form of coercive intervention, the rehabilitative ideology proposed to restore and reintegrate people who committed crimes or who had fallen into poverty.[82] Within a decade of juvenile courts' founding, the medicalization of delinquency led to increased emphasis on adolescent psychology and psychopathy. G. Stanley Hall's theory of adolescence posited that "every individual recapitulated the stages of human civilization. This theory had lent scientific legitimacy to the idea that children were qualitatively different from adults, and also focused attention on adolescence (the period in one's life from the onset of puberty to one's early twenties) as a particularly difficult developmental stage."[83]

Industrialization led to a material prosperity previously unknown to most people, and reformers eschewed radical alternatives to the existing political and economic system. Confident in their social order, they emphasized changing individuals and improving their morals and character rather than addressing structural causes of crime like urbanization, poverty, inequality, and limited social mobility. Although Progressives recognized that social factors contributed to delinquency, they designed their programs to care for damaged individuals rather than to change the structural root causes. They blended a liberal humanitarian inclination to use state power to help the less fortunate with a conservative impulse to control and repress those who differed or posed a threat to social order.[84]

The juvenile court melded the new ideology of childhood with the new strategies of crime control. One goal was to divert youths from the criminal justice system and to substitute the state as *parens patriae*.[85] Reformers viewed young offenders as innocent albeit misguided children, attributed their delinquency to adverse social conditions and inadequate parenting, and focused on control, guidance, and welfare rather than blame and punishment.[86] They believed that children were less blameworthy than were adults for criminal behavior and more amenable to change.[87] Because they viewed children as malleable, their coercive strategies emphasized both child welfare and social control—to eliminate causes of delinquency and to reform delinquents.[88] In addition to diverting youths from the criminal justice system, reformers viewed juvenile courts as agencies that would prepare youths for citizenship in the new republic.[89]

Most histories of juvenile courts emphasize their rehabilitative or interventionist purpose. In this view, intervention by child-welfare experts would produce positive outcomes and benefit the community and the child simultaneously. By contrast, Franklin Zimring argues that an important, albeit less prominent function of juvenile courts was to divert youths from criminal courts and to allow them to grow up in the community. "[A] child-centered juvenile court could avoid the many harms that criminal punishment visited on the young. The reformers believed that penalties were unnecessarily harsh and places of confinement were schools for crime, where the innocent were corrupted and the redeemable were instead confirmed in the path of chronic criminality. From this perspective, the first great virtue of the juvenile court was that it would not continue the destructive impact of the criminal justice system on children."[90] Avoiding the harms that processing children as criminals would be beneficial regardless of whether juvenile courts' treatment produced positive outcomes.

Progressive child-savers described the juvenile court as a benign therapeutic agency, although analysts differ whether their primary motivation was a humanitarian desire to save poor and immigrant children or to expand state control over them.[91] Some critics argued that "the juvenile court's founders intended from the very beginning to use procedural informality as a mechanism for social control rather than to rehabilitate wayward youth. . . . [I]t was not a benevolent enterprise gone awry but the very effective execution of social coercion operating behind the veil of rehabilitative informality."[92] *Parens patriae* legitimated intervention and undergirded claims that juvenile courts were civil welfare rather than criminal agencies. Characterizing intervention as welfare proceedings rather than criminal prosecutions gave reformers greater flexibility to supervise and control children. Like other diversionary reforms, analysts contend that juvenile courts had a net-widening effect, brought more youths under their control, and addressed behavior that criminal courts previously ignored or handled informally.[93]

Juvenile courts' role as agencies of assimilation and acculturation led them to distinguish and discriminate between children of European immigrants and Black youths. In *The Condemnation of Blackness*, Khalil Gibran Muhammad argues that Northern Progressives' collection of crime statistics by race and emphases on disproportionate rates of Black arrests and prison confinement reinforced whites' beliefs in Black inferiority and cultural pathology and supported discriminatory social welfare and public policies. "Progressive era white social scientists and reformers often reified the racial criminalization process by framing white criminals sympathetically as victims of industrialization. They described a 'great army of unfortunates' juxtaposed against an army of self-destructive and pathological blacks who were their 'own worst enem[ies].'"[94]

Juvenile courts' status jurisdiction enabled reformers to regulate non-criminal misbehavior—sexual activity, immorality, truancy, or living a wayward, idle, and dissolute life.[95] This broad jurisdiction focused on a child's status or circumstances.[96] Progressives did not distinguish between children who committed crimes and those who engaged in non-criminal misconduct or whose parents neglected them—all required support and moral guidance. Juvenile courts' status jurisdiction enabled reformers to impose their middle-class manners and morals on those who did not subscribe to them. The status jurisdiction embodied the new vision of childhood innocence and vulnerability, furthered the legal differentiation between children and adults, and expanded state authority over child rearing and family functions. Juvenile courts' truancy jurisdiction enabled them to enforce compulsory school attendance laws and to protect working-class and immigrant children from parental pressures to work and contribute to the family economy.[97]

The status jurisdiction had special implications for girls, many of whose parents brought them to court for "sexual precocity" or fear they would become "lost women."[98] "Girls who got in trouble exemplified new economic, social, and sexual opportunities available to urban young women in the early twentieth century. . . . 'Delinquency' was a label that families, reformers, and public officials applied to socially precocious and/or sexually active young women whom they sought to protect from the perceived risks of their behavior."[99] The industrial economy required family members to contribute to the household economy, but sending young women to work exposed them to moral corruption, unscrupulous men, and the threat of prostitution.[100] Sexually active girls contradicted Progressives' vision of childhood innocence and offended their Victorian sensibilities. Girls appeared in juvenile court far more often than did boys for immorality or sexual experimentation and judges confined proportionally more girls than boys for noncriminal behavior.[101] Although judges committed foreign-born white boys to institutions twice as often as native ones, their commitment rates for native-born and immigrant white girls did not differ significantly. "This suggests a more general concern with regulating the behavior and development of white girls, reflecting patriarchal interests in enforcing gender norms, and linked to racial politics of Americanizing the stock of potential mothers and wives for future white American families."[102] Reflecting prevailing racial attitudes, judges sanctioned white girls for status offenses far more often than Black girls, leading one analyst to conclude that "white, male-dominated juvenile court communities were indifferent to the precocious sexuality of black girls and little concerned with their equal protection."[103]

Juvenile Court Procedures

Some standard features of juvenile courts—private hearings, confidential records, separate detention facilities and courtrooms, and professional probation staff—were not part of the court's original design, but later additions—a "work-in-progress."[104] David Tanenhaus argues that those threatened by state intervention—poor and working-class people, immigrants, and Catholics—challenged some of its central elements.[105] For example, at their inception, juvenile courts opened hearings to the public to allay fears that judges would discriminate against Catholic youths or commit them to Protestant institutions.

A relationship exists between procedure and substance in juvenile courts. Issues of procedure implicate youths' competence to exercise rights. Issues of substance involve juveniles' culpability or criminal responsibility and appropriate dispositions. Because juvenile courts separated children from adults and provided a rehabilitative alternative to punishment, reformers rejected most criminal procedural safeguards. They assumed that children lacked the understanding or judgment to exercise legal rights.[106] Juvenile courts excluded lawyers and juries, abjured rules of evidence, and used a euphemistic vocabulary.[107] Progressives' conception of juvenile court procedures

> was to focus on the child or adolescent as a person in need of assistance, not on the act that brought him or her before the court. The proceedings were informal, with much discretion left to the juvenile court judge. Because the judge was to act in the best interests of the child, procedural

safeguards available to adults, such as the right to an attorney, the right to know the charges brought against one, the right to trial by jury, and the right to confront one's accuser, were thought unnecessary. Juvenile court proceedings were closed to the public and juvenile records were to remain confidential so as not to interfere with the child's or adolescent's ability to be rehabilitated and reintegrated into society.[108]

Juvenile courts' child-welfare theory likened delinquency proceedings to a visit to a doctor rather than a court trial.[109] Just as a lawyer would not accompany a patient to a physician's examination, juvenile court judges viewed lawyers as an unnecessary intrusion. Judges enjoyed broad discretion and there was very little attorneys could do to affect the outcome of a case.[110]

Judges assumed that youths who appeared before them needed some type of correction and their goal was to determine what form it should take rather than to adjudicate the underlying facts.[111] Judges held an informal meeting in their chambers to make proceedings feel more personal and less threatening. Court personnel reviewed a child's circumstances, family, and background before the hearing to identify why she was in trouble and what could be done to ameliorate it.[112]

Reformers viewed young offenders as innocent and vulnerable—victims of their circumstances—rather than as criminally responsible actors. Theoretically, a youth's delinquency was only a symptom of her actual needs; her social circumstances and future welfare guided dispositions.[113] Because juvenile courts existed to help children rather than to punish them, judges did not need to determine criminal responsibility or consider doctrines like insanity or infancy that might defeat jurisdiction.[114]

Juvenile courts' dispositions combined social welfare with crime control. States defined their jurisdiction based, in part, on violations of criminal laws and crimes provided the most common basis for intervention. The tension between a welfare orientation—the child's best interests—and control of criminal behavior created a fundamental and perhaps irreconcilable tension in juvenile courts' administration and dispositions from their inception.

Juvenile courts deemphasized their criminal foundations, rejected notions of criminal responsibility and punishment, blurred distinctions between criminal violators and noncriminal children, and acted to improve their future welfare.[115] Their broad jurisdiction enabled probation officers to supervise youths in their home, transfer them to another caretaker, or place them in a reformatory or institution.[116] Judges imposed indeterminate and nonproportional dispositions that could continue for the duration of minority. Indeterminate dispositions had no set limit and could continue indefinitely until adulthood. Nonproportional dispositions rejected limits on the length of disposition based on what the child did.[117] Each child differed, dispositions addressed her future needs, and her offense did not limit the duration or intensity of intervention.[118]

Reformers envisioned a specialized judge assisted by social service personnel and probation officers. They assumed that understanding and diagnosing a child's circumstances would lead to a prescription that would change a youth's character and behavior and prevent future delinquency. The juvenile court was a social welfare agency. "Children who had needs of any kind could be brought into the juvenile court, where their troubles would be diagnosed and the services they needed provided by court workers or obtained from other agencies."[119] Judges decided cases individually, exercised broad discretion, and factors that influenced one decision did not necessarily govern the next.[120]

Juvenile courts handled most cases informally and probation was the most common disposition.[121] As a diversionary alternative to criminal courts, community supervision constituted a modest intrusion, did less harm than criminal processing or penal confinement, and allowed the court to exercise control cheaply.[122] Probation enabled courts to handle youths efficiently, avoided nullification and dismissal if the state processed minor cases in criminal court, and expanded regulation to include noncriminal offenders.[123] Probation officers served as intermediaries who gave the court information about the child and supervised youths whom judges returned to the community.[124] Probation exposed youths' families to state supervision as well. "[T]he entire family, not just the child, became the subject for extended case work, which could involve demands to change jobs, find a new residence, become a better housekeeper, prepare different meals, give up alcohol, and abstain from sex."[125]

Although juvenile courts exercised probationary supervision over most youths who appeared before them, judges could and did sentence substantial numbers of youths to institutions.[126] Reformers expanded on the cottage-plan model of reformatories, added academic and vocational programs, and relabeled institutions as vocational schools or industrial training schools.[127] Despite Progressives' rehabilitative rhetoric, juvenile institutions and reformatories were essentially custodial, punitive, and ineffective.[128] They almost inevitably subordinated rehabilitative ambitions to custodial considerations because of institutional needs to maintain order and control, protect staff, and forestall external criticisms. As Ellen Ryerson notes, the "fusion of social control with greater humaneness is a tenuous one which typically dissolves, leaving the machinery for social control firmly entrenched—even if it is ineffective—after the spirit of humanitarianism has departed."[129] Similarly, Zimring argues that those who created the juvenile court did not expect training schools to be significant places of reform and their primary virtue was that they were not prisons.[130]

The residents of these punitive institutions disproportionately were the children of the poor and immigrants.[131] Progressives created juvenile courts to Americanize and acculturate poor and immigrant children who made up the vast majority of those who appeared before it. They expected them to discriminate between "other people's children" and their own middle-class offspring.[132] David Rothman argues that juvenile courts operated a dual justice system: "one brand for the poor, another for the middle and upper classes. Judicial discretion may well have promoted judicial discrimination."[133] At the beginning of the twentieth century, the vast majority of Blacks still lived in the rural South and those who administered juvenile courts in the North reserved the institutions for white youths.[134]

Judges could transfer cases of some young offenders to criminal courts. They used this authority sparingly to deal with the most serious or visible crimes committed by older youths.[135] The ability to transfer a few cases provided a safety valve that protected juvenile courts' jurisdiction to address the needs of or divert most youths from criminal courts. I argue in Chapter 5 that at the end of the twentieth century, law makers launched a frontal assault on juvenile courts' diversionary mission with get tough policies that shifted waiver discretion from judges to prosecutors, relegated about two hundred thousand chronological juveniles a year to criminal courts, and disproportionately affected minority youths.

The ethnic and class discrimination embedded in juvenile justice administration reflected the structural context within which courts operated. Poor and immigrant children had more and greater needs than did children of those better off. They were more likely to come into contact with police, social welfare agents, and schools who identified them for intervention and less able to defend themselves. "Once consideration shifted from the crime to the criminal, class distinctions came almost inevitably to assume new significance when punishments were meted out."[136] The individualized justice of juvenile courts legitimated differing responses based on who youths and their family were, rather than what they did.

The creation of juvenile courts in Northern cities coincided with the emergence of Jim Crow justice in the South, where most Blacks lived. Unlike the assimilationist and citizen-building agenda of Northern reformers, Southern states tried Black youths in criminal court, committed them to adult prisons, subjected them to chain gangs and convict leasing, and executed them.[137] White Southerners did not expect Black children to become economically self-sufficient or political equals and excluded them from juvenile courts' citizen-building mission.[138] Matters were only marginally better for Black youths in the north in the early twentieth century. "Blacks were portrayed as heralding from an inferior culture, one so scarred by centuries of slavery that government intervention would be of little help until blacks uplifted their own race on their own. In short, white criminality was considered society's problem, but black criminality was considered blacks' problem."[139] As Chicago's Black population grew, the private Catholic and Protestant institutions to whom juvenile court judges committed youth accepted only white co-religionists. By drawing a clear color line, private institutions limited juvenile court judges' dispositional options. As a consequence, judges committed Black youths to state-run facilities sooner than they did other ethnic children and they remained confined longer than white youths.[140] "Whereas religion had been the most important consideration in the processing of the cases of children from 'foreign' families at the end of the century, as European immigrants were slowly becoming white Americans and more 'colored' people migrated to American cities in the North and Midwest, the significance of race became more visible and tangible as the color line became more entrenched after World War I."[141]

Conclusion

Progressive reformers defined young people as vulnerable and malleable, and enacted laws to supervise, control, and guide them. Child-saving laws formalized their dependency and excluded them from adult activities. Compulsory school attendance laws required youths to attend school. Child labor laws excluded them from the workplace. Juvenile courts' delinquency and status jurisdiction extended state control potentially to all youth. These laws isolated children from adults, limited their social and economic roles, confined them with age-graded peers in schools, and prolonged their dependency. Progressives evinced special concern for poor and immigrant children whose parents' economic necessity might cause their children to assume adult roles prematurely.

Despite their benevolent rhetoric, Progressive reformers intended juvenile courts to discriminate between "our children" and "other people's children" whom they would acculturate, assimilate, and control.[142] "Unlike blacks and other nonwhites, European immigrants and their embryonic-citizen child could potentially be reformed into whiteness, a requirement for eventual assimilation into the white body politic."[143] White philanthropy was the primary source of crime prevention funding and immigrant children and native-born whites were the primary recipients, even though African American children's needs were greater.[144] Reformers viewed white people's criminality as society's problem, but regarded Blacks' crimes as a problem for them to solve alone. Reformers recognized that structural factors caused poor and immigrant whites to offend, but attributed the same behavior by Blacks to racial inferiority and cultural pathology which could not solved.[145] In the South, white supremacy and racial exclusion defined juvenile justice policies toward Black children.[146]

Although social structural features—urbanization, economic inequality, and political processes—create criminogenic conditions, Progressives focused on individual deficiencies rather than those structural factors.[147] Although family, economic, and social influences contributed to delinquency, Progressives opted to minister to affected individuals rather than to alter the conditions that caused their misbehavior.[148] Changing individuals and reforming their character was a less radical agenda than understanding crime as consequence of social inequality and reducing it.[149] In the South, where most Black youths lived, juvenile courts arrived later, implemented the rehabilitative ideal more tentatively, and practiced racial exclusion and segregation.[150]

Progressives situated juvenile courts on several legal and criminological fault lines that rested on binary distinctions: child or adult; dependent or responsible; determinism or free will; treatment or punishment; procedural informality or formality; discretion or rules. I argue in later chapters that during the last third of the twentieth century, court decisions, structural and racial demographic changes, an increase in youth crime, disillusionment with rehabilitation, and the politics of race shifted juvenile courts' emphases from the former to the latter of each of these alternative constructs. From their inception, juvenile courts seldom achieved rehabilitative goals, but they kept the vast majority of youths out of the more damaging criminal justice system. During the Get Tough Era, lawmakers repudiated Progressives' assumptions that children differ from adults, rejected rehabilitation as a goal, reinvigorated classical views of crime as rational choice by responsible individuals, and sought to punish many more youth as adults.

PART II

The Due Process Era

2

The Due Process Revolution and the Juvenile Court

For the first two-thirds of the twentieth century, juvenile courts avoided sustained public, judicial, or legal scrutiny, although a few academics expressed concerns about their procedural deficiencies and judges' broad discretion. In 1937, Harvard Law dean Roscoe Pound, a strong proponent of juvenile courts, insisted that the judges who presided should be exceptionally well qualified because court procedures were so limited and discretion so great. "The powers of the Star Chamber were a trifle in comparison with those of our juvenile courts. . . . It is well known that too often the placing of a child in a home or even in an institution is done casually or perfunctorily or even arbitrarily."[1] In 1946, Paul W. Tappan strongly criticized these hybrid judicial case-work agencies. He described the processes as "informal, unofficial probation supervision or institutional remand before a hearing is held and hearings in which there is no determination as to guilt of an offense, where personality factors and the 'total situation' determine adjudication."[2] He condemned juvenile courts' "treatment without trial," in which rumors or speculation about a child or his family determined outcomes rather than proof of a crime using basic procedural protections.[3] He complained that juvenile courts presumed guilt or ignored it and left discretion "in the hands of judicial and probation personnel unhampered by statutory definitions or limitations, undirected save by a very general principle of treating, reforming, rehabilitating."[4]

Despite concerns expressed by a few academics, however, juvenile courts languished in a legal backwater that insulated judges and court personnel from systematic examination because of their closed confidential operation, the absence of lawyers who practiced in them, and their clients' disadvantaged status. The Supreme Court's 1967 decision in *In re Gault* began the transformation of the juvenile court from a welfare agency into a legal institution. This, in turn, subjected its practices to closer evaluation by lawyers, criminologists, and public officials. *Gault*

was part of the Warren Court's larger project to expand civil rights, reform states' criminal procedures, and protect minorities.

This chapter examines the social and legal context within which the
Court's due process revolution occurred and its juvenile justice decisions. It focuses first on the decades prior to and after World War II,
during which the Great Migration of Blacks from the rural South to
the North and West increased minority populations in urban ghettos,
heightened national visibility of racial discrimination, and provided political and legal impetus for the Court's civil rights decisions.[5] The chapter's later sections examines the Court's civil rights decisions, criminal
procedure rulings, and juvenile court judgments during the 1960s.[6] The
Court's decisions transformed juvenile courts and led to a procedural
and substantive convergence with criminal courts.

The Great Migration

In the nineteenth century, the cotton gin made growing cotton com-
mercially viable and slavery became the economic foundation of the
pre–Civil War Southern economy. At the start of the twentieth century,
over 90% of Blacks lived in the South, three-quarters in rural areas. The
Great Migration of African Americans in the decades before and during
World War II increased their urbanization and placed issues of racial
inequality and civil rights on the national political agenda.[7] Between the
outbreak of World War I in 1914 and its end in 1918, European immigration to the United States plunged by more than 90%.[8] As World War I
increased demand for industrial production and simultaneously reduced
the flow of immigrants, Northern labor recruiters solicited Southern
Blacks to fill jobs in factories, railroads, and packing houses.[9]

The Great Migration during the first two-thirds of the twentieth century profoundly changed American society, politics, and law. "The configuration of the cities as we know them, the social geography of black
and white neighborhoods, the spread of the housing project as well as
the rise of a well-scrubbed black middle class, along with the alternating
waves of white flight and suburbanization—all of these grew directly
or indirectly, from the response of everyone touched by the Great Migration."[10] Between World Wars I and II, the mechanization of cotton-
picking, the collapse of cotton prices, and the Mexican boll weevil's

damage to cotton production shifted Southern agricultural from cotton to food and livestock. These changes decreased demand for Black tenant sharecroppers contemporaneously with increased demand for labor in the Northern factories.[11] Between 1910 and 1920, more than a half-million Blacks migrated to non-Southern states, followed by more than three-quarters of a million in the 1920s. An additional 400,000 Blacks left for Northern cities during the Great Depression. In the 1940s, Black migration increased to 160,000 per year, during the 1950s it averaged 146,000 per year, and in the 1960s, it was about 102,000 per year.[12]

Many Blacks joined the exodus to escape Southern racial hostility— Jim Crow laws, Ku Klux Klan violence, beatings and lynching, poor segregated schools, lack of employment, and job discrimination.[13] It is difficult to overstate the oppressed and brutalized plight of Blacks in Southern states.[14] Although the Thirteenth Amendment to the Constitution abolished slavery and involuntary servitude, it exempted "punishment for crime whereof the party shall have been duly convicted." Southern sheriffs and local officials used criminal laws to punish vagrancy and other vague offenses with a system of repression and peonage labor on chain gangs.[15]

When the outbreak of World War I curtailed European immigration, 85% of Blacks lived in the South. Three-quarters still lived there when the United States entered World War II. Opportunities to work in war production industries in the 1940s induced more than one and a half million Blacks to move as labor shortage forced employers to hire Black and female workers whom they had previously excluded.[16] During World War II, twelve million men and women entered the armed forces and fifteen million civilians relocated for defense jobs.[17] Between 1940 and 1944, defense contractors integrated their work forces and Black populations in urban areas increased dramatically.[18] For example, during the 1940s, California's population of Blacks quadrupled as they sought work in shipyards and defense industries.[19] In the 1950s and 1960s, an additional one and a half million Blacks migrated from the South. Between the end of World War II and 1960, about one-third of African Americans who had remained in the South moved to other parts of the country, the vast majority to live in central cities.[20] Between 1940 and 1970, five million Blacks left the South and reduced the proportion of the total U.S. Black population who remained there from three-quarters to about half.[21]

When Blacks migrated, they almost always moved to cities.[22] Between 1910 and 1930, New York's Black population tripled, Chicago's quintupled, and Detroit's increased twenty-fold.[23] During the first half of the twentieth century, there was a massive demographic shift as Blacks moved from the countryside to the city: in 1910, less than one-quarter of Blacks lived in cities. By 1940, half lived in cities, and by 1960, more than three-quarters did.[24] In 1870, 80% of Black Americans lived in the rural South; by 1970, 80% resided in urban locales, half in the North, Midwest, and West.[25] In 1910, African Americans comprised 2% of Northerners; by 1960, they accounted for 7% of Northerners and 12% of Northern urban residents.[26]

When Blacks moved to cities, racist public policies and private discrimination forced them to live almost exclusively in racial ghettos.[27] Although the term "ghetto" originally referred to certain quarters of European cities in the sixteenth and seventeenth centuries where Jews lived due to forced separation, it has come to describe a densely populated urban slum in which relatively homogenous minority groups are compelled to live because of social, legal, or economic pressure. As racial diversity outside the South increased, whites reacted to Blacks in their midst with fear and hostility.[28] Whites' violence—including arson and bombings—reinforced segregation in housing, education, and employment and buttressed racial isolation.[29] White-on-Black violence in St. Louis in 1917 and Chicago in 1919 killed forty-eight and thirty-eight people respectively as working-class whites reacted to the perceived menace of Blacks in their midst.[30] "[I]ndividual blacks were attacked because of the color of their skin. Those living away from recognized 'black' neighborhoods had their houses ransacked or burned. Those unlucky or unwise enough to be caught trespassing in 'white' neighborhoods were beaten, shot, or lynched."[31]

During the post–World War II era, as Blacks entered cities, whites increasingly moved to suburbs.[32] Federal mortgages subsidized single-family homes in rapidly growing suburbs.[33] Federal interstate highway building facilitated suburban expansion and easy credit enabled more commuters to buy automobiles.[34] Building contractors mass produced houses and developed vast suburban tracts.[35] Federal mortgage, housing, and tax policies subsidized construction of white suburbs and bank lending policies reinforced neighborhoods' racial stability and contributed to white suburbs surrounding urban minority residents.[36]

> Federal policy ensured that housing development happened in suburbs rather than within cities and favored the white middle classes rather than minorities and the poor. . . . [T]he actions of the federal government accelerated the exodus to the suburbs. These included a vast postwar expansion of the Federal Housing Administrations (FHA) mortgage guarantee program, the growth of a federally sponsored secondary mortgage market, and the income tax deduction for home ownership. At the same time, zoning ordinances restricted most suburban residential development to single-family housing, and the FHA placed racial restrictions on its mortgages until the 1960s. Together, these policies kept the suburbs white.[37]

The federal government cut subsidies to construct urban rental units and reduced mortgage and home improvement loans in Black sections of cities. During the 1950s and 1960s, federal highways facilitated white suburban development and urban planners located interstate arteries to create physical barriers and curtail expansion of Black communities. Local elites manipulated housing and urban renewal projects to clear Black neighborhoods that threatened white business interests.[38] Urban planners consciously located public housing projects to maintain residential racial segregation.[39]

Emerging Civil Rights Movement

Despite America's postwar affluence and growth, Blacks' subordinate legal, political, economic, and social status demanded fundamental societal and legal reforms. During the 1950s and 1960s, a more assertive civil rights movement initially challenged segregation in the South and subsequently emerged as a social movement against racism throughout the nation. During the 1950s, the civil rights movement contested the social construction of race.

> It was this process which created what we call "the great transformation" of racial awareness, racial meaning, racial subjectivity. Race is not only a

matter of politics, economics, or culture, but all of these "levels" of lived experience simultaneously. It is a pre-eminently *social* phenomenon, something which suffuses each individual identity, each family and community, yet equally penetrates state institutions and market relationships. The racial minority movements of the period were the first *new social movements*—the first to expand the concerns of politics to the social, to the terrain of everyday life.[40]

Demands for racial equality and social justice confronted the racist ideology of segregation and ultimately transformed American politics. Blacks' migration away from state-mandated segregation and toward economic opportunities in the North made them a newly potent electoral force in key states, heightened demands for civil rights for themselves and those left behind, and ultimately altered the constituencies of the respective political parties.[41] Several factors—economic, demographic, and ideological—changed American politics. As Blacks moved from farms to Northern cities, they gained the right to vote, obtained better jobs and higher incomes, and acquired resources with which to challenge the racial status quo.[42]

Divisions within the Democratic Party between racial and social policy liberals and conservatives—predominantly Northerners and Southerners, respectively—emerged after World War II. The Democrats' New Deal coalition included white southerners, urban ethnic groups, and recent Black migrants to Northern cities. In 1948, President Harry S. Truman ordered the end of racial segregation in the armed forces, supported elimination of state poll taxes that discriminated against Black voters, and championed federal anti-lynching laws. In 1948, the Democratic Party convention platform included a strong civil rights plank in response to Northern Blacks' growing political influence and liberal whites' opposition to segregation.[43] In reaction, then Democrat South Carolina governor Strom Thurmond bolted the party, ran for president on the States Rights Party line—the "Dixiecrats"—carried Alabama, Louisiana, Mississippi, and South Carolina, and demonstrated the role race would play in the political realignment of the South and the nation.[44] The Dixiecrat revolt revealed that the votes of Southern whites as well as Blacks would be in play and gave both parties incentives to adopt policies to attract them.[45] Subsequent Democratic efforts to win back disaffected white Southern voters enabled Republicans to garner 21% of the Black vote in the 1952 and 39% in the 1956 presidential elections.[46] As I describe in Chapter 4, since the 1960s national Republican politicians pursued an electoral strategy to appeal to white Southern voters' racial antipathy and resistance to school integration, engineer a conservative backlash, and realign the parties around race and public policy issues.[47]

Although presidents Truman and Eisenhower took some steps to reduce racial inequities, conservative Southern Democrats in Congress resisted anti-discrimination laws, voting rights laws, open housing laws, federal aid to education, and national health insurance.[48] Even as the nation became more urbanized and racially diverse, long-serving Southern Democrats chaired pivotal congressional committees and blocked laws to address racial inequality, social justice, or urban programs.[49] Despite conservatives' resistance to racial reforms, Hitler's racist crimes and postwar competition between the United States and Soviet Union for the allegiance of decolonizing countries in the Third World required a national response to Southern apartheid.[50]

During the 1950s and 1960s, the Warren Court's desegregation, civil rights, and criminal procedure decisions aimed to dismantle the Jim Crow system of white supremacy.[51] Between *Brown v. Board of Education* in 1954 and passage of the Civil Rights Act in 1964 and Voting Rights Act in 1965, the Court and Congress imposed equality norms on the South to end formal legal apartheid.[52]

Constitutional Jurisprudence and "Discrete and Insular" Minorities

The Great Migration increased the visibility of Blacks' plight and highlighted the magnitude of America's racial dilemma.[53] "In an era of relatively primitive communications—no radio or television and few national news magazines—rural southern blacks could be disenfranchised, coerced in their labor, cheated out of public school funds, and even lynched—all without most northern whites even being aware of what was happening."[54] Southern segregation and legally enforced inequality were grounded in theories of racial inferiority. During the first third of the twentieth century, a new paradigm questioned so-called scientific theories of biological racial differences and attributed Blacks' condition to social, cultural, and environmental forces.[55] Assumptions of inherent racial inferiority conflicted with American ideals of democracy, equality, and justice. Resolving this contradiction required integrating Blacks into American society.[56] Changing racial demography and its political impact moved segregation and de jure inequality to the center of the nation's and Supreme Court's concerns about civil rights.

During the 1937–38 term, the Court reviewed the constitutionality of New Deal laws and distinguished the scope of review it would apply to economic legislation—where it gave Congress and states broad regulatory authority—and its scrutiny of laws that affected individual rights. In the famous Footnote Four of *United States v. Carolene Products,* the Court announced that it would review more closely state laws that affected political rights and those protections enumerated in the Bill of Rights.

> Nor need we enquire whether similar considerations [of deference] enter into the review of statutes directed at particular religious, or national, or racial minorities, whether the prejudice against *discrete and insular minorities* may be a special condition, which tends seriously to curtail the operation of those political processes ordinarily to be relied upon to protect minorities, and which may call for a correspondingly more searching judicial inquiry.[57]

The Court proposed to use the Equal Protection Clause to strictly scrutinize laws that affected the political process and racial minorities—discrete and insular minorities—whose rights might suffer continually from majoritarian domination.[58] Discrete and insular minorities, such as Blacks, were members of groups who historically had been discriminated against, who had immutable characteristics—unchangeable and highly visible—and who were powerless to protect themselves from oppression through the political process.

The Court recognized that those in power could pervert the political process to entrench themselves and that racial minorities could be perpetual losers because of their subjugation and vulnerability to scapegoating and race-baiting.[59] "The theory of Footnote Four suggests that even if African-Americans in the South could vote, they could not win elections and might be subject to such prejudice that legislation hostile to them would be forthcoming. When that occurs, the Court must step in to protect the discrete and insular minority that otherwise lacks the normal means—joining electoral coalitions—that we expect to protect people."[60] The political process failed because white groups would not form alliances with emancipated Blacks because of deeply entrenched racist sentiments.

The Warren Court acted to protect minority groups' civil rights because "the questions associated with the Black experience in America raised, as no others could, the spectre of internal conflict between the values of a free and open political life . . . and of fair treatment of 'minorities.'"[61] Until the 1960s, laws, customs, and extra-legal violence in the South combined to create and enforce a caste system of white supremacy. During the 1950s, Southern Blacks attended segregated schools, rode segregated buses, and used segregated bathrooms. They could not drink from whites-only water fountains, eat in whites-only restaurants, or sleep in whites-only hotels.[62] They had little voice in government and scant hope for fair treatment from white police or the white judiciary. They were systematically disenfranchised and excluded from juries. Blacks were subject to racial domination and subordination through duly enacted Jim Crow laws and violent extra-legal terrorism.[63]

Southern racial terrorism flourished because local sheriffs were politically elected and nonprofessional. Whites readily resorted to organized violence when Blacks challenged racial mores or threatened lines between superiors and subordinates.[64] Without intervention from outside the region, the combinations of private terror by white-hooded Klansmen, formal legal discrimination, abuse of the justice system, and political exclusion assured Southern Blacks' continued disenfranchisement and subordination.

The modern civil rights movement's campaign for equal rights, the right to vote, and the end of legally sanctioned segregation gained national prominence with the Montgomery bus boycott in 1955 led by Rev. Martin Luther King, Jr.[65] The struggle for racial equality continued throughout the South for the next decade with protests, demonstrations, sit-ins, and violent clashes with the defenders of segregation.

The task fell to the Court to pursue racial equality and dismantle segregation. In 1896, *Plessy v. Ferguson* held that "separate but equal" facilities did not deny Blacks equal protection of the law and remitted racial issues to the states.[66] For the next half century, *Plessy* provided the constitutional foundation for segregated public facilities and Jim Crow laws, and contributed to a long downward spiral in Southern race relations.[67] In the 1950s and 1960s, racial injustice and urban problems presented volatile issues that the Congress was unable or unwilling to address because of Southern committee chairs' dominance. "The Supreme Court probably was a better gauge of national opinion on race than was a United States Congress in which white supremacist southern Democrats enjoyed disproportionate power because of Senate seniority and filibuster rules."[68]

By default, the Warren Court began to address the public policy void through decisions to protect individual rights and minorities' civil liberties. Although the NAACP Legal Defense Fund attacked the segregation in a variety of fora, the crucial battle for racial justice and to end Southern apartheid was fought to desegregate schools. In *Brown vs. Board of Education*, the Warren Court concluded that separate no longer could be equal.[69] The implications of overruling *Plessy* were profound.

> *Brown* involved a major social problem, racial discrimination, translated into a legal question, the constitutionality of separate but equal public schools. It posed an issue that no other branch of government was anxious to address. It raised questions that had distinctively moral implications: in invalidating racial segregation the Court was condemning the idea of racial supremacy. And it affected the lives of ordinary citizens, not merely in the South, not merely in public education, for the Court's series of per curiam decisions after *Brown* revealed that it did not consider racial segregation any more valid in other public facilities than it had in schools. The Warren Court had significantly altered race relations in America.[70]

Although *Brown II* ordered states to desegregate schools with "all deliberate speed," Southern political leaders denigrated the Court's decision and urged "massive resistance" to judicial usurpation. Maintaining segregated public schools ranked near the top of white supremacists' hierarchy of racial goals.[71] White southern leaders castigated *Brown* as a decision by "a lawless Court, abandoning the Constitution ('a mere scrap of paper') for the personal and political values of the unelected judges."[72] Southern congressional Democrats drafted the Southern Manifesto, which denounced *Brown* as an abuse of judicial power and advocated noncompliance with an illegitimate decision.[73] The few Southern congressmen who declined to endorse the Manifesto suffered defeat in the next Democratic primary. In the aftermath of *Brown*, Southern racial moderates virtually disappeared under pressure from more hardline racists as Southern politics moved even farther to the right.[74] "*Brown* radicalized southern politics, leading candidates for office to maneuver for the most extreme segregationist position, and turning 'moderation' into a derisive terms."[75] After George Wallace lost the 1958 Alabama governor's race to an avowed racist, he swore that he was "not goin' to be out-niggahed again,"[76] and he refined race-coded appeals in subsequent gubernatorial and presidential campaigns. White Southerners viewed *Brown* as federal interference with race relations, which elicited historical memories of Reconstruction and carpetbag government.[77] "The Ku Klux Klan reasserted itself as a powerful terrorist organization, committing castrations, killings, and the bombing of black homes and churches. NAACP leaders were beaten, pistol-whipped, and shot."[78] As I explain in Chapter 4, Southern resistance to desegregation in the 1950s, Senator Barry Goldwater's Republican presidential campaign in 1964, and George Wallace and Richard Nixon's presidential campaigns in 1968 demonstrated the political salience of a racialized Southern strategy.[79]

The initial civil rights struggle attempted to end legal segregation, to secure equal rights, and to guarantee the right to vote. The norm of racial equality emerged during the 1950s and 1960s as cultural leaders and influential elites attacked segregation, lynching, police brutality, and political exclusion.

> Cultural leaders increasingly communicated the notion that racial inequality was an immoral principle. The norm of racial equality gained momentum through landmark legislation and court rulings that signaled that racial equality should now be the injunctive norm. The norm of racial equality was also furthered by the civil rights movement, through its moral rhetoric and through actions that prodded and enabled landmark

legislation and discredited the white southern adherents of the old in-
egalitarian norm.[80]

The civil rights movement generated political pressure and nationally
televised violent attacks on Black protesters and Freedom Riders led
Congress to pass the Civil Rights Act of 1964 banning discrimination
in schools, employment, and public accommodations, and the Voting
Rights Act of 1965 prohibiting procedures designed to impede Blacks'
exercise of the franchise.[81] The proportion of registered Black voters in
Southern states more than doubled from 23% in 1964 to 61% by 1969.[82]

The passage of the Civil Rights and Voting Rights Acts formally ended
American apartheid. Southern Democrats cast 104 of the 130 congressional votes against the Civil Rights Act and understood how it would
affect their constituents.[83] The laws created a national norm—formal
legal equality—on matters of race to which 70% of the members of Congress and the Supreme Court required the South to conform. Racial
equality became the dominant cultural value and no politician wanted
to be perceived as racist.[84] However, formal equality belies America's
deep racial divisions, which conservative politicians later would exploit
to foster a political realignment.

Due Process Revolution in Criminal and Juvenile Justice

Criminal justice cases often raise implicit issues of racial inequality.[85]
Beginning in the 1920s and 1930s, Supreme Court cases like *Moore v.
Dempsey*, *Powell v. Alabama*, and *Brown v. Mississippi* sporadically used
the Fourteenth Amendment Due Process Clause to review criminal justice administration and protect Blacks against Southern injustice.[86] Those
earliest decisions involved egregious injustices—confessions extracted by
torture, mob-dominated proceedings, sham trials, and the death penalty.[87]
Southern state supreme courts regarded the formality of any trial, regardless of its procedural deficiencies, as preferable to extra-judicial lynching,
whereas the Supreme Court believed that trials should actually determine defendants' guilt or innocence.[88] The Court's oversight of Southern
states' criminal proceedings became especially important in cases that
challenged white supremacy or that heightened national visibility of the
injustice afforded Black criminal defendants.[89] Southern justice

was not a pretty sight. Jim Crow reigned supreme. Blacks were systematically disenfranchised and excluded from juries. . . . The states virtually had a free hand in the administration of justice. Trials often proceeded without counsel or jury. Convictions were allowed to stand even though they turned on illegally seized evidence or on statements extracted from the accused under coercive circumstances. There were no rules limiting the imposition of the death penalty.[90]

The Court's limited role in overseeing Southern criminal justice marked its initial efforts to eradicate regional deviation from elementary procedural expectations.

The Supreme Court's race-related criminal procedure decisions of the interwar period almost certainly were consonant with dominant national opinion. Most of the country was appalled by these farcical proceedings in which southern black defendants, quite plausibly innocent of the offenses charged, were tortured into confessing and then rushed to the death penalty in mob-dominated trials without effective assistance of counsel. Black criminal defendants certainly were not treated this way in the North. While northern blacks were segregated in ghetto neighborhoods and discriminated against in employment and public accommodations, the administration of justice in northern courts was relatively nondiscriminatory.[91]

Although the Court's early decisions had limited impact on routine Southern justice, they served important non-legal purposes. They offered Blacks hope that progress was possible and apartheid might end. They provided cases around which to organize protests and educate Blacks about their rights. Finally, they exposed Northern whites to the abuses of Jim Crow justice and helped to turn white Americans against segregation and disenfranchisement.[92]

By the 1960s, questions of race became linked with concerns about rising crime rates, urban disorders, the crisis of law and order, and the Court's due process decisions. During the decade, the children of the baby boom reached adolescence and crime increased dramatically. The number of males aged fifteen to seventeen years doubled and rates of serious violent and property crimes increased by more than

75% (Figure 3.1). Demographic changes in the population age structure and improved data collection accounted for much of the recorded
crime rise, but it nonetheless generated a heightened sense of insecu-
rity and fear.[93] Higher rates of crime occur in urban settings and the
greater numbers of Blacks in cities increased the visibility of crime in
minority areas.[94]

Due Process Revolution and Criminal Procedure

The Warren Court's criminal procedure decisions responded to the
previous half century of racial demographic changes, attempted to
protect minority citizens, and sought to limit states' abuses of the
criminal justice system.[95] During the 1960s, it used adversarial procedures and judicial *per se* rules to limit police discretion and protect
defendants' rights.[96] Several themes animated its due process jurisprudence: an emphasis on individual liberty and equality, distrust of state
power, an unwillingness to rely on officials' benevolent motives, and
recognition that their discretion decisions adversely affected minorities.[97] The Court used the Fourteenth Amendment and Bill of Rights
to impose procedural restraints and protect minorities from state officials.[98] Its criminal procedure decisions closely connected with its civil
rights opinions because states disproportionately accused the poor,
minorities, and young with crimes.[99] Those decisions redefined the
relationship between individuals and the state and highlighted the connection between race, civil rights, and criminal justice.[100] It reflected
Carolene Products' shift from protecting private property and economic
interests to protecting civil rights and criminal suspects' constitutional
safeguards.[101]

During the 1960s, the Court used three constitutional strategies—
incorporation, reinterpretation, and equal protection—to decide state
criminal procedure cases.[102] First, it used the Fourteenth Amendment
Due Process Clause to incorporate provisions of the Bill of Rights and
apply them to the states. The Bill of Rights offered national standards
for criminal procedure and the Court applied those provisions to states
to establish a minimum requirement of fairness in criminal trials.[103]
Applying the Bill of Rights to state criminal proceedings redefined the
relationship between the Court and state police practices and justice ad-

ministration. Second, it reinterpreted those provisions to expand constitutional rights and exercise greater oversight over state officials.[104] Finally, it used the Equal Protection Clause to redress imbalances between white and non-white and rich and poor defendants in states' criminal justice systems.

The Court's decisions extending constitutional rights to criminal defendants, many of whom were guilty, coincided with the baby boom increase in crime rates and urban race riots in the 1960s.[105] Decisions such as *Mapp v. Ohio*—exclusionary rule—and *Miranda v. Arizona*—warning prior to custodial interrogation—expanded defendants' rights, restricted police power, and provided a remedy for constitutional violations.[106] These decisions elicited hostile criticism from law enforcement officials, conservative politicians, and the public.[107] While earlier criminal decisions like *Powell*, *Moore*, and *Brown* involved egregious injustice and were veiled cases about race, by the mid-1960s many whites viewed the Court's decisions as overtly racial because of their concurrence with urban riots and rising crime rates.[108] Richard Nixon's 1968 presidential campaign emphasized law and order, decried decisions that he claimed handcuffed police, and made connections between the Court, crime, and race explicit.

Due Process in Juvenile Justice: *In re Gault* and Its Progeny

Penal policy should not be viewed in isolation from but rather as part of a broader framework of social welfare and social control policies.[109] Are social problems like crime and poverty the result of individual bad choices or determined by larger structural factors? Answers to these questions would focus politicians' attention on personal responsibility or the state's role in ameliorating root causes—for example, a choice between punishing individuals and promoting social welfare. Until the 1960s, the rehabilitative ideal dominated penal ideology and emphasized treatment to promote offenders' well-being.[110] Concomitant social welfare policies viewed the poor and disadvantaged as people in need of government intervention rather than as responsible for their own condition.

From its Progressive origins until the early 1970s, the rehabilitative ideal provided the intellectual framework, cultural vocabulary, and shared understandings that animated criminal and juvenile justice professionals.[111]

> Its basic axiom—that penal measures ought, where possible, to be rehabil-itative interventions rather than negative, retributive punishments—gave rise to a whole new network of interlocking principles and practices. . . . [T]he rehabilitative ideal . . . was the hegemonic, organizing principle, the intellectual framework and value system that bound together the whole structure and sense of it for practitioners. It provided an all-embracing conceptual net that could be cast over each and every activity in the penal field, allowing practitioners to render their world coherent and meaning-ful, and to give otherwise unpleasant, troublesome practices something of a benign, scientific gloss.[112]

The rehabilitative enterprise focused on the individual offender and relied on judges and professionals to make welfare-oriented decisions.[113]

Support for the rehabilitative ideal presumes a cultural consensus about the goals of change and the means to achieve them.[114] Progressives believed that the new social sciences gave them the tools with which to modify people's behavior, and they had no qualms about imposing their middle-class values on immigrants and the poor.[115] They affirmed the state's responsibility to care for, as well as to control, offenders. "The state was to be an agent of reform as well as of repression, of care as well as control, of welfare as well as punishment. . . . [T]he criminal justice state became, in part, a welfare state, and the criminal subject, especially one who was young, or disadvantaged, or female, came to be seen as a subject of need as well as guilt, a 'client' as well as an offender."[116]

Beginning in the 1960s, the politics of race and crime precipitated a sharp decline in states' support for social welfare. Justice system poli-cies shifted from a belief that penal measures should rehabilitate and promote positive change to a more negative and punitive orientation.[117] Several forces eroded support for the rehabilitative ideal. Left-wing crit-ics characterized individualized treatment as a paternalistic veneer that masked coercive social control and oppressed the poor, the young, and minorities.[118] They argued that no correctional programs could coun-teract the racial, economic, and social inequality in the larger society.[119] Liberals criticized judges and social workers whose discretionary decisions did not rely on science or evidence, but which resulted in unequal treatment of similarly situated offenders, and they questioned the state's ability to deal justly with its most vulnerable citizens.[120] Conservative critics perceived a moral crisis in rising crime rates, civil rights protests, and urban race riots, advocated for law and order, and favored repression over rehabilitation.[121]

It was against this backdrop that the Court scrutinized juvenile justice administration in the 1960s.[122] In 1966, *Kent v. United States*, which I discuss in Chapter 5, required procedural safeguards in transfer hearings.[123] In 1967, *In re Gault* reviewed states' juvenile court procedures, found them constitutionally deficient, and required a substantial overhaul.[124] David Tanenhaus, in *The Constitutional Rights of Children*, and Christopher Manfredi, in *The Supreme Court and Juvenile Justice*, provide excellent analyses of the litigation strategy and tortured route from an obscure delinquency hearing in rural Arizona to a constitutional landmark.[125]

Gault involved the hearing and institutional confinement of an Arizona boy who allegedly made a telephone call to a neighbor of the "irritatingly offensive, adolescent, sex variety."[126] The offending words purportedly included "Are your cherries ripe? Do you have big bombers? Do you give any away?"[127] Police took fifteen-year-old Gerald Gault into custody and held him overnight without notifying his parents. The next day, a juvenile court judge held an informal hearing to consider a delinquency petition that simply alleged he needed care and custody. The judge questioned Gault about the telephone call, which he admitted dialing, but insisted a companion spoke the offending words. No witnesses testified and there was no transcript or record of the proceeding. The judge did not advise Gault or his parents of the right to remain silent or to counsel and did not provide an attorney. A week later, the judge committed Gault to the State Industrial School "for the period of his minority [that is, until 21], unless sooner discharged by due process of law."[128] A judge could have sentenced an adult convicted of the same crime to a $50 fine or two months' imprisonment, rather than potential confinement of up to six years.[129]

Gault identified two fatal disjunctions between juvenile justice rhetoric and reality: the theory versus the practice of rehabilitation and the procedural safeguards criminal defendants and delinquents received.

Although Progressives envisioned informal meetings, the Court examined actual practices and required adversarial hearings to protect delinquents from the state.

A survey conducted contemporaneously with *Gault* by the President's Commission on Law Enforcement and the Administration of Justice (known as the President's Crime Commission) reported data on the 207 largest juvenile courts serving populations of one hundred thousand or more.[130] Three-quarters (74%) reported that non-white juveniles comprised 40% of delinquents; in 5%, minorities comprised 60% of delinquents. Some of these racial disparities were by-products of Blacks' migration to the North, adaptation from a rural to an urban life, and experience with economic dislocation and discrimination, which contributed to higher rates of delinquency.[131]

Studies of mid-century juvenile courts reported racial bias in handling Black youths compared with whites. In the Jim Crow South, correctional institutions still were segregated, separate, and unequal for those Black youths fortunate enough to be sentenced as delinquents rather than committed to prisons.[132] Elsewhere, juvenile courts more often referred Black juveniles for formal processing and committed them to institutions than they did whites with similar crimes and prior records.[133] A study of institutionalized delinquents found that Black youths were younger, had fewer prior appearances, committed fewer and less serious crimes, but received probation less often than their white counterparts.[134] Although they were less seriously delinquent, a lack of community alternatives contributed to higher rates of commitments.

Although juvenile courts' Progressive founders and Dean Roscoe Pound aspired to exceptionally well qualified judges—mature, wise, and sophisticated, versed in law and social sciences—the survey conducted by the President's Crime Commission reported that "half had not received undergraduate degrees; a fifth had received no college education at all; a fifth were not members of the bar . . . and judicial hearings often are little more than attenuated interviews of 10 or 15 minutes' duration."[135] Nearly all delinquents appeared before judges without counsel. Only 3% of courts reported that lawyers accompanied delinquents in 40% or more of cases and only one-tenth (10.8%) reported that counsel appeared in more than 20% of delinquency cases.[136]

Gault examined juvenile courts' actual operations rather than to accept uncritically their rehabilitative rhetoric.[137] It reviewed their historical justifications to deny procedural safeguards: they were civil rather than criminal proceedings; delinquents received treatment rather than punishment; and when the state acted as *parens patriae*, the child was entitled to custody rather than liberty. It noted that absence of procedures often resulted in judicial arbitrariness rather than "careful, compassionate, individualized treatment."[138] Youths could not challenge judges' discretion even when they imposed punitive sanctions.[139] *Gault* did not reject juvenile courts' rehabilitative goals, but emphasized their high rates of recidivism, stigma of a delinquency label, access to court records by military, law enforcement, and employers, and arbitrary decision making as reasons to require procedural safeguards. It examined the institutions in which states purported to treat delinquents:

> [H]owever euphemistic the title, a "receiving home" or an "industrial school" for juveniles is an institution of confinement in which the child is incarcerated for a greater or lesser time. His world becomes "a building with whitewashed walls, regimented routine, and institutional hours. . . ." Instead of mother and father and sisters and brothers and friends and classmates, his world is peopled by guards, custodians, state employees, and "delinquents" confined with him for anything from waywardness to rape and homicide. . . . [U]nder our Constitution, the condition of being a boy does not justify a kangaroo court.[140]

Gault ruled that juvenile courts must conduct fundamentally fair proceedings: notice of charges, an impartial hearing, assistance of counsel, opportunity to confront and cross-examine witnesses, and the privilege against self-incrimination.[141] The Court did not address juveniles' rights prior to trial—intake and detention—or at disposition, but focused on the adjudication of guilt or innocence.[142] Because *Gault* involved a delinquency case—a youth charged with a crime facing institutional confinement—the Court did not consider noncriminal-status offenders' rights.

The Court endorsed adversary procedures both to determine what happened—factual accuracy—and to preserve individual freedom and limit state power—prevent governmental oppression. *Gault* based delinquents' rights to notice, counsel, and confrontation on the Fourteenth Amendment's due process requirement of fundamental fairness. "Fundamental fairness is a context-sensitive approach in which the procedural guarantees required in any specific case vary according to the proceeding under review and the nature of the rights at stake in those proceedings."[143] The Arizona Supreme Court used the same fundamental fairness approach when it rejected Gault's pleas for procedural protections.[144] By contrast, the Sixth Amendment provides, "In all criminal prosecutions, the accused shall enjoy the right to a *speedy and public trial*, by an *impartial jury* ... and to be *informed* of the nature and cause of the accusation; to be *confronted* with the witnesses against him; ... and to have the Assistance of *Counsel* for his defence."[145]

Gault did not rely on the Sixth Amendment, but held that "[d]ue process of law requires notice of the sort we have described—that is, notice which would be deemed constitutionally adequate in a civil or criminal proceeding."[146] Although *Gault* deemed delinquency proceedings "comparable in seriousness to a felony prosecution," it based his right to counsel on notions of due process rather than the language of the Sixth Amendment.[147] It based his right to confront and examine witnesses on "our law and constitutional requirements" rather than the Sixth Amendment.[148] As I explain in Chapter 9, the Court's reliance on Fourteenth Amendment fundamental fairness, rather than the Sixth Amendment, has resulted in a procedurally deficient justice system compared with rights formally available to adults.

The Court explicitly granted delinquents the Fifth Amendment privilege against self-incrimination. It held that "juvenile proceedings to determine 'delinquency,' which may lead to commitment to a state institution, must be regarded as 'criminal' for purposes of the privilege against self-incrimination. ... It is incarceration against one's will whether it is called 'criminal' or 'civil.'"[149] Granting the privilege against self-incrimination negated claims that delinquency hearings were civil nonadversarial proceedings, and "challenged a core principle of traditional juvenile jurisprudence, that admissions of wrongdoing are an indispensable element of the rehabilitation process."[150] The Fifth Amendment privilege buttresses the adversary system to maintain equality between the individual and the state. Its policies include our preference for an accusatorial rather than an inquisitorial system of criminal justice; our fear that self-incriminating statements will be elicited by inhumane treatment and abuses; our sense of fair play which dictates "a fair state individual balance by requiring the government to leave the individual alone until good cause is shown for disturbing him and by requiring the government in its contest with the individual to shoulder the entire load," . . .[151]

Gault's Fifth Amendment holding reflected the two roles of constitutional procedures: to assure accurate fact finding *and* to protect against government oppression.[152] If *Gault* was concerned only with reliability of juvenile confessions and fact finding, then it could have relied on previous decisions that required confessions be made "voluntarily." As I explain in Chapter 9, *Gallegos v. Colorado* and *Haley v. Ohio* considered juveniles' confessions, used the Fourteenth Amendment voluntariness test, and concluded that youthfulness adversely affected the reliability of statements.[153] By contrast, *Gault* recognized that the Fifth Amendment not only enhanced fact-finding, but also struck a balance between the individual and the state and prevented governmental oppression.[154] *Gault* recognized that the interests of delinquents and the state conflicted and that judges or probation officers could not adequately protect youths.[155]

Justice Hugo Black concurred in *Gault*, but argued that delinquents should enjoy the same criminal procedural safeguards as adult defendants based on the Fifth and Sixth Amendments, rather than watered-down safeguards based on vague notions of fundamental fairness. For Justice Black, once the state charged a youth with a crime for which it could confine him, delinquency proceedings were functionally criminal prosecutions.

Where a person, infant or adult, can be seized by the State, charged and convicted for violating a state criminal law, and then ordered by the State to be confined for six years, I think the Constitution requires that he be tried in accordance with the guarantees of all the provisions of the Bill of Rights. . . . Undoubtedly this would be true of an adult defendant, and it would be a plan denial of equal protection of the laws—an invidious discrimination—to hold that others subject to heavier punishment could, because they are children, be denied these same constitutional safeguards.[156]

The functional equivalence between delinquency and criminal trials required comparable procedures.

Both *Gault*'s majority and Black's concurring opinion assumed that juveniles were competent to exercise their newly granted rights in conjunction with counsel.[157] *Gault* quoted from the President's Crime Commission that "no single action holds more potential for achieving procedural justice for the child in the juvenile court than provision of counsel. The presence of an independent legal representative of the child, or his parent, is the keystone of the whole structure of guarantees that a minimum system of procedural justice requires."[158] The Court recognized that providing counsel and other safeguards could make proceedings more formal, adversarial, and complex, but concluded that delinquents needed "advocates to speak for them and guard their interests."[159] *Gault* acknowledged that delinquents could waive counsel, but presumed they could do so knowingly, intelligently, and voluntarily.[160]

Subsequent decisions further criminalized delinquency trials. *In re Winship* held that the state must prove delinquency by the criminal standard—beyond a reasonable doubt—rather than by the lower civil standard of proof—preponderance of the evidence.[161] Because the Bill of Rights does not define the standard of proof in criminal cases, *Winship* first held that the Constitution required states to prove criminal defendants' guilt beyond a reasonable doubt . It endorsed the highest standard to prevent governmental overreach, to avoid wrongful convictions, and to assure public confidence in justice administration. It then required the same standard of proof in delinquency proceedings. "[I]ntervention cannot take the form of subjecting the child to the stigma of a finding that he violated a criminal law and to the possibility of institutional confinement on proof insufficient to convict him were he an adult."[162]

Breed v. Jones held that the double jeopardy protection of the Fifth Amendment barred criminal prosecution of a youth whom a juvenile court previously found delinquent for the same crime.[163] *Breed* posited the same constitutional interests in delinquency and criminal trials:

Although the juvenile-court system had its genesis in the desire to provide a distinctive procedure and setting to deal with the problems of youth, including those manifested by antisocial conduct, our decisions in recent years have recognized that there is a gap between the originally benign conception of the system and its realities.

. . . [I]t is simply too late in the day to conclude . . . that a juvenile is not put in jeopardy at a proceeding whose object is to determine whether he has committed acts that violate a criminal law and whose potential consequences include both the stigma inherent in such a determination and the deprivation of liberty for many years.[164]

The Court found that policies that underlay the double jeopardy prohibition applied equally to delinquency and criminal prosecutions.[165]

McKeiver v. Pennsylvania denied delinquents the constitutional right to a jury trial. Previously, in *Duncan v. Louisiana* the Court held that adults enjoyed the Sixth Amendment right to a jury trial in state criminal proceedings.[166] By contrast, *McKeiver* ruled that Fourteenth Amendment due process required only accurate fact-finding, which a judge could do as well as a jury.[167] *McKeiver* marked a departure from the Court's approach to constitutional rights in state criminal proceedings. During the previous decade, it incorporated specific provisions of the Bill of Rights and applied them to states to expand defendants' rights and rejected the fundamental fairness approach *McKeiver* used.[168] *McKeiver* did not explain why it did not follow *Duncan* but simply asserted that juvenile courts were not criminal prosecutions.[169] "[T]he juvenile court proceeding has not yet been held to be a 'criminal prosecution,' within the meaning and reach of the Sixth Amendment, and also has not yet been regarded as devoid of criminal aspects merely because it usually has been given the civil label."[170] It cautioned that granting delinquents a jury trial "will remake the juvenile proceeding into a fully adversary process and will put an effective end to what has been the idealistic prospect of an intimate, informal protective proceeding."[171]

McKeiver's singular focus on accurate fact-finding departed from *Gault* and *Winship*, which emphasized the *dual* functions of procedural safeguards—accurate fact finding *and* protection from the state. *Gault* relied on the Fifth Amendment to strengthen the adversarial process and prevent governmental overreaching, despite any adverse effect it might have on accurate fact-finding. Similarly, Justice Brennan's concurring-dissenting opinion in *McKeiver* concluded that delinquents required either a jury or a public trial to guard against governmental oppression.[172]

The *McKeiver* plurality feared that jury trials would impair juvenile courts' informality, flexibility, and confidentiality, and undermine their rehabilitative mission. It worried that a jury would bring "the traditional delay, the formality, and the clamor of the adversary system and, possibly, the public trial."[173] However, *Gault* already had considered and rejected those concerns. "[I]nformality has no necessary connection with therapy. . . . It is quite possible that in many instances lawyers, for all their commitment to formality, could do more to further therapy for their clients than can the small, overworked social staffs of the courts."[174] Despite *McKeiver*'s concerns, in the states that provide a jury right, it has, at most, a modest impact on justice administration.[175]

McKeiver denied that delinquents needed protection from the state. It invoked the mythology of the paternalistic juvenile court judge and rejected concerns that closed hearings could prejudice fact-finding.[176] I explain in Chapter 9 that there are many reasons to question fact-finding in a system in which police and probation officers testify regularly before the same judge who has reviewed a juvenile's social history and prior delinquency record while dealing with the case at earlier stages.[177] I argue in Chapter 5 that the get tough policies of the 1980s and 1990s increased direct and collateral consequences of delinquency convictions and repudiated *McKeiver*'s unsupported premise that juvenile courts treat rather than punish delinquents.

Conclusion: Due Process and Criminal Convergence

Gault triggered a procedural revolution that transformed juvenile courts from welfare agencies into scaled-down criminal courts. Progressives focused on a child's social circumstances and need for rehabilitation. Criminality was a symptom of delinquency, but its formal proof was secondary. Despite *McKeiver*'s denial of a jury, *Gault* and *Winship* endorsed the adversarial model, attorneys, privilege against self-incrimination, and criminal standard of proof as a prerequisite to intervention. By adopting some criminal procedures, the Court shifted delinquency hearings' focus to proof of crimes, formalized the relationship between crimes and consequences, and launched a procedural and substantive convergence between juvenile and criminal justice systems.[178]

Franklin Zimring contrasts the implications of providing procedural safeguards for the interventionist and diversionary rationales of juvenile courts. He argues that "standards of proof and defense lawyers are a major drawback to identifying children in need and providing them with help. If that is the mission of the juvenile court, then due process will be a major handicap to its achievement. But if saving kids from the gratuitous harms inflicted by the criminal process is the aim, there is no inherent conflict between due process and the court's main beneficial functions."[179] I argue in Chapter 9 that robust procedural safeguards would create financial and administrative incentives to divert more youths from the formal process and provide greater protections for those facing a punitive juvenile system.

The Court's decisions reflected competing visions of children. In granting delinquents legal rights, *Gault* assumed that young people were competent to exercise them—"a new conception of childhood that embodied a broader understanding of children's capacity for independent judgment and action."[180] By contrast, *McKeiver* viewed youths as immature and unable to benefit from rights available to adults. The Court's contradictory characterizations of youth provide rationale with which to deny juveniles' claims either for procedural parity with criminal defendants or safeguards to compensate for their disabilities.

The Court did not intend its decisions to impair juvenile courts' rehabilitative efforts, but subsequent judicial and legislative responses fostered their convergence with criminal courts. Prior to *Gault*, probation officers presented delinquents' cases in court and recommended dispositions. After *Gault* gave delinquents a right to counsel, states introduced prosecutors to offset defense lawyers' presence. Prosecutors socialized in criminal courts to maximize convictions and punishment began to import those norms into juvenile courts.[181]

Although *Gault*'s safeguards were less extensive than those granted adults, the Court provided no mechanisms to implement or enforce them. *Gault* did not give delinquents a constitutional right to appellate review, thereby limiting higher courts' ability to oversee compliance.[182] Similarly, it remitted delinquents' right to counsel to state legislatures to appropriate funds to implement it. In Chapter 9, I explain that local authorities have financial and administrative reasons to underfund public defenders and discourage youths from asserting rights.

Contemporary juvenile courts have become wholly owned subsidiaries of the criminal justice system. A modicum of procedural justice, however inadequate, enabled states to subordinate juvenile courts' rehabilitative goals and impose harsher sanctions. Although racial concerns drove the Court to focus on civil and procedural rights, granting delinquents even meager protections legitimated the escalation of penalties that fall heavily on minority youths.

PART III

The Get Tough Era

3

The Get Tough Era I

Structural Change and Youth Crime

At the beginning of the twentieth century, modernization transformed
America from a rural agrarian society into an urban industrial one. By
the middle of the century, Blacks' migration from the rural South to the
urban North and West and whites' movement from cities to suburbs
further changed American society. In the 1960s, a rise in lawbreaking
and urban riots heightened whites' fears of crime and racial discord.[1]
Between the mid-1960s and late 1970s, the number of serious and violent crimes doubled and led to more conservative public opinion about
crime and punishment.[2] Macro-structural industrial change in the 1970s
and 1980s led to the loss of manufacturing jobs for low-skilled workers
in cities, where most minorities lived. By the late 1980s, these changes
contributed to escalating youth violence and provided political impetus
for get tough policies that transformed criminal and juvenile justice.

This chapter examines what happened in the 1970s and 1980s that led
to concentrated poverty in the inner city and drug-related violent crime.
The first section examines macro-structural economic and racial demographic changes in American cities. The second section examines how
the epidemic of crack cocaine in the 1980s spurred gun violence and
youth homicide in devastated inner-city neighborhoods.[3] Black youth
homicide provided the nexus between race, crime, and fear that enabled
the politics of crime and set the stage for mass incarceration of adults
and harsher punishment of juveniles.

Macro-Structural Transformation

In wealthy democratic countries, a strong relationship exists between
social and economic inequality and homicide rates—the greater the
income and wealth disparities, the higher the rates of killings; the United

States is among the most economically stratified and unequal countries in Western society.[4] The United States' uniquely high homicide rates reflect the country's pronounced inequalities in wealth and income, historic racial discrimination, and gun policies that make firearms readily available. People who aspire to cultural goals of wealth and success but who lack access to legitimate means to achieve those goals experience frustration and anger that can lead to behavior destructive both to self and others.[5] Robert Sampson and William Julius Wilson argue that "macro-social patterns of residential inequality give rise to the social isolation and ecological concentration of the truly disadvantaged, which in turn leads to structural barriers and cultural adaptations that undermine social organization and hence the control of crime."[6]

Between the prosperous post–World War II years and the early 1970s, automobile, steel, construction, and manufacturing industries provided high school graduates with well-paid union jobs, health insurance, and retirement pensions.[7] This was the era of the middle class in which all segments of the population benefited from economic growth.[8] The United States emerged from World War II with its industrial base intact and became the economic engine that rebuilt the world for the next quarter century. Federal programs like the Servicemen's Readjustment Act—the GI Bill—provided funds for returning veterans to pursue college degrees and obtain low-cost home loans.[9] Mass-produced consumer goods led to growth of markets at home and abroad. The expansion of trade unions and rising incomes enabled more people to enter the middle class and enjoy access to goods and services—cars, single-family homes, foreign travel—previously available only to the wealthy.[10]

Black men who moved to cities during the Great Migration benefitted from blue-collar jobs that provided the foundations of working-class communities.[11] For more than a quarter century, the country enjoyed sustained economic expansion and prosperity fueled by industrial production, consumer demand, and low energy costs. The postwar period of unprecedented material well-being, economic growth, and public confidence supported inclusive social policies and the rehabilitative ideal. David Garland argues that "[p]enal-welfare policies, like the welfare state itself, were developed against a background of economic conditions that were favourable to welfare provision, public spending, and a measure of redistribution. . . . To the extent that penal-welfare policies required public legitimation, this was forthcoming in an expanding economy, where middle class derived tangible benefits from public expenditure, and were broadly supportive of welfare policies."[12] As long as the economic pie grew and the middle class felt that they received a fair share of the benefits, the public supported or at least did not strongly object to social welfare and rehabilitative penal policies adopted by more liberal elites.[13] While economic growth in the 1950s and 1960s made redistributive government policies tolerable, later economic contraction and income inequality undermined popular support for government intervention and welfare.[14]

Transition to a Post-Industrial Economy

Between the end of World War II and the early 1970s, programs implemented during the New Deal, enhanced educational opportunities, and economic expansion contributed to declining poverty, increasing median income, and a reduction in income inequality.[15] Beginning in the early 1970s, the transition from an industrial to an information and service economy reduced employment prospects for lower-skilled factory workers. Oil crises in 1973 and 1979 and the decline in manufacturing led to periods of economic recession, inflation, and high unemployment, and steadily decreasing union membership.[16] The job security, income, and benefits blue-collar workers had enjoyed for a quarter century began to disappear.

The transition to a post-industrial economy produced bifurcated opportunities based on education and technical skills.[17] Globalization, outsourcing, and technologically sophisticated manufacturing eliminated many jobs of less skilled workers. In a decade and a half, employment in manufacturing sectors decreased from 26% to 19% of the workforce, while full-time employment in the service sectors—finance, insurance, real estate—more than doubled and surpassed manufacturing employment.[18] Beginning in 1973, and for the first time since the post–World War II period of growth, inflation-adjusted real hourly wages stagnated and then declined.[19] The structure of cities reflected the transformation of the economy, racial demography, and urban space—shiny towers of banks, finance, and commercial centers near the closed factories of the industrial districts, wealthy young professionals living in gentrified older neighborhoods, and impoverished African Americans living in concentrated poverty.[20]

During the 1970s, the globalizing economy and international competition in the auto and steel industries had profound consequences. William Julius Wilson argues that these changes adversely affected Blacks more than other groups because of their more recent arrival into and greater vulnerability within the manufacturing economy.[21] Manufacturing sectors in which blue-collar workers and unions had previously experienced the strongest gains were among the primary victims of the economic decline of the 1970s and 1980s. White factory workers saw their wages, benefits, and middle-class status eroded and resented liberal affirmative action programs to extend jobs and seniority to Blacks against whom unions and employers previously discriminated.[22] They understood conservative political attacks on affirmative action policies—couched as reverse discrimination—in terms of racial competition.[23] White workers' anxiety and anger over their economic vulnerability and government failure to address their concerns enabled some politicians to scapegoat Blacks and increased their receptiveness to racial appeals.[24] With the decline in manufacturing jobs, lower-skilled and less educated workers could find alternative work only in retail and service industries, which paid lower wages, lacked health benefits, and provided less stability.[25]

Inequality in America increasingly operates through education.[26] The earnings gap between high school and college graduates widened as those with more education and technical training prospered and those with fewer skills foundered.[27] In the 1970s, college-educated people only earned about 25% more than did those with a high school education.[28] Two decades later, differences in earnings were almost 100%, because college graduates' income grew substantially while high school graduates' declined.[29] Increasingly, success in the labor market correlated with education. The education-earning differential exacerbated racial inequality because only 13.1% of Blacks aged twenty-five to thirty-four had college degrees, compared with 24.5% of whites; the proportion of Blacks aged eighteen to twenty-four enrolled in college declined while that of whites increased during this period.[30] Better-paying jobs—professional, technical, and managerial—employed disproportionately more white workers and grew faster than did those that employed proportionally more Black workers—machine operators, service, clerical, and household workers.[31] These economic changes had regional and political ramifications. Employment declined most in the Northeast and Midwestern rust-belt industries—steel, rubber, and auto—while high-technology industries—electronics and computers—expanded in the more conservative Sunbelt states.[32] "The great economic losers of the new inequality were men with only a high school education. Without a college degree, these less-skilled men missed out on the technical and white-collar jobs that retained their value through the 1970s and 1980s. Young black men in urban areas were hit the hardest. As urban labor markets buckled under the loss of industrial jobs, minority neighborhoods in the Northeast and the Midwest descended into poverty and chronic joblessness."[33]

Tax policies enacted during the Reagan administration fostered wealth and income inequality and shifted the tax burden from the wealthy to the middle class.[34] Reductions in capital gains and dividend tax rates directed more than 80% of tax benefits and savings to the wealthiest 10% of the population.[35] At the same time, the Reagan administration cut half a million families from welfare rolls, slashed one million from food stamps, and dropped 2.6 million children from school lunch programs.[36] Since 1980, the country has experienced overall growth similar to that during the prosperous postwar era, but as a result of those political decisions, the incomes and wealth of those at the top have grown substantially, while that of the middle class have stagnated, and the condition of the poor has deteriorated.[37]

Parental education and wealth confer intergenerational advantages to their children. Over the past quarter century, the net worth of college educated households with children increased by 47%, whereas that of high school–educated households fell by 17%.[38] Tax policies skewed toward the top wealth holders enable them to disproportionally benefit from economic and productivity growth, to compound their cumulative advantage, and to produce the greatest income and wealth inequality in American history.[39]

The 1964 Civil Rights Act included women in its employment discrimination provisions; women's entry into the work force eroded traditional patriarchy and the economic position of white men. As financial pressures made one-earner male-headed households increasingly untenable, the proportion of married women entering the workforce grew from about one-third in 1965 to more than half by 1980.[40] Since the early 1970s, average family income has increased little, real wages of typical male workers have declined, and only the entry of women into the workforce has sustained median family incomes.[41] Although some women entered the labor force to take advantage of expanding opportunities and changing gender roles, economic necessity forced many others to enter the workforce to supplement declining family incomes and to maintain a middle-class status. Women married later, had fewer children, and reentered the workforce sooner after giving birth.[42] Professional opportunities for college-educated women and service and light-manufacturing employment for working-class women changed the operation of families. As more women entered the workforce, parents' ability to supervise and control their children declined. Changes in family structure and gender roles have become a central part of political and cultural debates—"family values"—over the past quarter century.

Public Policies Created the Urban Ghetto

The experiences of Blacks during and after the Great Migration differed substantially from those of earlier generations of European immigrants and placed them at a significant economic and structural disadvantage during the post-industrial transition.[43] Unlike the situation around the turn of the century, when companies sought immigrants' labor during industrialization, by the 1970s manufacturing jobs had begun to decline. Black men leaving the South entered the manufacturing economy as demand for industrial workers was contracting.[44] Notwithstanding discrimination against earlier immigrant groups, Blacks faced much more intense exclusion and segregation in education, residence, and employment, which impeded their integration and upward mobility.[45]

Racism reinforced residential segregation and limited Blacks' ability to live near employment opportunities.[46] As Blacks moved to cities, automobile ownership and federal highway policies contributed to white suburban growth.[47] Since 1980, more than two-thirds of manufacturing and retail employment growth has occurred in suburbs rather than in central cities.[48] Job growth in the suburbs coupled with inadequate public transportation posed obstacles for urban workers who could not afford cars and created a job-spatial mismatch—people and employment opportunities located in different places.[49] Spatial and social isolation from informal job networks exacerbated Black poverty and limited chances for economic integration and mobility.[50]

As noted in Chapter 2, federal housing policies, bank redlining, disinvestment and mortgage policies, real estate block-busting and related sales practices, and interstate highway construction contributed to white suburbs surrounding increasingly poor minority urban cores.[51] In the 1950s and 1960s, urban renewal eliminated about 20% of central cities' housing stock and freeway construction destroyed or quarantined many viable low-income Black communities.[52] As the urban Black population grew, municipalities concentrated public housing units in inner-city ghettos, withdrew services from Black neighborhoods, and contributed to urban decay. [53] During the Reagan era, cuts in direct aid to cities reduced revenues for transit, social services, public works, education, job training, and the like.[54] These cuts particularly affected the older cities of the Northeast and Midwest and contributed to consolidation of inner-city ghettoes. Even as cities faced increasingly complex problems—crime, drugs, the AIDS epidemic and public health costs, joblessness, and failing schools—many lacked the resources with which to address them.[55]

The segregation of many Blacks in urban ghettos did not happen by chance or simply reflect personal housing preferences. Public policies, private institutions, and individuals' actions created and sustained racial segregation and concentrated poverty.[56] A half century ago, the National Advisory Committee on Civil Disorders—the Kerner Commission—stated that "segregation and poverty have created in the racial ghetto a destructive environment totally unknown to most white Americans. . . . White institutions created it, white institutions maintain it, and white society condones it."[57] Robert Sampson and Janet Lauritsen argue that "even given the same objective socioeconomic status, blacks and whites face vastly different environments in which to live, work, and raise their children."[58] They attribute racialized concentrated poverty to deliberate public policies to contain and isolate minorities and to white communities' opposition to public housing in their neighborhoods.[59] In 1980, 70% of poor whites live in non-poverty areas compared with only 16% of poor Blacks. Conversely, fewer than 7% of poor whites live in areas of concentrated poverty compared with 38% of poor Blacks.[60] As corollaries of deindustrialization, Black family income dropped from 61% of that of white families in 1970 to 54% in 1992.[61] In short, Blacks are far more likely than whites to be poor and, if they are poor, far more likely to live in segregated areas of concentrated poverty. As Marie Gottschalk observes, "there are virtually no white neighborhoods as poor as the poorest black neighborhoods. The 'worst' urban neighborhoods in which whites reside are considerably better off than those of the average African American community, and the most advantaged black neighborhoods are no better off than the typical white neighborhood."[62] Concentrated poverty for Black families is far more likely to be intergenerational than it is for whites.[63]

Segregation and concentrated poverty created an inhospitable environment to which ghetto residents struggled to adapt and which sustained outlooks and behaviors that impede social mobility.[64] Disorganized slum communities foster a milieu in which crime and drug use, joblessness, welfare dependency, teenage childbearing, and unwed parenthood become normal.[65] Whites' fears strengthens their desire to insulate themselves from those whom they perceive as dangerous and threatening.[66]

The structural changes—deindustrialization, suburban job growth, and economic bifurcation based on education—and demographic transformations—white migration to suburbs, Black concentrated poverty in inner cities—altered the nation's political balance.[67] Efforts to reduce residential and school segregation contributed to white flight to the suburbs.[68] After the Supreme Court in *Milliken v. Bradley* stopped busing across school district boundaries to achieve *Brown*'s desegregation goals, "suburban municipalities built on white flight were permitted to set up virtually all-white enclaves operating as if 1954 had never happened."[69]

Between 1970 and 1986, the suburban population, already overwhelmingly white, grew from 40 to 45% of the national electorate.[70] As a result of economic stratification, more families now live either in uniformly affluent or poor neighborhoods and fewer live in mixed- or moderate-income neighborhoods.[71] Residential sorting and school quality go hand in hand because well-educated parents will move to districts that provide their children with better educational opportunities.[72]

The emergence of the suburbs as a virtual electoral majority enables white voters to address their own public service needs—schools, parks, police, and roads—through local and county government while weakening their ties to cities increasingly populated by Blacks and other minorities.[73] Suburban whites' ability to fund public services through local taxes and divisions between urban and suburban municipalities reduced whites' incentives to contribute to state or federal programs for the poor. The concentration of Black voters in urban areas has limited their influence over politicians who represent predominantly white suburban districts.[74] While investments in public services and, especially, public schools is imperative to address condition of segregated poverty, urban-suburban political divisions reduce whites' incentives to contribute.[75]

Where children live determines the quality of schools they attend. During the period of deindustrialization, increased income-based residential segregation has reinforced de facto class-based school segregation.[76] The twenty-five largest central-city school districts enroll 27.5% of all Black students and 30% of all Hispanic schoolchildren, but only 3.3% of all white children.[77] With more affluent students attending private schools or better suburban schools, the quality of urban schools deteriorated and further limited educational opportunities for minority youths. Underperforming urban schools and low expectations undermine Black youths' prospects to escape the effects of concentrated poverty.[78] In an economy that places a premium on education, skills, and training, many poor and urban children of color are at a significant disadvantage compared with their white suburban counterparts. I argue in Chapter 7 that these changes have fueled a school-to-prison pipeline for urban Black male students.

Deindustrialization and the Black Underclass

The post-industrial economic transition and racial reorganization of cities contributed to an urban underclass living in cultural isolation and concentrated poverty.[79] In *The Truly Disadvantaged*, William J. Wilson argues that the transformation of inner cities reduced Black males' employment prospects, increased rates of out-of-wedlock childbirths, contributed to the decline of two-parent Black households, and increased child poverty.[80] Limited employment opportunities for low-skilled workers reduced the pool of Black men who could support a family.[81] Households headed by unwed mothers increased as marriage to unemployed or unemployable Black males became less attractive.[82] Children reared in single-parent households experience higher rates of poverty than do those raised in two-parent households. Sixty percent of Black children live in single-parent households and they are four times more likely than white children to live in poverty.[83]

Following passage of federal housing laws in the mid-1960s, many middle-class Blacks took advantage of economic and housing opportunities to leave the ghettos.[84] "The out-migration of middle-class families from ghetto areas left behind a destitute community lacking the institutions, resources, and values necessary for success in post-industrial society."[85] While most African Americans live conventional lives, about 30 to 40% live in segregated areas of concentrated poverty outside the economic mainstream.[86] Middle-class Blacks' residential mobility deprived the truly disadvantaged who remained of the human capital and economic and cultural resources necessary for social stability and amplified the effects of concentrated poverty.[87] Their social isolation deprives them of resources, role models, cultural learning, and informal networks that could facilitate social and economic advancement.[88]

Crack Cocaine and Black Youth Homicide

In the 1980s, the introduction of crack cocaine into inner cities led to a proliferation of guns and a sharp increase in Black youth homicides.[89] The connection between race and youth crime provided a powerful incentive to politicize crime policies.[90] Because rates of offending for some crimes differ by race, political decisions to get tough on violence and drugs meant targeting young Black men.[91] The media depict and the public perceive crime and juvenile courts' clientele primarily as urban Black males.[92] Politicians manipulated and exploited these perceptions with demagogic pledges to crack down on "youth crime," which white voters understood as code words for Black males.[93]

The Federal Bureau of Investigation's *Uniform Crime Reports* reveal that arrest rates for serious crime, juvenile crime, and violent juvenile crime followed similar patterns—increasing from the mid-1960s until 1980, declining somewhat in the mid-1980s, and increasing to another

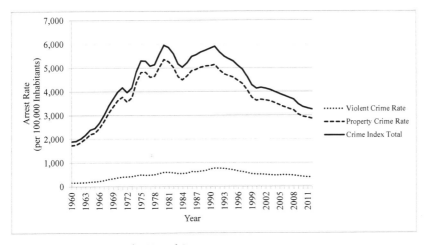

Figure 3.1. Arrest Rate in the United States
Sources: Federal Bureau of Investigation—Uniform Crime Reporting, *Crime in the United States*, https://ucr.fbi.gov; Disaster Center, *United States Crime Rates*, www.disastercenter.com.

peak in the early 1990s, since which time they have fallen precipitously.[94] Between 1965 and 1980, violent crime and homicide rates doubled, followed by a second upsurge between 1986 and 1994.[95] Elizabeth Hinton attributes part of the perceived increases in crime in the 1960s and 1970s to Great Society crime legislation that funded improved state data collection and expanded the deployment of police resources in African American communities.[96]

The FBI Crime Index includes arrests for both violent and property crimes. The Violent Crime Index records four crimes—murder and non-negligent manslaughter, forcible rape, robbery, and aggravated assault. The Property Crime Index records four crimes—burglary, larceny-theft, motor vehicle theft, and arson. Arrests may be reported either as absolute numbers or as rates per 100,000 population to control for changes in population, which allows for comparisons between years.

Figure 3.1 depicts arrest rates for violent, property, and total index crime for all offenders—juveniles and adults—from 1960 to 2011. In the early 1960s, police arrested offenders for violent crimes at a rate around 160 per 100,000, for property crimes at a rate about 1,750 per 100,000, and for total crimes at rate of less than 2,000 per 100,000. Over the next two decades, arrests rates for violent, property and total index crimes more than doubled and first peaked in the early 1980s. In 1980, the total

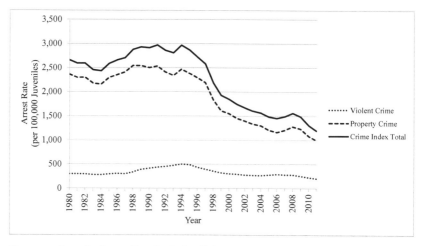

Figure 3.2. Juvenile Arrest Rate for Index Crimes
Source: Office of Juvenile Justice and Delinquency Prevention, *Statistical Briefing Book*,
www.ojjdp.gov.

arrest rate was 5,950 per 100,000, nearly three times that of the early
1960s. Violent arrest rates nearly quadrupled and comprised about 10%
of that total. After a mid-1980s dip, arrest rates peaked again in the early
1990s, since which time they have fallen steadily. At the second peak in
1991, the overall arrest rate reached 5,898 per 100,000, but violent crime
arrest rates comprised 12.9%, a larger proportion of the total. After two
decades of decline, overall crime and violent arrest rates are currently
about half of what they had been at their peak.

Juveniles' arrest rates mirrored the pattern reflected in Figure 3.1.
Figure 3.2 shows their rates dipping in the mid-1980s, peaking in the
mid-1990s, and then falling. In 1980, the arrest rate for juveniles aged ten
to seventeen for violent crimes was 295 per 100,000, or about 11% of all
juvenile arrests. At the peak in 1994, the juvenile arrest rate for violent
crimes was 497 per 100,000, a 68% increase and comprised 16.8% of all
juvenile arrests. Violent crimes are a smaller component of the overall
Crime Index and police arrest juveniles for a smaller proportion of violent crimes than they do adults. But the increase in juveniles' arrest rates
in the late 1980s and early 1990s for violence outstripped that of adults,
especially for homicide.

In the mid-1990s, police arrested juveniles for about one in seven
homicides. In 1995, for example, they arrested 2,560 juveniles for mur-

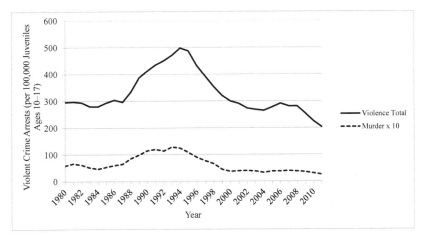

Figure 3.3. Juvenile Violence and Homicide Arrest Rate
Source: Office of Juvenile Justice and Delinquency Prevention, *Statistical Briefing Book*, OJJDP, www.ojjdp.gov.

der compared with 14,141 adults. Figure 3.3 displays the juvenile arrest rates for homicide and for all violent crimes. To place them on the same graph, I multiplied the homicide rate by ten (10). Between 1984 and 1994, the juvenile arrest rate for violent crimes increased from 279 per 100,000 to 497 per 100,000, a 78% increase. In 1984, juvenile homicide arrests comprised about 1.6% of all arrests for violence. Over the next decade, the juvenile homicide arrest rate increased 267%. In 1994, homicides comprised 2.5% of all juvenile arrests for violence. In 1995, police arrested juveniles under the age of fifteen for 5.6% of all violence and 13.5% of all homicides.[97] Juvenile arrests for violence and homicide increased at a faster rate than did those of adults and included younger juveniles.

Two elements of youth violence—race and guns—drove get tough transfer and delinquency sentencing laws in the 1980s and 1990s. Arrest rates of Black youth for violent crimes and the use of guns to murder changed significantly.[98] Since the mid-1960s, police have arrested Black juveniles for violent crimes and homicide at rates about five times those of white youths.[99] Lethal violence and victimization are highly concentrated in the interstices of social disadvantage and closely linked with race.[100] For example, the twenty largest cities comprise slightly more than one-tenth of the nation's population but experience more than one-third of all homicides.[101] Sampson and Wilson attribute the relationship

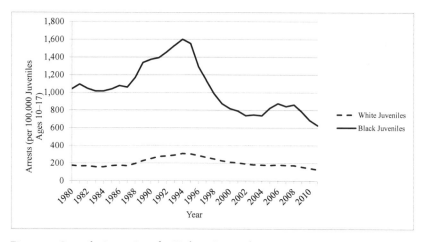

Figure 3.4. Juvenile Arrest Rate for Violent Crimes, by Race, 1980–2011
Source: Office of Juvenile Justice and Delinquency Prevention, *Statistical Briefing Book*, www.ojjdp.gov.

between race and violent crime to the "differential distribution of blacks in communities characterized by (1) *structural social disorganization* and (2) *cultural social isolation*, both of which stem from the concentration of poverty, family disruption, and residential instability."[102]

Figure 3.4 depicts Black and white juveniles' arrest rates for violent crimes and the divergence by race between 1984 and 1994. In 1984, police arrested white youths for violent crimes at a rate of 157 per 100,000. By 1994, their arrest rate had nearly doubled to 307 per 100,000. Black youths' Violent Crime Index arrests started at a rate six times that of white youths—1015 per 100,000—and by 1994 rose to 1600 per 100,000, a 58% increase. By 2011, white youths' violent arrest rate had fallen to 126 per 100,000, a 244% decline. Black youths' arrest rate decreased to 627 per 100,000, a similar decline albeit from a much higher base rate. For youths of both races, arrest rates for violence surged between the mid-1980s and the mid-1990s and then fell even more precipitously.

Figure 3.5 reports juvenile homicide arrests rates by race. In 1984, police arrested white youths for homicide at a rate of 3 per 100,000, Black youths at a rate of 14.3 per 100,000, and other youths at a rate of 4.2 per 100,000. A decade later, the white youth homicide arrest rate had doubled to 6.1 per 100,000, while the Black youth homicide arrest rate rose even more sharply to 46.4 per 100,000, a 325% increase. Although ho-

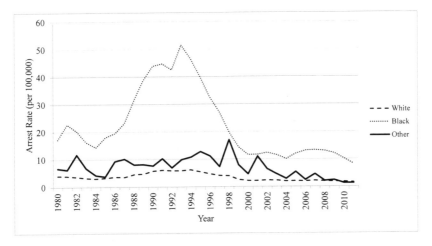

Figure 3.5. Juvenile Arrest Rates for Homicides, by Race, 1980–2011
Source: Office of Juvenile Justice and Delinquency Prevention, *Statistical Briefing Book*, www.ojjdp.gov.

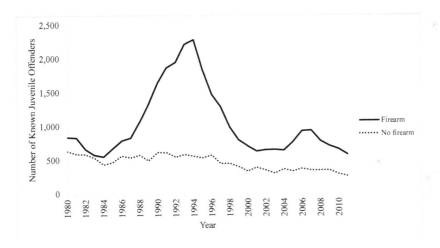

Figure 3.6. Juvenile Homicides, by Use or Nonuse of Firearm
Source: Office of Juvenile Justice and Delinquency Prevention, *Statistical Briefing Book*, www.ojjdp.gov.

micide arrests increased for youths of all race, the rise for Black youths was greater than that of whites and other youths.[103] By 2011, arrest rates for white youths had declined to 1.5 per 100,000, half of what it had been before the surge began in 1984. The arrest rate for Black youths had declined to 8.1 per 100,000, or 57% less than before the surge, but still quintuple that of white youths. Racial differences in homicide arrests reflect the structural location of Black youths in segregated urban slums.[104]

Figure 3.6 shows that juveniles' use of guns accounted for the sharp increase in homicide. Juveniles used knives, blunt objects, and other means to cause around 570 deaths per year.[105] By contrast, between 1984 and 1994, the number of people they killed using firearms increased from 543 to 2,271, a 418% jump.[106] Over that decade, juveniles' arrests for murder nearly tripled, guns accounted for most of the increase, and urban Black males accounted for most of those killed.[107]

Crack Cocaine and Violent Drug Markets

Analysts attribute the dramatic increase in gun murders to the violent crack cocaine industry that appeared in large cities in the mid- to late 1980s.[108] Alfred Blumstein and others ascribe the disproportional racial increase to several factors: introduction of crack cocaine into inner-cities ghettos in the mid-1980s; recruitment of young Black males to sell drugs in open-air street markets; drug sellers arming themselves for self-protection; circulation of guns among drug dealers' peers; young peoples' irresponsible use of guns; and a contagion effect that changed attitudes about and behaviors involving gun use.[109] The low price of crack cocaine increased the numbers of buyers and sellers to accommodate demand. Selling drugs attracted juveniles because they faced less severe penalties than adults. They lacked economic alternatives and naïvely believed they could earn large amounts of money selling drugs. Youths armed themselves for self-protection and to resolve disputes.[110] Adolescents engage in riskier behavior than do adults and the presence of guns increases the likelihood lethal violence. As guns proliferated, more youths armed themselves for self-defense and social status and homicide escalated.[111]

Social context strongly influences adolescent development and participation in criminal activity. As a result of concentrated poverty, social disorganization, and economic and racial inequality, inner-city youths may be socialized in what Elijah Anderson describes as a "code of the street" that encourages violent responses to disrespect.[112] They are more likely to witness violence, to learn the instrumental value of violence, and to have violent role models. The drug industry, in turn, contributed to deterioration of urban neighborhoods by driving out stable families, undermining community leaders, weakening inhibitions against violence, and providing attractive criminal role models.[113]

Each separate factor—urban, Black, and youth—affects the prevalence and rate of crime; the Black youth homicide rate reflects the pernicious intersection of all three factors in certain structural niches. Political economy—macro-economic forces, public policy choices, and private business decisions—and social processes create the conditions that generate high levels of lethal violence in areas of concentrated poverty.[114]

By the early 1990s, random gang violence, drive-by shootings, and disproportionate minority homicides inflamed public fears and left people vulnerable to law and order demagoguery.[115] Politicians promoted and exploited the public's fears for electoral advantage, warned of a young generation of super-predators whose stunted empathy derived from moral poverty, and demonized them to muster support for wars on crime, drugs, and youth.[116] Although predictions about a future threat cannot be proven or falsified, they advocated preemptive get tough policies to transfer youths to criminal court and incarcerate them.[117]

Conclusion: Childhoods Are Different

The types of childhoods that children experience are strongly shaped by social structure, race, and class. In *Our Kids: The American Dream in Crisis*, Robert Putnam poignantly describes how these factors affect family formation, parenting styles, schools, and the communities in which they live, and strongly influence their opportunities and life trajectories.[118] The post-industrial processes that emerged in the 1970s have amplified differences between the childhoods of middle-class white children of college-educated parents growing up in safe suburbs attending quality schools and those of Black children growing up in concentrated poverty in dangerous inner-city neighborhoods attending failing schools.

Economic forces, government policies, and institutional decisions create the conditions that determine the varieties of childhood. Public policies and private institutional decisions created the urban ghetto. Federal housing policies, disinvestment in cities, the siting of public housing projects, bank loan policies, real estate sales practices, and interstate highways facilitated white suburban growth and created poverty-stricken urban slums in which Blacks are forced to live. Deindustrialization disproportionately affected Black male factory workers, undermined family formation, and exacerbated poverty for children growing up in single-parent households. These structural conditions contributed to racial differences in gun violence in the 1980s and 1990s and led to disproportionate deaths and woundings within the urban Black male population. Regardless of how we feel about adults, children are innocent bystanders and victims of their parents' circumstances who cannot escape the criminogenic environments to which the larger society consigns them. Their childhoods are very different from those of their more affluent peers.

4

The Get Tough Era II

Politics of Race and Crime

Macro-structural changes, rising crime rates, and social unrest in the 1960s realigned both political parties around race-related issues.[1] Republicans employed a Southern strategy to appeal to white voters' racial antipathies by politicizing crime and welfare policies.[2] They attributed race riots and crime to Warren Court decisions and liberal Democrat policies that rewarded bad behavior and fostered welfare dependency.[3] They described young offenders as dangerous criminals—super-predators—rather than as children and attributed their violence to lenient juvenile court dispositions.[4] By the early 1990s, lawmakers' politicization of crime policies led to mass incarceration of adults and get tough juvenile justice measures—transfer, delinquency sentencing, public hearings, record sharing, and the like.

The causes of social problems such as welfare or crime may be understood in different ways and lead to different policy prescriptions. Indeed, the definition of a particular condition as a social problem emerges through a process of social construction.[5] Politicians compete for public acceptance of their interpretations and use mass media to shape popular culture about crime and race.[6] In the 1960s and 1970s conservative politicians shaped a law-and-order message that focused on crime in the streets, which they implicitly attributed to Blacks.[7] They ascribed the causes of crime to individual choices rather than to structural forces and promoted policies to crack down on criminals as part of a racialized electoral strategy.[8] Ian Haney Lopez describes this tactic as strategic racism—"purposeful efforts to use racial animosity as leverage to gain political power."[9] Since the 1970s, a reactionary attitude has dominated American political discourse—reactionary not simply as a political characterization, but as a desire to reverse the directions of social, cultural, and legal changes and to restore a previous halcyon social order.[10]

This chapter examines the politics of race and crime that laid the foundation for get tough policies in juvenile courts and schools. It focuses first on the political and social changes that emerged in the 1960s and fostered realignment of the Democratic and Republican parties around race, welfare, and crime policies. Next it describes Republicans' Southern strategy, which used policy issues associated with race—crime, welfare, and affirmative action—to attract white Southern and suburban voters. Finally, it describes their use of coded language to convey a message that its recipients readily understood as a racial appeal while allowing them to deny its racist content.

Racial Political Realignment: Welfare, Crime, Riots, and Backlash

During the second half of the 1960s, the civil rights struggle shifted from ending apartheid and Jim Crow discrimination to even more difficult issues of political, economic, and social inequality nationwide.[11] Politicians and the public increasingly appreciated the magnitude of the changes wrought by the Great Migration and the racial transformation of cities.

> [T]he migration hardly created a harmonious, racially synthesized country. It was disruptive; it engendered hostility. The fabric of city life in the United States changed forever. Some of the bitterness of race relations leached into city politics. The ideal of high-quality universal public education began to disappear. Street crime became an obsessive concern for the first time in decades. The beginning of the modern rise of conservatism coincides exactly with the country's beginning to realize the true magnitude and consequences of the black migration, and the government's response to the migration provided the conservative movement with many of its issues.[12]

The civil rights agenda frayed the coalition of Blacks, liberals, Northern ethnic and Southern white voters, and polarized the Democratic and Republican parties over matters of race.[13] The pre-1964 civil rights agenda focused on citizenship rights—the right to vote, equal access to housing and public accommodations. The post-1964 agenda focused on broader issues—welfare, housing, and employment sometimes pursued through racial preferences—which conservatives and the Republican Party strongly opposed.[14] Beginning in the 1960s, crime and welfare became central issues in partisan politics and acquired a racial coloration as conservatives cast Blacks and their Democratic allies as the villains.[15]

Welfare and Poverty

The Great Migration swelled the Northern Black population and the ranks of the urban poor. The original federal Aid to Families with Dependent Children (AFDC) welfare program granted states considerable latitude to set benefit levels and eligibility requirements. AFDC was means-tested, stigmatized recipients, and created financial disincentives to work or to marry.[16] Southern states with large Black populations provided low benefits and excluded most Black mothers from those meager grants.[17] Changes in the law, the amount of federal matching grants, and the migration of African Americans to the North increased the percentage of eligible Black AFDC recipients from 14% in 1936 to 46% in 1973.[18] As Blacks' enrollment on welfare expanded, rates of out-of-wedlock childbirth increased and conservative politicians asserted a link between welfare dependency and race.[19]

Whites' attitudes toward welfare distinguish between the *deserving* and *undeserving* poor and soured as the relationship between welfare, poverty, and race emerged.[20] Americans value individualism, self-reliance, and personal responsibility—values that emphasize personal choices rather than structural determinants of behavior.[21] The American Dream posits that anyone can succeed through hard work; those who fail to realize its promise are lazy, profligate, or immoral.[22] Whites recognize that structural forces cause hardships when poor people resemble themselves—people trapped by social forces or misfortune.[23] They shift to a belief in personal failings when they see the poor as non-white and unlike themselves.[24] They blamed the Black emigrants from the South—undeserving poor—rather than structural conditions for family breakdown, unemployment, unwed parenthood, and welfare dependency.[25]

During the 1960s, as poor Blacks came to the attention of the media and public, the longstanding distinctions between deserving and undeserving poor and the stereotypic belief that Blacks were lazy became more strongly intertwined.[26] Lyndon Johnson's War on Poverty extended welfare benefits to non-whites and the number of recipients doubled during the 1960s because so many children of color lived in poverty.[27] Poverty in minority communities was closely connected with racial segregation in schools, housing, and employment, and resistance to integration became tightly linked with opposition to welfare.[28] Martin Gilens argues that most Americans hate welfare because they believe that it rewards the undeserving poor, that the majority of welfare recipients are Black, and that Blacks evince less commitment to the work ethic than other groups.[29] Conservatives exploited cultural narratives about personal responsibility and individual choice over structural constraints.[30]

Conservatives attributed Black poverty and criminality to individuals' character failings and cultural shortcomings rather than structural factors.[31] According to this narrative, government assistance is futile because only Blacks themselves can reform their dysfunctional culture and avoid self-defeating behavior.[32] Negative media coverage reinforced public opinion and political depictions of Blacks as criminals and undeserving.[33] The concurrence of rising crime rates with poverty programs enabled conservatives to attribute Black-white socioeconomic disparities and criminality to personal pathologies and fostered resistance to policies to ameliorate structural factors that contributed to those differences.[34] Punitive measures such as eligibility time limits and work requirements were necessary to goad the reluctant poor to seek gainful employment.[35]

Two social norms that sustained the traditional nuclear family began to unravel. One was a patriarchal division of labor in which a working man supported his family and his wife maintained the domestic sphere. The second was a strong norm against out-of-wedlock child bearing and rearing.[36] In 1965, the prescient Moynihan Report—*The Negro Family: The Case for National Action*—warned that urban Black male unemployment threatened the stability and viability of Black families and communities.[37] In the rapid transition from a rural agrarian to urban industrial life, many unskilled Black men suffered unemployment.[38] Without financial ability to support families, men deserted their women and children and illegitimacy and welfare dependency increased.[39] The

Moynihan Report argued that "[a]t the heart of the deterioration of the fabric of Negro society is the deterioration of the Negro family. It is the fundamental source of weakness of the Negro community at the present time. . . . Unless this damage is repaired, all the efforts to end discrimination and poverty and injustice will come to little."[40] Both Black and liberal critics attacked the Moynihan Report for "blaming the victims," but the structural and economic problems he identified—Black male unemployment, out-of-wedlock childbirth, concentrated poverty, and violent crime—remain primary issues of contemporary urban, welfare, and criminal justice policy.[41]

The trends in family formation/dissolution and child-rearing arrangements that affected Blacks a half century ago now affect whites as well. Among the high-school-educated lower third of the population, white children's parents increasingly fail to marry, divorce, and many raise offspring in single-parent households and poverty.[42] While only about 10% of college-educated women give birth to children outside of wedlock, almost two-thirds of women with a high school education or less are unmarried when they have children. Today, family formation among college-educated Blacks looks more like that of college-educated whites while that of less educated whites looks more like that of less educated Blacks.[43] In the Epilogue, I argue that changes in family formation and child poverty require class-based economic reforms as well as racial amends to improve children's life chances.

Urban Race Riots

Race riots rocked American cities in the 1960s as Blacks reacted violently to decades of segregation, deprivation, and alienation.[44] In 1964, a white police officer in Harlem shot and killed a fifteen-year-old Black youth and set off the largest race riot since World War II. The following summer, five days after President Johnson signed the 1965 Voting Rights Act, the Watts district of Los Angeles exploded in riot and television viewers watched Blacks battle police and loot stores.[45] Thirty-eight riots in 1966 and 164 riots in 1967 raised fears of a national race war.[46] Three summers of riots left more than two hundred dead, thousands injured, and tens of billions of dollars in property damage. In 1968, the assassination of Martin Luther King, Jr., provoked another spate of urban riots.[47]

Black Power advocates challenged church-based civil rights leaders for prominence. Their violent rhetoric and the urban riots frightened many white voters who felt that Blacks had failed to take advantage of their invitation to citizenship.[48]

President Lyndon Johnson established the National Advisory Commission on Civil Disorders—the Kerner Commission—in the aftermath of the riots. The commission attributed the riots to the nation's history of racial discrimination in employment, education, social services, and housing.[49] It warned that the country was moving "toward two societies, one black, one white—separate and unequal."[50] It cautioned that the historical legacy of segregation and discrimination and continuation of current policies would "make permanent the division of our country into two societies; one, largely Negro and poor, located in the central cities; the other predominantly white and affluent, located in the suburbs."[51] As I explained in Chapter 3, by the 1970s and 1980s, many American cities already had become white doughnuts surrounding a Black center of segregated neighborhoods and schools.

Despite the Kerner Commission's sympathetic analysis of the structural causes of urban crime and racial disorder, crime and welfare emerged as potent political issues in the 1960s. The riots changed many whites' perceptions of the legitimacy of Blacks' grievances and led to the subsequent race-based politicization of public policies.[52] Republicans appealed to whites' racial animus and promoted beliefs that the time for remediation had passed and Blacks had failed to take advantage of their new opportunities.[53]

Liberals and conservatives attributed increases in crime and welfare dependency to different sources. Liberals focused on structural conditions of racial and economic inequality to explain crime and poverty.[54] Conservatives rejected the causal roles of discrimination in housing, education, and employment, and argued that people became criminal or poor because they made bad choices that social welfare programs only encouraged.[55] They simplistically attributed rising crime and urban racial disorders to Supreme Court decisions protecting civil rights and criminal defendants.[56] Heightened media attention to crime gave credence to their claims that the Court had undermined deterrence, made it harder to arrest and convict criminals, increased whites' fears of victimization, and created a receptive audience for advocates of punitive policies.[57]

Politics of Race and Crime

Following *Brown v. Board of Education*, conservative Southerners linked race with crime.[58] Civil rights activists challenged Southerners' "massive resistance" to integration with direct action, civil disobedience, and sit-ins to desegregate public facilities.[59] *Brown* radicalized Southern racial politics.[60] Diehard segregationists had stronger commitments to their position than did racial moderates and used repressive tactics to create an appearance of monolithic resistance.[61] When activists protested or used disruptive strategies, law enforcement violently suppressed them and politicians denounced them as Communists, criminals, and mobs of "outside agitators."[62] They conflated crime with political dissent, claimed that civil disobedience caused crime, and urged forceful repression of criminals and protesters alike.[63]

Although most Americans agreed in theory with principles of equality, many opposed the remedies that courts and government agencies adopted to address racial injustice. While whites outside the South repudiated white supremacy and endorsed racial equality, their support for the civil rights agenda plummeted once it called for changes that affected them.[64] Many Northern whites believed that the 1964 Civil Rights Act had removed barriers to racial equality and that further progress was a matter of Blacks' efforts rather than state remediation.[65] By the 1960s and 1970s, the burdens of integrating schools, housing, and employment fell more heavily on working- and lower-middle-class ethnic groups than on white professionals, who could insulate themselves in gated suburbs and send their children to private schools.[66]

The expanding rights revolution—involving minorities, women, and gays—and cultural changes disturbed and angered white working-class people who bore the brunt of these changes—civil rights for minorities, employment and reproductive rights for women, protection for criminal defendants, affirmative action and racial hiring preferences.[67] Politicians appealed to whites' social conservatism and blamed the shiftless poor for increased welfare expenditures and higher taxes, Blacks for crime in the streets, and liberal elites for a permissive culture that encouraged anti-social behavior.[68]

The civil rights movement forced the Democratic Party to choose between its white Southern and its Black, Northern, and liberal constituencies.[69] Under Presidents Kennedy and Johnson, it loosened its bonds with whites in the South and aligned the party with civil rights and African Americans. Conservative Republicans countered to win white Southerners' support and topple the pro–civil rights Eastern wing of their party.[70] They attacked liberal social policies and ascribed baby boom crime, race riots, welfare dependency, and domestic social changes to Warren Court decisions and liberal Democrats' policies.[71]

Differences between the two parties clearly emerged in the 1964 presidential race between Lyndon Johnson, whose leadership led to passage of the 1964 Civil Rights Act, and Senator Barry Goldwater, a staunch conservative and ideological opponent of the law.[72] The 1964 Republican Party convention rejected a party platform favoring civil rights by a two-to-one margin.[73] Goldwater's 1964 campaign linked street crime with civil rights protest and appealed to whites' growing concerns about racial violence.[74] Democratic support for Blacks' civil rights alienated white Southern voters and presaged political realignment as the divide on race-related issues between the two parties deepened.[75]

The confluence of the 1960s cultural changes with shifts in crime, welfare, and race relations created a combustible political environment. "[T]he *fusion* of race with an expanding rights revolution and with the new liberal agenda, and the fusion, in turn, of race and rights with the public perception of the Democratic party, and the fusion of the Democratic party with the issues of high taxes and a coercive, redistributive government, that created the central force splintering the presidential coalition behind the Democratic party through the next two decades."[76] In 1966, Republicans made significant electoral gains—forty-seven House seats, three Senate seats, and Ronald Reagan's landslide gubernatorial victory in California—by blaming liberals' "soft social programs" and the Court for race riots and rising crime rates.[77]

Republican politicians used crime, affirmative action, and welfare as wedge issues to attract Southern white, suburban, and ethnic voters.[78] During the turbulent 1960s, they blamed street crime and riots on dangerous and undeserving individuals and issued cries for law and order.[79] They promoted punitive crime policies rather than social welfare measures.[80] For the first time, crime policies became a partisan political issue and a fallback position for white Southern politicians who no longer could explicitly promote segregation in education and public accommodations.[81]

While liberals argued that the state bore some responsibility to reduce causes of crime and poverty, conservatives argued that social programs encouraged irresponsible individuals to make poor choices and contributed to dependency and criminality.[82] President Johnson's War on Poverty coincided with increasing crime rates and conservatives argued that social welfare programs contributed to crime and a culture of dependency.[83]

Civil rights changed public perceptions of the Democratic and Republican parties. Increasingly, people viewed Democrats as promoting new rights and government entitlements for marginalized and disenfranchised groups at the expense of traditional constituencies.[84] In the public mind, Court decisions to end racial segregation and protect criminal defendants became associated with the liberal Democratic agenda.[85] Finally, structural economic changes induced many middle-class voters to reconsider support for progressive social welfare policies that they perceived no longer benefited them.[86]

In 1968, Alabama governor George Wallace's presidential campaign mobilized a white right-wing populist backlash against moral, racial, and cultural liberalism.[87] He denounced efforts by elitist lawyers, judges, academics, and government bureaucrats to impose their values and social policies on beleaguered working people.[88] His populist rhetoric helped to forge an alliance between working-class whites and traditionally affluent Republican voters in common opposition to liberal elites collecting taxes to conduct social experiments.[89] Richard Nixon's 1968 presidential campaign attributed urban riots and rising crime rates to Warren Court decisions that "coddled criminals" and "handcuffed police."[90] Three years of riots, rising crime rates, Vietnam War protests, and the assassinations of Robert F. Kennedy and Martin Luther King, Jr., created a climate of fear and anger and clamor for law and order with a racial subtext.[91]

Republicans' Southern Strategy

Divisions within the Democratic Party over civil rights, crime, welfare, and other cultural issues made the South politically competitive.[92] Republican tacticians concluded that a Southern strategy employing coded racial appeals could foster a political realignment among white Southerners, suburbanites, and socially conservative ethnic voters.[93] They stoked hostility toward integrating schools and neighborhoods and fueled resentment toward government programs to help non-whites.[94] They coupled economic concerns—taxes, inflation, and the decline of manufacturing—with racially tinged social issues—crime, urban disorder, family breakdown, and expanding welfare rolls.[95]

In the decades after World War II, millions of middle-class white voters moved to more Republican suburbs.[96] Republican theoretician Kevin Phillips's Southern strategy courted the new constituencies through racial code words that indirectly invoked racial themes without explicitly challenging egalitarian ideals.[97] Nixon straddled the conflict by professing support for the abstract principle of racial equality while simultaneously opposing government efforts to enforce civil rights.[98] He adopted his coded racial appeals from Goldwater's 1964 campaign successes in the South and Wallace's 1968 campaign in the North, but played the race card with deniability.[99] He found a message acceptable to the majority of white Americans who believed that it was wrong to deny Blacks basic rights of citizenship, but who opposed residential, economic, and educational integration.[100]

Law-and-order rhetoric appealed to blue-collar and working class whites who opposed school integration, felt the brunt of social changes, and became disenchanted with Democrats' support for civil rights.[101] Thomas and Mary Edsall argue that "[r]ace was central . . . to the fundamental conservative strategy of establishing a new, non-economic polarization of the electorate, a polarization isolating a liberal, activist, culturally-permissive, rights-oriented, and pro-black Democratic Party against those unwilling to pay the financial and social costs of this reconfigured social order."[102]

Republicans' Southern strategy succeeded in rupturing Democrats' New Deal coalition and realigning the parties around race.[103] After violent confrontations at their 1968 Chicago convention, Democrats introduced reforms that proved more advantageous to better-educated veterans of civil rights, women's, and anti-war movements than to traditional blue-collar union representatives and ward politicians. Designed to increase diversity and access to the nominating process, the new rules empowered liberal activists at the expense of more conservative white male leaders of ethnic and working-class constituents.[104] As more progressive forces dominated the Democratic Party and embraced historically marginalized groups, conservative Republicans depicted them as liberal elitists bent on imposing an alien racial and cultural agenda.[105] They courted anxious and resentful whites with a veiled message connecting civil rights activism and Black criminality.[106] Divisive issues such as busing to integrate schools highlighted the impact of the progressive agenda for white residents of bigger cities.[107]

Since the 1960s, the Republican Party has successfully politicized crime and welfare policies.[108] Because of the association between race, on the one hand, and crime and welfare, on the other, Democrats inadequately addressed increasingly conservative public attitudes. They resisted information about rising crime rates and unmarried childbearing because confronting criminality and welfare dependency could shift focus from whites' responsibility for the legacy of discrimination to blaming victims and stigmatizing Blacks for a culture of poverty.[109]

In the 1960s, conservative Republicans decried crime in the streets and advocated law and order. In the 1970s, they supported a war on crime. In the 1980s, Ronald Reagan launched a war on drugs. By the 1990s, they waged a war on youth. From the beginning, they favored repression in response to rising crime rates, civil rights marches, and urban and campus turmoil. In the Get Tough Era, sound bites and demagogic rhetoric shaped penal policies and reflected political calculus rather than criminological research, which questioned the efficacy of tougher penalties and increased imprisonment.[110] Politicians' fear of being labeled as "soft on crime" obviated thoughtful discussions of crime policy and relegated penal strategies to political advisers and focus-group-tested themes.[111] Only in the early 1990s did Democrats under Bill Clinton respond to Republicans' exploitation of crime by embracing equally tough rhetoric and punitive policies.[112] As a result, both parties competed to demonstrate who was tougher on crime and more concerned about public safety.

Political Rhetoric and Coded Racial Appeals

It is politically incorrect to express overtly racist sentiments. Research on modern racism identifies closely intertwined racial sentiments—anti-Black emotional affect, beliefs that Blacks make excessive and unreasonable demands, views that Blacks do not value hard work or take personal responsibility, attitudes that Blacks receive undeserved government benefits, denial that discrimination continues to exist, and the like—as indirect indicators of racial animus.[113]

Code words are symbols or phrases that implicate racial themes but without directly challenging egalitarian ideals. Racial appeals must remain implicit so as not to defy democratic values but still be recognizable to whites who harbor negative attitudes toward Blacks.[114] They convey a known but implicit meaning while resisting overtly racist interpretation and maintaining deniability.[115] Ian Haney Lopez uses the term "dog-whistle politics" to describe coded talk centered on race that triggers strong reactions in its auditors even as it hides explicit racism.[116] Many conservative politicians employed a new vocabulary to channel racial prejudices but without providing objective evidence of racism or intent to discriminate.[117]

Race provides a nexus for political conflicts over values, culture, and allocation of material resources. It implicates diverse policy arenas—welfare, housing, neighborhood schools, taxes, crime, drugs and violence, and family structure. Crime and welfare, in particular, enable politicians to use coded language and exploit white Americans' negative views about Blacks without being explicitly racial.[118] For many, perhaps most, whites the connection between minorities and crime is "an 'obvious' truth that, while rooted in social structures and cultural beliefs, is nevertheless accepted simply as reality."[119] David Garland argues that politicized discourse about crime evokes images and archetypes that play to public anxieties and depict criminals as fundamentally different and threatening—the "alien other."[120] Martin Gilens argues that many white Americans' hostility to welfare reflects their erroneous perception that most welfare recipients are Black and that they evince less commitment to the work ethic than do whites, do not deserve assistance, and their privation results from feckless choices and a culture of poverty.[121] Media coverage and political discourse about welfare and crime reinforce public views of Blacks as overly demanding, undeserving, and threatening.[122] Ronald Reagan popularized the image of the Black "welfare queen," driving "behind the wheel of a Cadillac, tooling around in flashy splendor . . . [and] propagating the stereotypical image of a lazy, larcenous black woman ripping off society's generosity without remorse."[123]

By the 1970s, conservative politicians appreciated that they could deploy concerns about states' rights, law and order, individual rights, and even equality to invoke racial themes. By the 1980s, words like "welfare," "fairness," and "groups" had acquired racial meanings within the context of a backlash against liberal policies.[124] Republicans recast hostility to civil rights enforcement into principled support for fairness, equality, and opposition to special privileges for minorities, women, and gays. Conservatives' emphasis on "egalitarianism" shifted public resentment away from structural and economic inequality and toward minorities, the poor, and federal redistributive efforts.[125]

Media Sensationalism: Violence and the Black Face of Youth Crime

About three-quarters of whites live residentially segregated lives in cities and suburbs whose populations are less than 5% Black.[126] Most of their knowledge about Blacks comes indirectly from media coverage of crime, welfare, or unemployment, which tends to activate racial stereotypes and reinforce prejudices.[127]

Stereotypes are fast, intuitive, and largely unconscious ways of thinking.[128] They are socially constructed and enable people to make sense of a complex world, automatically classify people into racial categories, and activate culturally internalized racial meanings.[129] Historically, racism has been one of American's most conspicuous and enduring cultural stereotypes. Some whites' beliefs in Blacks' biological or cultural inferiority provide rationalizations for their inferior social position.[130] Stereotypes of Blacks operate as perceptual filters that admit confirmatory evidence and block contradictory information, and media depictions subliminally reinforce them.[131]

Television news producers are located in urban areas with large Black populations, which provide easy access to report about crime and welfare.[132] Local news favors an action format—violence and crime—to attract audiences, bolster ratings, and increase revenues.[133] Its standard script consists of two elements: crime is violent and the usual suspects are minority perpetrators.[134] "If it bleeds, it leads." It systematically distorts reality by overreporting violent crime and minorities' roles as perpetrators, and reinforces public stereotypes of race with crime.[135] Portrayals of crime victims are equally racialized and disproportionately depict victims as white female suburbanites, even though they experience less victimization than other groups, especially Blacks.[136] Media coverage shows Blacks as more involved in violent crimes than their actual rates and more frequently portrays them anonymously, poorly dressed, or in police custody than they do violent white offenders.[137] Viewers see non-whites as racial archetypes—murderers, rapists, or gang members—which generalizes to all Blacks.[138]

Whites generally have more punitive attitudes and greater confidence in the evenhandedness of the justice system than do Blacks.[139] Racial depiction of violent crime activates whites' stereotypes and views about crime and punishment.[140] During the last third of the twentieth century, conservative politicians used anti-crime rhetoric as a coded message to appeal to white voters, conflated Blackness and crime in public consciousness, promoted get tough policies for electoral advantage, and fostered a moral panic.[141] Politicians generated crime-news stories in populist emotive terms to shape public attitudes, reinforce conservative interpretations of crime, and put a Black face on it.[142] After Republican politicians declared a war on drugs during the 1980s, media coverage of drug stories increased sharply, shifted focus from powder to crack cocaine, and depicted drug users and dealers as Black.[143] The media saturated viewers with images of "crack whores" and "crack babies" that confirmed the worst negative stereotypes of poor inner-city residents.[144] Michael Tonry argues that Republicans' war on drugs represented a cynical political strategy to assert toughness about crime despite having a disastrous impact on the Black community and doing little to alleviate the causes of drug use or crime.[145] The Federal Sentencing Guidelines' crack versus powder cocaine sentencing differentials were part of the policies that led to mass incarceration and adversely affected young Black men's subsequent employability, marital prospects, and consigned them to lives of marginality and criminality.[146] Contrast the harsh media coverage of crack users with the more sympathetic portrayal of whites addicted to heroin and opioids in small towns and rural America today and the greater policy emphasis on treatment rather than punishment.

Conclusion

There is a correlation between punitiveness and hostility toward Blacks; those who report greater racial prejudice also support more punitive crime control policies.[147] Whites tend to associate crime and violence with Blacks and those who harbor racial resentments endorse tougher penalties and deny that the criminal justice system discriminates against Blacks.[148] Michael Tonry argues that Evangelical Protestants, more closely aligned with the Republican Party, tend to see criminal justice policy issues in moralistic terms of right and wrong that brook no compromise and detract from empathy or compassion.[149] Law-and-order rhetoric and other veiled racial references encourage such attitudes and the political success of those who employ coded racial appeals guarantees their continued use.[150]

In *Punishment and Inequality in America*, Bruce Western argues that policies of mass incarceration have institutionalized racial inequality in America.[151] In *Punishing Race*, Michael Tonry argues that the paranoid streak in American politics—a tendency to see policy options as black-and-white or right-and-wrong—coupled with religious moralism and a highly politicized justice system has led to severe and vindictive punishment without regard to its inefficacy.[152] Loïc Wacquant argues that urban deindustrialization and the movement of jobs and whites to the suburbs enabled policy makers to wage a war on drugs that marooned Blacks in segregated urban areas.[153] In *The New Jim Crow*, Michelle Alexander contends that the racial dimension of mass incarceration reinforces the longstanding stigmatization of Blacks. "Like Jim Crow, mass incarceration marginalizes large segments of the African American community, segregates them physically (in prisons, jails, and ghettos), and then authorizes discrimination against them in voting, employment, housing, education, public benefits, and jury service."[154]

These and other analysts focus on how the war on drugs, the politics of race and crime, and mass incarceration adversely affected young Black men and their communities. The next three chapters explore how those get tough policies transformed the juvenile justice system and social control of youths. Chapter 5 examines changes in juvenile court transfer and sentencing laws. Chapter 6 explores juvenile courts' handling of female delinquents. Chapter 7 analyzes the school-to-prison pipeline, which disproportionately affects urban minority youths and sets them on a path for criminal involvement as adults.

5

The Kid Is a Criminal

Transfer and Delinquency Sanctions

Social welfare and social control operate in fundamental tension. How do we balance young offenders' best interests with punishment for their offenses? How do we safeguard children and protect communities?[1] The interventionist juvenile court asserted a social welfare mission in which children's and society's interests were congruent, but get tough politicians subordinated welfare to crime control.[2] This imbalance inevitably occurs because states define delinquency jurisdiction based on criminal behavior rather than children's welfare needs. Jurisdiction based on crimes diverts attention from the criminogenic conditions in which many youths live, for which they are not responsible, and from which they cannot escape—concentrated poverty, failing schools, dysfunctional families, dangerous neighborhoods, and the like—that contribute to delinquency. Defined by criminal behavior, juvenile courts highlight that their clients are young criminals and reinforce public antipathy against other people's children.[3]

The social construction of adolescent culpability is part of the larger framing of welfare versus individual responsibility that changed abruptly during the Get Tough Era. Conservatives promoted a stereotype of dangerous super-predators—cold-eyed young killers suffering from moral poverty—rather than traditional images of disadvantaged youths who needed help.[4] Based on erroneous demographic projections, they predicted a bloodbath of youth crime, even as juvenile violence declined precipitously.[5] Relying on those flawed predictions, legislators preemptively enacted get tough laws that emphasized suppression of crime rather than efforts to change children. They expressed popular anger and symbolized toughness despite the ineffectiveness of punishment to reduce delinquency.

A moral panic occurs when the public, politicians, and media react to a perceived social threat with fear and alarm and adopt a disproportionate punitive response. The violence and homicide of the late 1980s and early 1990s, sensationalized media depictions, and public and political attribution of crime to urban Black males precipitated such a panic.[6] Policy makers portrayed adolescents as young criminals and sharply shifted juvenile justice policy from rehabilitation to punishment. Efforts to prosecute more youths as adults represented an assault on juvenile courts' historic diversionary mission to shelter them from criminal prosecution. Harsh delinquency sanctions belied the claims of juvenile courts that their rehabilitative programs required fewer procedural safeguards.

Questions about effectiveness of rehabilitation emerged in the 1960s, eroded juvenile courts' interventionist rationale, and evoked a sense of failure among practitioners and the public.[7] Conservatives claimed that juvenile courts' lenient sanctions failed to protect the public and emphasized punishment.[8] Legislative changes included a shift from individualized sentences to just deserts, from rehabilitation to retribution, from amenability to treatment and best interests to public safety, accountability, and proportionality, and of decision-making authority from judges to prosecutors.[9] The unifying theme is punitive segregation—to incapacitate and exclude offenders rather than to change and reintegrate them.[10]

During the 1970s, Progressives' optimism about human malleability foundered on empirical evaluations of rehabilitation that questioned its effectiveness.[11] In 1974, Robert Martinson's essay "What Works?" concluded that "[w]ith few and isolated exceptions, the rehabilitative efforts that have been reported so far have had no appreciable effect on recidivism."[12] "Nothing works" became the conventional wisdom for several decades thereafter and undercut efforts to treat offenders.[13] It reinforced conservatives' distrust of government efforts to reduce crime or ameliorate social problems. Politicians promoted policies to punish, deter, and incapacitate criminals.[14] Juvenile justice shifted from a welfare to a penal orientation and assumed responsibility to manage and regulate delinquents rather than to cure them.[15]

In the 1970s, just deserts and retribution displaced rehabilitation as rationales for juvenile and criminal sentencing.[16] Deserts-based sentences focus on offenders' past behavior rather than utilitarian considerations like treatment, deterrence, or incapacitation. Determinate sentences impose backward-looking penalties based on offense, culpability, or criminal history.[17] In *The Struggle for Justice*, the American Friends Service Committee argued that indeterminate sentences gave judges too much discretion, produced racial disparities, and violated norms of proportionality, and recommended short fixed sentences and abolition of parole.[18] However, offense-based sanctions enabled conservative politicians to openly express punitive thoughts and enact draconian laws.[19]

Disillusionment with rehabilitation and the renaissance of retribution produced awkward political bedfellows: radicals who viewed the criminal justice system as an instrument of state oppression; liberals disturbed about discretion and discrimination; civil libertarians concerned about individual liberty and autonomy; and conservatives who advocated law and order and a reduced state welfare role.[20] Conservatives argued that indeterminate sentences allowed dangerous offenders' premature release and emphasized crime in their political agenda.[21] Their emphases on personal and justice system accountability challenged the legitimacy of the welfare state and governmental programs. Liberals had criticized rehabilitation as ineffective and discriminatory, lacked coherent alternatives to proposals to crack down on criminals, and eventually joined the law-and-order bandwagon to avoid being labeled soft on crime.[22]

Race played an increased role in national domestic politics—starting with the civil rights movement's struggle for racial equality and culminating in conservative crime policies of the Reagan and, later, Clinton administrations. Anti-state populism aimed to dismantle programs to reduce racial, economic, and gender inequalities, and to strengthen states' police powers.[23] Politicians focused on the effects of crime rather than its causes and on crime control rather than social welfare.[24] The racially skewed impact of crime policy changes—mass incarceration, disproportionate minority confinement, and harsher delinquency sanctions—reversed some of the progress achieved by the civil rights movement.[25]

Doubts about juvenile courts' ability to treat young offenders or protect public safety bolstered get tough policies. In the 1980s and 1990s, states amended their juvenile codes to expedite transfer of youths to criminal courts, where they faced substantial sentences as adults. States required juvenile court judges to impose determinate or mandatory sentences on delinquents who remained in an increasingly punitive system.[26] Both strategies deemphasized treatment in favor of personal and justice system accountability. Cumulatively, they reflect an inversion of juvenile justice jurisprudence and practice—from rehabilitation to retribution, from offender to offense, and a shift of discretion from judges to prosecutors.

This chapter traces the impact of the Get Tough Era, the ascendance of punitive policies, and their disproportionate impact on children of color. It focuses on three critical decisions that affect youths' custody and whether they receive treatment or punishment. First, it focuses on transfer of youths to criminal court for punishment as adults. It describes changes from assessment of youths' amenability to treatment to decisions based on their offense and the rising role of prosecutors. It examines whether transfer laws accomplish their legislative intent, their iatrogenic effects, and their racially disparate impacts. Next, the chapter focuses on juveniles' pretrial detention. Detention laws give judges broad discretion to confine youths prior to trial. Judges overuse and abuse it and disproportionally detain children of color. The chapter's middle sections review reforms to reduce inappropriate use of pretrial confinement. The chapter's final sections examine delinquency sanctions and the shift from treatment to punishment. *McKeiver* assumed with no empirical basis that juvenile courts solely provided delinquents with rehabilitative treatment, that they thus did not require protection from the state, and consequently denied them a jury right. Get tough changes emphasized offense-based punishment and eviscerated *McKeiver*'s benign premise. Juvenile codes' purpose clauses and court opinions endorse punishment. Statutes authorize determinate and mandatory minimum sentences. Judicial practices focus on the crime committed rather than a youth's needs. Conditions of confinement reflect custodial rather than therapeutic goals. Even as delinquency sanctions became more punitive, however, juvenile courts diverted most youths from the criminal justice system. Despite their limited ability to rehabilitate youths, they sheltered them from even worse criminal punishment.

Transfer for Criminal Prosecution

States pursue several goals when they transfer youths to criminal courts. They transfer some charged with serious crimes whom they believe deserve longer sentences than juvenile courts can impose and to symbolically affirm retribution. They seek long-term incapacitation of chronic recidivists to protect public safety.[27] They transfer youths to deter offenders and would-be lawbreakers. During the 1980s and early 1990s, get tough politicians transformed the theory and practice of transfer, changed the legal construction of adolescence, and increased the numbers of youths tried as adults.

Juvenile courts traditionally focused on offenders' best interests and individualized treatment. Criminal courts emphasize offenses and proportional punishment. Transfer implicates many sentencing issues: balancing rehabilitation, incapacitation, deterrence, and retribution; focusing on offender or offense; promoting discretionary or mandatory decisions; and defining the roles of judges, legislatures, and prosecutors. Transfer laws embody contradictory crime control strategies and conflicting construction of youth as immature or as adult-like.[28] State uses one or more often overlapping transfer strategies: judicial waiver, legislative offense exclusion, and prosecutorial direct file.[29] They emphasize different sentencing goals, rely on different actors, and elicit different information to decide youths' criminal status.

Transfer to Criminal Court

The vast majority of states have judicial waiver statutes on their books, but judges account for the fewest number of youths transferred.[30] Forty-five states' laws specify ages and types of offenses for which a judge may waive juvenile court jurisdiction and transfer a youth to criminal court after conducting a hearing to determine his or her amenability to treatment or threat to public safety.[31]

Legislatures create juvenile courts and may define their jurisdiction to exclude youths based on age and offense.[32] Some states exclude youths sixteen or older charged with murder, while others exclude more extensive lists of offenses.[33] A few states set their juvenile courts' age jurisdiction at fifteen or sixteen years, rather than seventeen, which results in the largest numbers of youths tried as adults.[34]

Prosecutorial direct file is a third method by which states transfer youths to criminal courts.[35] In these states, juvenile and criminal courts share concurrent jurisdiction over some ages and offenses—older youths and serious crimes—and prosecutors decide in which forum to charge a youth.[36]

Blended sentences provide another juvenile/criminal court sentencing option.[37] Some states allow juvenile court judges to impose extended delinquency dispositions backed by stayed criminal sentences. Other states authorize a criminal court judge to impose a delinquency disposition reinforced by threat of a criminal sentence. If juveniles successfully complete their delinquency dispositions, then judges do not execute the criminal sentences. Blended sentencing laws give youths all criminal procedural safeguards, including a jury trial, to preserve the option of a criminal sentence.[38]

States annually try nearly two hundred thousand youths under age eighteen as adults because juvenile courts' jurisdiction ends at fifteen or sixteen, rather than seventeen years of age.[39] They transfer another fifty thousand youths via judicial transfer, offense exclusion, or direct-file laws.[40] Judges waive about seventy-five hundred cases annually, prosecutors direct file about twenty-seven thousand youths, and they charge the remainder with excluded offenses in criminal courts.[41] It is difficult to calculate precise numbers of youths tried as adults because most states collect data only on judicial transfers, which account for the fewest number waived, and do not count chronological juveniles tried in criminal court.[42]

Amid predictions of a bloodbath of youth violence in the late 1980s and early 1990s, states adopted get tough laws to transfer more juveniles to criminal court.[43] Judges' neutrality and relative autonomy from political pressures impelled legislators to shift control of transfer decisions to prosecutors.[44] They assumed that juveniles' criminal responsibility equaled that of adults and expected criminal courts to punish them similarly.[45] As I explain in Chapter 8, the Supreme Court finally halted states' most draconian sanctions.

Get tough laws lowered the age of eligibility for transfer, increased the numbers of excluded offenses, and shifted discretion to prosecutors making charging decisions.[46] Although fourteen is the minimum age for transfer in most jurisdictions, some states set no minimum age or permit criminal prosecution of children as young as ten; others require prosecution of children as young as thirteen.[47] By 1999, half the states enacted mandatory transfer provisions for serious crimes.[48] Although forty-five states have judicial waiver statutes, prosecutors' excluded-offense or direct-file charging decisions determine the adult status of 85% of youths.[49]

Judicial Waiver: Individualized Sentencing and Impetus for Alternatives

From juvenile courts' inception, judges could transfer some youths to criminal courts.[50] In *Kent v. United States*, the Supreme Court required judges to conduct a procedurally fair hearing before transferring a youth.[51] *Kent* concluded that loss of juvenile courts' benefits—access to treatment, confidentiality, limited collateral consequences, and the like—was a critical action that required a hearing, assistance of counsel, access to probation reports, and written findings for appellate review. *Breed v. Jones* applied the Fifth Amendment double jeopardy prohibition to delinquency adjudications and required states to decide whether to prosecute a youth in juvenile or criminal court before proceeding to trial.[52]

Until Get Tough Era changes, judges made transfer decisions by assessing a youth's amenability to treatment or threat to public safety. *Kent* appended to its opinion a list of criteria for judges to consider. State court decisions and statutes incorporated those criteria.[53] Judges typically focus on three groups of factors. First, a youth's age and time remaining within juvenile court jurisdiction—typically to age nineteen, twenty-one, or twenty-five—provide impetus to transfer older youths more readily than younger ones.[54] Second, clinical evaluations and prior interventions influence judges' appraisals of amenability to treatment, especially if youths have received or exhausted available options.[55] Third, judges base threat to public safety on a youth's offense, prior record, gang involvement, or weapon use.[56]

Despite these factors' seeming relevance, judges have broad discretion to interpret them. Lists of factors like those appended in *Kent* allow them to emphasize different variables and justify any decision. Like the capital punishment statutes invalidated in *Furman v. Georgia*, transfer laws lack meaningful standards to guide discretion.[57] Liberals complained that vague criteria produce inconsistent outcomes, racial disparities, and urban/rural differences within a state.[58] Conservatives attributed rising crime rates to judges' reluctance to transfer cases.[59]

Studies of judicial waiver clearly document inconsistent rulings, justice by geography, and overrepresentation of racial minorities. Waiver rates for similar offenders vary between and within states.[60] Geographic context affects whether prosecutors file waiver motions or judges grant them.[61] Where youths live, rather than what they did, influences transfer outcomes, producing justice by geography.[62] Judges in the same urban county decide cases of similar offenders differently.[63]

For decades, studies reported racial disparities in judicial transfer decisions.[64] Get tough laws to limit judges' discretion, expand prosecutors' power, or exclude youths from juvenile court amplify racial disparities. Judges transfer minority youths more often than white youths, especially those charged with violent and drug crimes.[65] In some states, judges transferred minority youths at five times their proportion of the population.[66] Los Angeles judges were 6.2 times more likely to transfer minority youths than white youths and 7 times more likely to imprison them.[67] In the seventy-five largest counties in the United States, racial minorities comprised more than two-thirds of juveniles tried in criminal court and the vast majority of those sentenced to prison.[68]

Just Deserts, Criminal Careers, and Transfer without a Hearing

A few states historically excluded capital murder or serious crimes from juvenile court jurisdiction, but in the 1970s and 1980s many states expanded offense exclusion and direct-file laws to evade *Kent*'s hearing requirement.[69] In the 1970s, jurisprudential changes—just deserts—and criminological research—criminal careers—provided intellectual legitimacy and rationale for offense-based transfer laws.

Proponents of just deserts advocated offense-based determinate and proportional criminal sentences rather than indeterminate penalties. They argued that indeterminate sentences gave judges too much discretion and produced racially disparate outcomes.[70] By the mid-1980s, half the states enacted determinate sentences for adults, ten eliminated parole boards, and many used sentencing guidelines to decide confinement, supervision, and release.[71]

In juvenile courts, just deserts provided an offense-based alternative to judicial waiver.[72] Deserts advocates questioned whether judges could assess amenability to treatment or predict dangerousness, criticized indeterminate criteria and discretionary processes, and condemned discriminatory results.[73] Twenty-nine states exclude some offenses from juvenile court jurisdiction, typically murder by older youths.[74] Many exclude longer lists—crimes against the person, property, drugs, or weapons offenses—and expanded them during the Get Tough Era.[75]

Research on criminal careers in the 1970s and 1980s initially offered the prospect that judges could identify and incapacitate active offenders.[76] Marvin Wolfgang's seminal *Delinquency in a Birth Cohort* and subsequent research on delinquent careers provided an empirical rationale to incapacitate chronic offenders.[77] A small subset of chronic offenders committed most serious and violent crimes as by-products of persistent law breaking.[78] Delinquent offenders do not specialize in particular crimes, and we cannot predict a future crime from an initial offense, but an extensive prior record is a good indicator of likely future criminal behavior.[79]

Researchers distinguish between most youths who commit some crimes as a normal part of growing up but then desist—adolescent-limited offenders—and those who become chronic or life-course persistent offenders.[80] Those youths who engage in persistent antisocial behavior into adulthood have personal characteristics—low IQ, psychomotor clumsiness, minor birth defects, or neuropsychological deficits that heighten impulsivity—that interact with their environments—poverty, stress, harsh or abusive parenting—and contribute to continued offending.[81] In Wolfgang's study of all boys born in 1945 who lived in Philadelphia from their tenth to their eighteenth birthdays, police arrested more than one-third, but nearly half of those had no further police contact.[82] Those arrested for a violent crime desisted at the same rates as those arrested for other offenses.[83] Chronic offenders—those arrested five or more times—comprised 6% of the cohort, continued into adulthood, and committed most of the serious and violent crimes perpetrated by their age-mates.[84] A second Philadelphia cohort study confirmed that a small subset of youths became life-course persistent offenders.[85]

Chronic offenders exhibit behavior problems during childhood—aggression, risk taking, impulsiveness, and the like—which increase in frequency and severity in adolescence.[86] Age of onset is an indicator of who will become a chronic offender—those who become delinquent before twelve years of age are two or three times more likely to become chronic offenders than those who begin later.[87] Criminal career research held promise that justice system personnel could identify and incapacitate chronic offenders to prevent crime, but their pattern only emerges retrospectively.[88] Although chronic offenders differ from their less delinquent peers, they need time to distinguish themselves—a luxury most legislators are unwilling to indulge.

Transfer laws based on a just deserts rationale would exclude older youths charged with serious crimes who deserve more severe punishment. Policies to incapacitate career offenders would focus on extensive prior records. In the 1980s and 1990s, legislators augmented lists of excluded offenses, excluded combinations of present offense and prior record, lowered the ages to criminally prosecute youths, and expanded prosecutors' authority.[89] Politicians expected that increased certainty and severity of punishment also would deter young offenders.[90]

Legislative Offense Exclusion

Offense-exclusion and direct-file laws focus on offenses and ignore youths' amenability to treatment. Appellate courts uniformly reject youths' claims that prosecuting them for an excluded offense denies *Kent*'s procedural safeguards. In *United States v. Bland*, the prosecutor charged Bland in criminal court with an excluded offense.[91] The *Bland* dissent criticized offense exclusion as a transparent effort to evade *Kent*, warned that it precluded consideration of the offender, and argued for procedural parity between judges' waiver and prosecutors' charging decisions. The *Bland* majority relied on the doctrine of separation of powers, which denies judges authority to control executive branch discretionary decisions—whether and whom to charge and with what crime—and rejected procedural limits.[92]

Prosecutorial Direct File

In fifteen states, juvenile and criminal courts share concurrent jurisdiction over serious crimes.[93] Prosecutors decide both the charge and forum: did the youth commit a direct-file offense and should it be tried in juvenile or criminal court? Under offense exclusion, the crime charged determines the venue; direct-file laws allow prosecutors to select either system to try the crime. Direct file elevates prosecutors' power at judges' expense and creates a model more typical of criminal courts.[94]

Most direct-file laws provide no criteria to guide prosecutors' choice of forum.[95] Even if prosecutors adopt self-imposed guidelines, they have little impact on their forum decisions.[96] They lack access to personal, social, or clinical information about a youth that a judge would consider and base their decisions primarily on police reports.[97] While trained to evaluate evidence and charges, they have no professional expertise or non-offense information with which to decide to try a youth as a juvenile or adult. Prosecutors in Virginia direct filed about one-quarter of eligible youths and focused on offense, weapons, and victim's injury.[98] Compared with youths whom judges previously waived, they deemphasized clinical information, prior record, or culpability.[99]

Critics of direct file contend that locally elected prosecutors exploit crime issues like get tough legislators, introduce justice by geography, and exercise their discretion as subjectively as do judges but without being subject to appellate review.[100] Prosecutors who view the position as a stepping stone to higher office may get tough on crime at the expense of young offenders.[101] Assistant prosecutors for whom juvenile court is their first assignment lack judges' experience to make such important decisions.[102]

Youths' challenges to prosecutors' direct-file authority fail. The California Supreme Court in *Manduley v. Superior Court of San Diego County* reviewed Proposition 21—a 1998 voter-approved get tough initiative—that authorized district attorneys to direct file youths as young as fourteen in criminal court.[103] *Manduley* reasoned that youths do not have a right to be tried in juvenile court, so prosecutors' decision to charge them in criminal court did not violate due process.[104] Although prosecutors charge some youths in criminal court and others with the same crime in juvenile court, they have no equal protection recourse unless prosecutors selected them for harsher treatment because of race, religion, or other discriminatory purpose.[105]

Even though most states have judicial waiver statutes, prosecutors transfer the vast majority of youths without any hearing.[106] Florida allows prosecutors to direct file *any* sixteen- or seventeen-year-old charged with *any* felony and younger juveniles charged with more serious crimes. They direct filed about 10% of eligible juveniles, about the same number as juvenile court judges transferred in the country.[107] Nationally, prosecutors determined the criminal status of 85% of youths tried as adults and acted as gatekeepers to the juvenile justice system, a role previously reserved for judges.[108] Judicial waiver vests discretion in more experienced, better informed, and less politicized judges, whereas offense exclusion and direct file allow less knowledgeable, politically motivated prosecutors to make adulthood determinations.[109]

Blended Sentencing: Juvenile and Criminal Court Convergence

Juvenile courts lose jurisdiction when youths reach the age of majority or other dispositional age limit—nineteen, twenty-one, or twenty-five. As a result, judges may be unable to sentence appropriately older offenders convicted of serious crimes.[110] Juvenile courts' time-limited opportunity to treat or punish youths provides impetus to increase their sentencing powers.[111] Blended sentences meld delinquency dispositions with threat of criminal sanctions and provide longer confinement options than otherwise available in juvenile court—to treat with the possibility of punishment.

States use several versions of blended sentences. Some allow juvenile courts to impose extended delinquency sentences; others give criminal courts power to use a delinquency disposition in lieu of imprisonment.[112] In some states, juvenile courts impose a delinquency disposition coupled with a stayed criminal sentence pending successful completion of the juvenile probation.[113] In others, when a youth reaches the juvenile court's jurisdictional age limit, a judge decides whether he should serve the remainder of the criminal sentence.[114] Regardless of approach, all blended sentencing laws require criminal procedural safeguards, including the right to a jury trial, to enable a judge to punish and thereby gain greater flexibility to treat. Critics charge that blended sentences and punishment blur juvenile courts' rehabilitative mission with respect to other delinquents.[115]

Although states adopted blended sentences as an alternative to transfer, juvenile court judges frequently impose them on less serious offenders whom they previously handled as delinquents.[116] Net-widening occurs when reformers introduce a new sanction to be used instead of another more severe sanction—e.g., blended sentences in lieu of transfer—but which judges then apply to those whom they previously treated more leniently.[117] Evaluation of Minnesota's blended sentencing law found that judges transferred the same numbers and types of youths whom they previously waived *and* imposed blended sentences on many younger, less serious offenders whom they previously dealt with as delinquents. Judges subsequently revoked the probation of more than one-third of youths who received blended sentences, primarily for technical violations, and doubled the number of youths sent to prison.[118] Prosecutors used the threat of transfer to coerce youths to plead to blended sentences, to waive procedural rights, to increase punishment imposed in juvenile courts, and to risk exposure to criminal sanctions.[119] Franklin Zimring criticized blended sentencing as a prosecutorial power grab. "If the enhancement of prosecutorial power was sought and the creation of a structure of outcomes where plea bargaining was encouraged, then blended sentencing is just what the district attorney ordered."[120]

Relocating Discretion: Reverse Waiver and Transfer Back

Progressive reformers created juvenile courts to remove youths from adult prisons. However, many excluded offenses carry mandatory prison sentences. As explored in more detail below, juveniles sentenced as adults are more likely to be imprisoned, to be victims of violence, to experience sexual assaults, and to commit suicide than youths confined in juvenile facilities.[121] Some states allow criminal court judges to transfer back to juvenile court youths whose excluded-offense or direct-file cases originated in criminal court. Reverse waiver restores some flexibility to a prosecutor-dominated process and about half the states allow a judge to return a youth to juvenile court for trial or disposition.[122]

Although *Kent*'s procedural requirements prompted the adoption of offense-exclusion and direct-file laws, reverse waiver relocates *Kent*-type hearings in criminal courts in which judges review a presentence report and consider *Kent* criteria.[123] No reasons exist to believe that criminal court judges are better able than juvenile court judges to decide whether a youth is amenable to treatment.[124]

Juveniles in Prison

In the absence of reverse waiver or blended dispositions, criminal court judges sentence transferred youths like adults. Imprisoning juveniles increases rather than reduces subsequent offending.[125] While all inmates face the possibility of abuse, adolescents' lesser size, physical strength, and social skills, and lack of sophistication increase their risk for physical, sexual, and psychological victimization.[126] Although staff- and inmate-on-inmate violence occurs in juvenile settings, youths housed in adult facilities more often are victimized and commit suicide.[127] Although we lack research on youths' prison experiences, "placements in prisons and jails put less mature, less experienced adolescents into a social environment that stresses survival and toughness. Such an arrangement seems to inevitably increase an adolescent's chances of being involved in a physical confrontation, either through efforts to establish a reputation or to resist assaults or sexual advances."[128] To prevent victimization, some states place vulnerable youths in solitary confinement for twenty-three hours a day.[129]

Prisons are developmentally inappropriate places for youths to form an identity, acquire social skills, or make a successful transition to adulthood.[130] Identity formation requires positive adult relationships, healthy peer interactions, and opportunities to make decisions.[131] Prison confounds these tasks where a criminal identity can be self-protective, peer relationships entail schooling for crime, decision-making authority is stripped away, and guards focus on security rather than developmental concerns. Most states put juveniles in the general inmate population, perhaps to be victimized or to learn better criminal skills.[132]

Confining youths in prison exacts different and greater developmental opportunity costs than those experienced by adults.[133] The normal adolescent life course—forming an identity, finishing school, finding work, developing relationships, starting a family—is integrative and draws youths into society.[134] Completing education, finding a job, and forming relationships impose structure and routine and create social bonds that promote desistance from offending.[135] Imprisonment disrupts normal development; ground lost may never be regained. Most adolescents sentenced to prison already exhibit social and developmental delays.[136] Young inmates are less likely than the general population to have a high school diploma or High School Equivalency Certificate.[137] Imprisonment imposes stigma and civil disabilities, discourages employers from hiring ex-offenders, undermines marriage prospects, and increases likelihood of future offending.[138] Young Black men bear the burden of stigma and exclusion most heavily.[139] Collateral consequences of criminal convictions are extensive—civic participation, public housing restrictions, ineligibility for school loan, sex offender registration, licensure, bonding, and employment restrictions, and many others.

Policy Justifications for Waiver: Unarticulated and Unrealized

States will prosecute some youths in criminal court as a matter of public safety and political reality.[140] Retributivist would argue that serious crimes deserve longer sentences than juvenile courts can impose. Consequentialists would punish to deter youths or other would-be offenders or to incapacitate them. Youths' immaturity, impulsiveness, and lack of self-control may frustrate these goals. *Roper*, *Graham*, and *Miller*, which I discuss in Chapter 8, concluded that youths' reduced culpability weakens retributive justification and their impaired judgment and limited self-restraint undermines deterrence.

If transfer and criminal court sentencing practices are incongruent, then some youths may fall between the cracks.[141] Prior to get tough changes, judges transferred the largest plurality of youths for property crimes and criminal court judges typically sentenced them as if they were adult first offenders.[142] Judges placed the majority on probation and imposed jail and prison sentences within the range of those available to juvenile courts on many.[143]

The Get Tough Era targeted violent and drug crimes and increased the likelihood and severity of criminal sentences. Judges incarcerate transferred youths convicted of violent crimes more often and for longer sentences than youths retained in juvenile courts.[144] Three-quarters of those convicted of violent felonies went to prison.[145] For nonviolent youths sentenced as adults, however, about half received probation and most received confinement sentences comparable to those in juvenile facilities.[146] Nearly half of youths tried in criminal court are not convicted or are placed on probation, fewer than 25% are sentenced to prison, and 95% are released from custody by their twenty-fifth birthday.[147] Many youths prosecuted as adults are not among the worst of the worst, receive sentences similar to those that juvenile courts could impose, and the vast majority return to their communities within a few years.

Deterrence

Legislators in the Get Tough Era assumed that threat of transfer and criminal punishment would deter youths. *Roper v. Simmons* questioned whether the risk of a sanction altered youths' calculus. "[T]he absence of evidence of a deterrent effect is of special concern because the same characteristics that render juveniles less culpable than adults suggest as well that juveniles will be less susceptible to deterrence."[148] *Roper's* intuition appears more accurate than legislators' expectations.

Studies of juvenile crime rates before and after passage of get tough laws found no general deterrent effect. New York's juvenile offender law had minimal impact on arrest rates for excluded offenses especially for youths in high-crime urban areas.[149] A comparison of arrest rates in Washington and Idaho before and after Idaho adopted a broad exclusion law reported that arrests there actually rose.[150] After Washington enacted get tough laws, no differences were observed between its arrest rates and national rates over the same period.[151] Comparisons of arrests rates in states where juvenile court jurisdiction ended at sixteen and at seventeen years of age found no age impact on crime rates.[152] Analyses of arrest rates five years before and after states adopted offense-exclusion and direct-file laws concluded that neither strategy significantly affected arrests for violent crimes.[153]

Studies of special deterrence report that transferred youths had higher recidivism rates than did those sentenced as delinquents.[154] Jeffrey Fagan compared recidivism rates of four hundred fifteen- and sixteen-year-old boys charged with robbery and burglary in criminal court in New York with four hundred New Jersey boys tried in juvenile court and found the former reoffended more quickly and frequently than their juvenile compatriots.[155] Fagan subsequently expanded the comparative research to twenty-four hundred juveniles charged with robbery, burglary, and assault and found that police rearrested those prosecuted in criminal courts more quickly and for more serious offenses than those processed in juvenile courts.[156]

Florida researchers matched 2,738 pairs of youths tried as juveniles and adults, used several measures of recidivism after twenty-four months and seven years, and found that police rearrested direct-filed youths more often, more quickly, and for more serious offenses than those sentenced as juveniles.[157] A subsequent study with more equivalent comparison groups again found that police rearrested transferred youth for violent crimes more quickly and more often than those retained in juvenile court.[158]

The Center for Disease Control's Task Force on Community Preventive Services reviewed studies that compared outcomes of youths transferred to criminal courts with those who remained in juvenile courts.[159] It concluded that youths tried as adults had higher and faster recidivism rates, especially for violent crimes, than their delinquent counterparts.[160] Any short-term public protection of incarceration is offset by developmental disruption and increased likelihood of future recidivism.[161]

Youthfulness as an Aggravating Factor in Sentencing

Although judges do not imprison all transferred youths, they sometimes treat youthfulness as an aggravating rather than a mitigating factor when they do.[162] Virginia sentencing law prescribes youthfulness as an aggravating factor, a policy inconsistent with ideas about youths' reduced culpability.[163] Florida judges sentence direct-filed youths to longer terms than young adults convicted of the same crimes.[164] More youths convicted of murder receive life-without-parole sentences than do adults sentenced for murder.[165] A study in thirty-nine urban counties in nineteen states reported that transferred juveniles are more likely to be convicted and incarcerated than adult offenders.[166] Compared with young adult offenders, juveniles convicted of the same crimes received longer sentences.[167]

Constructing Culpability: Accountability and Race

States prosecuted more youths in criminal court during the Get Tough Era.[168] They recast youths as responsible near-adults rather than as immature children.[169] Alfred Regnery, director of the Office of Juvenile Justice and Delinquency Prevention during the Reagan administration, described sixteen-year-olds as "criminals who happen to be young, not children who happen to commit crimes."[170] Politicians' get tough sound bites—"adult crime, adult time," "old enough to do the crime, old enough to do the time"—depicted teenagers as responsible. They viewed their crimes as rational choices, rather than socially influenced conduct, and ignored immaturity, impulsivity, and youthful mitigation.[171] Simplistically emphasizing rational choice ignored a century of criminological research, but justified severe penalties and accountability over a rehabilitative approach.[172]

Punitive transfer laws targeted violent crimes, which Black youths commit more often.[173] Even prior to the Get Tough Era, studies reported racial disparities in judicial transfer decisions.[174] Subsequently, judges transferred youths of color more often than white youths charged with similar violent and drug crimes.[175] The vast majority of juveniles transferred to criminal court and sentenced to prison are youths of color, primarily Blacks.[176]

Waiver Policy: What Should a Rational Legislature Do?

Expansive transfer policies adopted a quarter century ago do not further any legitimate penal goals. Equating younger and older offenders ignores developmental differences and disproportionately punishes less blameworthy adolescents. No credible evidence exists that transfer deters youths. Immature judgment, short-term time perspective, and preference for immediate gains lessen the threat of sanctions. Youths tried as adults reoffend more quickly and more seriously, thereby negating any short-term crime reduction. Transfer increases risk to public safety because criminal prosecution *per se* aggravates youths' recidivism, regardless of the sentence imposed.

Despite offense-based get tough laws and prosecutors' dominant role, the vast majority of juvenile justice scholars agree that *if some youths must be transferred*, then it should occur in a judicial waiver process that is used rarely.[177] A state should waive only those youths whose serious *and* persistent offenses require minimum lengths of confinement that greatly exceed the maximum sanctions available in juvenile court.[178] A retributive policy would limit severe sanctions to youths charged with homicide, rape, robbery, or assault with a firearm or substantial injury. However, severely punishing *all* youths who commit serious crimes would be counterproductive because youths arrested for an initial violent offense desist at similar rates to other delinquents.[179] Chronic offenders may require sentences longer than those available in juvenile court because of persistent criminality and exhaustion of rehabilitative resources.[180]

Legislatures should also prescribe minimum ages of eligibility for criminal prosecution. In Chapter 8, I review developmental psychological and neuroscience research that reports a sharp drop-off in judgment, self-control, and appreciation of consequences for youths fifteen years of age or younger. In Chapter 9, I review developmental and criminological research on youths' competence to exercise procedural rights, which also reports a sharp drop-off in ability to exercise legal rights among those fifteen years of age or younger. The minimum age for transfer should be sixteen years of age.

A juvenile court hearing guided by offense criteria and clinical considerations and subject to rigorous appellate review is the only sensible way to make transfer decisions.[181] Criteria should focus on offenses, prior record, offender culpability, criminal participation, clinical evaluations, and aggravating and mitigating factors that, taken together, distinguish youths who deserve sentences substantially longer than juvenile courts can impose from those who do not. Appellate courts should closely review waiver decisions and develop substantive principles to define a consistent boundary of adulthood. Although waiver hearings are less efficient than prosecutor's charging decisions, it should be difficult to transfer youths—juvenile courts exist to keep them out of the criminal justice system. An adversarial hearing at which prosecution and defense present evidence about offense, culpability, and treatment prognoses will produce better decisions than will politically motivated prosecutors acting without clinical information.

Offense-exclusion and direct-file laws have not obviated the need for judicial discretion, which reappears as transfer back or delinquency sanctions in lieu of imprisonment. However, offense-based laws symbolize a reorientation of juvenile jurisprudence from diversion and rehabilitation to retribution, incapacitation, and deterrence. They represent a legal and cultural reconstruction of youth from innocent immature children to responsible mature offenders. They allow politicians to express punitive vengeful sentiments without regard to their laws' iatrogenic and counterproductive impact on children and public safety.

Pretrial Detention of Delinquents

Pretrial detention involves a youth's interim custody status pending trial. When police take a youth into custody, they can release her to a parent or take her to a detention facility. There, probation officers can release a youth to her parent or detain her pending a hearing. Finally, a juvenile court judge can hold a youth in detention pending trial if she finds that the youth poses a danger to him or herself, a threat to others, or will not appear for further proceedings.[182] Of youths referred to juvenile courts, states hold about 20% in pretrial detention facilities—between one-quarter and one-third of a million juveniles annually.[183] In 2011, judges detained a larger proportion of youths arrested for person offenses (25.6%) than they did for property crimes (16.8%), but because police arrested so many more youths for property than person crimes, they confined roughly equal numbers.[184] Rates of detention rose and peaked between 1998 and 2007, even as the absolute numbers of youths referred to juvenile courts declined. Courts detained older youths at higher rates than younger juveniles, more boys than girls, and more children of color than white youths.[185]

In 1984, the Supreme Court in *Schall v. Martin* reviewed a New York statute that authorized preventive detention if a judge found there was a "serious risk" that the child "may . . . commit an act which if committed by an adult would constitute a crime."[186] The law did not specify the type of present crime, the likelihood or seriousness of a future crime, burden of proof, or criteria or evidence a judge should consider to make the prediction. Despite these flaws, the *Schall* majority held that preventive detention "serves a legitimate state objective, and that the procedural protections afforded pre-trial detainees" satisfy constitutional requirements.[187]

The Court noted that crime prevention is an important goal, juveniles commit a substantial amount of crimes, and victims suffer the same harm regardless of a perpetrator's age.[188] *Schall* minimized juveniles' liberty interests. "Juveniles, unlike adults, are always in some form of custody. . . . [T]he juvenile's liberty interest may, in appropriate circumstances, be subordinated to the State's *parens patriae* interest in preserving and promoting the welfare of the child."[189] Detention protected juveniles from the injuries they might suffer from a victim's resistance or police arrest.[190] *Schall* recognized that a negative ruling would invalidate similar preventive detention laws in every state.[191]

The district court and Court of Appeals' decisions in *Schall* concluded that judges detained youths to impose pretrial punishment for unproven offenses, rather than as a crime-prevention measure. The *Schall* litigation involved the Spofford Detention Facility, which had been the subject of extensive litigation, judicial scrutiny, and critical reports.[192] A previous court described it as a penal institution—inmates wore uniforms, marched in line, and staff locked them in dormitories, classes, and dining halls.[193] The Court of Appeals in *Schall* concluded that judges used detention to punish youths because they dismissed many cases before trial and returned most youths to the community after trial. By contrast, the Supreme Court described institutional conditions and release practices as collateral aspects of "legitimate governmental regulation" rather than as pretrial punishment.[194]

The Court considered whether detention hearing procedures provided adequate protection. *Gerstein v. Pugh* required a prompt probable cause determination for arrested adults facing continued detention.[195] *Schall* concluded that the procedures satisfied *Gerstein* because a judge advised the juvenile of their charges, the right to remain silent, and to counsel at an initial appearance. Although the majority implied that a judge made a probable cause determination, the dissent asserted that it did not occur until three days or longer after the initial appearance, which would violate *Gerstein*.[196]

To detain a youth, a judge must predict that whether he or she would commit a crime before the next court appearance. *Schall* rejected the district court's findings that it is "virtually impossible to predict future criminal conduct with any degree of accuracy," and insisted that judges regularly predict future crimes.[197] "[F]rom a legal point of view there is nothing inherently unattainable about a prediction of future criminal conduct. Such a judgment forms an important element in many decisions, and we have specifically rejected the contention, based on the same sort of sociological data relied upon by appellees and the district court, 'that it is impossible to predict future behavior and that the question is so vague as to be meaningless.'"[198] Despite the majority's confidence in judges' predictive powers, they declined to specify the burden of proof, criteria, or evidence they should consider.

Ends and Means: Legitimate State Objective and Adequate Procedures?

The *Schall* dissent questioned the substantive goals and procedural means used to make detention decisions. The dissenters argued that neither judges nor clinicians could reliably predict who would commit a crime in the future.[199] Decision makers use different methodologies—statistical or actuarial versus clinical—to make predictions. Statistical prediction relies on correlations between independent characteristics and behavior to be predicted, assesses the individual to determine whether he or she has those traits, and then makes a prediction based on the aggregate risk of people with those features.[200] Clinical prediction relies on expert evaluation of the individual and a hypothesis about how that person might act in the future.[201] Despite *Schall*'s confidence in judges' clinical prognostication, social scientists question its assumption.[202] Studies compare the relative accuracy of statistical versus clinical prediction and strongly support the superiority of actuarial instruments over professional judgments.[203] The American Psychiatric Association long has disclaimed psychiatrists' competence to predict future dangerousness because they tend to not use information reliably, to disregard base rate variability, to consider factors that are not predictive, and to assign inappropriate weights to factors.[204] Under the best conditions, clinical predictions are wrong about two times out of three—an error rate that would result in confining many people who would not have offended.[205] The fallibility of prediction is compounded because judges at an initial appearance often lack access to information—psychometric tests, professional evaluations, and social histories—on which clinicians would rely. *Schall*'s dissent argued that most detained youths would not have committed crimes if released and their loss of liberty conferred little benefit to the community.[206]

Conditions of Confinement

The *Schall* majority denigrated juveniles' liberty interests—"juveniles are always in some form of custody"—and trivialized conditions of confinement. Judges confine far more juveniles in detention facilities than they subsequently commit to correctional institutions. An earlier court found that conditions at Spofford violated the Constitution—that it was a jail-like facility "fraught with problems related both to architectural layout and to maintenance," "poorly designed," and where staff and inmates physically abused juveniles.[207]

Inadequate and dangerous conditions have characterized detention facilities for decades.[208] Get tough policies in the 1990s exacerbated overcrowding as states detained youths to impose short-term punishment or to house those awaiting post-adjudication placement.[209] According to a recent summary of conditions of confinement,

> Many detention centers are overcrowded, elevating the risks to the safety of both youths and staff. The overcrowding, high volume of juveniles (many of whom are there for very brief periods), and high rates of staff turnover make it difficult for detention centers to offer quality services. Conditions of confinement may be poor, including understaffing, insufficient supervision, poor design, or deteriorating facilities. Children of color are greatly overrepresented in detention compared with their percentages in the general population. Many detained youths have substance abuse problems and/or mental health conditions that may never have been diagnosed, let alone treated. . . . Overcrowded facilities tend to be at elevated risk for a number of other problems. These include injuries to youth and staff, more use of short-term isolation, more suicidal behavior, and higher staff turnover.[210]

In *Conditions of Confinement: Juvenile Detention and Corrections Facilities*, the Office of Juvenile Justice and Delinquency Prevention reported deficient conditions, inadequate health care, poor education, lack of treatment services, and excessive use of solitary confinement and

physical restraints.[211] Although *Schall* described institutional practices as equivalent to parental supervision, detention staff conduct
suspicionless strip searches of female status offenders prior to their
admission.[212]

The *Schall* dissenters objected that pretrial detention disrupted life,
weakened ties to family, school, and work, stigmatized youth, and impaired legal defenses. Judges convict and institutionalize detained youths
more often than those released pending trial.[213] The dissent questioned
the procedures used to detain youths because the statute did not specify
the type of crime, the burden of proof, or evidence to support the prediction. Despite the majority's confidence that attorneys participated at
detention hearings,

> juvenile codes in certain states do not even require courts to appoint at-
> torneys at the detention stage. . . . [E]ven when state law does afford ju-
> veniles the right to counsel at the pretrial hearing, juveniles frequently
> waive counsel's appearance. . . . In some jurisdictions, as many as 80 to
> 90 percent of youth waive their right to an attorney because they do not
> know the meaning of the word 'waive' or understand its consequences.
> And finally, when attorneys do appear at detention hearings, they are
> frequently untrained in juvenile court procedures, inexperienced, and
> overburdened.[214]

Without objective criteria, a standard of proof, or time to prepare, an
attorney can do little. The informality, vagueness, and subjectivity of
detention proceedings lend themselves to erroneous, arbitrary, and discriminatory decisions.[215]

Racial Disparities in Detention

Judicial discretion leads to racial disparities in detention.[216] To be
sure, some differences reflect differences in serious offending by race.
As noted in Chapter 3, police arrest Black youths for violent crimes at
higher rates than white youths; juvenile courts detain a larger proportion of violent offenders than those arrested for other crimes.[217] But,
after controls for present offense, prior record, and other variables,
judges more frequently detain Black youths than white offenders.[218]

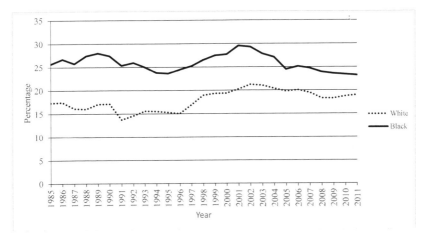

Figure 5.1. Detention for All Offenses, by Race, 1985–2011
Source: Office of Juvenile Justice and Delinquency Prevention, *Easy Access to the Census of Juveniles in Residential Placement: 1985–2011*, www.ojjdp.gov.

While race affects detention decisions, detention adversely affects youths' subsequent case processing and compounds disparities at disposition. Michael Lieber reported race effects of detention on disposition in Iowa.[219] Nancy Rodriguez reported that Arizona juvenile courts detained Black, Hispanic, and Native American youths at higher rates than they did comparable white offenders and that "youth who were detained pre-adjudication were more likely to have petitions filed, less likely to have petitions dismissed, and more likely to be removed from home at disposition."[220]

Between 1985 and 2011, juvenile court judges detained about one-fifth of all youths referred to them. Figures 5.1, 5.2, and 5.3 show rates of detention by race over a quarter century. Figure 5.1 reveals that between 1985 and 2011, judges on average detained 18.2% of white youths compared with 26.0% of Black youths. Judges detain youths charged with person offenses at higher rates than youths charged with other crimes. Figure 5.2 indicates that on average, judges detained 22.4% of white youths charged with person offenses compared with 28.4% of Black youths. Figure 5.3 reports detention rates for youths charged with drug offenses. Even as detention rates for drug crimes peaked during the Get Tough Era, racial disparities persisted. On average, judges placed 17.1% of white youths in detention for drug offenses. In 1990, judges de-

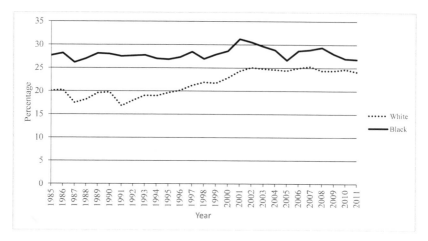

Figure 5.2. Detention for Person Offenses, by Race, 1985–2011
Source: Office of Juvenile Justice and Delinquency Prevention, *Easy Access to the Census of Juveniles in Residential Placement: 1985–2011*, www.ojjdp.gov.

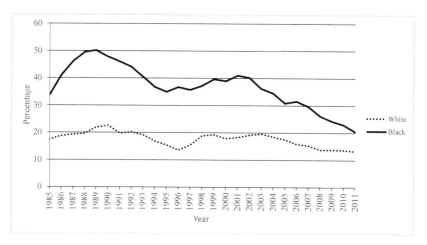

Figure 5.3. Detention for Drug Offenses, by Race, 1985–2011
Source: Office of Juvenile Justice and Delinquency Prevention, *Easy Access to the Census of Juveniles in Residential Placement: 1985–2011*, www.ojjdp.gov.

tained less than one-quarter (23.5%) of white youths for drug crimes. By contrast, they detained more than one-third (36.7%) of Black youths charged with drug offenses—more than double white youths' rate. Between 1988 and 1991—the peak of the crack cocaine panic and the Get Tough Era—judges detained about half of all Black youths charged with drug offenses, a rate twice that of white youths. The racial disparities for drug crimes are especially disturbing because, since the 1970s, self-report research consistently reports that Black youths use and sell drugs at *lower* rates than do white youths.[221] Despite these racial differences in drug use, police resource and enforcement decisions result in higher arrests rates of Blacks than whites.[222]

Reform Efforts

Beginning in the late 1980s, the Annie E. Casey Foundation launched the Juvenile Detention Alternatives Initiative (JDAI). JDAI aimed to reduce use of detention, develop alternatives to institutions, reduce overcrowding, improve conditions of confinement, and lessen racial disparities.[223] JDAI reforms enlist justice system stakeholders to develop consensus rationales for detention, to adopt objective intake and risk assessment criteria, to use alternatives to secure detention—home detention, electronic monitoring, after-school or day-reporting centers—and to expedite cases to reduce pretrial confinement.[224] JDAI screening tools are not validated actuarial prediction instruments. Rather, stakeholders develop consensus criteria about which youths are appropriate to detain based on present offense, prior record, and other factors.[225] JDAI expanded from one Florida county in the 1980s to hundreds of sites in more than two dozen states. Although not all of these efforts have been equally successful, many sites have reduced the numbers of youths detained with no increases in crime or failures to appear. Despite use of objective screening tools, JDAI efforts to reduce racial disparities among detained youths have proved less successful.[226]

Policy Recommendations

The *Schall* dissent maintained that the harms of pretrial confinement outweighed any benefits to the juvenile or community and opined that clearer statutes and procedures could improve decision making. The *Schall* majority responded that its role was to determine whether the statute met minimum constitutional standards and noted that "we are neither a legislature charged with formulating public policy nor an ABA committee charged with drafting a model statute."[227] The legislatures that pass laws and the judges who implement them bear primary responsibility for reform. Statutes should specify more explicit offense-based criteria. Juvenile court judges in collaboration with other stakeholders and social scientists should develop risk-assessment instruments to better identify who *might* offend in the future. Laws should presume release of all non-felony offenders and place a heavy burden—clear and convincing evidence—on the state to prove that a youth needs secure detention and that non-secure alternatives—house arrest, electronic monitoring, shelter care, day reporting—would fail. Other than youths who pose a risk of flight or who have absconded from an institution, states should reserve detention for youths charged with serious crimes—felonies, violence, or firearms—for whom, if convicted, commitment to a secure facility would likely result. States should bolster procedures with a non-waivable right to counsel and an opportunity to meet prior to the hearing.

Delinquency Dispositions: Treatment or Punishment?

What are the goals of delinquency dispositions—rehabilitation, punishment, incapacitation, deterrence?[228] How do delinquency sanctions differ from criminal punishment? How do juvenile court judges decide with whom to intervene and what disposition to impose? How effective are these interventions? Progressives' rehabilitative ideal empowered judges to impose indeterminate nonproportional dispositions in a child's best interests. Despite good intentions, historians question whether they were rehabilitative either in theory or in practice.[229] After *Gault*, delinquency sanctions became more punitive and Get Tough Era laws shifted them even further toward punishment.[230] If rehabilitation is the justification for fewer procedural safeguards in juvenile courts than in criminal courts, then how do we know what it is or whether it occurs?

Certain markers distinguish between punishment and treatment.[231] Punishment involves state-imposed consequences—stigma, denunciation, or confinement—on people who violate criminal law.[232] It assumes that responsible actors make blameworthy choices and deserve prescribed penalties.[233] Rehabilitative treatment assumes that deterministic forces caused a person's behavior and can be changed.[234] Interventions are concerned with the person's future welfare rather than past crime.[235]

This section examines juvenile courts' dispositions. It first considers whether juvenile courts treat or punish delinquents and why that distinction matters. *Gault* rejected claims that delinquency prosecutions were civil proceedings, but *McKeiver* denied that they were criminal prosecutions. Juvenile court procedure—the process to determine delinquency—and substance—consequences imposed—rest on purported differences between treatment and punishment. The section first identifies factors to which courts look to distinguish between the two: legislative purpose clauses, sentencing statutes, sentencing practices, conditions of confinement, and intervention outcomes. It examines the impact of legislative changes during the Get Tough Era. Judged by these criteria, it argues that juvenile courts punish delinquents and that those harsher sanctions fall disproportionately heavily on minority youths. In Chapter 9, I argue that because juvenile courts punish delinquents, they require all adult criminal procedural safeguards *and* additional protections to offset their developmental limitations.

Why Does It Matter Whether Juvenile Courts Treat or Punish?

Whether juvenile courts treat or punish delinquents has procedural and substantive significances. *McKeiver* denied a jury trial based on its assumption that delinquency sanctions differed from criminal punishment, but without elaborating how. Procedurally, whether juvenile courts treat or punish would affect youths' right to a jury, protection from collateral consequences of adjudications, and use of delinquency convictions for criminal sentence enhancement. Substantively, whether they treat or punish implicates delinquency dispositions that exceed maximum sentences adults convicted of the same crime receive.[236] The differences bear on juveniles' claims that conditions of confinement violate the Eighth Amendment ban on cruel and unusual punishment. Finally, the distinction affects whether the state has denied their Fourteenth Amendment Due Process Clause "right to treatment" when it confines them.[237]

Whether the question arises in a procedural or substantive context, courts have to decide whether sanctions are punishment or treatment.[238] *Kennedy v. Mendoza-Martinez* pondered whether stripping a dual-nationality person of United States citizenship for avoiding the draft during World War II was punishment and described factors to consider.

> Whether the sanction involves an affirmative disability or restraint, whether it has historically been regarded as punishment, whether it comes into play only on a finding of *scienter,* whether its operation will promote the traditional aims of punishment—retribution and deterrence— whether the behavior to which it applies is already a crime, whether an alternative purpose to which it may rationally be connected is assignable for it, and whether it appears excessive in relation to the alternative purposes assigned are all relevant to the inquiry, and may often point in different directions.[239]

Allen v. Illinois relied on *Mendoza-Martinez* to decide whether an adult in a Sexually Dangerous Persons Act commitment proceeding could invoke the Fifth Amendment privilege against self-incrimination. Even though criminal charges triggered commitment proceedings, the Court concluded that the confinement was civil, denied Fifth Amendment protections, and required him to submit to clinical evaluation.[240] The Court noted that the statutory purpose was to provide "care and treatment," the state disavowed a punitive purpose, commitment was indeterminate, the state purportedly provided treatment, and inmates theoretically could be released after brief confinement.[241] *Allen* acknowledged that some conditions of confinement could amount to punishment, which would require criminal procedural protections, but the complainant failed to show his conditions were "essentially identical to that imposed upon felons with no need for psychiatric care."[242] *Allen* distinguished *Gault*, which granted delinquents Fifth Amendment protections, by noting, "Here, by contrast, the State serves its purpose *of treating* rather than punishing sexually dangerous persons by committing them to an institution expressly designed to provide psychiatric care and treatment."[243]

Justice White's *McKeiver* concurrence highlighted differences between juvenile court treatment and criminal punishment. The criminal law punishes offenders for blameworthy conduct, whereas juvenile courts view delinquents as less culpable or responsible.

For the most part, the juvenile justice system rests on more deterministic assumptions [than the criminal justice system]. Reprehensible acts
by juveniles are not deemed the consequence of mature and malevolent
choice but of environmental pressures (or lack of them) or of other forces
beyond their control. . . . Coercive measures, where employed, are considered neither retribution nor punishment. Supervision or confinement
is aimed at rehabilitation, not at convincing the juvenile of his error simply by imposing pains and penalties. Nor is the purpose to make the juvenile delinquent an object lesson for others, whatever his own merits
or demerits may be. A typical disposition in the juvenile court where
delinquency is established may authorize confinement until age 21, but
it will last no longer and within that period will last only so long as his
behavior demonstrates that he remains an unacceptable risk if returned
to his family. Nor is the authorization for custody until 21 any measure of
the seriousness of the particular act that the juvenile has performed.[244]

Justice White concluded that juvenile courts' nonproportional indeterminate dispositions eschewed notions of blameworthiness and
punishment.[245]

The Court's decisions—*Mendoza-Martinez*, *Allen*, and *McKeiver*—
identify factors with which to distinguish between punishment and
treatment: legislative purpose, indeterminate or determinate sentences,
judges' sentencing practices, institutional conditions, and intervention
outcomes.[246] The Get Tough Era fostered a punitive convergence between juvenile and criminal courts' sentencing policies and practices.

Punishment vs. Treatment: Juvenile Courts' Legislative Purpose

Most states' juvenile codes contain a purpose clause to aid courts to
interpret the law. In 1899, the Cook County juvenile court's purpose was
"[t]hat the care, custody and discipline of a child shall approximate as
nearly as may be that which should be given by its parents, and in all
cases where it can properly be done the child be placed in an improved
family home and become a member of the family by legal adoption or
otherwise."[247] Illinois later added the purpose to provide "such care
and guidance, preferably in his own home, as will serve the moral,

emotional, mental, and physical welfare of the minor and the best interests of the community; . . . removing him from the custody of his parents only when his welfare or safety or the protection of the public cannot be adequately safeguarded without removal; and, when the minor is removed from his own family, to secure for him custody, care, and discipline as nearly as possible equivalent to that which should be given by his parents."[248] Many states' juvenile codes used similar language to emphasize non-penal goals—counseling, supervision, and treatment.[249]

Since the 1970s, states have amended their juvenile codes' purpose clauses to endorse punishment.[250] The revised language focused on accountability, responsibility, culpability, punishment, and public safety rather than, or in addition to, a child's welfare or best interests.[251] "[T]he intent was to shift from accountability *to* youths toward the accountability *of* youths. . . . Government's role was, not to safeguard the interests of troubled youths, but to protect society from them."[252]

As accountability became synonymous with retribution, deterrence, and incapacitation, state courts affirmed punishment as a legitimate element of juvenile courts' treatment regime.[253] The Nevada Supreme Court opined that "[b]y formally recognizing the legitimacy of punitive and deterrent sanctions for criminal offenses juvenile courts will be properly and somewhat belatedly expressing society's firm disapproval of juvenile crime and will be clearly issuing a threat of punishment for criminal acts to the juvenile population."[254] After Washington adopted a just deserts juvenile sentencing framework, its supreme court observed that "sometimes punishment is treatment" and concluded that "accountability for criminal behavior, the prior criminal activity and punishment commensurate with age, crime and criminal history does as much to rehabilitate, correct and direct an errant youth as does the prior philosophy of focusing upon the particular characteristics of the individual juvenile."[255]

Punishment vs. Treatment: Indeterminate versus Determinate Sentencing Statutes

Traditionally, juvenile courts imposed indeterminate nonproportional dispositions. If delinquency was only a symptom of a child's needs, then what she did had little bearing on what she might need to change. The shift from an interventionist court to a criminalized one culminates a trend that *Gault* set in motion. In 1978, the Twentieth Century Fund Task Force report, *Confronting Youth Crime*, recommended determinate and mandatory minimum sentences for violent young offenders.[256] In 1980, the American Bar Association's *Juvenile Justice Standards Relating to Juvenile Delinquency and Sanctions* recommended that juvenile court judges' authority be "rigorously limited in type and duration according to the age and prior record of the juvenile and the seriousness of his or her offense."[257] Proposals to impose proportional and determinate sentences reflected the impact of just deserts jurisprudence, a desire to reduce judges' discretion, and an aspiration to reduce racial disparities.

During the Get Tough Era, states amended laws to emphasize individual responsibility, justice system accountability, and determinate or mandatory minimum sentences.[258] Some now use determinate sentencing guidelines based on age, offense, and prior record.[259] Others impose mandatory minimum sentences or define security level placements based on a youth's offense.[260] States' departments of corrections use offense-based administrative or parole-release guidelines to determine length of stay.[261] The National Research Council's analysis of juvenile court sentencing laws concluded that "[s]tate legislative changes in recent years have moved the court away from its rehabilitative goals and toward punishment and accountability. Laws have made some dispositions offense-based rather than offender-based. Offense-based sanctions are to be proportional to the offense and have retribution or deterrence as their goal. Strategies for imposing offense-based sentences in juvenile court include blended sentences, mandatory minimum sentences, and extended jurisdiction."[262] These crime-based sentences enable legislators to symbolically demonstrate their toughness by repudiating juvenile courts' commitment to treating youth.

Punishment vs. Treatment: Judicial Sentencing Practices—Offense and Race

Two sets of factors influence why juvenile court judges sentence delinquents as they do. First, states define juvenile courts' delinquency jurisdiction based on criminal law violations. As a result, the same factors that influence criminal court sentences—present offense and prior record—strongly influence juvenile court sentences as well.[263] Juvenile courts are complex bureaucracies, they routinely collect information about present offenses and prior records, and these provide easily administered criteria with which to triage serious and minor offenders and manage heavy caseloads. Judges can avoid scandal and adverse political repercussions of leniency by imposing restrictive sentences on serious or chronic offenders.[264]

The second consistent finding of delinquency sentencing research is that after statistical controls for legal variables, juveniles' race affects dispositions.[265] Analysts attribute disparities in justice administration to several factors: differences in rates of offending by race; differential selection by justice system personnel; and juvenile courts' context—the interaction of urban locale with minority residency.[266] As a result, juvenile courts' punitive sanctions fall most heavily on African American youths.

Delinquency case processing entails a succession of decisions by police, court personnel, prosecutors, and judges—arrest, referral, intake, petition, detention, waiver or adjudication, and disposition. The compounding effects of even small disparities produce larger cumulative differences between white youths and children of color.[267] As indicated in Figure 5.4, Black youths comprised about 16.6% of the population aged ten to seventeen, 31.4% of juvenile arrests, 33.2% of delinquency referrals, 38.1% of juveniles detained, 40% of youths charged, and 40% of youths placed out of home.[268] Although the greatest disparities occur at earlier less visible stages of the process, differences compound and Blacks and other racial minorities comprise the largest plurality of youth in institutions.[269]

Differential Offending

If juvenile court judges focus on legal variables—present offense and prior records—then differences in rates of offending would contribute to racial differences in dispositions. As reflected earlier in Figures 3.4 and 3.5 and by other measures of delinquency—self-reports and crime victim surveys—Black youths commit violent crimes at higher rates than white juveniles.[270] While police arrest Black youths for drug offenses at somewhat lower rates than they do for violent crimes, self-report studies report higher rates of drug use by white youths than by Blacks.[271]

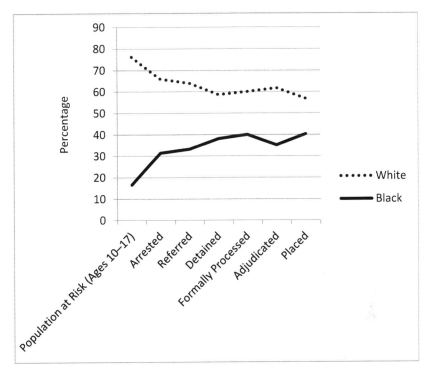

Figure 5.4. Case Processing Summary Counts, by Race, 2011
Source: Office of Juvenile Justice and Delinquency Prevention, *National Disproportionate Minority Contact Databook*, www.ojjdp.gov.

Victims more often report violent crimes to police, judges more read-ily confine youths convicted of those offenses, and differences in rates of violence contribute to disparities in confinement.[272] While present offense and prior record strongly influence judges' dispositions, a prior record reflects previous justice system decisions and masks some racial disparities.[273]

In Chapter 3, I attributed higher rates of violent offending by Black youth to their greater exposure to risk factors associated with criminal involvement, most of which are corollaries of poverty.[274] Concentrated poverty, unemployment, dysfunctional families, poor supervision, harsh discipline, abuse or maltreatment, failing schools, gang-infested neighborhoods, and community disorder contribute to higher crime and violence in segregated urban areas.[275] Some inner-city

youths may be socialized in a code of the street that emphasizes mas-
culinity, risk taking, autonomy, and violent responses to challenges or
disrespect.[276]

Differential Selection

While differences in rates of offending contribute to racial disparities,
justice system personnel's decisions amplify those differences. Police
stop and arrest youths of color more frequently than white youths.[277]
Factors that contribute to heightened risk of arrests include: self-
fulfilling deployment of police to high-crime neighborhoods, racial
profiling, aggressive stop-and-frisk practices, and youths' attitude and
demeanor during encounters.[278] After referral to juvenile court, discretionary decisions increase racial disparities and lead to more severe
outcomes for Black than for white youths.[279] As noted above, disparities
in detention rates by race have prevailed for decades and pretrial detention affects subsequent out-of-home dispositions. Probation officers
who decide whether or not to detain and to file formal petitions often
perceive minority juveniles as more threatening than white juveniles.[280]
The National Research Council reported

> pronounced differences in [probation] officers' attributions about the
> causes of crime committed by white and minority youth. For black chil-
> dren, crime was attributed to negative attitudinal traits and personality
> defects. Among white children, their offenses were thought to be primar-
> ily caused by external environmental factors (e.g., family dysfunction,
> drug abuse, negative peer influence). Furthermore, they found that these
> differences contributed significantly to differential assessments of the risk
> of reoffending and to sentence recommendations, even after adjusting for
> legally relevant case and offender characteristics.[281]

Experimental studies examined unconscious racial stereotypes held
by police and probation officers and reported that subliminal exposure
to racially primed words—"ghetto," "homeboy," and "dreadlocks"—
elicited more negative assessments, imputations of greater culpability,
and support for harsher punishment regardless of respondents' race.[282]
If decision makers perceive Black youths as more serious or culpable

than white offenders, their unconscious racial perceptions may produce more severe sanctions without their awareness.[283]

Juveniles courts' *parens patriae* ideology legitimates individualized dispositions and exposes disadvantaged youths to more extensive controls. "[Y]oung people with greater resources are more likely to have parents who intervene, hire lawyers and counselors, and take responsibility for addressing the problem, all of which will be viewed favorably by judges and probation officers."[284] By contrast, children of color have both greater needs and greater risk of intervention because of economic inequality and their parents' inability to purchase private services.

Decision-Making Context

The structural context of juvenile courts also contributes to racial disparities. Urban courts are more procedurally formal and sentence all delinquents more severely than do suburban or rural courts.[285] Urban courts have greater access to detention facilities, judges detain minority youths at higher rates than white youths, and detained youths receive more severe sentences than those who remain at liberty.[286] Larger proportions of minority youths live in urban settings, experience higher rates of detention, and have their cases adjudicated in more formal courts. As a result, the structural context of juvenile courts interacts with racial demography to produce disproportionate minority confinement.[287] As I discuss in Chapter 7, inner-city youths are more likely to attend poor-performing schools with a heightened police presence. Urban schools are more likely to suspend or expel Black males, refer them to juvenile court, and fuel the school-to-prison pipeline.

Racial Disparities of Juveniles in Confinement

Figures 5.5, 5.6, and 5.7 provide indicators of Get Tough laws' impact on racial disparities in confinement. Figure 5.5 shows the percentage of youths by race who receive out-of-home placements. Over the quarter century beginning in 1985, the proportion of white youths removed from home declined by about 10% while that of Black youths increased by 10%. In 1985, states removed 105,830 delinquents from their homes and placed them in residential facilities. The number of youths who received out-of-home placements increased steadily during the 1990s,

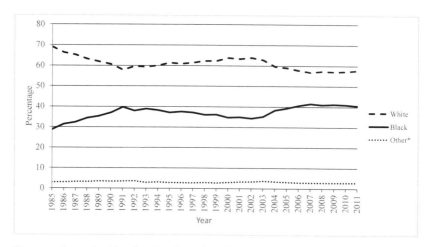

Figure 5.5. Juveniles Placed in Residential Facility, by Race
* Includes American Indian and Asian/Native Hawaiian and Pacific Islander (NHPI).
Source: Office of Juvenile Justice and Delinquency Prevention, *Easy Access to the Census of Court Statistics: 1985–2012*, www.ojjdp.gov.

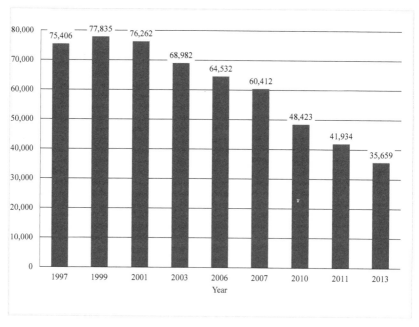

Figure 5.6. Number of Juveniles in Residential Facility, 1997–2013
Source: Sickmund, M., Sladky, T.J., Kang, W., and Puzzanchera, C., *Easy Access to the Census of Juveniles in Residential Placement: 1997–2013*, www.ojjdp.gov.

peaked at 168,395 delinquents in 1997, a 59% increase, and reflects Get Tough Era changes and judicial sensitivity to the punitive ethos. Since the peak in the late 1990s, the number of youth removed from home has declined dramatically. In 2012, judges placed 87,540 youths in residential facilities, 21% fewer than in 1985 and 92% lower than the peak.[288] We do not know why residential placements have declined. Perhaps lawmakers and judges moderated their commitment to punish youths or better appreciated the damage of institutional placements.

Despite the overall decline, the racial composition of youths in confinement changed substantially. As reflected in Figure 5.5, in 1985, judges removed 68.5% of non-Hispanic and Hispanic white youths, 28.5% of Black youths, and 2.9% of youths of other races from their homes. By 2012, the proportion of white youths removed from home declined to 57.8% of all youths—a 10.7% decrease—while the proportion of Black youths increased to 39.3%—an offsetting 10.8% increase.

Figure 5.6 uses a one-day count of juveniles in residential placements. One-day counts report standing population, as distinguished from annual admission and release data, which measure population flow. These data distinguish between non-Hispanic white youths and Hispanic

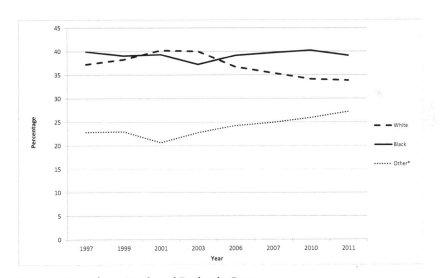

Figure 5.7. Juveniles in Residential Facility, by Race
* Includes Hispanic, American Indian, Asian, Pacific Islander, and Other.
Source: Office of Juvenile Justice and Delinquency Prevention, *Easy Access to the Census of Juveniles in Residential Placement: 1997–2011*, www.ojjdp.gov.

144 | THE KID IS A CRIMINAL

youths in confinement. Hispanic youths comprise more than 80% of the racial category "other," along with Native American, Asian, and Pacific Islander youths. The numbers of youths in confinement reached their apex in the late 1990s at the peak of the Get Tough Era and have declined steadily since. The numbers of youths confined on a given day fell from 75,406 in 1997 to 35,659 in 2013, a 111% decrease.

Despite dramatic reduction in youths in confinement, the racial composition of institutionalized inmates became ever darker. During the decade, the proportion of white inmates declined from 37.2% to 33.8% of all residents, the proportion of Black inmates hovered around 40%, and the proportion of other youths of color increased.

Congress amended the Juvenile Justice and Delinquency Prevention Act (JJDPA) in 1988 to require states receiving federal juvenile justice funds to examine sources of minority overrepresentation in detention and institutions.[289] It amended the JJDPA in 1992 to make disproportionate minority confinement a core requirement and again in 2002 to require states to reduce disproportionate minority contact.[290] States responded to the 1988 JJDPA requirement, conducted evaluations, and reported disproportionate overrepresentation of minority youths in institutions.[291] Minority juveniles receive disproportionately more out-of-home placements, while whites receive more probationary dispositions.[292] Judges commit Black youths to public institutions at rates three and four times that of white youths, and send larger proportions of white youths to private residential treatment programs.[293] Black youths serve longer terms than do white youths committed for similar offenses.[294]

Punishment vs. Treatment: Community-Based and Institutional Confinement

Juvenile courts' dispositional options run the gamut from community service, probation, and placement in small local group homes that house half a dozen residents, to large correctional facilities and training schools with hundreds of inmates and prison-like custodial features—fenced perimeters, razor wire, armed guards, and locks and bars.[295] Facilities may be privately run or administered by local or state government. Juvenile court judges place the majority (60%) of adjudicated delinquents on probation and put more than one-quarter (27%)

in residential facilities.[296] Of those removed from home, judges place less than one-third (30.3%) in community-based group homes, about 3% in boot camps, and 7% in ranch/wilderness challenge facilities. More than two-thirds of delinquents removed from their homes are housed in facilities with more than fifty inmates and 42% are in long-term secure training schools and youth prisons.[297] Despite the prevalence of small privately run and community-based programs, states confine the vast majority of youth (69%) in large public institutions.[298]

Since Martinson's pessimistic "What Works?," researchers have evaluated programs in community and residential settings to determine what works, how well, and at what costs. The diversity of facilities and programs and variability of populations they serve make assessing outcomes difficult. Correctional evaluations typically lack control groups, which makes it difficult to attribute positive outcomes to intervention or to sample selection bias of the youths committed to them.

Meta-analyses combine independent studies to measure effectiveness of different strategies to reduce recidivism or other outcomes.[299] Evaluations have compared generic strategies—counseling, behavior modification, and group therapy—more sophisticated assessments and replications of brand-name programs, and cost/benefit appraisals of different treatments.[300] A substantial literature exists on effectiveness of probation and other forms of noninstitutional treatment.[301] Community-based programs are more likely to be run by private (usually nonprofit) service providers, to be smaller and less overcrowded, and to offer more treatment services than do publicly run institutions.[302]

Delbert Elliot developed the Blueprints for Prevention program, which certifies programs as proven or promising. Proven programs demonstrate reductions in problem behaviors with rigorous experimental design, continuing effects after youths leave the program, and successful replication by independent providers.[303] Although some proven programs treat delinquents, most programs aim to prevent school-aged youths' involvement with the juvenile justice system.[304] Mark Lipsey's ongoing meta-analyses report that treatment strategies such as counseling and skill building are more effective than those that emphasize surveillance, control, and discipline.[305] The Campbell Collaboration conducted meta-analyses of rigorous empirical evaluations of treatment programs for serious delinquents in secure institutions. A review of thirty studies concluded that cognitive-behavioral treatment reduced overall and serious recidivism.[306] Cost-benefit studies use meta-analytic methods to evaluate program costs and benefits to the individual and community—recidivism reduction, costs to taxpayers, and injury or losses to potential victims.[307] While there is a paucity of high-quality evaluations, available research suggests that prevention programs— preschool enrichment and family-based interventions outside of the juvenile justice system—provide benefits that exceed their costs and improvements in education, employment, income, mental health, and other outcomes.[308]

Cumulatively, evaluations conclude that states can handle most delinquents safely in community settings with cognitive-behavioral models of change.[309] The most successful Blueprints programs—Functional Family Therapy and Multisystemic Therapy—focus on altering family interactions, improving family problem-solving skills, and strengthening parents' ability to deal with their children's behaviors.[310] But effective programs require extensive and expensive staff training, for which most state and local agencies are unwilling to pay. Despite decades of research, "only about 5% of the youths who could benefit from these improved programs now have the opportunity to do so. Juvenile justice options in many communities remain mired in the same old tired options of custodial care and community supervision."[311]

Punishment vs. Treatment: Juvenile Correctional Institutions

Conditions of confinement provide another indicator of whether inmates receive treatment or punishment.[312] *Gault* mandated procedural safeguards because of conditions in training schools.[313] Accounts of early Progressive training schools corroborate *Gault's* observation that those institutions more closely resembled prisons than clinics.[314] Cases contemporaneous with *Gault* described inmates beaten by guards, hog-tied, or becoming psychotic through prolonged isolation.[315] Recent law suits challenging institutional conditions reveal gang conflict, sexual abuse of inmates by guards, inadequate education, mental health and health care services, suicide, and inmate deaths at the hands of staff.[316] Analysts criticize training schools as sterile and unimaginative facilities, as inappropriate venues in which to treat juveniles, as schools for crime where children learn from more delinquent peers, and as settings in which staff and residents abuse and mistreat inmates.[317] During the 1960s and 1970s, investigators conducted in-depth ethnographic research in correctional facilities.[318] Studies in different states reported similar findings—violent environments, minimal treatment or educational programs, physical abuse by staff and inmates, make-work tasks, extensive use of solitary confinement, and the like. States confined half of all youths in overcrowded facilities, more than three-quarters in large facilities, and more than one-quarter in institutions with two hundred to one thousand inmates.[319] Unfortunately, for the past quarter century, we have had no ethnographic studies of juvenile institutions. Corrections officials' recalcitrance and institutional review boards strictures have severely limited criminologists' ability to study institutions because they involve confined populations who derive no immediate benefits and minors for whom they are unable to obtain parental consent.[320]

I was introduced to Massachusetts's training schools in 1970. Under the leadership of Dr. Jerome Miller, the Department of Youth Services initially attempted to devolve large custodial institutions into small therapeutic communities in each residential cottage. Some cottages housed fewer than a dozen residents, provided a one-to-one staff inmate ratio, and offered group therapy, whereas in other cottages, staff physically beat inmates and did little to curb physical abuse and rape of other inmates.[321] In the face of staff resistance to reform, Miller closed the state's training schools, returned nearly one thousand residents to the community, and housed youths who posed a threat to the community in small, secure facilities with fifteen beds or fewer.[322] Evaluations of institutional closure and community-based alternatives indicated that quality of care improved without adversely affecting public safety.[323] By the 1980s, get tough policies overtook the Massachusetts experiment, and it would be decades before other states replicated institutional closures and relied more heavily on community placements.

Punishment vs. Treatment: Right to Treatment

Over the past four decades, juvenile inmates have filed nearly sixty lawsuits that challenge conditions of confinement, asserting that they violate the Eighth Amendment's prohibition on cruel and unusual punishment

and deny their Fourteenth Amendment right to treatment.[324] Eighth
Amendment litigation is proscriptive, defines constitutionally imper-
missible practices, and delineates the floor below which institutional
conditions may not fall. Judicial opinions from around the country
describe youths housed in dungeons, beaten with paddles, drugged for
social control, tear-gassed, locked in solitary confinement, housed in
overcrowded and dangerous conditions, and subjected to other punitive
practices.[325]

The Fourteenth Amendment litigation is prescriptive. *McKeiver* denied delinquents a constitutional right to a jury trial because the Court
assumed that they received treatment. Juveniles claim that denial of
criminal procedural protections imposes a substantive right to treatment and creates a duty on states to provide beneficial programs.[326] In
most cases, judges appoint a special master to mediate between inmate-
plaintiffs' attorneys and state department of corrections to ameliorate
unconstitutional conditions.

The right to treatment raises difficult issues of federalism and separation of powers. When inmates file constitutional claims in federal court,
their suits pit federal judges against a state's department of corrections.
Remedies to improve conditions require a state legislature to allocate
more funds for treatment services. In response to the flood of litigation over conditions in institutions, the Supreme Court in *Youngberg
v. Romeo* limited the doctrinal foundation of the right to treatment.[327]
Youngberg required reasonably safe conditions, freedom from unnecessary restraint, and minimally humane conditions, and instructed trial
judges to defer to correctional professionals.[328] To further discourage
litigation, in 1996, Congress passed the Prison Litigation Reform Act,
which restricts the power of state and federal courts to order prospec-
tive relief from conditions that violate inmates' limited constitutional
rights.[329]

Punishment vs. Treatment: What Works?

Do treatment programs reduce recidivism, enhance psychological well-
being, improve educational attainments, provide vocational skills, or
boost community readjustment? There are no standard measures of
recidivism—rearrest, reconviction, or recommitment—and most states

do not collect data on programs' effectiveness or recidivism, which complicates judges' ability to distinguish treatment from punishment.[330] Measuring outcomes is further complicated because programs' populations vary with states' juvenile court age of jurisdiction and disposition, the crimes for which judges commit youths, and whether facilities are large or small, public or private, community-based or institutional.

Despite these limitations, evaluations of training schools provide scant evidence of effective treatment.[331] Programs that emphasize deterrence or punishment—institutions and boot camps—may lead to increased criminal activity following release.[332] Correctional boot camps, reflecting punitive policies of the 1990s, emphasized physical training, drill, and discipline. Despite their popularity, they did not reduce recidivism and some studies reported increases.[333]

Evaluations of training schools report that police rearrest half or more of the juveniles who have been sent to them for a new offense within one year of release.[334] "There is virtually no evidence that juvenile facilities produce positive results in reducing future law-breaking behavior. Moreover, there is growing evidence that youths who more deeply penetrate the juvenile justice system, especially those who are securely confined, have the worst long-term public safety outcomes."[335] More than half of incarcerated youth have not completed the eighth grade and more than two-thirds do not return to school following release.[336] Young Black men involved with the justice system who have not completed high school have bleak life prospects.[337]

Jamie Fader's *Falling Back* poignantly describes confined minority youths' transition from a rural correctional facility to an inner-city Philadelphia neighborhood of failing schools, high crime, aggressive policing, and lack of jobs. They encountered myriad barriers in their quest for employment. They were unable to complete an electronic application for an entry-level job, lacked "soft" or "people" skills like smiling and making eye contact with demanding customers, suffered from the spatial mismatch between their urban residence and suburban jobs, failed employer drug tests and criminal background checks, and confronted other barriers.[338] Within three years of the fifteen youths' release, one was dead, half were reincarcerated, several more were on the run, and only two (14%) had avoided rearrest.[339] Their experience reflects the larger structural barriers young Black men confront in segregated neighborhoods, reared in the code of the street, who drop out of failed schools, and lack access to labor markets.

Juvenile Corrections Policy: What Would a Responsible Legislature Do?

Justice system involvement impedes youths' transition to adulthood and aggravates minority youths' social disadvantage.[340] Like the Hippocratic oath, the first priority of juvenile court intercession should be harm reduction—to avoid or minimize practices that leave youths worse off. Franklin Zimring argues that "harm reduction creates the opportunity to use concerns about the impact of the system on minority kids as a wedge to reduce the harmful impact of the system on all processed through it."[341]

Adolescence is a developmentally fraught period of rapid growth and personality change. Most delinquents will outgrow adolescent crimes without extensive treatment and interventions should be short-term, community-based, and as minimally disruptive as possible. "The best-known cure for youth crime is growing up. And the strategic logic of diversion and minimal sanctions is waiting for maturation to transition a young man from male groups to intimate pairs and from street corners to houses and workplaces."[342]

More than four decades ago, Massachusetts closed its training schools and replaced them with community-based alternatives—group homes, mental health facilities, and contracts for services for education, counseling, and job training.[343] Evaluations reported that more than three-quarters of the young people overseen by the state's Department of Youth Services were not subsequently incarcerated, juvenile arrest rates decreased, and the proportion of adult prison inmates who had graduated from juvenile institutions declined.[344]

More recently, Missouri has replicated and expanded on the Massachusetts experiment. Missouri relies on continuous case management, decentralized residential units, staff-facilitated positive peer culture, and a rehabilitative environment.[345] Although proponents claim reduction in recidivism rates, no rigorous evaluations demonstrates its effectiveness.[346] Other states have adopted deinstitutionalization strategies. The California Youth Authority has closed five large institutions and reduced its incarcerated population from about ten thousand juveniles to around sixteen hundred.[347] New York's Office of Children and Family Services (OCFS) announced plans to close six youth correctional facilities after a study found that nearly 80% of young people released from its facilities were rearrested within three years.

Punishment or Prevention

During the last two decades of the twentieth century, offenses trumped offenders as get tough lawmakers shifted sentencing policy from treatment to punishment. Prosecutors' charging decisions—direct file or offense exclusion—superseded judges' assessment of amenability to treatment. Present offense and prior record dominate detention and disposition decisions. Just deserts—proportionality, determinacy, and responsibility—and punishment, incapacitation, and deterrence displaced the rehabilitative ideal. Juvenile courts' purpose clauses emphasize punishment, accountability, and public safety. States' use determinate and mandatory minimum sentences. Present offense and prior record explain most of the variance in judges' sentencing decisions. Offense criteria have redefined the meaning of rehabilitation. Previously, treatment was a welfare-oriented, client-centered endeavor in which an offense was a symptom of need and the goal was to improve offenders and deliver services. In its new guise, it is a strategy to manage risk, impose restrictions, reduce crime, and advance public safety rather than to promote offenders' welfare as an end in itself.[348]

Delinquency prevention programs provide an alternative to control or suppression and reflect the adage that "a stitch in time saves nine." Prevention intervenes with children and youths before they engage in delinquency. Risk-focused prevention identifies factors that contribute to offending and employs programs to ameliorate or counteract them. Some interventions apply to communities or families and others to individuals at risk to become offenders.[349]

Some prevention strategies identify individual risk factors—low intelligence or delayed school progress—and provide programs to improve cognitive skills, school readiness, and social skills. The Perry Preschool Project—an enhanced Head Start program for disadvantaged Black children—aimed to provide intellectual stimulation, improve critical thinking skills, and enhance later school performance.[350] Cost-benefit analyses and evaluations report that larger proportions of experimental than control youths graduated from high school, received post-secondary education, had better employment records and higher incomes, paid taxes, had fewer arrests, and reduced public expenditures for crime and welfare.[351]

Other delinquency prevention programs address the families in which at-risk youths live. Family-based risk factors include poor child-rearing techniques, inadequate supervision, lack of clear norms, and inconsistent or harsh discipline. Home visitation, nurse home visitation, and parent management training can produce positive outcomes in the lives of children.[352] Family interventions for adjudicated delinquents that operate outside of the juvenile justice system also produce positive outcomes—Multisystemic Therapy (MST), Functional Family Therapy (FFT), and Multidimensional Treatment Foster Care (MTFC).[353]

David Farrington and Brandon Welsh, in *Saving Children from a Life of Crime*, provide a comprehensive review of risk factors and effective interventions to prevent delinquency. They identify individual, family, and community level factors and effective programs to ameliorate delinquency. At each level, they report proven or promising programs to improve youths' lives and recommend risk-focused, evidence-based prevention programs.[354]

Peter Greenwood, in *Changing Lives: Delinquency Prevention as Crime-Control Policy*, provides a comprehensive review of prevention programs. He focuses on interventions across the developmental trajectory from infancy and early childhood through elementary-school-aged children, and into adolescence. Some prevention programs have been adequately evaluated and clearly do *not* work—for instance, Drug Abuse Resistance Education (DARE).[355] Many prevention programs have no evidentiary support—they either have not been evaluated or used such flawed design that researchers could draw no conclusions. Greenwood uses cost-benefit analyses to evaluate various delinquency and prevention programs. While cost-benefit analyses could rationalize delinquency policy and resource allocation decisions, politicians do not embrace prevention programs because they lack a punitive component and do not demonstrate immediate impact.[356] While highly visible crimes evoke fear and an immediate punitive response, delinquency prevention takes longer to realize and has a more diffuse impact. Despite effective programs, delinquency prevention "holds a small place in the nation's response to juvenile crime. Delinquency control strategies operated by the juvenile justice system dominate."[357]

Conclusion

Progressive reformers created juvenile courts to divert youths from the criminal justice system and rehabilitate them in a separate system. Politicians in the Get Tough Era assaulted the idea that children are different, repudiated the court's welfare role, and rejected its premise to keep youths out of prisons. States changed transfer laws to prosecute more children as adults. Despite their punitive turn, changes in juvenile justice were less extreme than the mass incarceration that overtook the criminal justice system.[358] Rates of transfer and incarceration of delinquents increased, but imprisonment rates of young adults aged eighteen to twenty-four more than tripled during the Get Tough Era.[359] Zimring argues that juvenile courts served their diversionary function even as the criminal justice system underwent a paroxysm of imprisonment.

> [T]he political forces that produced extraordinary expansion through the rest of the penal system had been stymied in juvenile courts. In that sense, the under-eighteen population became the last significant battleground for a get-tough orientation that had permeated the rest of the peno-correctional system. . . . [A]ngry assaults on juvenile courts throughout the 1990s are a tribute to the efficacy of juvenile justice in protecting delinquents from the incarcerative explosion that happened everywhere else. The largest irony of the 1990s from a diversionary standpoint is that the juvenile courts were under constant assault not because they had failed in their youth-serving mission, but because they had succeeded in protecting their clientele from the new orthodoxy in crime control.[360]

While juvenile courts served their diversionary function, lawmakers sharply shifted their interventions from rehabilitation toward offense-based punitive policies. Progressive reformers did not expect training schools to achieve great reforms; their principal virtue was that they were not prisons. While they envisioned positive programs administered by

child welfare experts, neither the Progressives nor subsequent generations ever achieved those goals. *Gault* mandated procedural safeguards
because it recognized that "a 'receiving home' or an 'industrial school'
for juveniles is an institution of confinement in which the child is incarcerated for a greater or lesser time."[361] During the last third of the
twentieth century, lawmakers forsook even nominal commitment to
treatment in favor of punishment. They changed juvenile codes' purpose from care and treatment to accountability and punishment. They
amended sentencing statutes to define length and location of confinement based on offense. In practice, judges focused primarily on present
offense and prior record when making dispositions. Although most delinquents received probation, between 1987 and 1997, institutional confinement rose by 54%. Training schools more closely resembled prisons
than clinics and seldom improved delinquents' life trajectories. Training
schools are the least effective way to respond to youths' needs. Meta-
analyses and other evaluations identify effective programs and most of
them are not administered by juvenile justice personnel.

I emphasize juvenile courts' explicitly punitive turn because it implicates their procedural safeguards. *McKeiver* denied delinquents a right
to a jury and *Gault* granted only watered-down safeguards because the
Court assumed that delinquents received treatment. Because juvenile
courts punish youths, their justification for reduced procedural safeguards evaporates. In Chapter 9, I argue that juveniles require more procedural safeguards that adult criminal defendants to protect them from
their developmental limitations, the harsh consequences of delinquency
adjudications, and the collateral consequences of convictions.

Finally, the turn toward punishment—waiver, detention, and
disposition—falls most heavily on Black youths. Progressive reformers intended juvenile courts to discriminate between "our children" and
"other people's children." A century ago, the court administered a different justice system for native-born and immigrant children. The courts'
interventionist role was to assimilate and Americanize miscreant youth,
and the children of the foreign born had a greater distance to travel and
required more extensive controls.

A century later, juvenile courts continues to discriminate between
"our children" and "other people's children," but now they are African
American children and other youths of color. At every critical custodial

decision, Black youths receive more punitive sanctions than white youths. Differences in rates of violence by race contribute to some disparity in justice administration. But many Black youths experience very different childhoods than do most white youths. Public policies and private decisions created segregated urban areas and consigned children of color to live in concentrated poverty with criminogenic consequences. Race affects decision makers' responses to children of color—the way they see them, evaluate them, and dispose of them. It is not coincidental that the turn from welfare to punishment and from rehabilitation to retribution occurred as Blacks gained civil rights and the United States briefly flirted with integration and inclusionary rather than exclusionary racial policies.

6

The Girl Is a Criminal

The Impact of Get Tough Policies on Girls

During the Get Tough Era, policy makers perceived an alarming increase in girls' violence. Official statistics reported that police arrests of female juveniles for crimes against the person—simple and aggravated assault—either increased more or decreased less than those of their male counterparts and portended a gender convergence in violence.[1] Popular media amplified public perceptions of increased girl-on-girl violence with features on "bad girls gone wild," "feral and savage" girls, and girl-gang violence.[2]

The perceived narrowing of the crime gender-gap might reflect gender-specific social or cultural changes that affected girls' criminality differently than boys' and caused more of them to act violently. Or the supposed increase in girls' violence might be socially constructed and reflect other get tough policies—decreased tolerance of violence, shifts in police responses to domestic violence, heightened surveillance, or changes in parental attitudes—that affected girls differently than boys.[3] Comparing boys' and girls' official arrest rates with self-report and victimization surveys that do not rely on justice system data conclude that the perceived increase in girls' violence is more likely a social construction than an empirical reality.[4] Changes in girls' arrest-proneness for violence may be attributed to three gender-specific policy changes: an increased probability to charge less serious conduct as assault, a criminalizing of domestic violence between intimates, and parents' diminished tolerance of females' acting-out behavior. While police practices may account for some changes in girls' arrests for violence, juvenile justice policies—especially the mid-1970s federal mandate to deinstitutionalize status offenders (DSO)—likely contributed as well.[5] After federal policies were initiated to deinstitutionalize status offenders, analysts warned that judges could bootstrap or relabel them as delinquents to retain access to secure facilities.[6]

This chapter contends that the perceived increase in girls' violence is an artifact of changes in police practices and get tough juvenile justice policies. Heightened concern about domestic violence lowered the threshold for assaults and mandated arrests in intra-family conflicts. Laws that prohibited confining status offenders with delinquent youth drove efforts to relabel them as delinquents to place them in institutions. The chapter first examines historical differences in juvenile justice responses to male and female offenders, focusing on the 1974 federal Juvenile Justice and Delinquency Prevention Act, which mandated deinstitutionalization of status offenders (DSO). It next analyzes boys' and girls' arrests for simple and aggravated assault and highlights differences in crime seriousness by gender. Examining offender-victim relationships indicates that girls' violence more often occurs within family conflicts and arrests for simple assault reflect a relabeling of status offenders as delinquents. Finally, the chapter focuses on boys and girls incarcerated for simple and aggravated assault; states confine girls more frequently for minor offenses. It concludes that the justice systems' responses to girls reflect collateral damage of get tough policies.

Girls in the Juvenile Justice System

The Progressive reformers who created juvenile courts combined two visions—one interventionist and the other divisionary.[7] They envisioned a specialized court to separate children from adults in courts, jails, and prisons—diversion—and to treat them rather than punish them for crimes—intervention.[8] Juvenile courts' delinquency jurisdiction initially encompassed only youths charged with crimes. However, reformers soon added status offenses—noncriminal misbehavior such as incorrigibility, runaway, truancy, immorality, and indecent conduct—to juvenile courts' jurisdiction.[9] The behaviors subsumed in the status jurisdiction enabled juvenile courts to reinforce parental authority, to reassert schools' controls over youth, and to enforce norms of childhood.[10] Juvenile courts' status jurisdiction rested on the idea of childhood dependency and provided a preemptive basis to intervene.[11]

Historically, juvenile courts responded to boys primarily for minor crimes such as theft or vandalism and to girls mainly for status offenses such as incorrigibility, immorality, or being beyond parental control—code words for being sexually active.[12] Status jurisdiction reflected Progressives' construction of childhood dependency, Victorian sensibilities, and their desire to control female sexuality.[13] Reformers feared that "the temptations of the city would corrupt girls' natural innocence" and lead to premarital sex, unintended pregnancies, and inability to attract respectable marriage partners.[14] Judges detained and confined girls largely for status offenses and at higher rates than boys.[15]

In the early 1970s, about three-quarters of girls in juvenile court appeared for status offenses.[16] Critics argued that confining status offenders with delinquents in detention facilities and training schools discriminated against females, stigmatized them with delinquency labels that led to secondary deviance, exposed them to more seriously delinquent role models, and provided few services.[17] Intervention at parents' behest exacerbated intra-family conflicts and enabled some caretakers to avoid their responsibilities.

The 1974 federal Juvenile Justice and Delinquency Prevention Act (JJDPA) prohibited states from confining status offenders with delinquents in detention facilities and institutions and withheld formula grant money from states that failed to remove them.[18] In many states, judges sent girls to non-secure shelter facilities but some ran away. Judges demanded a means to keep girls safe from themselves and from sexual predators. At the behest of the National Council of Juvenile and Family Court Judges, in 1980 Congress amended the JJDPA to allow states to continue to receive federal funds *and* to permit judges to commit status offenders to institutions for violating a "valid court order."[19] The valid court order exception, which continues to the present, allows judges to bootstrap or convert status offenders into delinquents by finding them in contempt of court for violating a condition of probation—obey your parents, go to school, or stay at home.[20] Although the 1992 JJDPA reauthorization required states to provide gender-specific services for females, most states just collected data about girls rather than develop new programs for them.[21]

By the early 1980s, DSO initiatives produced a seeming decline in the number of female status offenders in detention and institutions.[22] The

National Academy of Sciences reported reductions in confinement of status offenders in public facilities.[23] By 1988, the number of status offenders in secure facilities had reportedly declined by 95% from those held prior to the JJDPA.[24] However, the changes may have been more apparent than real: the number of status offenders committed to private institutions increased during the 1980s and roughly offset those removed from public institutions, a phenomenon known as trans-institutionalization.[25] At the same time, the number of female status offenders detained for violating a valid court order—bootstrapping—grew at an alarming rate.[26]

Although the JJDPA prohibited states from incarcerating status offenders, it did not require states to appropriate funds or develop community-based programs to meet girls' needs. Even as policy- and lawmakers struggled to find other options, analysts warned that states could relabel them as delinquents—charge them with simple assault rather than incorrigibility—and thereby circumvent DSO.[27] States' failure adequately to fund community services provided continuing impetus to use the delinquency system for social control.[28]

The punitive policies examined in Chapter 5 targeted boys, especially urban Black males, charged with violent or drug crimes.[29] But those punitive changes indirectly affected girls' susceptibility to arrest and prosecution for assault even though they were not the intended targets.[30] Girls' increased arrests for assault coincided with DSO, reflecting the juvenile system's increasingly punitive mission and its adaptive strategy to control females.

The Chimera of Girls' Violence

Police arrest and juvenile courts handle fewer females than their proportion of the juvenile population. Table 6.1 shows that in 2011 police arrested about 1.5 million juveniles. Girls comprised less than one-third (29%) of juveniles arrested and less than one-fifth (18%) of those arrested for Violent Crime Index offenses. Violent Crime Index offenses are a small proportion (4.6%) of all juvenile arrests and nearly two-thirds (59%) of them are for aggravated assaults.[31] Girls made-up one-quarter (25%) of juveniles arrested for aggravated assaults and more than one-third (36%) of those arrested for simple assault. More than four-fifths

TABLE 6.1. Juvenile and Female Arrests for Violence, 2011

Crime	Total Juvenile Arrests for All Offenses	Percentage Female Share of Arrests
Total	1,470,000	29
Violent Crime Index*	68,150	18
Aggravated Assault	40,700	25
Simple Assault	190,900	36

* Violent Crime Index includes murder and non-negligent manslaughter, forcible rape, robbery, and aggravated assault.

Source: Office of Juvenile Justice and Delinquency Prevention, *Juvenile Arrests 2011*, www.ojjdp.gov.

(81%) of girls' arrests for Violence Crime Index offenses were for aggravated assaults, whereas about half (54.3%) of boys' arrests were for aggravated assaults and the remainder for murder, rape, and robbery.[32]

Juveniles' arrests for violence may reflect real differences in rates of offending by gender or they may reflect differences in how police and courts respond to boys and girls.[33] Police arrest proportionally fewer girls than boys, but their arrest patterns have diverged over the past decades. In earlier years, male and females' offending followed similar patterns and small increases in girls' delinquency occurred primarily for minor property rather than violent crime.[34]

Recently, arrests of females for violent offenses have either increased more or decreased less than those of their male counterparts. Reflecting the juvenile crime decline (Figure 3.2), between 2001 and 2010 the numbers of juveniles arrested dropped about 21%, primarily because males' arrests decreased by 24%, while females' decreased half as much (10%).[35] Males' arrests for Violent Crime Index offenses decreased substantially more than did females'. Aggravated assaults comprise nearly two-thirds (59%) of all juvenile arrests for Violent Crime Index offenses. Boys' arrests for aggravated assaults decreased by one-third (-33%), while girls' declined by one-quarter (-27%). By contrast, girls' arrests for simple assaults decreased only 3%, while boys' declined 17%.[36] Thus, the major change in recorded juvenile violence over the past decade is the greater decrease in boys' arrest rate for aggravated and simple assaults than girls'.

Figure 6.1 shows changes in arrest rates per hundred thousand male and female juveniles aged ten to seventeen for Violent Crime Index offenses between 1980 and 2011. Overall, police arrested boys at much

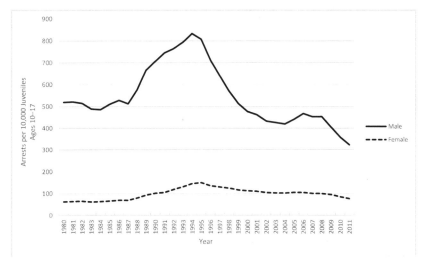

Figure 6.1. Male and Female Juvenile Arrest Rates, 1980–2011, Violent Crime Index
Offenses
Source: Office of Juvenile Justice and Delinquency Prevention, *Statistical Briefing Book*,www.ojjdp.gov.

higher rates than they did girls. Arrests rates for both genders peaked
in the mid-1990s, and then males' rates dropped off much more sharply
than did females'. Boys' arrest rates in 2011 for Violent Crime Index offenses were more than one-third (-37.7%) lower than they were in 1980,
whereas girls' arrests for these offenses *increased* 21.8% over the same period. In 1980, males' arrest rates for Violent Crime Index offenses were
eight times higher than those of females, whereas by 2011, they were
only four time higher. The crime drop of the past two decades primarily
reflects a decline in boys' arrests.

Aggravated assaults comprise the largest component of the Violent
Crime Index and simple assault constitutes the largest component of
non-index violent arrests. Over the past quarter century, clear changes
have occurred between boys' and girls' patterns of arrests for these offenses. As Figure 6.2 indicates, boys' and girls' arrests for aggravated
assault diverged conspicuously. Girls' arrest rate in 2011 was half again
larger (59.3%) than it was in 1980 (62 versus 40.3 arrests per 100,000).
Although police arrested males for aggravated assault about three times
as often as they did females, boys' arrest rate actually decreased 21.9%
over the same period (176.5 versus 215.2 arrests per 100,000).

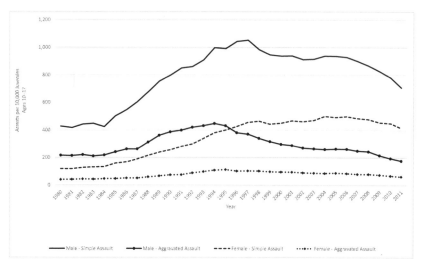

Figure 6.2. Male and Female Juvenile Arrest Rates, 1980–2011, Simple and Aggravated Assaults
Source: Office of Juvenile Justice and Delinquency Prevention, *Statistical Briefing Book*, www.ojjdp.gov.

Police arrest juveniles for simple assaults much more frequently than for aggravated assaults. Again, changes in females' arrests rates for simple assaults over the past third of a century greatly outstripped those of their male counterparts. Police arrested girls for simple assault in 2011 at a rate 3.5 times greater than they did in 1980 (413.5 versus 118.3 arrests per 100,000). Although males' simple assault arrest rate started from a much higher baseline than females', it increased by only 66% over the same period (708.3 versus 427.2 arrests per 100,000).

To gauge the relative seriousness of juveniles' arrests for violence by gender, Figure 6.3 depicts the ratios of arrest rates for simple and aggravated assaults for boys and girls. In 1980, police arrested girls for simple assaults about three times (2.9) as often as they did for aggravated assaults. Although boys started from a much higher base rate, police arrested them for simple assaults about twice (2.0) as often as for aggravated assaults. Boys' assaults are more frequently aggravated because they use weapons and physically injure their victims more often than do girls. By 2011, police arrested girls nearly seven times (6.7) as often for simple assaults as they did for aggravated assaults. By contrast, the boys' arrest ratio of simple to aggravated assaults only doubled

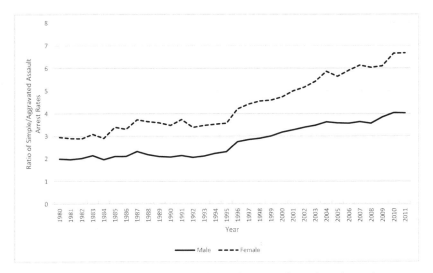

Figure 6.3. Ratios of Simple to Aggravated Assault Arrests for Male and Female
Juveniles Ages 10–17, 1980–2011
Source: Office of Juvenile Justice and Delinquency Prevention, *Statistical Briefing Book*,
www.ojjdp.gov.

(4.0). In short, police arrested girls for simple assault more than they
had previously and their ratio increased more than boys. By all official
measures—arrests, arrest rates, and simple/aggravated assault ratios—
girls' increased arrest rates for simple assaults and boys' decreased arrest
rates for aggravated assaults constitute the most conspicuous gendered
changes in youth violence.

Despite these gendered changes, one must ask whether girls' arrests
reflect real changes in their underlying behavior or police reclassifica-
tion of assault with a gendered dimension.[37] Unlike murder and robbery, which have relatively well defined elements and clearer indicators,
police exercise considerable discretion when they characterize behavior
as an assault, whether they classify it as a simple or aggravated assault,
and the meanings of these offenses have changed over time.[38] Because
elements of assault are not objective constants, their subjective definition may change from one observer to another.[39] Proactive policing of
disorder and minor crimes, a lower threshold to arrest or charge those
offenses, or more aggressive policing in private settings may create the
appearance of a juvenile crime wave where none exists. Police exercise

considerable discretion to classify low-level offenses, and policy changes rather than actual behavior may account for girls' increased arrests for minor assaults. Zimring argues that "since 1980, there is significant circumstantial evidence from many sources that changing police thresholds for when assault should be recorded and when the report should be for aggravated assault are the reason for most of the growth in arrest rates. . . . Any reduction in the threshold between simple and aggravated assault and any shift in the minimum standard for recording an offense would have the kind of statistical impact on assault arrests that has occurred since the late 1980s."[40]

Analysts compare ratios of aggravated assaults to homicide or robbery to demonstrate the malleability of classifications of assaults.[41] Because arrests for aggravated assaults increased *without* any corresponding rise in arrests for homicides or for robbery—both of which may include an assault—they attribute the rise in assault arrests to changes in law enforcement policies—lower thresholds of seriousness or responses to domestic violence—rather than to real increases in assaults *per se*. Similarly, Steffensmeier compared official FBI arrest statistics with crime victimization surveys and juveniles' self-report surveys to assess whether those indicators mirrored increases in official girls' violence over the same period.[42] These measures revealed no systematic changes in girls' rates of offending compared with boys, despite officially reported increases in girls' arrests for violence. They conclude that

> [r]ecent changes in law enforcement practices and the juvenile justice system have apparently escalated the arrest proneness of adolescent females. The rise in girls' arrests for violent crime and the narrowing of the gender gap have less to do with underlying behavior and more to do, first, with net-widening changes in law and policing toward prosecuting less serious forms of violence, especially those occurring in private settings and where there is less culpability, and, second, with less biased or more efficient responses to girls' physical or verbal aggression on the part of law enforcement, parents, teachers, and social workers.[43]

The line between status offenses and delinquency is as imprecise and malleable as the definition of assaults. Ambiguous differences between incorrigible or unruly behavior—status offenses—and disorderly conduct or simple assault readily lend themselves to relabeling girls' behavior. Steffensmeier argues that "female arrest gains for violence are largely a by-product of net-widening enforcement policies, like broader definitions of youth violence and greater surveillance of girls that have escalated the arrest-proneness of adolescent girls today relative to girls in prior decades and relative to boys."[44] The more than doubling (2.3) in the ratio of simple to aggravated assaults for girls over the past several decades indicates that police arrest girls for less serious violence.

Police's zero tolerance and mandatory arrest policies for domestic violence cumulatively lower the threshold for assault and lead to girls' arrests for behaviors previously addressed outside the purview of police or courts.[45] Such policies create an appearance of a girls' violent crime wave when their underlying behavior remains much more stable. Indeed, such policies "tend to blur distinctions between delinquency and antisocial behavior more generally, lump together differing forms of physical aggression and verbal intimidation as manifesting interpersonal violence, and elevate interpersonal violence (defined broadly) as a high-profile social problem (particularly among youth)."[46]

Girls' Violence and Domestic Disputes

Prior to the 1980s, police viewed domestic violence as a private matter. When police responded to a domestic disturbance, they most often either counseled the offender on the spot or removed him for a cooling-off period, but rarely made arrests. That began to change in the early 1980s as spousal assault gained national attention and women's groups advocated that police take them more seriously. In 1981–82, the Minneapolis Domestic Violence Experiment randomly instructed police to either counsel domestic disputants on the spot, to separate the disputants, or to make an arrest. Researchers reported that arrest had a significant deterrent effect: arrestees had significantly fewer subsequent domestic violence calls than those in the other two conditions.[47] The study had an extraordinary impact and by the late 1980s and 1990s, police departments across the country instituted mandatory arrest policies for domestic violence.

Changing public attitudes and police practices toward domestic assaults contributed to arrests for assaults that officers previously ignored.[48]

The apparent efficacy of mandatory arrests for domestic violence may have reduced tolerance for girls' delinquency.[49] "[A]n increased reliance on formal social control practices and a decreased tolerance of female delinquency by law enforcement are possible mechanisms influencing increases in arrests of girls for simple assaults, particularly because the majority of these incidents involve family conflicts."[50] Prohibitions on confining status offenders coupled with heightened sensitivity to domestic violence encourage police to arrest girls for assault rather than for incorrigibility and enable courts to circumvent DSO goals.[51]

Parents' differing expectations for their sons' and daughters' behavior may affect how the justice system responds to girls when they act out at home. Girls who deviate from traditional gender norms may be at greater risk of arrest for domestic violence than their brothers. "Girls who demonstrate aggression or violence, acts atypical to the female sex-type heuristics, are more likely to be judged as atypical for their sex role and therefor more in need of control than boys who show the same traits or commit the same acts."[52]

Girls fight with family members or siblings more frequently than do boys, while males more often fight with acquaintances or strangers.[53] Girls are three times as likely to assault a family member as are boys.[54] Police arrested larger proportions of girls than boys for assaulting a parent which, in the past, could have been charged as incorrigible behavior.[55] A study in California found that the female share of domestic violence arrests increased from 6% in 1988 to 17% in 1998.[56] Analysts attributed growth in girls' assault arrests "to the re-labeling of girls' family conflicts as violent offenses, the changes in police practices regarding domestic violence and aggressive behavior, [and] the gender bias in the processing of misdemeanor cases."[57]

Policies of mandatory arrest for domestic violence, initially adopted to restrain abusive males from attacking their partners, provide police and parents with a tool with which to control unruly daughters. A comparison of states with mandatory and discretionary domestic violence arrest laws reported higher arrest rates in mandatory than discretionary jurisdictions *and* a greater likelihood of police to arrest girls than boys for assaulting their parents.[58] Many girls charged with assault were involved a nonserious altercation with a parent who oftentimes was the initial aggressor.[59] Regardless of who instigates a domestic scuffle, it is easier and more practical for police to arrest a youth than a parent who takes care of other children in the home.[60] As one probation officer observed, "if you arrest the parents, then you have to shelter the kids. . . . So if the police just make the kids go away and the number of kids being referred to the juvenile court for assaulting their parents or for disorderly conduct or punching walls or doors . . . the numbers have just been increasingly tremendously because of that political change."[61] Analyses of girls' court referrals for assault report that half occurred within the family and involved conduct that previously could have been characterized as incorrigibility.[62] Probation officers describe most girls' assault cases as a fight with a parent at home or between girls at school over a boy.[63]

While girls' violence typically occurs at home or at school, boys more often commit violent acts against acquaintances or strangers. Two indicators of gender differences in offender-victim relationships support the inference that girls' violence more often involves domestic conflicts. Obviously, homicide is not a relabeled status offense, but the offender-victim relationship provides one indicator of gender differences in violent offending. An analysis of victim-offender relationships between 2001 and 2010 reported that in more than one-third (37%) of cases, girls killed a family member, as contrasted with only 8% of boys' homicides.[64] By contrast, boys murdered strangers more than twice as often as did girls (41% vs. 19%).

The offender-victim relationship of youths arrested for aggravated and simple assaults provides additional evidence of gender differences. The National Incident-Based Reporting System (NIBRS) includes information about offenders, victims, and their relationship.[65] More than one-quarter of girls (28%), as contrasted with less than one-fifth (18%) of boys, committed aggravated assaults against family members.[66] Similarly, police arrested girls for simple assaults within the family more frequently than boys. Girls' increased arrests for simple assault reflect their greater likelihood to victimize family members, decreased tolerance of domestic violence, and police's ability to classify incorrigibility as assault.[67]

Juvenile courts relabeled status offenders as delinquents to retain access to institutions. A comparison of petitions filed against girls before and after Pennsylvania eliminated its status jurisdiction in the mid-1970s reported that the proportion of girls charged with assaults more than doubled (from 14% to 29%).[68] A nationwide study of children in custody reported that the share of girls in training schools for status offenses declined from 71% in 1971 to 11% in 1987 in response to the DSO mandate, whereas the proportion of girls confined for minor delinquencies increased commensurately.[69] Moreover, states confined girls for less serious offenses than they do boys. In 1987, juvenile courts confined over half (56%) of girls for misdemeanors, compared with only 43% of boys.[70] "[T]he perceived increase in the delinquency of girls may actually reflect a relabeling of status offenses. With limited or nonexistent alternatives for girls who cannot or will not go back home, the juvenile court may be pressured to process girls as delinquents."[71]

Boys and Girls in Confinement

While juvenile court judges possess broad discretion to sentence delinquents, most research has focused on racial rather than gender disparities.[72] In the gender sentencing research that has been conducted, there have been two main strands of analysis—one that identifies chivalrous responses to girls charged with serious crimes, and another that finds paternalistic policies for those charged with less serious offenses. The former postulates that girls may receive more lenient treatment than similarly charged delinquent boys.[73] The latter contends that juvenile courts intervene more extensively with sexually active females and status offenders than they do with boys charged with minor offenses.[74] Earlier research consistently reported a gender double standard in which juvenile courts incarcerated more girls than boys for status offenses and more males than females for serious delinquency.[75] More recent research reports fewer gender differences in sentencing status offenders once analysts control for offense and prior record.[76] But others contend that the offenses for which researchers control—status offenses—already reflects gender bias.[77] For example, juvenile court judges used their contempt power covertly to perpetuate gender bias. They sentenced male and female status offenders who violated a valid court order differently and bootstrapped more girls into delinquents.[78] A summary of the inconsistent research findings on sentencing girls concludes that

[t]he traditional sex role model has more application to less serious types of violations, such as status offenses, for which females are given a more severe penalty than males for violating role expectation. It also has application for the sentencing of repeat offenders. Such behavior by girls is more strongly in violation of gender role expectations than it is for boys and should result in more punitive disposition for the girls. For the more serious violations of the law, the chivalry model may have the most relevance. Girls are more likely to receive leniency and protection from the consequences of the more serious crimes.[79]

The offenses for which judges commit boys and girls to residential facilities provide insight into gender differences. Police arrest and juvenile courts detain and place boys in institutions at higher rates and for more serious offenses than they do girls. Juvenile courts process girls for aggravated and simple assaults at higher rates than they do for other types of offenses.[80]

The Census of Juveniles in Residential Placement (CJRP) provides a one-day count of youths in confinement. Table 6.2 reports CJRP data on juveniles in residential confinement in 1997, 1999, 2001, 2003, 2006, 2007, 2010, and 2011. Over the past decade and a half, girls comprised 12.4% of all delinquents in confinement and 10.7% of delinquents confined for crimes against the person. Nearly three-quarters ($\approx$ 72.5%) of girls incarcerated for crimes against the person are confined for simple or aggravated assault. Across the census years, girls comprised about one-sixth (17.4%) of all delinquents confined for aggravated assault and nearly one-fourth (22.3%) of those confined for simple assault, the largest proportion for *any* offense.

States confine male and female delinquents for different types of offenses. In 2011, girls comprised about one in eight (12.5%) delinquents in confinement. States committed 17.1% of delinquents to residential placements for simple or aggravated assaults. However, they committed nearly one-quarter (23.7%) of delinquent girls for simple or aggravated assaults contrasted with about one-sixth (16.2%) of boys.

Reflecting changes in girls' arrests for assault, in each succeeding biennial census, the proportion of girls confined for aggravated and simple assaults increased. Even though males comprise 93% of all delinquents confined for Violent Crime Index offenses, the proportion of girls con-

TABLE 6.2. Juveniles Committed by Gender for Simple and Aggravated Assaults, 1997–2011

	1997	1999	2001	2003	2006	2007	2010	2011
Total Delinquents Confined	75,406	77,835	76,190	68,982	64,532	60,412	48,428	41,934
Female Proportion of All Delinquents Confined	11.9%	11.7%	12.9%	13.4%	12.2%	12.2%	12.3%	12.5%
Number of Girls Confined for All Person Offenses	2,413	2,835	3,050	2,972	2,615	2,398	1,894	1,654
Percentage of Delinquents Confined for All Person Offenses Who Are Female	9.1%	9.9%	11.5%	12%	11.4%	10.8%	10.4%	10.3%
Number of Females Confined for Simple and Aggravated Assault	1,650	2,040	2,189	2,125	1,988	1,816	1,345	1,226
Percentage of Delinquents Confined for Aggravated Assault Who Are Girls	14.1%	16%	18.1%	19.4%	19.4%	18.2%	17.2%	17.0%
Percentage of Delinquents Confined for Simple Assault Who Are Girls	20.1%	21.3%	22.9%	23.7%	24.4%	22.5%	22.6%	21%
Percentage of Girls Confined for Simple and Aggravated Assaults as a Proportion of All Delinquent Girls	18.4%	22.4%	22.3%	23%	20.9%	24.7%	22.8%	23.7%
Percentage of Boys Confined for Simple and Aggravated Assaults as a Proportion of All Delinquent Boys	15.1%	15.6%	14.9%	14.8%	14.8%	15.4%	15.2%	16.2%
Aggravated Assaults as a Proportion of All Girls' Assaults	42.5%	46.3%	49.1%	34.4%	36.2%	40.1%	36.5%	37.2%
Aggravated Assaults as a Proportion of All Boys' Assaults	62.5%	62.1%	54.6%	49.1%	52.3%	54.3%	54.9%	51.5%

Source: Office of Juvenile Justice and Delinquency Prevention, *Easy Access to the Census of Juveniles in Residential Placement: 1997-2011*, www.ojjdp.gov.

fined for aggravated assaults, as a percentage of all delinquents confined for aggravated assaults, increased from 10% in 1997 to 14.4% in 2003 and to 12.9% in 2011.[81] Across all eight biennial censuses, states confined a majority of boys for aggravated assaults ($\approx$ 55.2%), rather than simple assaults. By contrast, they confined the majority of girls for simple assaults, rather than aggravated assaults ($\approx$ 40.3%). Although violent girls may violate gender norms, their confinement primarily for simple assault further suggests a relabeling of status offenses.[82]

Conclusion

Juvenile courts evolve and adapt to change and their durability owes as much to organizational flexibility as it does to achieving rehabilitative goals.[83] The mutability of juvenile courts' mission—diversion, treatment, punishment—allowed personnel to maintain population stability in the face of the delinquent male crime-drop with an increase in female cases.[84] DSO coincided with the culture of control—emphases on proactive policing and aggressive responses to minor disorder.[85]

Girls are the historic and contemporary exception to juvenile courts' diversionary mission. Although Progressive reformers created juvenile courts to divert young offenders from criminal courts, they added status offenses to their delinquency jurisdiction to enable them to regulate girls' "sexual precocity." Victorian concerns about sexually active young women and class-based concerns about poor women's out-of-wedlock pregnancies impelled them to regulate girls differently than boys. While the 1974 JJDPA's DSO mandate attempted to remove status offenders from institutions, juvenile court judges were unsympathetic to its diversionary thrust and quickly obtained authority to maintain control and bootstrap them into delinquents.

Paternalistic attitudes toward girls, resistance to deinstitutionalization, and broad discretion enabled police and prosecutors to charge many status offenders as minor delinquents and bring them to court at rates nearly as great as prevailed prior to deinstitutionalization.[86] Courtroom observers reported that after states decriminalized status offenses, prosecutors charged many girls with criminal offenses for behavior previously charged as status offenses.[87] Washington State temporarily decriminalized status offenses and some police and courts redefined them as criminal offenders to retain court authority over them.[88] The gendered differences in system response to simple and aggravated assaults strongly suggests that perceived girl violence reflects a criminalizing of family conflict rather than a change in girls' behavior.[89]

After four decades of deinstitutionalizing status offenders, juvenile courts remain committed to controlling girls but without resources to respond to their real needs. When Congress passed the JJDPA in 1974, neither the federal nor state governments provided girls with adequate programs or services in the community. Although 1992 JJDPA amendments included provision for gender-specific services, implementing that mandate languished. States' failure to provide alternatives to institutions creates substantial pressures within the juvenile system to circumvent DSO by relabeling girls as delinquents.

7

The Student Is a Criminal

Get Tough Policies and the School-to-Prison Pipeline

From their inception, public schools have served important social control functions.[1] Their responsibilities included protecting students from corrupting influences, keeping them off the streets, preventing crime, and educating and preparing them to be workers. Prior to the Civil War, advocates of compulsory education described "the ideal school as a controlled environment for the Child. The school, ideally was not merely to be a casual, unstructured institution which the child encountered from time to time; it was to be as coextensive with childhood as conditions would permit. . . . [T]he proper 'culture' of childhood demanded a segregation of children from adults in asylum-like institutions called schools."[2] Progressives enacted compulsory attendance laws to assimilate and acculturate immigrant children and gave juvenile courts truancy jurisdiction over those who failed to attend.

The Court in *Brown v. Board of Education* began the struggle to dismantle segregated public schools. *Brown* recognized that education "is a principal instrument in awakening the child to cultural values, in preparing him for later professional training, and in helping him to adjust normally to his environment."[3] Recall from Chapter 3, as more racial minority students entered urban public schools in the decades after *Brown*, many white parents moved to racially homogenous suburbs or enrolled their children in private schools.[4] In many urban school districts, de facto segregation has replaced de jure segregation.[5] Indirectly, *Brown* shaped juvenile justice policies as well as education. It contributed to two education systems—one white and suburban, the other for children of color and urban—and the latter would become a pipeline to juvenile courts.

Over the past quarter century, the politics of race contributed to punitive juvenile justice policies and similar processes impelled schools to replicate their get tough policies. Responding to the moral panic of the 1990s, states and school districts espoused punitive practices, adopted zero-tolerance policies, expanded police presence, and employed surveillance technologies. Schools' control strategies treat all students like potential criminals, disproportionately affect urban children of color, and fuel the school-to-prison pipeline.[6]

Compulsory attendance laws congregate young people in schools. Because crime rates rise sharply during adolescence, schools confront unique problems. They must provide a safe learning environment and forestall guns, drugs, and violence on campus. Efforts by schools to maintain order may compromise their educational mission just as crime control trumps social welfare in juvenile justice. Schools impose extensive regulations and physically monitor students. Officials search students, their possessions, desks and lockers, and cars under a lower Fourth Amendment search standard—reasonable suspicion rather than probable cause—than that required to search adults. School resource officers, police liaisons, and canine partners sometimes initiate or accompany school personnel who conduct searches. Metal detectors and cameras increase the scrutiny to which schools subject students.[7]

Since the 1990s, schools increasingly have relied on exclusionary sanctions—expulsions, out-of-school suspensions, and juvenile court referrals.[8] While early-twentieth-century schools prepared workers to enter factories, Paul Hirschfield argues that contemporary discipline and security regimes "can be traced largely to deindustrialization, which shifted impacted [urban] schools and their disciplinary practices from productive ends toward a warehousing function . . . and these changes helped reorient school actors more toward the prevention and punishment of crime, and less toward the preparation of workers and citizens."[9]

The combination of lower Fourth Amendment search standards, ubiquitous police presence, heightened surveillance, zero-tolerance policies toward criminal and school misconduct, and financial incentives to exclude underperforming students have fueled a school-to-prison pipeline. The chapter's first section reviews the law governing school searches. The Court in *T.L.O. vs. New Jersey* allowed school officials to search students under a lower standard than that required to search adults. As a result, evidence that would be inadmissible in a criminal proceeding can be used to convict delinquents. The next section examines the presence of police in schools—school resource officers (SROs). They search students under the lower Fourth Amendment standard even when engaged in law enforcement activities. Schools' use of technology—metal detectors, cameras, and drug canines—and heightened police presence increases the likelihood of detecting wrongdoing. The third section considers schools' zero tolerance for student deviance and exclusionary responses. In the wake of school shootings in the 1990s, Congress passed the Gun-Free Schools Act of 1994 and school officials adopted zero-tolerance policies toward criminal and school misconduct. The fourth section weighs the impact of high-stakes testing on schools' financial incentives to rid themselves of underperforming students. The confluence of these laws and policies disproportionately affects Black male students.

Searching Students: *T.L.O. v. New Jersey*'s Watered-Down Fourth Amendment

A teacher discovered T.L.O.—a fourteen-year-old high school freshman—smoking in a bathroom in violation of a school rule that prohibited smoking except in designated student smoking areas.[10] Vice Principal Choplick confronted T.L.O., who denied smoking. When he opened her purse to find cigarettes, he saw rolling papers, which he associated with marijuana use. Based on that suspicion, he searched her purse and found some marijuana, a pipe, and other evidence which he gave to the police. In addition to school sanctions, the state convicted her of delinquency based on evidence seized from her purse. After the New Jersey Supreme Court reversed her conviction, the Supreme Court considered the Fourth Amendment's applicability to student searches.

    T.L.O. first ruled that public school officials are state actors bound by the Fourth Amendment.[11] The Court then defined the scope of reasonable searches conducted by school officials by balancing the degree of intrusion on a student's legitimate expectation of privacy against the school's need to intervene. "The determination of the standard of reasonableness governing any specific class of searches requires 'balancing the need to search against the invasion which the search entails.' On one side of the balance are arrayed the individual's legitimate expectations of privacy and personal security; on the other, the government's need for effective methods to deal with breaches of public order."[12]

The Court rejected the state's argument that students had no reasonable expectation of privacy in personal items because schools pervasively regulate them. It rebuffed the state's analogy between schools and prisons and officials' claim that their need to maintain order vitiated students' expectations of privacy.[13] It observed that students legitimately bring wallets, purses, backpacks, and other items to school and concluded that they have not "waived all rights to privacy in such items merely by bringing them onto school grounds."[14]

Both the majority and dissenting Justices in *T.L.O.* agreed that exigent circumstances—the need for flexible and immediate action—obviated the requirement that schools obtain a warrant before conducting a search. But when the Court balanced T.L.O.'s privacy interests in her purse against school officials' need to maintain order, it found that schools had "special needs" beyond those associated with law enforcement.[15]

While both opinions agreed that a warrant was not required, the majority and dissent disagreed about the level of suspicion needed to justify a search. Although warrantless searches ordinarily require probable cause, the majority opted for the lower reasonable suspicion search standard without explaining why it did so.[16] "Determining the reasonableness of any search involves a twofold inquiry: first, one must consider 'whether the . . . action was *justified at its inception*'; second, one must determine whether the search as actually conducted 'was *reasonably related in scope* to the circumstances which justified the interference in the first place.'"[17] A search would be justified at its inception if officials had reasonable suspicion to believe it would yield evidence of a crime or school rule violation. It would be reasonable in scope if officials confined their search to those items and did not use excessively intrusive methods "in light of the *age and sex* of the student and the *nature of the infraction*."[18] The Court did not explain the practical meaning of those limitations—age, sex, or nature of the infraction—when it upheld a male principal's search of a young female student's purse for cigarettes. Instead, *T.L.O.* adopted a vague reasonable suspicion standard that denied students the Fourth Amendment protections adults enjoyed and deferred to school officials to administer it.[19]

The *T.L.O.* dissent questioned why the majority approved a reasonable suspicion standard to conduct searches "whose only definite content is that it is *not* the same test as the 'probable cause' standard found in the text of the Fourth Amendment."[20] They argued that reasonableness provided no guidance to school officials or courts, allowed officials to conduct intrusive searches to enforce trivial rules, and effectively immunized officials from constitutional limits.[21] For them, opening T.L.O.'s purse constituted a search that required probable cause.[22] The Court in *Illinois v. Gates* had previously adopted a probable cause standard that it characterized as "practical," "fluid," "flexible," "easily applied," "nontechnical" and "commonsense." [23] The dissent questioned why school officials could not apply it.[24]

For decades, the Court has struggled to define probable cause and reasonable suspicion.[25] It first distinguished between the two standards in *Terry v. Ohio* which allowed police to stop-and-frisk suspects based on reasonable suspicion because those actions were less intrusive than an arrest and search.[26] The differing standards reflect the quantity and quality of information police must possess. Probable cause demands a "fair probability that contraband or evidence of a crime will be found in a particular place."[27] Reasonable suspicion requires "indicia of reliability" that an informant's tip justifies credence.[28] The verbal formulae do not lend themselves to easy quantification, clear distinction, or readily administered criteria. *Gates* observed that trying to quantify probable cause or reasonable suspicion is an exercise in futility. "[P]robable cause is a fluid concept—turning on the assessment of probabilities in particular factual contexts—not readily, or even usefully, reduced to a neat set of legal rules."[29]

The Court's definition of reasonable suspicion is equally unilluminating and requires "some objective manifestation that the [individual] is, or is about to be, engaged in criminal activity."[30] As with probable cause, reasonable suspicion is fact-specific and flexible. It is a "common-sense, nontechnical conception[ ] that deal[s] with the 'factual and practical considerations of everyday life on which reasonable and prudent men, not legal technicians, act.'"[31] *United States v. Sokolow* described reasonable suspicion as "something more than an inchoate and unparticularized suspicion or hunch. . . . [P]robable cause means a fair probability that contraband or evidence of a crime will be found, and [reasonable suspicion] is obviously less demanding than that for probable cause."[32] *Safford Unified School District #1 v. Redding* distinguished the two standards with the cryptic observation that "[p]erhaps the best that can be said generally about the required knowledge component of probable cause for a law enforcement officer's evidence search is that it raises a 'fair probability,' or a 'substantial chance,' of discovering evidence of criminal activity. The lesser standard for school searches could be as readily described as a moderate chance of finding evidence of wrongdoing."[33] The amount and reliability of information needed for reasonable suspicion is less than that to establish probable cause by some unquantifiable degree.

My criticism of *T.L.O.* is not that probable cause provides a more precise standard to search than reasonable suspicion. Rather, it is that the Court adopted a lower search standard when none was required and without giving any reasons for doing so. As a result, school officials search students and states introduce evidence against them that would be inadmissible if seized from an adult based on similar quantity and quality of information.

A quarter century after *T.L.O.*, the Court in *Safford Unified School District #1 v. Redding* found school officials violated the Fourth Amendment when they strip-searched a thirteen-year-old girl to find prescription-strength ibuprofen.[34] *Redding* characterized a strip search as a uniquely intrusive search that required individualized suspicion.[35] Despite the school's zero-tolerance policy for drugs, *Redding* found the search unreasonable without specific reasons to believe she had hidden drugs in her underwear.

Redding brought a § 1983 civil rights action against school officials. Although the Court found the strip search violated her Fourth Amendment rights, it denied her any relief for the constitutional violation. The Court's qualified immunity doctrine protects public officials acting in good faith from liability unless they violate "clearly established statutory or constitutional rights of which a reasonable person would have known."[36] The Court has balanced the need for a damages remedy for constitutional violations against "the need to protect officials who are required to exercise their discretion and the related public interest in encouraging the vigorous exercise of official authority."[37] A clearly established constitutional right is one whose contours "must be sufficiently clear that a reasonable official would understand that what he is doing violates that right."[38] Even if a teacher or principal violated a student's constitutional rights, the employer–school district would not be liable for damages caused by their employees unless they acted pursuant to an official policy or custom to violate students' rights.[39] *Redding* announced a constitutional right of imprecise contours and without any remedy for its violation.[40]

School Resource Officers

The Court in *T.L.O.* did not address whether a search conducted by police rather than the vice principal would require probable cause.[41] In the decades since *T.L.O.*, school resource officers (SROs) have become a ubiquitous presence. They investigate and interrogate youths, and arrest, search, and refer law violators to juvenile courts. In the 1980s, police departments began to assign officers to schools to combat drugs and in the 1990s to enhance security after several school shootings.[42] The Gun-Free Schools Act of 1994 allocated funds to public schools to develop violence-prevention programs with local police and 1998 amendments to the Omnibus Crime Control and Safe Street Act of 1968 encouraged schools to use SROs.[43] Between 1999 and 2005, the Department of Justice's Community Oriented Policing Services (COPS) awarded more than $750 million to more than three thousand agencies to fund SRO programs.[44] Although approximately seventeen thousand SROs serve in schools nationwide, analysts have not conducted rigorous evaluations of their actual as opposed to symbolic impact on school safety.[45] Funding from COPS and other federal programs also enabled schools to invest heavily in security hardware—metal detectors, surveillance cameras, and other technologies.[46]

Over the past quarter century, local police agencies have assigned SROs—armed and uniformed officers—to schools to perform traditional law enforcement duties—patrolling campus, investigating crimes, and dealing with students who violate school rules or the law.[47] Expanded use of metal detectors and canine partners to detect weapons and drugs accompanied heightened police presence and fostered a prison-like environment.[48] "Many schools became more prisonlike: locked doors, closed campuses, metal detectors, classroom lock-downs and simultaneous locker searches, heavily armed tactical police patrols, dogs, camera surveillance, uniforms, expansive disciplinary codes, interrogations, and informers—these are some elements that contributed to the criminalization of school life."[49] In addition to police functions, SROs collaborate with schools to increase student trust, prevent crime, and provide training and education in conflict resolution, drug abuse prevention (DARE), and the like. Comparisons of schools with and without SROs do not report that they increase positive perceptions or reduce offending, but SROs increase the numbers of students arrested and referred to juvenile courts.[50]

Heightened police presence increases opportunities for Fourth Amendment issues to arise, redefines problem behavior as criminal, and leads to escalation of punishments.[51] Teachers increasingly have withdrawn from enforcing school norms or law violations in favor of security personnel.[52] By virtue of their presence, police observe and school personnel report incidents that previously would not have come to the attention of law enforcement. They introduce a law-and-order mindset that leads to arrests and referrals for behaviors that previously would not have warranted police action.[53] Analysts warn that "law enforcement presence in public schools, particularly when combined with zero tolerance policies, creates an acute risk of utilizing the criminal justice system to handle incidents and behaviors that had been previously dealt with through school disciplinary processes."[54] The ubiquitous presence of security personnel significantly increases court referrals for minor offenses—simple assault or disorderly conduct—that schools previously handled internally.[55]

With police as regular fixtures in public schools, courts have grappled with whether to apply *T.L.O.*'s reasonable suspicion or *Gates*'s probable cause standard when they search students. In *People v. Dilworth*, the local police department assigned an SRO to prevent and detect criminal activity, arrest offenders, and transport them to the police station. The Illinois Supreme Court characterized the officer's search as an effort to maintain a proper educational environment and held that "reasonable suspicion, not probable cause, is the proper fourth amendment standard."[56] Even though the SRO performed regular police functions, the court focused on where the search occurred rather than on who conducted it. The *Dilworth* dissent emphasized his law enforcement role, described the SRO as a "police officer . . . permanently assigned to the school," and reasoned that probable cause standard should govern.[57] Most courts apply *T.L.O.*'s relaxed standard when police search and justify the lower standard to help maintain school safety.[58] Critics contend that SROs should be held to a probable cause standard because equating them with school officials conflates their substantially different roles, disregards their expanded presence, and ignores their increased referrals to juvenile courts.[59]

Schools on "Lock-Down": Metal Detectors and Canine Partners

Threats of violence and weapons are unfortunate facts of life in many schools, especially in segregated urban areas. Schools have become high-security environments with police, metal detectors, and surveillance cameras.[60] A survey of school security practices reported that drug-sniffing dogs conducted random searches in more than 60% of high schools and officials relied on surveillance cameras in 84% of high schools.[61] Another reported that 92% lock their doors during school hours and two-thirds use security cameras.[62] Although metal detectors are common in airports and public buildings, people can choose whether or not to enter those spaces. Compulsory attendance laws require students to attend school and to submit to technological surveillance.[63]

Many schools—especially those serving urban students of color—install metal detectors to limit weapons, a practice that implies that all students are potential criminals.[64] Courts do not require individualized suspicion to use metal detectors, which they view as minimally intrusive.[65] They routinely approve handheld metal detectors to randomly check students.[66] Schools serving low-income students are more likely to rely on metal detectors and hands-on policing than more affluent schools, which use surveillance cameras.[67] Buildings with armed guards, locked doors, metal detectors, and security cameras create an environment that feels more like a prison than a school.[68] Urban minority students socialized in a setting of electronic oversight and police presence may become alienated and mistrustful of school and the police and habituated to government surveillance.[69]

When police use canines to sniff students, lockers, or cars, a dog's alert may provide reasonable suspicion to search or it may itself constitute a search that requires preexisting individualized suspicion. *Illinois v. Caballes* held that a dog's sniff of a car for contraband during a routine traffic stop was not a search that intruded on any reasonable expectation of privacy.[70] Because a sniff is not a search, police do not need specific suspicion before they deploy canines.[71] Justice Souter's *Caballes* dissent objected that ruling that a sniff is not a search placed canines outside of Fourth Amendment regulation.[72] Justice Ginsburg's dissent argued that dogs qualitatively changed a police-citizen encounter and required reasonable suspicion.[73] She warned that the ruling "clears the way for suspicionless, dog-accompanied drug sweeps of parked cars along sidewalks and in parking lots."[74]

School officials regularly enlist police and their canine partners to sniff students, lockers, and cars in school lots without any suspicion.[75] A dog's alert then provides reasonable suspicion to search under *T.L.O.*'s lower reasonableness standard.[76] Courts conclude that schools' responsibility to protect students prevails whether a search for drugs and other illegal activities occurs inside the school or in its parking lot.[77]

Although courts routinely uphold sniffs of students' cars and lockers, they divide over whether officials must have reasonable suspicion for handlers to direct dogs at students themselves.[78] Sniffing a person is qualitatively different from smelling a locker, luggage, or a car and the Supreme Court has not decided whether an olfactory intrusion requires either reasonable suspicion or probable cause.[79] Some courts characterize canines in classrooms as a minimal intrusion—a brief interruption applied evenhandedly to all students.[80] Other courts conclude that smelling a person is more intrusive and offensive than sniffing objects and required officials to have reasonable suspicion or probable cause to deploy dogs against students.[81]

Zero Tolerance

The increased presence of police and surveillance technologies coincided with schools' adoption of zero-tolerance policies toward law violations, rule infractions, and misbehavior. Zero-tolerance policies reflect a "broken windows" theory of crime control that posits that failure to punish minor violations leads to more serious crime and disorder.[82] According to the theory, broken windows left unattended transmit a message of societal indifference to disorder, contributing to further vandalism, serious crime, and urban deterioration. In schools, broken windows theory promotes zero-tolerance policies "by drawing a clear line, giving no quarter to disruption or disrespect, and setting high expectations . . . [to] instill the obedient and cooperative values of a former era."[83] Zero tolerance mandates specific punishments for violations without regard to the seriousness of misconduct or child's intent.[84] Schools' embrace of uniform procedures, disciplinary guidelines that focus on offenses and reduce officials' judgment, mirror juvenile courts' shift from individualized treatment to nondiscretionary offense-based sanctions.[85] Zero tolerance ignores mitigating factors and replicates crime control policies of deterrence and incapacitation.

Increase in youth violence in the late 1980s and school shootings in the early 1990s prompted passage of the Gun-Free Schools Act of 1994, which required schools to expel students found on school property with firearms.[86] "Within a year, the federal prohibition was revised to 'dangerous weapon' rather than firearm, and the school exclusion stampede was launched. As states added drug possession, drug paraphernalia, or assaults on school personnel as a basis for suspension or expulsion, school exclusion skyrocketed."[87] Schools adopted zero-tolerance policies for weapons, made schools drug-free zones, and suspended or expelled students for violations on or near campus.[88] These punitive changes reflected a public and political consensus that schools could suppress violence with more security and strict enforcement.[89] The increased presence of SROs can escalate a minor problem into a justice system matter and zero-tolerance policies have dramatically increased rates of suspension and expulsion of students, especially in large urban districts.[90] Despite their prevalence, zero-tolerance policies do not increase the consistency of school discipline, create school climates more conducive to learning, or deter student misbehavior.[91]

The school-to-prison pipeline operates both directly and indirectly.[92] Administrators may refer students directly to juvenile court, thereby criminalizing school misconduct. Alternatively, they may suspend or expel offending students. Exclusion deprives students of the positive support and structure of school and provides time and opportunity to get in trouble.[93] Over the past three decades, school suspensions have doubled and factors like poverty, minority composition, and residential mobility are associated with greater use of exclusionary sanctions.[94] Suspended students are more likely to repeat a grade, drop out, and become criminally involved and incarcerated as adults.[95]

School officials increasingly refer trivial offenses for delinquency proceedings that they previously handled internally—reporting minor scuffles as assaults, cursing as disorderly conduct, or nail clippers as knives.[96] Schools suspend or expel students for misconduct they previously dealt with through detention or counseling.[97] Administrators cannot ignore acts that could be deemed criminal.[98] Fear of crime and civil liability has resulted in overly simplistic, harsh disciplinary policies without any evidence that they contribute to school safety.[99] Increased presence of police and zero-tolerance policies have reduced administrators' discretion and had a disparate impact on urban youths of color.[100]

Perverse Financial Incentives: High-Stakes Testing

Under No Child Left Behind (NCLB), passed in 2001, schools that receive federal funds must annually test students' reading, language arts, math, and science and demonstrate yearly progress and among all student subgroups.[101] A school that fails to make satisfactory annual progress may be labeled a failing school, placed on probation, or taken over by the state.[102] In 2015, congress passed the Every Student Succeeds Act (ESSA) which replaced the heavily criticized NCLB. ESSA also requires states receiving federal funds to implement student assessments in their public schools, but gives states greater autonomy to measure academic performance and accountability. States historically have a poor record of addressing the educational needs of marginalized students and greater autonomy may lead to greater disparities in student achievement. ESSA does little to address racial disparities in discipline or the punitive environments in schools serving students of color.

The family wealth or poverty of children taking standardized tests strongly influences their results. Children of affluent parents enrolled in preschool, "Baby Ivies," and Montessori programs from age two will have had about twice as much schooling as children of poor parents when they start taking standardized tests around third grade.[103]

NCLB and ESSA accountability provisions give schools financial incentives to narrow curricula, to "teach to the test," and "rewards schools for altering their student bodies. Schools that can restrict their student bodies to the better test takers will improve their scores and be financially rewarded (or at least escape punishment)."[104] NCLB and now ESSA create financial incentives to push out, suspend, or expel academically low-performing students who may also misbehave.[105] "African Americans may be more likely to be punished than whites, but it is largely because they are already marginalized within the official school status system due to poor academic performance. . . . School staff may not target black students per se, but they target students who struggle academically, and such students are more likely to be African Americans."[106] Under high-stakes testing, excluding disruptive or underperforming students provide quick-fix alternatives to improving schools and providing qualified teachers, counselors, and resources.[107] Strategies include suspending or expelling students, assigning them to alternative schools, ordering them to complete their secondary education through GEDs, and removing them from attendance records.[108] Schools that measure poorly in student tests and teacher qualifications are those most likely to rely on punitive disciplinary sanctions.[109]

Segregation, Racial Disparities, and the School-to-Prison Pipeline

Although *Brown v. Board of Education* prohibited racial segregation in schools, it took another decade for Congress to pass the 1964 Civil Rights Act and provide means to enforce desegregation of public schools. Efforts to integrate urban schools precipitated massive white flight to suburbs.[110] After a decade of progress toward integration, the 1974 Court decision in *Milliken v. Bradley* barred cross-district remedies for school segregation and led to substantial resegregation of schools—urban Black and suburban white.[111] Inequality in America operates increasingly through education, which correlates with parental socioeconomic status, education, and residence.[112] Residential segregation is deeply rooted, sustained by zoning regulations and home mortgage tax deductions. The Court's decision in *Parents Involved in Community Schools v. Seattle School District No. 1* in 2007 eliminated many of the tools available to school districts to design voluntary desegregation plans.[113]

The vast majority of children of color attend segregated schools. Almost 94% of Black and Latino students in urban areas—a central city with more than 250,000 residents—attend "predominantly minority" schools in which the student body is 50–100% minority students.[114] Approximately two-thirds attend "intensely segregated schools" in which only 0–10% of their classmates were white.[115] In major urban areas, about 2.5 million students attend "apartheid schools" in which enrollment is 99–100% non-white. One-sixth of African American students and one-ninth of Latino students attend apartheid schools.

During the 1980s and 1990s, as middle-class Blacks moved to inner-ring suburbs, residential and school segregation reemerged and intensified white flight to even more distant racial enclaves.[116] By 2012, despite increased suburbanization of non-white families, 80% of Latino students and 74% of Black students attend majority non-white schools, 43% of Latinos and 38% of Blacks attend intensely segregated schools (those with 0–10% white students), and 15% of Black students and 14% of Latino students attend "apartheid schools."[117]

As *Brown* recognized more than sixty years ago, attending segregated minority schools adversely affects educational opportunities and students' learning. Students who attend racially and socioeconomically diverse schools achieve higher test scores, earn better grades, graduate from high school more often, and attend and graduate from college at higher rates than comparable peers who attend schools with large proportions of poor and disadvantaged youth of color. Although students from all racial and socioeconomic backgrounds—including middle-class white students—can benefit from diverse schools, low-income disadvantaged minority youth derive the most advantage.[118]

By contrast, segregated schools suffer from high poverty levels, residential transience, rapid faculty turnover, less experienced or qualified teachers, lower academic achievement, and higher dropout rates than those enjoyed by white students. "Teacher flight from the challenges in such schools—violence and disorder, truancy, lower school readiness and English-language proficiency, less supportive home environments—means that students in these schools get a generally inferior education."[119] In *Savage Inequalities* and *The Shame of the Nation*, Jonathan Kozol documents the deplorable conditions under which most urban children of color attend schools. He describes in painful and heartbreaking detail the separate and unequal education they receive.[120]

For three decades, school policies have contribute to overrepresentation of Black youths in disciplinary suspensions, expulsions, and juvenile court referrals.[121] Youths reared in segregated urban areas of concentrated poverty are exposed to more risk factors for criminal behavior than their more privileged white peers. Those risk factors adversely affect students' learning as well. It is difficult to concentrate, learn, or behave when they come to school hungry, ill clothed, from chaotic households and violent neighborhoods.[122] They attend under-resourced schools that do not provide opportunities comparable with those enjoyed by their white suburban peers. States' failures to provide equal education for many urban youths is a prescription for school-leaving and justice system involvement.

Youths who perform poorly in school may become frustrated, fail to make academic progress, and become disruptive or drop out.[123] Dropping out of school culminates a process of disengagement that begins long before students leave. Youths from poor families who have poorly educated parents and are poor readers encounter academic failure, fall a grade or two behind in school, and exhibit behavioral problems or become chronic truants.[124] Schools' failure to support and remediate academically struggling students may cause the misbehavior that then leads to disciplinary sanctions.

In *Homeroom Security*, Aaron Kupchik summarizes the disproportionate impact of zero-tolerance policies on poor children and students of color.

> [B]lack students are twice as likely to be suspended as white students and, independent of race, being poor also increases a student's probability of being suspended. Other research concludes that black students' disproportionate likelihood of receiving school punishment is influenced by the fact that they receive poor grades, are perceived as less well-behaved, and have been disproportionately sanctioned at school in the past. Evidence also suggests that students of color are more likely to be referred for discipline because teachers and other school staff perceive their behavior to be more threatening, disrespectful, and inappropriate compared to the behavior of white students.[125]

In addition, parents of students who attend low-income schools have less social capital—education, white-collar jobs, two-parent households—than those who attend more affluent schools and may be less able to challenge school disciplinary practices effectively.[126]

Black and Hispanic students in Texas were twice as likely as white students to be suspended, disciplined, and referred to juvenile court.[127] Although national suspension rates for all students have doubled over the past three decades, schools are three times as likely to suspend Black students as their white counterparts even for the same conduct.[128] "African American students are more than 3.5 times more likely to be suspended or expelled than their white peers and more than 70 per cent of students involved in school-related arrests or referred to law enforcement are Hispanic or African American."[129] The U.S. Office of Civil Rights reported that one out of every six Black students had been suspended at least once, as contrasted with only one of twenty white students enrolled in K–12 public schools.[130]

Jason Nance's research controls for school size and location, school crime and disorder, neighborhood crime, and other variables, and reports that students' race and poverty strongly predicted schools' decisions to use surveillance and security measures—metal detectors, guards, random sweeps, and cameras.[131]

[L]arge, urban schools serving primarily low-income or minority students are more likely to create intense surveillance environments than other schools. . . . [S]chools with high percentage of minority or low-income students tend to rely on heavy-handed, punitive-based measures to maintain order and control crime. . . . [T]hese schools are more inclined to coerce students into compliance and to promote safety by identifying, apprehending, and excluding students that school officials perceive as being dangerous, disruptive, or low-performing.[132]

Schools that rely heavily on surveillance create poorer learning environments and deprive impoverished students of educational opportunities more affluent students enjoy. Differences in behavior by race or socioeconomic class do not account for differences in school discipline practices.[133] Rather, schools serving large proportions of Black students are more likely to suspend, expel, or refer them to juvenile courts and less likely to use reprimands, meeting with a counselor, or in-school detention than those serving predominantly white students.[134]

School personnel may perceive poor Black males as troublemakers, dangerous, or a threat to their control in the classroom.[135] Poor youths of color who are not as fully socialized in white middle-class norms may respond inappropriately to criticism of their conduct.[136] Many incidents for which teachers sanction students involve subjectively defined misbehavior—disorderly conduct, insubordination, or disrespect—which can be characterized as assault but which may reflect a racialized perceptions of minority youths.[137] Perceived threat of loss of control in the classroom for infractions such as tardiness, disrespect, and defiance leads to punitive responses.[138]

Once school staff and SROs identify youths as troublemakers, they may monitor them more closely, which increases the likelihood of future disciplinary action and academic failure.[139] Disproportionately sanctioning youths attending underperforming schools and experiencing higher dropout rates reinforces a negative life trajectory.[140] While more than three-quarters of white youths graduated from school, only about half of Black and Hispanic youths do.[141] Fewer than one-quarter of Black male high school dropouts will find full-time employment; by their early twenties, most will be involved in criminal activity, convicted and incarcerated, and suffer economic consequences the rest of their lives.[142]

By the late 1990s, the majority of young Black men who did not graduate from high school were likely to be imprisoned.[143] Hirschfield argues that whereas schools a century ago prepared youths to work in industrial factories, contemporary "criminalization practices reflect increased perceptions of troublesome students as future criminals or prisoners. The needs of such students fall outside of the traditional school disciplinary paradigm, which is tied to images of students as future workers and citizens. . . . Owing to a dominant image of black males as criminals and prisoners, many school authorities view chronically disobedient black boys as 'bound for jail' and 'unsalvageable.'"[144] Similarly, Loïc Wacquant argues that impoverished inner-city schools have "deteriorated to the point where they operate in the manner of *institutions of confinement* whose primary mission is not to educate but to ensure 'custody and control.'" He asserts that "the carceral atmosphere of schools and the constant presence of armed guards in uniform in the lobbies, corridors, cafeteria, and playground of their establishment habituates the children of the hyperghetto to the demeanor, tactics, and interactive style of the correctional officers many of them are bound to encounter shortly after their school days are over."[145]

Conclusion

T.L.O. created a school search exception to the Fourth Amendment where none was needed. *Terry*'s stop-and-frisk authority enables teachers to conduct less intrusive investigations and *Gates*'s probable cause standard provides a workable requirement for searches. *T.L.O.*'s lower standard enables schools to subject students to a regime more suitable to prisons than to educational environments—suspicionless drug testing, surveillance, canine sniffs, and strip searches.[146] The Supreme Court and lower courts minimized students' privacy interests and expanded state control and intrusion. Public and political panics about drugs and violence encouraged schools to adopt heavy-handed, counterproductive strategies that deny students any expectation of privacy. A dearth of legal protections, heightened police presence, increased surveillance, and school officials' zero-tolerance repudiation of common sense have fostered a school-to-prison pipeline.

Schools are the incubators of future citizens and convey moral lessons by their actions. The Court in *West Virginia State Bd. of Educ. v. Barnette* emphasized that schools "educating the young for citizenship is reason for scrupulous protection of constitutional freedoms of the individual, if we are not to strangle the free mind at its source and teach youth to discount important principles of our government as mere platitudes."[147] By contrast, school disciplinary practices discourage students from questioning power and encourage passivity and obedience to authority.[148] School practices socialize students to accept police scrutiny, surveillance cameras, and other security practices in their workplaces and communities.

Providing young people with real Fourth Amendment protection will better socialize them to participate effectively as adults in a democratic society. Although the Court insists that "students do not shed their constitutional rights . . . at the schoolhouse gate,"[149] *T.L.O.*'s lesson is that we inculcate the values of citizenship by denying students basic rights. Schools that create inclusive climates in which students feel respected and rewarded for positive behavior experience less crime and disorder than do those that rely on harsh discipline and rigid security.[150]

Local property taxes fund schools in most states. Disparities between wealthy suburban districts with high home values and fewer tax-exempt businesses and those in poor urban communities replicate and reinforce social inequality. Broader structural features define schools' behavioral expectations, instructional content, and educational strategies. Schools reproduce social inequality because skills and behaviors that have economic values are not equally distributed and not all students are similarly socialized in them.[151]

Educational opportunities in high-poverty urban schools are more limited than those in wealthier districts in physical infrastructure, academically enriched courses, highly trained teachers, extracurricular activities, and the like.[152] Funding inequalities in large urban districts result in larger classrooms with fewer opportunities for individualized instruction and create more opportunities for failing students to be disruptive. Overwhelmed teachers rely on rigid discipline to maintain order. Intense surveillance and heavy security damage schools' social climate by implying distrust and suspicion and treating students as suspects.[153] It skews students' perceptions of government and normalizes surveillance.[154]

PART IV

The Kids Are Different Era

8

The Criminal Is a Kid

Adolescents' Diminished Culpability

The edifice of juvenile justice is built on binary categories—either child or adult, treatment or punishment, past offense or offender future welfare. Binary categories detract from viewing the transition to adulthood as a developmental continuum and from considering how immaturity should affect punishment of youths sentenced as adults.

Penal proportionality requires a principled relationship between the seriousness of a crime—harm caused and actor's culpability—and the sentence imposed. Until recently, courts rejected juveniles' proportionality challenges and used a circular logic that a crime is serious because of the harm inflicted without regard to a youth's culpability.[1] *Harris v. Wright* rebuffed a fifteen-year-old's challenge to a sentence of mandatory life without parole for murder. "Youth has no obvious bearing on this problem: If we can discern no clear line for adults, neither can we for youths. Accordingly, while capital punishment is unique and must be treated specially, mandatory life imprisonment without parole is, for young and old alike, only an outlying point on the continuum of prison sentences. Like any other prison sentence, it raises no inference of disproportionality when imposed on a murderer."[2] Lower courts found no impediment to imposing lengthy or mandatory sentences on very young children as long as they possessed criminal intent.[3]

The Supreme Court developed its jurisprudence of youth—"children are different"—in response to get tough laws that ignored adolescents' reduced culpability. The increased numbers and immaturity of many juveniles sentenced as adults impelled the Court to review states' laws and to judicially assert that "enough is enough." Recall from Chapter 5, states annually try upward of two hundred thousand youths as adults.[4] The predictions in the early 1990s of an impending bloodbath by superpredators propelled preemptive punitive policies.[5] States lowered the age for transfer, increased the number of excluded offenses, and shifted discretion from judges to prosecutors.[6] Get tough transfer laws exacerbated racial disparities.[7] Racial stereotypes taint culpability assessments and reduce the mitigating role of youthfulness.[8] Children of color comprise the majority of juveniles tried in criminal court and three-quarters of those who enter prison.[9] Over the twentieth century, Black youths comprised 70% of all juveniles executed, primarily in the South.[10] States' get tough criminal laws lengthened sentences, set mandatory minimums, and imposed mandatory life without parole for homicide and other crimes.[11] They apply equally to juveniles as to adults; judges sentenced them as if they were adults and sent them to the same prisons.[12]

In a trilogy of cases beginning in 2005, the Court applied the Eight Amendment prohibition on cruel and unusual punishment to juveniles. *Roper v. Simmons* prohibited states from executing offenders for murder committed prior to eighteen years of age.[13] The Justices concluded that youths' immature judgment and lack of self-control, susceptibility to negative influence from peers, and transitory personalities reduced their culpability and precluded the most severe sentence. *Graham v. Florida* extended *Roper*'s diminished responsibility rationale and prohibited states from imposing sentences of life without parole (LWOP) for non-homicide offenses.[14] It repudiated the Court's Eighth Amendment doctrine that "death is different."[15] *Miller v. Alabama* extended *Roper* and *Graham*'s diminished responsibility rationale and barred *mandatory* LWOP sentences for youths convicted of murder.[16] *Miller* required judges to make individualized culpability assessments and to weigh youthfulness as a mitigating factor.

Despite the Court's repeated assertions that "children are different," *Graham* provided non-homicide offenders very limited relief—"some meaningful opportunity to obtain release"—without requiring either rehabilitative services or eventual freedom. *Miller* required a judge to make an individualized assessment of a juvenile murderer's culpability but did not preclude an LWOP sentence. State courts and legislatures have struggled to implement juveniles' diminished responsibility when sentencing them as adults.

This chapter first analyzes the Court's abolition of the juvenile death penalty. *Roper* held that youths are categorically less criminally responsible than adults. However, the Court relied more on intuition—"as every parent knows"—than on the growing body of developmental psychological and neuroscience research that bolsters its conclusion. The second section examines *Graham's* rejection of the Court's "death is different" jurisprudence and its reformulation of proportionality analyses to account for the doubly diminished responsibility of juveniles who did not kill. The third section analyzes *Miller's* repudiation of *mandatory* LWOP sentences for juveniles who murder. *Miller* relied on death penalty precedents to require individualized assessments and to weigh youths' diminished responsibility. The fourth section reviews how state courts and legislatures have struggled unsuccessfully to implement the Court's "children are different" jurisprudence. Its limited constitutional authority to review state sentencing laws and the opinions' broad language provide scant guidance on several critical questions. The final section proposes a Youth Discount—shorter sentences for younger offenders—to formally recognize youthfulness as a mitigating factor.

Juveniles and the Death Penalty: *Roper v. Simmons* and Diminished Responsibility

The Eighth Amendment prohibits states from inflicting "cruel and unusual punishments."[17] Prior to *Roper v. Simmons*, the Court thrice considered whether it prohibited states from executing juveniles convicted of murder. *Eddings v. Oklahoma* reversed a sixteen-year-old youth's death sentence because the trial court failed to consider youthfulness as mitigating factor.[18] In *Thompson v. Oklahoma*, a plurality of Justices concluded that offenders fifteen years of age or younger lacked sufficient culpability to warrant execution.[19] In 1989, *Stanford v. Kentucky* upheld the death penalty for sixteen- or seventeen-years-olds convicted of murder and allowed juries to assess their individual culpability.[20]

In 2005, *Roper* overruled *Stanford* and prohibited states from executing youths for crimes committed prior to age eighteen.[21] *Roper* relied on *Atkins v. Virginia*, which barred execution of defendants with mental retardation.[22] *Atkins* found a national consensus against executing them because thirty states barred the practice and few states put them to death. *Atkins* concluded that intellectually impaired defendants lacked sufficient culpability to warrant execution. *Roper* found a similar national consensus: the number of states opposed to executing juveniles equaled that in *Atkins*; after *Stanford*, five states raised the age of death-eligibility, and only three states executed juveniles in the interim.[23]

Criminal responsibility is about an actor's degree of blameworthiness for his or her harmful acts. *Roper* gave three reasons why states could not punish juveniles as severely as adults. First, their immature judgment and limited self-control causes them to act impulsively and without adequate appreciation of consequences. "[A] lack of maturity and an underdeveloped sense of responsibility are found in youth more often that in adults and are more understandable among the young. These qualities often result in impetuous and ill-considered actions and decisions."[24] Second, their susceptibility to negative influence from peers and inability to escape criminogenic environments reduced their responsibility. "Juveniles are more vulnerable or susceptible to negative influences and outside pressures, including peer pressure. . . . Their own vulnerability and comparative lack of control over their immediate surroundings mean juveniles have a greater claim than adults to be forgiven for failing to escape negative influences in their whole environment."[25] Third, their transitory personality provides less reliable evidence of blameworthiness. "[T]he character of a juvenile is not as well formed as that of an adult."[26] Because juveniles' character is transitional, "[f]rom a moral standpoint it would be misguided to equate the failings of a minor with those of an adult, for a great possibility exists that a minor's character deficiencies will be reformed."[27]

For *Roper*, youths' diminished responsibility undermined retributive justifications for the death penalty. "Retribution is not proportional if the law's most severe penalty is imposed on one whose culpability or blameworthiness is diminished, to a substantial degree, by reason of youth and immaturity."[28] Similarly, the Court concluded that impulsiveness and limited self-control weakened any deterrent effect.[29]

The *Roper* majority and dissents disagreed whether to impose a categorical ban or to allow juries to evaluate youths' culpability individually.[30] Justice Kennedy opted for a categorical ban:

The differences between juvenile and adult offenders are too marked and well understood to *risk* allowing a youthful person to receive the death penalty despite insufficient culpability. An *unacceptable likelihood* exists that the brutality or cold-blooded nature of any particular crime would overpower mitigating arguments based on youth as a matter of course, even where the juvenile offender's objective immaturity, vulnerability, and lack of true depravity should require a sentence less severe than death.[31]

The American Psychiatric Association's *Diagnostic and Statistical Manual of Mental Disorders, Fifth Edition,* precludes clinicians' diagnoses of antisocial personality disorder—psychopathy—in people younger than eighteen because its criteria require longstanding enduring behavior patterns and adolescents' personalities continue to develop and change. *Roper* declined to let jurors make culpability assessments that psychiatrists eschew. Because a brutal murder could overwhelm the mitigating role of youthfulness, *Roper* used age as a categorical proxy for reduced culpability.

Developmental Psychology and Adolescent Culpability

Roper reasoned that immature judgment, susceptibility to peer and environmental influences, and transitional personalities reduced adolescents' criminal responsibility. But it relied more on intuition—"as any parent knows"—than on scientific evidence.[32] Although several *amicus* briefs presented developmental psychological and neuroscience research, the Court did not identify on which studies or evidence it relied.

Roper—and subsequently *Graham* and *Miller*—analyzed youths' reduced culpability within a retributive sentencing framework—proportionality and deserved punishment. Retributive sentencing proportions punishment to a crime's seriousness.[33] A crime's seriousness is defined by two elements—harm and culpability—which determine how much punishment an actor deserves.[34] An offender's age has no bearing on the harm caused—children and adults can cause the same injuries. But proportionality requires consideration of an offender's culpability and immaturity reduces youths' blameworthiness.[35] Youths' inability to fully appreciate wrongfulness or control themselves lessens, but does not excuse, responsibility for causing harms.[36] They may have the minimum capacity to be criminally liable—the ability to distinguish right from wrong—but still deserve less punishment.[37] Cognitive or behavioral impairment—mental illness or retardation, emotional arousal, youthfulness and developmental immaturity, or coercive influences—lessen a person's capacity to make as blameworthy decisions.[38]

Developmental psychology focuses on how children and adolescents' thinking and behaving change with age. Developmental tasks include forming a sense of self, separating from parents, exercising greater autonomy, acquiring social skills, and attaining educational and vocational competencies in the transition to adulthood.[39] During adolescence, youths explore identities, create a social self, interact with groups, and develop interpersonal skills and relationships.[40] Experimenting and risk taking serve adaptive functions to reach those goals.[41] Normal antisocial behavior—defying authority, lawbreaking, and risk taking—disrupts ties to parents and schools in the process of a child's becoming independent.[42]

By mid-adolescence, most youths reason similarly to adults.[43] For example, they make comparable informed-consent medical decisions.[44] But the ability to make reasonable decisions with complete information under laboratory conditions differs from the ability to act responsibly under stress with incomplete information.[45] Emotions influence youths' judgment to a greater extent than adults' and researchers distinguish between "cold" and "hot" cognition.[46]

> [A]dolescents are much less capable of making sound decisions when under stressful conditions or when peer pressure is strong. Psychosocial researchers have referred to cognition in these different contexts as *cold* versus *hot*. The traits that are commonly associated with being an adolescent—short-sightedness (i.e., inability to make decisions based on long-term planning), impulsivity, hormonal changes, and susceptibility to peer influence—can quickly undermine one's ability to make sound decisions in periods of hot cognition.[47]

Emotionally charged situations compromise adolescents' decision making and self-control.[48] Sensitivity to rewards suppresses judicious consideration of risk.[49] As the next section explains, youths are more heavily influenced by the reward centers of the brain, which contributes to riskier decisions.[50]

In response to states' get tough frenzy, in 1995 the John D. and Catherine T. MacArthur Foundation sponsored the Research Network on Adolescent Development and Juvenile Justice (ADJJ). Over the next decade, the ADJJ network conducted research on adolescent decision-making, judgment, and adjudicative competence.[51] The research distinguishes between cognitive abilities and judgment and self-control—controlled thinking versus impulsive behaving.[52] Cognitive capacities involve understanding—the ability to comprehend information—and reasoning—the ability to use information logically. Self-control requires the ability to think before acting, to choose between alternatives, and to interrupt a course in motion.[53] Although sixteen-year-olds' understanding and reasoning approximate adults', their ability to exercise mature judgment and control impulses takes several more years to emerge.[54]

The ADJJ research describes the disjunction between cognitive ability and judgment as the "immaturity gap."[55] Youths differ from adults in risk perception, appreciation of consequences, impulsivity and self-control, sensation seeking, and compliance with peers.[56] The regions of the brain that control reward seeking and emotional arousal develop earlier than do those that regulate executive functions and impulse control.[57]

Immature Judgment, Impulse Control, and Risky Behavior

Higher rates of accidents, suicide, drinking and drug use, unsafe sex, and crime reflect adolescents' greater propensity to engage in risky behavior.[58] To calculate risks, a person has to identify potential outcomes, estimate their likelihood, and make valuations of alternatives.[59] Adolescents underestimate the amount and likelihood of risks, emphasize immediate outcomes, and focus on anticipated gains rather than possible losses to a greater extent than adults.[60] They consider fewer options.[61] While youths and adults take similar time to solve simple problems, the amount of time used to solve complex problems increases with age.[62]

Youths' perception of risk declines during mid-adolescence before increasing into adulthood. Sixteen- and seventeen-year-olds perceive fewer risks than do younger or older subjects.[63] They weigh costs and benefits differently, apply dissimilar subjective values to outcomes, and more heavily discount negative future consequences than more immediate rewards.[64] They have less experience and knowledge to inform decisions about consequences.[65] They prefer an immediate albeit smaller reward than do adults, who can better delay gratification.[66]

In a risk-benefit calculus, youths may view *not* engaging in risky behaviors differently than adults.[67] For adolescents, risky behavior provides access to resources, opportunities to explore adult behaviors, and chances to increase status within their peer group.[68] They crave novel sensation and excitement.[69] Emotional arousal affects both impulsivity—the inability to inhibit responses—and sensation seeking—an affirmative quest for stimulating experiences.[70] Researchers attribute youths' impetuous decisions to a heightened appetite for emotional arousal and intense experiences, which peaks around sixteen or seventeen.[71] Feelings of invulnerability heighten risk propensity.[72]

Neuroscience and Adolescent Brain Development

Neuroscience research reports that the human brain continues to mature until the early to mid-twenties. Adolescents on average do not have adults' neurobiological capacity to exercise mature judgment or control impulses.[73] A commonly used analogy is that a teenager's brain is like a car with a powerful, responsive accelerator but slow and weak brakes. The relationship between two brain regions—the prefrontal cortex (PFC) and the limbic system—underlie youths' propensity for risky behavior.[74] The PFC is responsible for judgment and impulse control. The amygdala and limbic system regulate emotional arousal and reward-seeking behavior.[75] The PFC performs executive functions—reasoning, planning, and impulse control.[76] These top-down capabilities develop gradually and enable individuals to exercise greater self-control.[77]

During adolescence, two processes—myelination and synaptic pruning—enhance the PFC's functions.[78] Myelin is a white fatty substance that forms a sheath around neural axons and facilitates more efficient neurotransmission.[79] It acts like insulation on a wire to increase the speed of neural electro-conductivity and make communication between different brain regions faster and more reliable.[80] Synaptic pruning involves selective elimination of unused neural connections—use it or lose it.[81] The gray matter or brain cell neurons that cover the top layer of the brain begin to thin and eliminate unused connections.[82]

This promotes greater efficiency, speeds neural signals, and strengthens the brain's ability to process information.[83]

The limbic system controls emotions, reward seeking, and instinctual behavior—the fight-or-flight response.[84] It detects rewards and threats in the environment and activates responses.[85] The PFC and limbic systems mature at different rates and adolescents rely more heavily on the limbic system—bottom-up emotional processing rather than the top-down cognitive regulatory system.[86] The developmental lag between the PFC regulatory system and the reward- and pleasure-seeking limbic system contributes to impetuous behavior driven more by emotions rather than reason.[87] The imbalance between the impulse-control and reward-seeking systems contributes to youths' poor judgment, impetuous behavior, and criminal involvement.[88]

Poverty and Children's Brain Development

One in five children in the United States live in poverty and around 40% of children are poor or near-poor.[89] Brain plasticity is a physical process by which neural connections are forged and strengthened or weakened and severed as experiences reorganize neural pathways. Children's brains are biologically programmed to interact with their environment; neuroplasticity enables them to learn and adapt to their surroundings.[90] Positive and negative environmental factors affect critical functions—cognitive development, emotional regulation, impulse control, and planning—during children's brains' protracted development.[91] Early stress and trauma can disrupt circuitry between the PFC and limbic system and impair children's ability to control emotions.[92]

Neuroscience research has explored the relationship between socioeconomic status (SES) and cortical thinning—a process related to synaptic pruning.[93] Research on brain development reports differences among low- and high-SES children in regions of the brain responsible for language, executive function, selective attention, memory, mood dysphoria, and stress regulation with the strongest negative impact on neurocognitive abilities among the most disadvantaged children.[94]

Several factors associated with poverty affect brain development: material deprivation; toxic stress; and environmental toxins.[95] Children in poverty experience heightened exposure to in utero pollutants and toxins, nutritional deficits, high levels of stress associated with family turmoil and disruption, violence, and economic and residential instability.[96] Parents under stress of poverty may feel depressed or angry, which results in harsh and inconsistent child rearing, disrupts relationships, and less verbal communication.[97]

> [S]evere and chronic stress, especially if unbuffered by supportive adults, can disrupt the basic executive functions that govern how various parts of the brain work together to address challenges and problems. Consequently, children who experience toxic stress have trouble concentrating, controlling impulsive behavior, and following direction.
>
> Extreme stress causes a cascade of biochemical and anatomical changes that impair brain development and change brain architecture at a basic level. Stress caused by unstable and consistently unresponsive caregiving, physical or emotional abuse, parental substance abuse, and lack of affection can produce measurable physiological changes in the child that lead to lifelong difficulties in learning, behavior, and both physical and mental health.[98]

Environmental factors like trauma and violence in the home and chronic stress have especially toxic effects on the PFC and adversely affect cognitive abilities and self-control.[99]

Compared with higher-SES youngsters, poor children's brains receive less exposure to stimulation and enrichment—parents reading to them, providing age-appropriate toys and educational resources, and engaging them in conversations—which affect cognitive development and impulse control.[100] While heritability accounts for most of the IQ variability among higher-SES subjects, at lower-SES levels, environmental factors explain most of the variation and suggests that "as environmental adversity increases, these variations in environment become more important determinants of cognitive development compared to genetic inheritance."[101] Researchers attribute neurobiological differences in brain development among low- and high-SES children to prenatal factors, cognitive stimulation, and child-rearing practices that affect language acquisition and executive function.[102] Poor parents have less time and resources with which to foster children's cognitive development than do wealthier ones because of erratic work schedules, the absence of a second parent to share child-rearing responsibilities, more dangerous and chaotic communities, and limited options to seek respite.[103] Children's early cognitive development affects how they perform in school and puts them on different life trajectories.[104] Both school-based and family-based interventions can provide cognitive and behavioral gains for poor children and modest increases in family income in the first few years of life can produce large differences in adult outcomes.[105]

Limitations of Neuroscience

Neuroscience research about brain development bolsters social scientists' observations about adolescents' impulsive behavior and impaired self-control.[106] Despite impressive advances, neuroscientists have not established a direct link between brain maturation and behavior or found ways to individualize assessments of developmental differences.[107]

> [I]t is not possible to use brain imaging to assess immaturity in an individual adolescent, either alone or in combination with psychological assessment. . . . [T]here is not yet sufficient evidence linking age differences in specific aspects of brain structure to real-world behaviors that might mitigate adolescent culpability. It simply is not possible to point to a scan of a normally developing brain and identify a structural feature that clearly marks the brain as an "adolescent" brain rather than an "adult" brain. . . . Finally, many of the most important changes in the brain that occur over the course of adolescence and young adulthood are changes in how the brain functions, rather than simply changes in brain anatomy, or structure.[108]

Notwithstanding these limitations, the research helps to explain why adolescents make riskier decisions and respond more robustly to peers than do adults.

Peer Group Influences

Roper attributed juveniles' diminished responsibility to greater susceptibility to peer influences. Adolescents separate from parents—individuation—and develop a sense of self—identity formation—through peer interaction.[109]

Research across primate species suggests that peer socializing helps individuals develop adaptive behaviors—social skills, access to mates, and ability to survive without parental protection.[110] As their orientation shifts toward peers, youths' quest for acceptance and affiliation makes them more susceptible to influences than they will be as adults.[111]

Adolescents gauge their own behavior through peer comparison and adopt their friends' behavior and attitudes as their own.[112] Youths in a group context may engage in risky behavior out of fear of rejection or desire for approval.[113] Among the most dangerous things a teenager can say to another is "you're chicken" or "I dare you."[114] Peers increase youths' propensity to engage in unsafe behavior more often together than they would if they were alone.[115] Their presence stimulates neural activity in the brain's reward centers and makes them more sensitive to all kinds of rewards including risky behavior.[116]

Juveniles commit their crimes in groups to a greater extent than do adults.[117] Their ability to withstand pressure approaches that of adults only in the late teens and early twenties.[118] Because group criminality reflects normal behavior, it provide less compelling evidence of culpability than if an adult made the same choice.[119] Group offending increases youths' risks for prosecution as accessories to crimes they did not intend or personally commit and exposes them to the same penalties as principals.[120] All three defendants in *Roper*, *Graham*, and *Miller* committed their crimes with one or more co-offenders.

Roper recognized that juveniles' dependency on their families made them less able than adults to escape criminogenic environments.[121] The opportunity to develop self-control is socially constructed, and families, schools, and communities affect children's developmental prospects and risks of criminality.[122] Chapter 3 described structural conditions that contribute to high crime rates in inner-city neighborhoods, expose children of color to criminal subcultural norms that affluent youth do not confront, and consign them to inferior schools.[123]

Graham v. Florida: Reframing Proportionality

Roper's diminished responsibility rationale presumably would reduce juveniles' blameworthiness for non-capital crimes as well. Prior to *Graham v. Florida*, the Court had insisted that "death is different"—"a sentence of death differs in kind from any sentence of imprisonment, no matter how long."[124] It did not apply death penalty jurisprudence to term-of-years sentences and appellate courts rejected juveniles' challenges to lengthy, mandatory, or LWOP sentences.[125]

Graham extended *Roper's* diminished responsibility rationale to non-homicide offenders who received LWOP sentences. *Graham* arose at the intersection of two lines of Eighth Amendment cases. One group of cases examined whether some sentences were grossly disproportional to the seriousness of the crime. The other barred the death penalty for certain categories of offenders or offenses—those with mental retardation, juveniles, or convicted of non-homicide offenses.[126]

The Court has vacillated over whether the Eighth Amendment imposed proportionality limits on non-capital sentences. *Rummel v. Estelle* held that sentencing a three-time, minor property offender to life in prison *with* the possibility of parole did not violate the Eighth Amendment.[127] Three years later, *Solem v. Helms* held that a sentence of life *without* possibility of parole for a property crime *did* violate the Constitution.[128] *Solem* focused on "(i) the gravity of the offense and the harshness of the penalty; (ii) the sentences imposed on other criminals in the same jurisdiction; and (iii) the sentences imposed for commission of the same crime in other jurisdictions."[129] *Harmelin v. Michigan* upheld a life *without* parole sentence for a first-time drug dealer.[130] After *Harmelin*, courts rarely reviewed sentences that crossed some undefined threshold of gross disproportionality and declined to overturn long sentences for minor crimes.[131]

Categorical challenges to the death penalty affect entire classes of offenses or offenders. Some decisions barred execution for non-homicide crimes and some felony-murders.[132] Others prohibited states from executing less culpable offenders—juveniles and the mentally disabled.[133]

Graham raised "a categorical challenge to a term of years sentence"—a life without parole sentence applied to the category of juveniles.[134] *Graham* repudiated the Court's "death is different" distinction, extended *Roper's* reduced culpability rationale to term-of-year sentences, and "declare[d] an entire class of offenders immune from a noncapital sentence."[135] *Graham* replicated *Roper's* analyses and found a national consensus against imposing LWOP sentences on non-homicide juvenile offenders. Although thirty-seven states authorized LWOP sentences,

Florida imprisoned two-thirds of the 123 juveniles serving LWOP for non-homicide crimes.

Graham rested on three features—offender, offense, and sentence. It reiterated *Roper's* rationale that juveniles' reduced culpability warranted less severe penalties than those imposed on adults convicted of the same crime. Unlike *Roper*, *Graham* explicitly based young offenders' diminished responsibility on developmental and neuroscience research. "[D]evelopments in psychology and brain science continue to show fundamental differences between juvenile and adult minds. For example, parts of the brain involved in behavior control continue to mature through late adolescence."[136]

Focusing on the offense, *Graham* invoked the Court's felony-murder death penalty decisions and concluded that even the most serious non-homicide crimes "cannot be compared to murder in their 'severity and irrevocability.'"[137] The combination of diminished responsibility and a non-homicide crime made an LWOP sentence grossly disproportional. "[W]hen compared to an adult murderer, a juvenile offender who did not kill or intend to kill has a twice diminished moral culpability. The age of the offender and the nature of the crime each bear on the analysis."[138]

Finally, the Court equated an LWOP sentence for a juvenile with the death penalty—"the sentence alters the offender's life by a forfeiture that is irrevocable" and denies any hope of release.[139] *Graham* found no penal rationale—retribution, deterrence, incapacitation, or rehabilitation—justified the penultimate sanction for non-homicide juvenile offenders. While incapacitation might reduce future offending, judges could not predict at sentencing whether a juvenile would remain incorrigible or pose a future danger to society. Most states denied vocational training or rehabilitative services to youths sentenced to LWOP in favor of those who might return to the community.[140]

As in *Roper*, the majority and dissenting Justices in *Graham* differed on whether to bar LWOP for non-homicide juveniles categorically or allow judges to impose LWOP on a case-by-case basis. The majority ruled categorically and denied trial judges the option. *Graham* reiterated *Roper's* misgivings about clinicians' ability to distinguish between most juveniles who would change and the few who might remain incorrigible. *Graham* also recognized that youths' immaturity increased judges' risks of error in assessing culpability.

[T]he features that distinguish juveniles from adults also put them at a significant disadvantage in criminal proceedings. Juveniles mistrust adults and have limited understandings of the criminal justice system and the roles of the institutional actors within it. They are less likely than adults to work effectively with their lawyers to aid in their defense. Difficulty in weighing long-term consequences; a corresponding impulsiveness; and reluctance to trust defense counsel seen as part of the adult world a rebellious youth rejects, all can lead to poor decisions . . . [and] impair the quality of a juvenile defendant's representation.[141]

As I explain in Chapter 9, developmental differences impair youths' competence to exercise rights, ability to work with counsel, and capacity to make legal decisions.[142]

Although *Graham* adopted a categorical rule, it gave the 123 youths convicted of non-homicide crimes and serving LWOP sentences very limited relief. It required states only to provide "some meaningful opportunity to obtain release based on demonstrated maturity and rehabilitation."[143] It did not prescribe states' responsibility to provide resources with which to change or specify when youths might become eligible for parole. Parole consideration would not guarantee young offenders' release and some might remain confined for life.[144]

Justice Thomas's dissent criticized the *Graham* majority for repudiating the Court's "death is different" jurisprudence.[145] He argued that trial judges could balance a crime's seriousness with a youth's diminished responsibility and decide individually whether LWOP was warranted. He chided the majority for failing to define what a meaningful opportunity to demonstrate maturity was or when it would occur.[146] He observed that barring LWOP sentences for non-homicide offenders but permitting it for juveniles who murdered was disproportionality based on offenses rather than offenders.

Miller v. Alabama—"Children Are Different"

When the Court decided *Miller v. Alabama*, forty-two states permitted judges to impose LWOP sentences on any offender—adult or juvenile—convicted of murder.[147] In twenty-nine states, LWOP sentences were mandatory for those convicted murder. Mandatory sentences precluded consideration of actors' culpability or degree of participation, and equated juveniles' criminal responsibility with adults. Courts regularly upheld mandatory LWOP and extremely long sentences imposed on youths as young as twelve or thirteen years of age.[148] One of six juveniles who received an LWOP sentence was fifteen years or younger; for more than half (59%), it was their first-ever conviction.[149] States may not execute a felony-murderer who did not kill or intend to kill, but one-quarter to one-half of juveniles who received LWOP sentences were convicted as accessories to a felony-murder.[150] Although *Eddings, Thompson,* and *Roper* viewed youthfulness as a mitigating factor, many trial judges treated it as an aggravating factor and sentenced young murderers more severely than adults convicted of murder.[151]

Prior to the 1970s, few states imposed LWOP sentences and most relied on indeterminate sentences and parole release.[152] In the 1970s, states resumed executions *and* expanded LWOP sentences.[153] During the Get Tough Era, states enacted mandatory and LWOP sentences to restrict judges' discretion and eliminated parole boards.[154] Death penalty abolitionists supported LWOP sentences as an alternative to execution and by 2005, forty-eight states and the District of Columbia enacted them.[155] Despite states' adoption of LWOP sentences, the number of murderers sentenced to death remained stable and judges imposed LWOP sentences on many defendants who would not have been death-eligible, for example, felony-murderers. Between 1992 and 2003, the number of inmates on death row rose from 2,575 to 3,374—a 31% increase—while the number of prisoners who received LWOP sentences grew from 12,453 to 33,633—a 170% increase.[156] By 2008, the number of LWOPs had increased to 41,095, a 330% increase.[157]

In 2004, 2,225 people were serving LWOP sentences for crimes they committed as juveniles and the number rose to 2,500 by 2009.[158] Prior to 1980, judges rarely sentenced children to LWOP; now they impose LWOPs on youths three times as often as they did in 1990.[159] Sixteen was the average age at which juveniles committed the crimes for which they received LWOP, but judges imposed them on many younger children as well.[160] Judges impose LWOP on Black juveniles at higher rates than they do white youths and they comprise 60% of all youths serving LWOP.[161] Black youths who killed a white victim were twice as likely to receive LWOP as white youths who killed a Black person.[162]

Miller v. Alabama extended *Roper* and *Graham* and banned *mandatory* LWOP for youths convicted of murder.[163] Although Justice Thomas's *Graham* dissent claimed that the majority ruled on categories of crimes rather than characteristics of offenders, Justice Kagan responded that "none of what it said about children—about their distinctive (and transitory) mental traits and environmental vulnerabilities—is crime specific."[164] She postulated that "[t]he concept of proportionality is central to the Eighth Amendment," and precludes "sentencing practices based on mismatches between the culpability of a class of offenders and the severity of a penalty."[165]

Graham equated a non-homicide LWOP sentence with the death penalty. *Miller* invoked death penalty cases that barred *mandatory* capital sentences and required an individualized culpability assessment before a judge could impose LWOP on a juvenile murderer.[166] *Miller* noted that in the fifteen states in which judges had discretion to impose LWOP sentences, only 15% of youths received them, but in the twenty-nine states in which it was mandatory, 85% received them. Justice Kagan emphasized that "children are constitutionally different from adults for purposes of sentencing" and "mandatory penalties, by their nature, preclude a sentence from taking account of an offender's age and the wealth of characteristics and circumstances attendant to it."[167] The Court asserted that once judges considered a youth's diminished responsibility individually, very few cases would warrant LWOP. "[W]e think appropriate occasions for sentencing juveniles to this harshest possible penalty will be uncommon."[168]

Justice Thomas's *Miller* dissent argued that *Harmelin v. Michigan* upheld mandatory LWOP for an adult.[169] Justice Kagan responded that sentences valid for adults could be unconstitutional applied to children. "We have by now held on multiple occasions that a sentencing rule permissible for adults may not be so for children. . . . So if (as *Harmelin* recognized) 'death is different,' children are different too."[170] Chief Justice Roberts's dissent argued that no national consensus against mandatory LWOP sentences existed because most states approved them for adult *and* juvenile murderers.[171] Justice Kagan responded that *Miller* did not preclude LWOP for a juvenile murderer, but required individualized assessment and consideration of youthfulness.[172] The Court reiterated concerns expressed in *Thompson v. Oklahoma* that interaction of transfer statutes and LWOP laws could produce harsher results than legislators intended because many states excluded youths charged with murder.[173] The Court in *Roper*, *Graham*, and *Miller* recognized what get tough legislators did not—"children are different"—and halted the most extreme sanctions.

Miller required judges to conduct individualized assessments and consider youthful mitigation. Like *Graham*'s ambiguous instruction to provide a meaningful opportunity to obtain release, *Miller* did not give legislators or judges practical guidance how to conduct individualized culpability assessments or consider youthfulness in sentencing decisions.

The Uncertain Meaning of *Graham* and *Miller*: Confusion and Contradiction

The Court's recognition that children are different reflected a belated corrective to states' punitive excesses, but its Eighth Amendment authority to regulate their sentencing policies is very limited. *Graham* and *Miller* raised as many questions as they answered. After *Miller* held mandatory LWOP unconstitutional, would courts apply the rule retroactively to more than twenty-five hundred youths sentenced prior to the decision? *Miller* did not categorically ban LWOP sentences for juvenile murderers, so how should states' sentencing laws frame culpability assessments? What factors should judges consider when they make individualized evaluations? Does *Miller*'s ban on mandatory LWOP apply to other mandatory sentences for juveniles? Does *Graham*'s prohibition on LWOP for youths convicted of non-homicide crimes apply to those who receive very long or consecutive sentences that exceed their life expectancy? Are states obligated to provide rehabilitative resources to give youths a meaningful opportunity to change? States' contradictory answers to these questions require a clearer approach to youth sentencing policy.

Retroactivity

When the Court announces a new constitutional rule as in *Miller*, it must decide whether to apply it retroactively to youths who previously received sentences now deemed invalid. About twenty-five hundred prisoners had received mandatory LWOP for murders committed as juveniles and some had been confined for decades.[174] The Court hesitates to apply new constitutional rules retroactively because of concerns about undermining finality of judgments, federalism, and risks of overturning convictions that states could not prosecute years later.[175] Its retroactivity jurisprudence distinguishes between defendants who raise a constitutional issue on direct appeal and those who seek collateral relief through habeas corpus proceedings after their convictions have become final.[176] Its retroactivity doctrine also distinguishes between substantive rules—those that more narrowly interpret the scope of a criminal statute or place particular conduct beyond the state's power to punish—and procedural rules—constitutionally infirm procedures that merely raise the possibility of an erroneous conviction.[177]

After *Miller*, dozens of state and federal appellate courts considered whether it was a substantive or procedural ruling.[178] When the Court resolved the issue in 2016, twelve state courts had applied *Miller* retroactively as a substantive rule and five state and federal appellate courts held that it was a procedural rule and denied retroactive application.[179] *Montgomery v. Louisiana* resolved lower courts' conflicting decisions, held that *Miller* announced a substantive rule, and ruled that youths who received a mandatory LWOP prior to *Miller* would be eligible for resentencing or parole consideration.[180] *Montgomery* concluded that "[p]rotection against disproportionate punishment is the central substantive guarantee of the Eighth Amendment and goes far beyond the manner of determining a defendant's sentence."[181] *Montgomery* concluded that applying *Miller* retroactively would not undermine the finality of youths' convictions or require states to relitigate every sentence. "A State may remedy a *Miller* violation by permitting juvenile homicide offenders to be considered for parole, rather than by resentencing them."[182]

Individualized Culpability Assessments: Judicial and Legislative Criteria

What factors should sentencing laws and trial judges consider to make culpability assessments and decide whether or not to impose LWOP? *Miller* gave lawmakers and judges minimal guidance. The factors it described—age, immaturity, impetuosity, family and home environment, circumstances of and degree of participation in the offense, youthful incompetence, and amenability to treatment—give expression to judges' subjective discretion.[183] State courts' interpretations of *Miller* vary substantially. Some direct judges to consider "*Miller factors*," or "factors in mitigation," while others provide comprehensive lists of factors.[184] The California Supreme Court in *Gutierrez v. People* analyzed *Miller's* criteria and directed sentencing judges how to fully consider each factor.[185] One court summarized the *Miller* inquiry and concluded that "the enumerated factors are not ends in themselves but rather are, when considered together in a reasoned manner, the useful and necessary means by which a sentencing court must determine whether transient immaturity requires some degree of leniency or irreparable corruption must be punished as severely as possible."[186] While *Roper* and *Graham* emphasized that "children are different," *Miller* enables judges to decide that "this kid is different," emphasize callousness, maturity, or dangerousness, and impose the harshest penalty. *Miller* is difficult to implement fairly and consistently because "the framework is based on subjective criteria, whereby judges must somehow decide based on very limited evidence whether juvenile offenders have adult capacities."[187] Without clear guidelines and appellate control, judges are unlikely to recognize youths' reduced culpability.

Miller required twenty-nine states to revise mandatory LWOP statutes and provide individualized assessments.[188]

> Some states have heeded the call of the *Miller* Court and have comprehensively reconsidered LWOP and extreme custodial sentences as they apply to children. To begin, nine states have abolished juvenile LWOP, and three more have banned it for some categories of juveniles. . . . On the other end of the spectrum, some states have missed the mark by replacing mandatory juvenile LWOP with another mandatory juvenile sentence and, in some cases, still leaving juveniles exposed to an LWOP sentence. For example, two states have enacted post-*Miller* legislation that replaces mandatory LWOP with a mandatory minimum of 40 years for juveniles convicted of homicide. Other states have imposed similarly steep mandatory minimums and still permit juvenile LWOP. . . . Of the 13 states that have passed legislation in response to Miller, nine still permit juvenile LWOP, and none set an alternative minimum sentence at less than 25 years.[189]

Some states adopted *Miller* factors for a judges to consider.[190] A few states abolished juvenile LWOP sentences entirely; others replaced them with sentences ranging from twenty-five years to life with periodic reviews, or determinate sentences of forty years to life.[191] The Iowa Supreme Court in *State v. Sweet* categorically prohibited imposition of LWOP on juveniles convicted of murder because there was no basis on which a judge at the time of sentencing could determine that a youth would be forever incorrigible.[192] Other states provide age-tiered minimum sentences for parole consideration—twenty-five years for youths fourteen or younger convicted of murder; thirty-five years for those fifteen or older.[193] None of these legislative changes approximate the American Law Institute's Model Penal Code recommendations that juveniles should be eligible for parole consideration after ten years.[194]

Life without Parole vs. Lengthy Aggregate Sentences

Graham barred LWOP for juveniles convicted of a non-homicide crimes, but many more youths are serving de facto life sentences—aggregated mandatory minima or consecutive terms totaling 50–100 years or more—than those formally sentenced to LWOP.[195] Do consecutive or multiple sentences for non-homicide crimes equal an LWOP sentence that violates the Eighth Amendment? The California Supreme Court in *People v. Caballero* found that a 110-year-to-life sentence imposed on a juvenile convicted of several non-homicide offenses did not provide a meaningful opportunity to obtain release.[196] The Iowa Supreme Court in *State v. Null* held that a 52-year minimum sentence based on aggregated mandatory sentences violated *Miller* because "an offender sentenced to a lengthy term-of-years sentence should not be worse off than an offender sentenced to life in prison without parole who has the benefit of an individualized hearing under *Miller*."[197] *Null* also held that long mandatory minimum violated *Graham* because "The prospect of geriatric release, if one is to be afforded the opportunity for release at all, does not provide a 'meaningful opportunity' to demonstrate . . . 'maturity and rehabilitation' . . . ."[198]

By contrast, other courts read *Graham* narrowly, limit its holding to formal LWOP sentences, and uphold consecutive terms that exceed youths' life expectancy. *Bunch v. Smith* reasoned that *Graham* involved an LWOP sentence for a single crime and "did not clearly establish that consecutive, fixed-term sentences for juveniles who commit multiple nonhomicide offenses are unconstitutional when they amount to the practical equivalent of life without parole."[199]

Non-Homicide Mandatory Sentences

Although *Miller* required an individualized culpability assessment, Chief Justice Roberts's dissent observed that there is "no clear reason that [*Miller's*] principle would not bar all mandatory sentences for juveniles or any juvenile sentence as harsh as what a similarly situated adult would receive."[200] State courts divide over whether *Miller* applies to mandatory sentences that preclude consideration of youthful mitigation. Several post-*Miller* courts have approved twenty-five-year mandatory minimum sentences without any individualized culpability assessments.[201] By contrast, the Iowa Supreme Court in *State v. Lyle* found all mandatory minimum sentences violated the state constitution.[202] *Lyle* found no reason to prohibit mandatory sentences for murder but to deny judges' discretion to consider mitigating evidence when sentencing juveniles for other crimes.[203]

Mandatory Waiver

In Chapter 5, I likened judicial transfer to the death penalty because of its low incidence, standardless discretion, repudiation of youthfulness, and inconsistency with juvenile courts' rehabilitative premises. After *Furman v. Georgia* condemned discretionary capital punishment, states adopted mandatory death penalty provisions, which *Woodson v. North Carolina* struck down as too rigid and inflexible. *Miller* relied on *Woodson* to require individualized consideration of youthful mitigating factors. Does *Miller's* prohibition of mandatory LWOP apply to transfer provisions—offense exclusion and prosecutorial direct file—that do not provide individualized assessments? *Miller's* observation that "criminal procedure laws that fail to take defendants' youthfulness into account at all would be flawed" may preclude automatic transfer laws.[204] Offense exclusion is a mandatory sentence—the offense charged equals automatic adulthood. Prosecutorial direct file is not just a charging decision

THE CRIMINAL IS A KID | 217

but a sentencing decision made without any standards, knowledge of a juvenile's circumstances, formal reasons, or appellate review. Just as the Court's death penalty jurisprudence allows a defendant to present mitigating evidence to a judge to avoid execution, "a juvenile facing transfer should be able to present mitigating evidence to spare him a permanent disbarment from the benefits of childhood."[205]

Access to Rehabilitative Services

Graham required states to provide juveniles with a "meaningful opportunity to obtain release based on demonstrated maturity and rehabilitation."[206] But many states abolished parole boards and others required inmates to serve substantial fractions of fixed-term sentences before eligibility for release.[207] *Graham* required states to reinstate some discretionary release. Although parole will not always be granted, it expected that most youths would be released at some point. The Court remitted to states the responsibility to develop procedures for compliance and to provide a meaningful opportunity to obtain release. State correctional systems typically denied juveniles serving life sentences access to counseling, education, and rehabilitation programs in favor of those eligible for parole. *Graham* provides a modest nudge to improve conditions of confinement and provide rehabilitative services, because absent some affirmative obligation, the Court's injunction would be meaningless.

Youth Discount

There is a straightforward alternative to the confusion and contradiction reviewed above. States should formally incorporate youthfulness as a mitigating factor in sentencing statutes. *Roper, Graham,* and *Miller* affirm that youthful mitigation applies both to capital and non-capital sentences.[208] Youths who produce the same harms as adults are not their moral equals and do not deserve the same consequences.[209] Youthful mitigation does not excuse criminality, holds juveniles accountable for their crimes, but proportions punishment to their diminished responsibility.[210] Other countries routinely recognize youthfulness as a mitigating factor as a "principle of fundamental justice."[211]

Categorical Recognition of Youthful Mitigation

Despite the Court's preference for individualized culpability assessments, *Roper* and *Graham* adopted a categorical prohibition because "[t]he differences between juvenile and adult offenders are too well marked and well understood to risk allowing a youthful person to receive the death penalty despite insufficient culpability."[212] The Court feared that a judge or jury could not properly consider youthful mitigation when confronted with an especially brutal or heinous crime. Because clinicians cannot accurately distinguish between the vast majority of immature juveniles who deserve leniency and the rare youth who might possess adult-like culpability, it would not allow a jury to do so.

The Court in *Miller*, Chief Justice Roberts's concurrence in *Graham*, and the dissenting Justices in all three cases advocated for individualized assessments. *Roper and Graham* endorsed categorical rule rather than guided discretion even though the Justices recognized individual variability in culpability.[213] The Court reasoned that a rule which occasionally "under-punishes the rare, fully-culpable adolescent still will produce less aggregate injustice than a discretionary system that improperly, harshly sentences many more undeserving youths."[214]

The seriousness of a crime reflects the blameworthiness of the actor's choice to cause harm.[215] Adolescents' deficits of judgment and self-control reflect common developmental processes and should provide categorical reductions of all adult sentences.[216]

There are two reasons to prefer a categorical rule over individualized discretion.[217] First, judges and legislators cannot define or identify what constitutes adult-like culpability. Culpability is not an objectively measurable thing, but a subjective judgment about criminal responsibility.[218] Development is highly variable—a few youths may achieve competencies prior to eighteen years of age, while many others may not attain maturity even as adults.[219] Despite individual developmental differences, clinicians lack tools with which to assess youths' impulsivity, foresight, and preference for risk, or a metric by which to relate maturity of judgment with criminal responsibility.[220] The inability to define, measure, or diagnose immaturity or validly to identify a few responsible youths could introduce a systematic bias toward overpunishing less culpable juveniles.[221] When there is no objective basis on which to exercise individualized discretion, case-by-case assessments are error prone, likely to reflect factors other than immaturity, contribute to racial disparities, and overpunish less blameworthy youths.[222] The law uses age-based categorical lines to approximate the level of maturity required for particular activities—voting, driving, and consuming alcohol—and restricts youths without individualized assessments of their maturity or ability to make competent decisions.[223]

The second reason to adopt a categorical rule of youthful mitigation is judges' or juries' inability to fairly weigh the abstraction of diminished responsibility against the aggravating reality of a horrific crime.[224] *Roper* rightly feared that jurors could not distinguish between a person's diminished responsibility for causing a harm and the harm itself, and the heinousness of a crime trumped reduced culpability.[225] When courts sentence minority offenders, unconscious racial stereotypes compound the difficulties of assessing immaturity.[226] Although *Miller* requires individualized culpability assessments, states' conflicting and inadequate responses require a more workable alternative. Treating youthfulness categorically is a more efficient way to address immaturity because every juvenile exhibits some degree of diminished responsibility.[227]

Age as a Proxy for Diminished Responsibility

The abstract meaning of culpability, the inability to measure or compare moral agency of youths, the administrative complexity of individualization, and the tendency to overweigh harm require a clear-cut alternative. A categorical Youth Discount would give all adolescents fractional reductions in sentence lengths based on age as a proxy for culpability.[228] While age may be an incomplete proxy for maturity or culpability, no better bases exist on which to distinguish among young offenders.[229] *Miller* recognized that same-length sentences exact a greater penal bite from younger offenders than older ones.[230] Imprisonment *per se* is more developmentally disruptive and onerous for adolescents than adults.[231]

A statutory Youth Discount would require a judge to give substantial reductions to youths off the sentence an adult convicted of the same crime would receive. It creates a sliding scale of diminished responsibility and gives the largest reductions to the youngest offenders.[232] If tried as an adult, a fourteen-year-old would receive a sentence substantially shorter than those an adult would receive—perhaps 10% or 20% of the adult length. A sixteen-year-old would receive a maximum sentence no more than one-third or one-half the adult length. Deeper discounts for younger offenders correspond with their greater developmental differences in judgment and self-control. A youth would need only a birth certificate to establish her eligibility for and the amount of discount. A judge can more easily apply a Youth Discount in states that uses sentencing guidelines under which the present offense and prior record dictate presumptive sentences. In less structured sentencing systems, a judge would have to determine the going rate or appropriate sentence for an adult convicted of that offense and then reduce it by the Youth Discount.

The Youth Discount's diminished responsibility rationale would preclude mandatory, LWOP, or de facto life sentences for young offenders.[233] LWOP is inherently indeterminate. For youths convicted of an offense for which an adult would receive LWOP, states should apply a Youth Discount to a presumptive sentence of forty years—the average age at which adult murderers enter prison and their shorter life expectancy.[234] A Youth Discount recognizes that recidivism decreases with age while the costs of confining geriatric inmates increases.[235] Although some legislators may find it difficult to resist penal demagoguery, states can achieve all of their legitimate penal goals by sentencing youths to a maximum of no more than twenty or twenty-five years for even the most serious crimes. The American Law Institute's Model Penal Code recommends that

> [n]o sentence of imprisonment longer than [25] years may be imposed for any offense or combination of offenses. For offenders under the age of 16 at the time of commission of their offenses, no sentences of imprisonment longer that [20] years may be imposed. For offenders under the age of 14 at the time of commission of their offenses, no sentence of imprisonment longer than [10] years may be imposed.[236]

Several juvenile justice analysts and policy groups have endorsed the Youth Discount as a straightforward way to proportionally reduce sentences for younger offenders. David Tanenhaus and Steven Drizin "endorse Feld's proposals [for a youth discount] because they respect the notion that juveniles are developmentally different than adults and that these differences make juveniles both less culpable for their crimes and less deserving of the harsh sanctions, which now must be imposed on serious and violent adult offenders."[237] In *Rethinking Juvenile Justice*, Elizabeth Scott and Laurence Steinberg conclude that "[p]roportionality supports imposing statutory limits on the maximum duration of adult sentences impose[d] on juveniles—a 'youth discount,' to use Feld's term."[238] The Reporter's Note to the Model Penal Code § 6.11A acknowledges that the framework of its recommendation for "specialized sentencing rules and mitigated treatment of juvenile offenders sentenced in adult courts, owes much" to Feld's proposal for a Youth Discount—"a sliding scale of developmental and criminal responsibility." The National Institute of Justice sponsored a study group that concluded that "[y]ouths' diminished responsibility requires mitigated sanctions to avoid permanently life-changing penalties and provide room to reform."[239]

The American Bar Association condemned juvenile LWOP sentences and proposed that statutes formally recognize youthfulness as a mitigating factor and provide for earlier parole release consideration.[240] The American Law Institute's revised Model Penal Code states that when judges sentence offenders convicted of crimes committed prior to the age of eighteen, "the offender's age shall be a mitigating factor, to be assigned greater weight for offenders of younger ages,"[241] and that youth sanctions should rehabilitate and reintegrate young offenders rather than simply punish them.

Although a small subset of chronic or life-course persistent offenders pose a risk of future offending, *Roper* observed that "it is difficult even for expert psychologists to differentiate between the juvenile offender whose crime reflects unfortunate but transient immaturity, and the rare juvenile offender whose crime reflects irreparable corruption."[242] *Graham* and *Miller* reaffirmed judges' inability to identify future high-risk individuals at the time of their trial and sentencing.

Proportionality is a retributive concept, not a utilitarian one. *Roper, Graham,* and *Miller* rest firmly on retributive grounds—reduced culpability—and examined and disposed of utilitarian arguments.[243] Accordingly, there is no basis on which to disregard the mitigating role of youthfulness or to allow judges to incapacitate some youths based on speculation they might be life-course persistent offenders.

Roper, Graham, and *Miller* emphasized that juveniles' personalities are more transitory and less fixed than adults', their crimes provide less reliable evidence of "irretrievably depraved character," and "a greater possibility exists that a minor's character deficiencies will be reformed."[244] Adolescence is a period of rapid growth and transition and youths change more quickly and to a greater degree in the years following a crime than older offenders. Some criminal offending is normal for adolescents, major interventions may be unnecessary, and punitive sanctions may be counterproductive.[245] Although crime rates increase rapidly among teenage males, their desistance rates are equally high as they mature into their early twenties and most will outgrow delinquency.[246] The Progressives recognized a century ago that youths in adult institutions are vulnerable to victimization, at greater risk of psychological harm and suicide, and more likely to reoffend in the future.

A Youth Discount enables young offenders to survive serious mistakes with a semblance of their life chances intact.[247] We can hold them accountable, manage the risks they pose, and provide them with a meaningful opportunity to reform without extinguishing their lives.[248] A young person who committed a terrible crime at fourteen or fifteen is a very different person than the adult who remains incarcerated decades later. Because youths eventually will return to the community, states should provide resources with which to reform them as they mature.

Conclusion

Roper, Graham, and *Miller*'s diminished responsibility rationale recognizes youthfulness as a mitigating factor. Adolescents deserve shorter sentences than adults when they cause the same harms because of their reduced culpability. It is unjust and irrational to continue harshly punishing a fifty- or sixty-year-old person for a crime that an irresponsible child committed many decades earlier. *Roper* and *Graham* used age as a proxy for culpability because no better, more reliable or accurate bases exist on which to individualize youths' sentences. Culpability is a normative construct. It is not an objective thing and there are no tools with which to measure how much culpability a youth possesses. Proportioning culpability is a moral judgment about deserved punishment. *Roper* and *Graham* feared that individualized culpability judgments would create a systematic bias and that judges would treat youthfulness as an aggravating rather than mitigating factor.

The Supreme Court has reached the limit of what it can accomplish through the Eighth Amendment to ameliorate harsh sentences for children. A Youth Discount provides a reasonable approximation of "what any parent knows"—kids are different and do stupid and dangerous things because they are kids. The amount by which to discount youths' sentences is a legislative policy choice, but states can achieve legitimate penal goals with maximum sentences of twenty or twenty-five years for even the most serious crimes. It will take political courage for legislators to enact laws that recognize young offenders' diminished responsibility. It will take bravery when a political opponent may charge a legislator with being soft on crime. The legislators who enacted unjust, disproportionate, and counterproductive transfer and sentencing laws must undo the damage they caused and adopt sensible laws for children.

9

The Defendant Is a Kid

Adolescents' Competence to Exercise Procedural Rights

A half century ago, the Supreme Court in *Kent v. United States* observed that "the child receives the worst of both worlds: he gets neither the protections accorded to adults nor the solicitous care and regenerative treatment postulated for children."[1] In Chapter 5, I argued that get tough changes have transformed juvenile courts' nominally "rehabilitative treatment" into sanctions that closely resemble criminal punishment. Here, I argue that delinquents do not receive the criminal procedural protections afforded adults prior to punishment. Two competing images of youth influence court procedures and assure that they receive the worst of both worlds. Judges and legislators sometimes depict young people as vulnerable children who need special safeguards to protect themselves from their own immaturity. At other times, they portray youths as mature and responsible and treat them just like adults. When policy makers choose between competing images of immaturity and responsibility, they ignore developmental differences that would justify stronger safeguards for youths. Instead, they treat juveniles just like adults when formal equality results in practical inequality and in other instances use juvenile court procedures that provide fewer protections than criminal defendants enjoy. These contradictory views raise questions about adolescents' competence to exercise rights and the reliability of court judgments. The answers implicate the accuracy of fact-finding, the quality of justice, the legitimacy of collateral consequences, and the dangers of wrongful convictions.

This chapter examines juvenile court procedures and youths' competence to exercise rights: *Miranda* rights, competence to stand trial, access to counsel, and jury trial. The first section briefly reviews policy makers' conflicted views of juveniles' competence to exercise rights, *Gault's* rationale to provide procedural safeguards, and the impetus it gave to divert and handle offenders informally. The second section analyzes juveniles' exercise of *Miranda* rights. It contrasts states' use of adult legal standards with psychological research that describes juveniles' questionable competence and vulnerability during interrogation. The third section reviews legal standards and developmental research on adolescents' competence to stand trial. The fourth section examines juveniles' competence to waive counsel, the impact of waivers on delivery of legal services, and appellate courts' inability to oversee justice administration. The fifth section examines juveniles' right to a jury trial. *McKeiver*'s denial of a jury undermines accurate fact-finding, makes it easier to convict delinquents than criminal defendants, and heightens risks of wrongful convictions. States use those flawed convictions to punish delinquents, to enhance criminal sentences, and to impose collateral consequences.

Competing Conceptions of Juveniles' Competence and Procedural Rights

A century ago, Progressive reformers created juvenile courts to divert children from criminal courts and to treat rather than punish them. Envisioned as a welfare agency, juvenile courts rejected criminal procedural safeguards and dispensed with formalities like lawyers, juries, and rules of evidence.[2] Questions about children's competence to stand trial or to exercise rights seldom arose because of delinquency proceedings' informality and welfare orientation.

In 1967, *In re Gault* began to transform the juvenile court from a social welfare agency into a more formal legal institution.[3] The Court emphasized juvenile courts' criminal elements—youths charged with crimes facing institutional confinement, stigma of delinquency labels and records, judicial arbitrariness, and high rates of recidivism—and required proof of guilt using fair procedures. Although *Gault* did not adopt adult procedural protections, it precipitated an operational convergence between juvenile and criminal courts. Progressive reformers depicted children as immature and rejected procedures, but *Gault* viewed delinquents as competent to exercise rights in an adversarial process. Subsequent decisions further emphasized delinquency proceedings' criminal character. *In re Winship* required states to prove delinquency beyond a reasonable doubt rather than by the civil standard of proof.[4] *Breed v. Jones* posited a functional similarity between juvenile and criminal trials and applied the Fifth Amendment's double jeopardy clause to delinquency prosecutions.[5] However, *McKeiver v. Pennsylvania* denied delinquents a jury trial and rejected procedural parity between delinquency and criminal proceedings.[6] Get tough changes have eroded *McKeiver*'s rationale and denial of a jury adversely affects accurate fact-finding and the presence and performance of counsel, and increases the likelihood of wrongful convictions.[7]

Progressives created juvenile courts to divert youths from the criminal justice system. *Gault*'s greater procedural formality increased the administrative burden of adjudicating delinquents and provided impetus to divert some youths from juvenile courts. Formal procedures pose no impediment to juvenile courts' diversionary mission to protect youths from the harms inflicted by criminal courts, jails, and prisons.[8] But enhanced safeguards could impede their ability to intervene with some youths for whom the state lacked adequate proof of guilt.

In 1967, the President's Crime Commission issued reports contemporaneously with *Gault* that proposed a two-track juvenile justice system—one informal, the other formal—for minor and serious offenders. It advised consensual, diversionary, and informal handling of less serious delinquents and status offenders.[9] Those proposals reflected criminologists' concerns that juvenile courts stigmatized and labeled delinquents and supported their calls for judicious nonintervention in response to most miscreants.[10] The Crime Commission's recommendation for a more formal juvenile court recognized that they intervened to control crime and protect the community and endorsed criminal procedural safeguards whenever the state proposed to remove a child from the home.[11]

Juvenile courts handle about half of the youths referred to them informally without filing a petition or proceeding to trial.[12] Court intake workers or prosecutors perform a triage function and conduct a rapid assessment to determine whether a youth's crime or welfare require formal juvenile court attention or can be discharged or referred to others for care. Diversion minimizes formal adjudication and provides supervision or services in the community. The original juvenile court diverted youths from criminal courts. In its current guise, diversion shifts youths who might otherwise enter the system from juvenile courts. Proponents of diversion contend that it is an efficient gate-keeping mechanism, avoids labeling minor offenders, and provides flexible access to community resources that referral after a formal process might delay. Because most youths desist after one or two contacts, it allows them to distinguish by recidivism those who need more formal controls and conserves judicial resources for those cases.

Critics of diversion contend that it widens the net of social control and exposes youths to informal supervision whom juvenile courts otherwise might have ignored. Probation officers or prosecutors who do preliminary screening of cases make low-visibility decisions that are not subject to judicial or appellate review. Many states do not use formal screening or assessment tools and discretion at intake constitutes the most significant source of racial disparities in case processing.[13] The criteria and administration of diversion raise many significant policy concerns. But cases handled informally do not raise the procedural issues of formal adjudication and seldom result in out-of-home placements that would require greater legal safeguards.

During the Get Tough Era, states adopted harsh policies that equated the crimes and culpability of adolescents with those of adults. In Chapter 5, I analyzed juvenile courts' sentencing policies and practices, identified the differences between treatment and punishment, emphasized that they penalized delinquents, and increased youths' needs for protection from the state. Progressive reformers assumed that children were incompetent and used informal procedures. *Gault* made delinquency hearings more formal, complex, and legalistic and required youths to participate in and make difficult decisions. Developmental psychologists question whether younger juveniles possess competence to stand trial and whether adolescents have the ability to exercise *Miranda* rights or to waive counsel. The developmental psychological research reviewed in Chapter 8 indicates that younger and mid-teens exhibit substantial deficits in understanding, maturity of judgment, and competence compared with adults. Despite clear differences between youths and adults, the Court and most states do not provide additional safeguards to protect them from their immaturity and increase the likelihood of erroneous outcomes.

Procedural Fairness and Legal Socialization

Youths' interactions with the justice system can promote or undermine legal socialization and their likelihood to cooperate or comply with legal actors.[14] People's perception of justice depends on the legitimacy of the process that determines the outcome and not simply whether they win or lose. People are more likely to perceive a court experience as legitimate and abide by its rules if they feel the system treated them fairly.[15] Children's experience with or awareness of others' encounters with the law shape their attitudes toward authority and rules.[16] Procedural justice rests on the equality and consistency of the process, the system's respectful treatment of parties, their ability to participate in and affect outcomes, and the neutrality and fairness of the fact-finder.[17] Juveniles are critical consumers of justice and the ways that court personnel treat them affects their ideas about laws, their perceptions of the process, and their feelings of obligation to obey the law.[18] Juvenile courts' procedures disregard youths' developmental limitations, deviate from accepted criminal procedural norms, use processes that few adults charged with a crime and facing confinement would accept, and undermine delinquents' feelings of fair treatment.

Police Interrogation of Juveniles

Police interrogation raises difficult legal and policy questions about justice administration and the relationship between the individual and the state. These questions become more acute when police interview juveniles who may be more vulnerable to interrogative pressures. The Court has decided more cases about interrogating youths than any other issue of juvenile justice.[19] Although it repeatedly has questioned juveniles' ability to exercise *Miranda* rights or make voluntary statements, it does not require special procedures to protect them. Rather, *Fare v. Michael C.* endorsed the adult standard—knowing, intelligent, and voluntary—to gauge juveniles' *Miranda* waivers.[20]

The law treats juveniles just like adults when formal equality results in practical inequality. This section examines how courts think about youthfulness when police interrogate juveniles. In most jurisdictions, the law on the books equates juveniles with adults. It then reviews developmental psychological research on juveniles' competence to exercise *Miranda* rights which questions adolescents' ability to understand warnings or exercise them effectively. It examines the law in action—empirical research on how youths respond to interrogation practices designed for adults. It highlights how developmental immaturity and susceptibility to manipulation increase juveniles' likelihood to confess falsely. It concludes with proposals of policies to redress the imbalance between legal expectations and developmental limitations.

Questioning Juveniles: The Law on the Books

Supreme Court decisions about youth reflect competing images of immaturity and vulnerability versus maturity and responsibility. These conflicting images elicit rulings that support protectionist or liberationist policies. A protectionist stance provides children with additional safeguards to offset their immaturity or restricts their rights because of their presumed inability to exercise them responsibly. A liberationist perspective portrays youths as autonomous and adult-like and treats them like other responsible actors.[21]

In the decades prior to *Miranda*, the Court adopted a protectionist stance and cautioned trial judges to examine closely how youthfulness affected the voluntariness of confessions. *Haley v. Ohio* emphasized that a fifteen-year-old boy's age and inexperience increased his vulnerability and rendered his confession involuntary. "That which would leave a man cold and unimpressed can overawe and overwhelm a lad in his early teens. This is the period of great instability which the crisis of adolescence produces. . . . [W]e cannot believe that a lad of tender years is a match for the police in such a contest."[22] *Gallegos v. Colorado* found that age was a special circumstance that rendered a boy's confession involuntary. "[A] 14-year old boy, no matter how sophisticated . . . is not equal to the police in knowledge and understanding . . . and is unable to know how to protect his own interests or how to get the benefits of his constitutional rights. . . . Without some adult protection against this inequality, a 14-year old boy would not be able to know, let alone assert, such constitutional rights as he had."[23] *Haley* and *Gallegos* found youthfulness, lengthy questioning, and the absence of a lawyer or parent rendered confessions involuntary. They recognized that children are not the equals of adults and required an attorney or parent to offset their vulnerability.

In re Gault reiterated concern that youthfulness adversely affected juveniles' statements. The Court repeated that "admissions and confessions of juveniles require special caution" and reminded that "[e]ven greater protection might be required where juveniles are involved, since their immaturity and greater vulnerability place them at a greater disadvantage in their dealings with police."[24] Recall from Chapter 2, *Gault* granted delinquents most procedural rights—notice, hearing, counsel, and cross-examination—based on the Fourteenth Amendment Due Process Clause. However, it relied explicitly on the Fifth Amendment to give delinquents the privilege against self-incrimination. "It would be entirely unrealistic to carve out of the Fifth Amendment all statements by juveniles on the ground that these cannot lead to 'criminal' involvement. . . . [J]uvenile proceedings to determine 'delinquency,' which may lead to commitment to a state institution, must be regarded as 'criminal' for purposes of the privilege against self-incrimination."[25] It recognized that the Fifth Amendment contributes to accurate fact-finding *and* maintains the adversarial balance between and protects the individual from the state.

> The privilege against self-incrimination is, of course, related to the question of the safeguards necessary to assure that admissions or confessions are reasonably trustworthy, that they are not mere fruits of fear or coercion, but are reliable expressions of the truth. . . . One of its purposes is to *prevent the state*, whether by force or by psychological domination, from overcoming the mind and will of the person under investigation and depriving him of the freedom to decide whether to assist the state in securing his convictions.[26]

Gault assumed that youths could exercise rights and participate in the legal process.

Fare v. Michael C. departed from *Haley, Gallegos,* and *Gault's* concerns about youths' vulnerability. *Michael C.* involved a sixteen-year-old who had several prior arrests, served time in a juvenile facility, and requested his probation officer prior to interrogation. The Court decided *Michael C.* as a *Miranda* case rather than as a juvenile interrogation case and held that legal standard used to evaluate adults' waivers—"knowing, intelligent, and voluntary under the totality of the circumstances"—governed juveniles' waivers as well.[27] *Michael C.* reasoned that *Miranda* provided an objective basis to evaluate waivers, denied that children's developmental differences demanded special protections, and required them to assert rights clearly.[28]

Miranda provided that if police question a suspect who is in custody—arrested or "deprived of his freedom of action in any significant way"—they must administer a warning.[29] The Court in *J.D.B. v. North Carolina* considered whether a thirteen-year-old juvenile's age affected the *Miranda* custody analysis.[30] The Court concluded that age was an objective factor that would affect how a young person might experience restraint.[31] The Court noted that in other contexts it treated features of childhood such as susceptibility to influence or outside pressure as objective facts.[32] An officer who knew or should have known a youth's age could properly assess how that would affect her feeling of custody.[33] *J.D.B.* recognized that juveniles could feel restrained under circumstances in which an adult might not. *J.D.B.* drew on *Roper* and *Graham*'s diminished responsibility rationale to emphasize their immaturity, inexperience, and heightened vulnerability during interrogation.[34]

Despite *J.D.B.*'s renewed concern about youths' vulnerability, the vast majority of states use the same *Miranda* framework for juveniles and adults.[35] *Miranda* only requires that suspects understand the words of the warning and not collateral consequences of a waiver. Most states do not require a parent or lawyer to assist juveniles.[36] When trial judges evaluate *Miranda* waivers, they consider characteristics of the offender—age, education, IQ, and prior police contacts—and the context of interrogation—location, methods, and length of interrogation. The leading cases provide long lists of factors for trial judges to consider.[37] Appellate courts identify many relevant elements, do not assign controlling weight to any one variable, and defer to trial judges' decisions whether a juvenile made a valid waiver.[38] Without decisive factors, *Michael C.* provides no meaningful check on judges' discretion to find that youths waived their rights.[39] Many youths claim to understand their rights to avoid admitting they do not, but police and judges will not probe further to determine what they know.[40]

Once judges find a valid waiver, appellate courts can only overrule them if the decision was clearly erroneous or an abuse of discretion—a very high standard. Trial judges failed to recognize that juveniles' waivers were involuntary or confessions coerced or false even when DNA evidence subsequently exonerated them.[41] Judges regularly find valid waivers made by children as young as ten or eleven years of age, with limited intelligence or significant mental disorders, with no prior police contacts, and without parental assistance.[42]

About ten states presume that most juveniles lack capacity to waive *Miranda* and require a parent or other adult to assist them.[43] Adopting a categorical *per se* rule—parental presence—avoids after-the-fact review to assess whether immaturity undermined a youth's waiver. Some states require a parent for juveniles younger than fourteen years, presume that those fourteen or sixteen years or younger are incompetent to waive, or oblige police to offer older youths an opportunity to consult.[44] Most commentators endorse parental presence, even though many question the value of their participation.[45]

States that require parental presence make several questionable assumptions. They posit an identity of interests between parent and child. They assume that parents possess greater abilities to make legal decisions than do their children. They believe that a parent will improve a child's understanding, provide legal advice, mitigate danger of unreliable statements, reduce feelings of isolation, and lessen coercive influences.[46] Because most states do not record interviews, a parent can witness and assure the accuracy of any statement obtained.[47] They may assist police to assess a youth's understanding and competency. They provide the means through which youths might obtain counsel. In the more punitive juvenile system, courts acknowledge youths need additional safeguards to achieve functional parity with adults.[48]

These protectionist assumptions and policies may not be valid. Parents' and children's interests may conflict, for example, if the juvenile assaulted or stole from a parent, victimized another sibling, or the parent is a suspect.[49] Parents may have a financial conflict of interests if they have to pay for their child's attorney. They may have an emotional reaction to their child's current arrest or chronic trouble.[50] They may expect their children to tell the truth, urge them to stop lying, or physically threaten them to confess.[51] Parents may not understand legal rights or consequences of waiver any better than their children.[52]

The Court's "children are different" jurisprudence emphasized developmental characteristics that heighten youths' vulnerability in the interrogation room. Despite its repeated references to youth's immaturity, most states use adult standards to gauge juveniles' waivers. If youths differ from adults in understanding *Miranda*, conceiving of or exercising rights, or susceptibility to pressure, then the law establishes a standard that few can meet and enables states to take advantage of their limitations.

Developmental Psychology and Juveniles' Legal Understanding

Developmental psychologists question whether juveniles can meet an adult waiver standard. *Miranda* requires police to advise suspects of their rights, but some juveniles do not understand the words or concepts. *Miranda* did not require police to use specific language to convey the substance of the rights and police departments around the country report more than five hundred different versions of the warning.[53] Psychologists studied the vocabulary, concepts, and reading levels required to understand warnings and concluded that they exceed many adolescents' abilities.[54] Key words require an eighth-grade level of education and most juveniles thirteen years or younger cannot grasp their meaning.[55] Some concepts—such as a "right," the term "appointed" to secure counsel, and "waive"—require a high school education and reduce many youths' *Miranda* comprehension. Many juveniles cannot define critical words in the warning.[56] Special dumbed-down juvenile warnings are often even longer and more difficult to understand.[57] If a demanding reading level or verbal complexity makes a warning unintelligible, then it cannot serve its protective function.[58]

Juveniles' Understanding of Miranda

Psychologist Thomas Grisso has studied juveniles' exercise of *Miranda* for more than four decades. He reports that many, if not most, do not understand the warning well enough to make a valid waiver.[59] He conducted his research under benign conditions—as a researcher in a laboratory rather than an officer in an interrogation room—and used simple warnings that required only a sixth- or seventh-grade reading level. Under these favorable conditions, most adults understood the warnings, but the majority of juveniles did *not* understand well enough to make a valid waiver. Although age, intelligence, and prior arrests correlated with *Miranda* comprehension, more than half (55.3%) of juveniles, as contrasted with less than one-quarter (23.1%) of adults, did not understand at least one of the four warnings and only one-fifth (20.9%) of juveniles, as compared with twice as many adults (42.3%), grasped all four warnings.[60] Juveniles fifteen years of age or younger exhibited significantly poorer comprehension of *Miranda* rights, waived more readily, and confessed more frequently than did older youths.[61] Other research reports that older youths understand *Miranda* about as well as adults, but many younger juveniles do not understand the words or concepts.[62]

Grisso developed and validated instruments to measure adolescents' understanding of *Miranda*.[63] These instruments ask youths to paraphrase the four warnings, to define six key words—"right," "attorney," "consult," "appoint," "interrogation," and "entitle"—and to interpret different sentences that had the same meaning as those in the warning.[64] Juveniles consistently underperformed compared with adults and most frequently misunderstood their right to consult with an attorney and to have one present when police questioned them.[65] Although older juveniles understood comparably with adults, substantial minorities of both groups failed to grasp some of the warnings.[66]

Age-related improvements in intellectual and verbal ability, attention, and *Miranda* comprehension appear in other studies.[67] A review of research concluded that "the understanding of adolescents ages 15–17 with near-average levels of verbal intelligences tends not to have been inferior to that of adults. But youths of that age with IQ scores below 85, and average youth below age 14, performed much poorer, often misunderstanding two or more of the warnings."[68] Understanding correlated with age—younger juveniles understood *Miranda* warnings less well than did mid-adolescents. One study found that 58% of eleven- to thirteen-year-olds, 33.3% of fourteen- and fifteen-year-olds, and 7.8% of sixteen- and seventeen-year-olds failed to understand one or more of the *Miranda* warnings.[69] Another study found more confusion by youths—78% of eleven- to thirteen-year-olds, 62.7% of fourteen- and fifteen-year-olds, and 35.3% of sixteen- and seventeen-year-olds—in *Miranda* comprehension.[70] Adolescents with low IQs perform more poorly than adults with low IQs and delinquent youths typically have lower IQs than do adolescents in the general population.[71] Larger proportions of delinquent youths have low IQs *and* mental disorders which interact with and further impair understanding.[72] The higher prevalence of mental disorders compounds juveniles' cognitive limitations, although police are seldom able to assess youths' impairments when they question them.[73]

Even youths who understand *Miranda*'s words may be unable to exercise rights. Juveniles do not appreciate the function or importance of rights as well as adults and they are less competent defendants.[74] They have greater difficulty conceiving of a right as an absolute entitlement that they can exercise without adverse consequences.[75] Juveniles view rights as something that authorities allow them to do, but which may be unilaterally retracted or withheld.[76] They misconceive the lawyer's role and attorney-client confidentiality. Youths raised in poverty exhibit poorer understanding than do middle-class youths, "because children from lower socioeconomic backgrounds are less likely to grow up believing they are entitled to rights and may have fewer opportunities to try out social roles in which they are able to assert their rights."[77] Youths with poorer understanding of rights waived them at higher rates than those with better comprehension.[78]

Roper, *Graham*, and *Miller* emphasized youths' susceptibility to social influences as among the factors that reduced their culpability. *Miranda* characterized custodial interrogation as inherently compelling because police dominate the setting and create psychological pressures to comply.[79] The differing legal and social status of youths and adults render children questioned by authority figures more suggestible. We expect youths to answer questions posed by police, teachers, parents, and other adults; social expectations and children's lower status increase their vulnerability during interrogation.[80] Juveniles may waive rights and admit responsibility because they believe they must obey authority.[81] They acquiesce more readily to negative pressure or critical feedback and accede more willingly to suggestions.[82] They weigh the interviewer's approval more heavily than the negative consequences of falsely admitting responsibility.[83] They impulsively confess to end an interrogation, rather than consider long-term consequences.[84] Experimental research also indicates a heightened sensitivity to peer influences.[85] Younger adolescents who initially chose to remain silent changed their decision more often than older adolescents or adults when informed that a peer made the opposite choice.

The Court requires suspects to invoke *Miranda* rights clearly and unambiguously.[86] However, members of some groups of people—juveniles, females, and racial minorities—tend to speak indirectly or tentatively to avoid conflict with those in power.[87] *Davis v. United States* recognized that to require suspects to invoke rights clearly and unambiguously could prove problematic for some. "We recognize that requiring a clear assertion of the right to counsel might disadvantage some suspects who—because of fear, intimidation, lack of linguistic skills, or a variety of other reasons—will not clearly articulate their right to counsel although they actually want to have a lawyer present."[88] If a suspect thinks she has invoked her rights, but police disregard it as an ambiguous request, then she may feel overwhelmed by their indifference and succumb to further questioning. The Court demands a level of assertiveness contrary to the way most youths respond when confronted by police.

Police Interrogation of Juveniles: The Law in Action

Research on police interrogation reports that about 80% of adults and 90% of juveniles waive their *Miranda* rights.[89] The largest empirical study of juvenile interrogation reported that 92.8% waived.[90] Juveniles' higher waiver rates may reflect lack of understanding or inability to invoke *Miranda* effectively.[91] As with adults, youths with prior felony arrests invoked their rights more often than those with fewer or less serious police contacts. Several factors likely contribute to experienced juveniles' higher rates of invocations. Youths who waived during prior arrests may have learned that they derived no benefit from cooperating. Those with prior felony arrests may have spent more time with lawyers and gained greater understanding of the adverse consequences of waiver.[92]

Once officers secure a juvenile's waiver, they question him just like an adult. They employ the same maximization and minimization strategies used with adults to overcome young suspects' resistance and to lead them to admit responsibility.[93] Maximization techniques intimidate suspects and impress on them the futility of denial; minimization techniques provide moral justifications or face-saving alternatives to enable them to confess.[94] Despite youths' greater susceptibility, police do not incorporate developmental differences into the tactics they employ.[95] Most do not receive any special training about questioning juveniles and use the same tactics as with adults.[96] Techniques designed to manipulate adults—aggressive questioning, presenting false evidence, and using leading questions—create unique dangers when employed with youths.[97]

Some states require a parent to assist juveniles in the interrogation room although analysts question their protective role.[98] Parents—as adults—may have marginally greater understanding of *Miranda* than their children, but both share misconceptions about police practices.[99] Parents erroneously believed that police must contact them prior to questioning their child and incorrectly believed that police would not lie.[100] They did not provide useful legal advice, increased pressure to waive rights, and many urged their children to tell the truth.[101] Parents may be emotionally upset or angry at their child's arrest, believe that confessing will produce a better outcome, or think they should respect authority or assume responsibility.[102] Juveniles rarely spontaneously request parents for a variety of reasons: estrangement from them; feeling that they cannot provide meaningful assistance; embarrassment or shame about their crime; or naïve hope that their parents will not learn of their arrest.[103] If a parent is present, police either enlist them as allies in the interrogation or neutralize their presence. Officers tell parents that they want to learn what happened and recruit parents as collaborators to learn the truth to help them help their child. If parents attend their child's interrogation, then police render them as passive observers, seat them behind their child, and instruct them not to intervene.[104] The largest empirical study of interrogations at which parents were present reported that most did not participate after police gave their child a *Miranda* warning, sometimes switched sides to become active allies of the police, and rarely played a protective role.[105]

Research on false confessions underscores juveniles' unique vulnerability.[106] Younger adolescents are at greater risk to confess falsely than older ones.[107] In one study, police obtained more than one-third (35%)

of proven false confessions from suspects younger than eighteen.[108] In another study, false confessions occurred in 15% of cases, but juveniles accounted for 42% of all false confessors and two-thirds (69%) of those aged twelve to fifteen confessed to crimes they did not commit.[109] Significantly, research on exonerated juveniles who confess falsely involves only the small group of youths prosecuted as adults. This reflects the seriousness of their crimes, the greater pressure on police to solve them, and the longer period available to youths and their attorneys to correct the errors.

Developmental psychologists attribute juveniles' overrepresentation among false confessors to reduced cognitive ability, developmental immaturity, and increased susceptibility to manipulation.[110] They have fewer life experiences or psychological resources with which to resist the pressures of interrogation.[111] They are more likely to comply with authority figures, tell police what they think they want to hear, and respond to negative feedback.[112] Their impulsive decision making and tendency to obey authority heightens those risks, especially for younger juveniles with limited understanding.[113] The stress and anxiety of interrogation intensify their desire to extricate themselves in the short run by waiving and confessing.[114] The vulnerabilities of youth multiply when coupled with mental illness, mental retardation, or compliant personalities. Juveniles' immature brains contribute to impulsive decisions and their limited ability to consider long-term consequences increases their vulnerability to confessing falsely.[115]

Policy Recommendations

Although *Miranda* purported to bolster the adversary system and protect citizens, the warnings failed to achieve those goals. Decisions since *Miranda* have limited its scope and reduced adverse consequences when police fail to comply.[116] *Miranda*'s assumption that a warning would empower suspects to resist pressures of interrogation is patently wrong. Post-*Miranda* research reports that the vast majority of suspects—80% of adults and 90% of juveniles—waive their sole protection in the interrogation room. Although *Miranda* recognized that the inherent coercion of custodial interrogation threatened the adversarial process, waivers provide police with an opportunity to conduct an inquisitorial examination. Perversely, *Miranda* allows judges to focus on ritualistic compliance with a procedural formality rather than to assess the voluntariness or reliability of a statement.[117] Judicial review of a *Miranda* waiver is the beginning *and* end of regulating interrogation.[118]

Research on false confessions underscores the unique vulnerability of younger juveniles.[119] Police obtained more than one-third of false confessions from suspects under eighteen years of age; younger adolescents are at even greater risk than older ones.[120] *Miranda* is especially problematic for younger juveniles who may not understand its words or concepts. Their incomplete understanding, impaired judgment, and heightened vulnerability warrant greater protections than those afforded adults. Psychologists distinguish between youths' cognitive ability— capacity to understand—and competence to make mature decisions and exercise self-control. *Miranda* requires only shallow understanding of the words, which developmental psychologists conclude most sixteen- and seventeen-year-old youths possess. By contrast, psychologists report that many, if not most, children fifteen or younger do not understand *Miranda* or possess competence to make legal decisions.[121]

Mandatory Counsel for Younger Juveniles

Younger juveniles' limited understanding and heightened vulnerability warrant greater procedural protections—a non-waivable right to counsel. The Court in *Haley, Gallegos, Gault, Fare, Alvarado*, and *J.D.B.* excluded statements taken from youths fifteen years of age or younger and admitted those obtained from sixteen- and seventeen year-olds. The Court's de facto functional line—fifteen and younger versus sixteen and older—closely tracks what psychologists report about youths' ability to understand the warning. Courts and legislatures should adopt that functional line and provide greater protections for younger juveniles.

Psychologists advocate that juveniles younger than sixteen years of age "should be accompanied and advised by a professional advocate, preferably an attorney, trained to serve in this role."[122] More than three decades ago, the American Bar Association endorsed mandatory, non- waivable counsel because it recognized that "[f]ew juveniles have the experience and understanding to decide meaningfully that the assistance of counsel would not be helpful."[123] Juveniles should consult with an attorney, rather than rely on parents, before they exercise or waive rights.[124] Requiring consultation with an attorney assures a functioning legal services delivery system and an informed and voluntary waiver. If youths fifteen years of age or younger consult with counsel prior to waiver, it will limit somewhat police's ability to secure confessions. However, if younger juveniles cannot understand or exercise rights without assistance, then to treat them as if they do enables the state to exploit their vulnerability. Constitutional rights exist to assure factual accuracy, promote equality, and protect individuals from governmental overreaching. *Michael C.* emphasized lawyers' unique role in the justice system, and *Haley*, *Gallegos*, and *Gault* recognized younger juveniles' exceptional need for their assistance.

Limiting the Length of Interrogation

The vast majority of interrogations are very brief; police complete nearly all interviews in less than an hour and few take longer than two hours.[125] By contrast, interrogations that elicit false confessions are usually long inquiries that wear down an innocent person's resistance—85% took at least six hours—and youthfulness exacerbates that danger.[126] The Court recognizes that lengthy interrogations can produce involuntary confessions; *Haley* and *Gallegos* found that five or six hours of questioning rendered a statement involuntary. States should create a sliding-scale presumption that a confession is involuntary and unreliable based on length of interrogation.[127]

Mandatory Recording of Interrogation

Within the past decade, legal scholars, psychologists, law enforcement, and justice system personnel have reached consensus that recording interrogations reduces coercion, diminishes dangers of false confessions, and increases reliability.[128] In recognition of the unique vulnerability of juveniles, the Wisconsin Supreme Court in *In the Interest of Jerrell C.J.* required police to electronically record all custodial interrogations.[129] About a dozen states require police to record interrogations, albeit some under limited circumstances—homicide or very young suspects.[130] Recording creates an objective record and provides an independent basis to resolve credibility disputes about *Miranda* warnings, waivers, or statements.[131] It enables a judge to decide whether a statement contained facts known to a guilty perpetrator or police supplied them to an innocent suspect.[132] Recording protects police from false claims of abuse and enhances professionalism. It enables police to focus on suspects' responses, to review details of an interview not captured in written notes, and to test them against subsequently discovered facts. Recording avoids distortions that occur when interviewers rely on memory or notes to summarize a statement.

Police must record all interactions with suspects—preliminary interviews and interrogations—rather than just a final statement—a "post-admission narrative."[133] Otherwise, police may conduct a pre-interrogation interview, elicit incriminating information, and then construct a final confession after the "cat is out of the bag." Only a complete record of every interaction can protect against a final statement that ratifies an earlier coerced one or against a false confession contaminated by non-public facts that police supplied a suspect.[134]

Competence to Stand Trial

Are delinquents competent to participate in more formal, punitive, and complex juvenile court proceedings? *Gault's* procedural rights would be of no value to youths unable to exercise them. The Court long has required that a defendant must be competent to preserve the integrity of trials, to promote factual accuracy, to reduce risk of error, and to enable defendants to play a part in proceedings.[135] *Dusky v. United States* held that a defendant must possess "sufficient present ability to consult with his lawyer with a reasonable degree of rational understanding . . . [and have] a rational as well as factual understanding of proceedings against him."[136] *Drope v. Missouri* held that "a person whose mental condition is such that he lacks the capacity to understand the nature and object of the proceedings against him, to consult with counsel, and to assist in preparing his defense may not be subjected to a trial."[137] The standard is functional and binary—a defendant either is or is not competent to stand trial.[138]

The standard for competency is not especially onerous because the more capability it requires of moderately impaired defendants, the fewer will meet it.[139] Juveniles must understand the trial process, have the ability to reason and work with counsel, and to rationally appreciate their situation.[140] If a person understands that he is on trial for committing crimes, knows he can be sentenced if convicted, and can communicate with his attorney, a court likely would find him competent.[141] Significant mental illness—psychotic disorders such as schizophrenia—or severe mental retardation typically impair adult defendants' ability to understand the process, make rational decisions, and assist counsel.[142] However, psychotic disorders typically do not emerge until late adolescence or early adulthood and the American Psychiatric Association's *Diagnostic and Statistical Manual* cautions against diagnosing profound illnesses in younger populations.[143] Despite that reservation, researchers report that the prevalence of mental disorders among delinquent youths are substantially higher than in the general population—one-half to three-quarters exhibit one or more mental illnesses.[144]

Developmental psychologists assert that immaturity *per se*—especially for younger juveniles—produces the same deficits of understanding and inability to assist counsel that mental illness or retardation engenders in incompetent adults. [145] Youths' developmental limitations adversely affect their ability to pay attention, absorb and apply information, understand proceedings, make rational decisions, and work with counsel.[146]

Significant age-related differences appear between adolescents' and young adults' competence, judgment, and legal decision making.[147] Developmental psychologists report that many juveniles younger than fourteen years of age were as severely impaired as adults found incompetent to stand trial.[148] Thirty percent of eleven- to thirteen-year-olds and 19% of fourteen- and fifteen-year-olds exhibited deficits of reasoning and understanding comparable to that of incompetent adults.[149] Some older youths also exhibited substantial impairments.[150]

Age and intelligence interacted and produced higher levels of incompetence among adolescents with low IQs than adults with low IQs.[151] Juveniles with below-average intelligence exhibited greater impairment than did either low-intelligence adults or juveniles with normal intelligence.[152] Mental retardation accounted for more than half of youths found incompetent to stand trial in Florida.[153] The MacArthur adolescent research network described in Chapter 8 reported that about one-fifth of fourteen- and fifteen-year-olds were as impaired as mentally ill adults found incompetent; those with below-average intelligence were more likely than juveniles with average intelligence to be incompetent.[154] Even nominally competent adolescents may suffer from cognitive deficits—borderline intelligence, limited verbal ability, short attention span, or imperfect memory—that adversely affect understanding and decisions.

While incompetence in adults stems from mental disorders that may be transient or treatable with medication, it is less clear how to accelerate legal capacities in adolescents whose deficits result from developmental immaturity.[155] Competency restoration may be especially problematic for younger juveniles who never possessed relevant knowledge or understanding to begin with.[156] Moreover, adolescents deemed incompetent due to mental retardation may be especially difficult to remediate or restore to competence.[157]

The Court in *Graham* noted that developmental characteristics— mistrust of adults, limited understanding of the justice system or its actors, inability to work with counsel—impaired juveniles' defenses.[158] Adolescents' questionable ability to work with counsel increases the risk that defenses will go unrecognized and compounds the danger they will confess falsely or enter unfounded guilty pleas.

The prevalence of mental illness among delinquents compounds their developmental incompetence. In many jurisdictions, the juvenile justice system has become a de facto mental health system as a result of inadequate mental health services for children.[159] Analysts estimate that half or more of male delinquents and a larger proportion of female delinquents suffer from one or more mental disorders.[160] Youths suffering from attention-deficit hyperactivity disorder (ADHD) may have difficulty concentrating or communicating with their attorney and those suffering from depression may lack the motivation to do so.[161]

The issue of competence to stand trial arises both for youths tried in criminal court and those prosecuted in juvenile court. For youths tried as adults, criminal courts apply the *Dusky/Drope* standard, but focus on mental illness rather than developmental immaturity.[162] For youths tried in juvenile courts, about half the states have addressed competency in statutes, court rules, or case law.[163] However, most statutes consider only mental illness or retardation as sources of incompetence rather than developmental immaturity.[164]

Even after states recognize juveniles' right to a competency determination in delinquency proceedings, they differ over whether to apply the *Dusky/Drope* adult standard or a juvenile-normed standard. This is another instance in which states have the option to provide delinquents with adult criminal procedural safeguards or use less stringent juvenile protections. Some courts apply the adult standard in delinquency as well as criminal prosecutions because both may result in a child's loss of liberty.[165] "[B]ecause dispositions in juvenile proceedings, including rehabilitative dispositions, may involve both punishment and a substantial loss of liberty, the level of competence required to permit a child's participation in juvenile court proceedings can be no less than the competence demanded for trial or sentencing of an adult."[166] Other jurisdictions opt for a relaxed competency standard on the theory that delinquency hearings are less complex and consequences less severe.[167]

Elizabeth Scott and Thomas Grisso advocate for a lower, watered-down standard of competence in delinquency proceedings. They contend that a youth who might be found incompetent to stand trial as an adult or if evaluated under an adult standard in juvenile court could still be found competent under a relaxed standard.[168] They insist that if delinquency sanctions are less punitive than criminal sentences and geared to promote youths' welfare, then they require fewer procedural safeguards.[169] Scott and Steinberg maintain that "if youths in delinquency proceedings do not face the *same jeopardy* that criminal defendants face, they may not need the same procedural safeguards."[170] However, *Breed v. Jones* clearly held that youths tried in either system confront the same legal jeopardy.[171]

The constitutional requirement of competence hinges on defendants' ability to participate in proceedings and not the punishment that may ensue.[172] It focuses on the legitimacy of the trial process and not the subsequent disposition.[173] Unlike *Roper, Graham,* and *Miller,* which treated youths' reduced culpability categorically, competence to stand trial is an individual property.[174] Although delinquency dispositions, especially for serious crimes, may be shorter than criminal sentences, *Baldwin v. New York* held that no crime that carried an authorized sentence of six months or longer could be deemed a petty offense. Scott and

Steinberg argue that a rule that immunizes some incompetent youths from adjudication could undermine juvenile courts' legitimacy.[175] But adjudicating immature youths under their relaxed standard enables the state to take advantage of their incompetence and undermines the legitimacy of the process.

The argument for a watered-down competency standard ignores the shift to punishment described in Chapter 5. Grisso acknowledges that get tough policies include "public protection as the primary purpose of the juvenile court (relegating rehabilitation to a secondary purpose), an increase in penalties and determinate sentences, and dispositional schemes that allowed for corrections jurisdiction . . . to extend well into the adult years."[176] A finding of delinquency requires proof of guilt. Either defendants understand the proceedings and can assist counsel or they cannot; if they cannot perform those minimal tasks, then they should not be prosecuted in any court.[177] The constitutional requirement of competence undergirds the legitimacy of the trial process, assures accurate fact-finding, and prevents the state from taking advantage of an impaired defendant's limitations.[178]

Juvenile courts do not routinely initiate competency evaluations even for young offenders and many delinquents may face charges without understanding the process or the ability to work with counsel.[179] Defense attorneys may be best positioned to detect whether a competency evaluation is warranted, but often fail to do so because of heavy caseloads, limited time spent with individual clients, and an inability to distinguish between generic immaturity and disabling incompetence.[180] Defense counsel tactically may not raise a juvenile's incompetence because of the consequent delays for competency evaluation and restoration.[181] Justice system personnel may lack evaluation instruments or clinical personnel who can administer them in a consistent and valid manner.[182] Juveniles' lack of competence to assist counsel undermines courts' ability to provide a fair trial or assure valid guilty pleas.

Access to Counsel

Gideon v. Wainwright applied the Sixth Amendment to the states to guarantee criminal defendants' right to counsel. *Gault* relied on *Gideon*, compared a delinquency proceeding to a felony prosecution, and granted delinquents the right to counsel.[183] However, *Gault* used the Fourteenth Amendment Due Process Clause rather than the Sixth Amendment and did not mandate automatic appointment of counsel.[184] *Gault*, like *Gideon*, left to state and local governments the task to fund legal services. Over the past half century, penurious politicians who want to get tough on crime and avoid coddling criminals have shirked their responsibility to adequately fund public defenders' offices and undermined the quality of justice.

Gault required a judge to advise the child and parent of the right to have a lawyer appointed if indigent, but ruled that juveniles could waive counsel. Most states do not use special procedural safeguards—mandatory non-waivable appointment or pre-waiver consultation with a lawyer—to protect delinquents from improvident decisions.[185] Instead, they use the adult standard—knowing, intelligent, and voluntary—to gauge juveniles' relinquishment of counsel. As with *Miranda* waivers, formal equality results in practical inequality—lawyers represent delinquents at much lower rates than they do criminal defendants.[186]

Despite statutes and court rules of procedure that apply equally throughout a state, juvenile justice administration varies with urban, suburban, and rural context and produces justice by geography.[187] Lawyers appear more frequently in urban courts than in more informal rural courts.[188] In turn, more formal urban courts hold more youths in pretrial detention and sentence them more severely. Finally, a lawyer's presence is an aggravating factor at disposition; judges sentence youths who appear with counsel more severely than they do those who appear without an attorney.[189] Several factors contribute to this finding: lawyers who appear in juvenile court may be incompetent and prejudice their clients' cases; judges may predetermine sentences and appoint counsel when they anticipate out-of-home placements; or judges may punish delinquents for exercising procedural rights.[190]

Presence of Counsel in Juvenile Courts

When the Court decided *Gault*, lawyers appeared in fewer than 5% of delinquency cases.[191] A study attributed the absence of counsel to "juvenile court judges' actively discouraging juveniles from retaining counsel and [to] the inability of attorneys to perform their traditional role in juvenile courts."[192] Although states amended their juvenile codes to comply with *Gault*, the law in action lagged behind the law on the books. Evaluations of initial compliance with *Gault* found that most judges did not advise juveniles of their rights and the vast majority did not appoint counsel.[193] A study of three urban juvenile courts before and after *Gault* reported that one judge did not inform juveniles of their right to counsel and a second only advised 3%.[194] Studies in the 1970s and 1980s reported that many judges did not advise juveniles and most did not appoint counsel.[195] Research in Minnesota in the mid-1980s reported that most youths appeared without counsel, that rates of representation varied widely in urban, suburban and rural counties, and that one-third of youths whom judges removed from home and one-quarter of those in institutions were unrepresented.[196] A decade later, about one-quarter of juveniles removed from home were unrepresented despite law reforms to eliminate the practice.[197] A study of delivery of legal services in six states reported that only three of them appointed counsel for a substantial majority of juveniles.[198] Studies in the 1990s described juvenile court judges' continuing failure to appoint lawyers.[199] In 1995, the General Accounting Office confirmed that rates of representation varied widely among and within states and that judges tried and sentenced many unrepresented youths.[200] Research in Missouri found urban, suburban, and rural variation in rates of representation and reported that an attorney's presence increased a youth's likelihood of receiving out-of-home placement.[201] Race, gender, and type of representation influenced sentencing severity in different court settings.[202]

In the mid-1990s the American Bar Association published two reports on juveniles' legal needs. *America's Children at Risk* reported that many children appeared without counsel and that lawyers who represented youth lacked adequate training and often failed to provide effective assistance.[203] *A Call for Justice* focused on the quality of defense lawyers, again reporting that many youths appeared without counsel and that many attorneys failed to appreciate the challenges of representing young clients.[204] Since the late 1990s, the ABA and the National Juvenile Defender Center have conducted more than twenty state-by-state assessments of access to and quality of counsel. They report that many, if not most, juveniles appeared without counsel and that lawyers who represented youths often encountered structural impediments to effective advocacy—heavy caseloads, inadequate resources, lack of training, and the like.[205]

Waivers of Counsel and Guilty Pleas in Juvenile Court

Several factors account for why so many youths appear in juvenile courts without counsel. Public defender services may be less available or non-existent in nonurban areas.[206] Judges may give cursory advisories of the right to counsel, implying that waivers are just legal technicalities. They may readily allow juveniles to waive counsel to ease their administrative burdens.[207] If judges expect to impose noncustodial sentences, then they may dispense with counsel.[208] Some jurisdictions charge fees to determine a youth's eligibility for a public defender and others base youths' eligibility on their parents' income.[209] Parents may be reluctant to retain or accept an attorney if, as in many states, they may have to reimburse the state for attorney fees if they can afford them.[210]

The most common explanation why so many juveniles are unrepresented is that they waive counsel.[211] The National Academy of Sciences reported, "In Louisiana, as many as 90 percent of youth waived their right to counsel and in many other states, including Florida, Georgia, and Kentucky, more than 50 percent of youth waived that right."[212] Judges in most states use the adult standard to gauge juveniles' waivers of counsel.[213] They consider the same factors—age, education, IQ, prior police contacts, or court experience—as those in *Miranda* waivers.[214] As with *Miranda* waivers, many juveniles do not understand their rights or the role of lawyers and waive counsel without consulting with either a parent or an attorney.[215] Although judges are supposed to conduct a dialogue to determine whether a child can understand rights and represent herself, they frequently failed to give any counsel advisory, often neglected to create a record, and readily accepted waivers from manifestly incompetent children.[216] Judges who give counsel advisories often seek waivers to expedite court dockets, which affects how they inform juveniles of their rights and interpret their responses.[217] As long as the law allows juveniles to waive counsel, judges can conclude that they did so validly regardless of youths' incompetence.

The research on juveniles' exercise of *Miranda* rights and adjudicative competence applies equally to their ability to waive counsel and subsequently to plead guilty. Even youths who understand a counsel advisory may not appreciate the importance of the right or the collateral consequences of relinquishing counsel.[218] Juveniles' diminished competence, inability to understand proceedings, and judicial encouragement to waive counsel results in delinquents being adjudicated without lawyers in larger proportions than adult criminal defendants.[219]

Pleas without Bargains

Like adult criminal defendants, nearly all delinquents plead guilty and proceed to sentencing.[220] Because most states deny juveniles the right to a jury trial, delinquents have very little plea bargaining leverage.[221] Juvenile court judges resist plea bargains by which prosecutors and defense counsel could restrict their sentencing discretion.[222] Even though pleading guilty is the most critical decision a delinquent makes, states use adult standards to evaluate their competence to enter a plea.[223] Judges and lawyers often speak with juveniles in complicated legal language and fail to explain long-term consequences of pleading guilty.[224]

A valid guilty plea requires a judge to conduct a colloquy on the record in which an offender admits the facts of the offense, acknowledges the rights being relinquished, and demonstrates that she understands the charges and potential consequences.[225] Because appellate courts seldom review juveniles' waivers of counsel, pleas made without counsel receive even less judicial scrutiny.[226] Guilty pleas by factually innocent youths occur because attorneys fail to investigate cases; assume their clients' guilt, especially if they have already confessed; and avoid adversarial litigation, discovery requests, and pretrial motions that conflict with juvenile courts' cooperative ideology.[227] Juveniles' emphasis on short-term over long-term consequences and dependence on adult authority figures increases their likelihood to enter false guilty pleas.

Counsel as an Aggravating Factor in Sentencing

Historically, juvenile court judges discouraged adversarial litigants and impeded effective advocacy.[228] Lawyers in juvenile courts may put their clients at a disadvantage when judges sentence them.[229] Research that controls for legal variables—present offense, prior record, pretrial detention, and the like—consistently reports that judges removed from home and incarcerated delinquents who appeared with counsel more frequently than unrepresented youths.[230] Law reforms to improve delivery of legal services actually increased the aggravating effect of representation on dispositions.[231]

Several factors contribute to lawyers' negative impact at disposition. Juveniles' developmental limitations and incomplete understanding of a lawyer's role may undermine effective representation.[232] Juveniles may not believe lawyers' explanations of confidential communications and withhold important information to their detriment. In addition, the lawyers assigned to juvenile court may be incompetent and prejudice their clients' cases.[233] Public defender offices may send their least capable or newest attorneys to juvenile court to gain trial experience.[234] Lack of adequate funding for defender services may preclude investigations, which increases the risk of wrongful convictions.[235] Defense attorneys seldom investigate cases or interview their clients prior to trial because of heavy caseloads and limited organizational support.[236] Court-appointed lawyers may place a greater premium on maintaining good relations with judges who assign their cases than on vigorously defending their revolving clients.[237] Juvenile courts' *parens patriae* ideology discourages zealous advocacy and engenders adverse consequences for attorneys who "rock the boat," as well as for their clients.[238] Most significantly, many defense attorneys work under conditions that create structural impediments to quality representation.[239] Observations and qualitative assessments in dozens of states report derisory working conditions—crushing caseloads, penurious compensation, scant support services, inexperienced attorneys, and inadequate supervision—that detract from or preclude effective representation.[240] Ineffective assistance of counsel, for whatever reasons, is a significant factor in one-quarter of wrongful convictions.[241]

Another explanation of lawyers' negative impact on dispositions is that judges may appoint them when they anticipate more severe sentences.[242] The Court in *Scott v. Illinois* prohibited "incarceration without representation" and limited indigent adult misdemeanants' right to appointed counsel to cases in which judges ordered defendants' actual confinement.[243] Judges' efforts to comply with *Scott* may explain the relationship between initial decisions to appoint counsel and subsequent decisions to remove youths from home. In most states, the same judge presides at a youth's arraignment, detention hearing, adjudication, and disposition and may appoint counsel if she anticipates a more severe sentence.[244] Judges typically appoint counsel, if at all, at the arraignment, detention hearing, or on the day of trial. At these initial proceedings when the only information theoretically available is the formal charging document, how would a judge know whether she intends to incarcerate a youth later? Perhaps from prior familiarity with a case or the juvenile. Perhaps from *ex parte* communications with prosecutor or court personnel. Can an attorney provide an effective defense if the judge has already prejudged the case?[245]

Finally, judges may sentence delinquents who appear with counsel more severely than those who waive because the lawyer's presence insulates them from appellate reversal.[246] Juvenile court judges may sanction youths whose lawyers invoke formal procedures, disrupt routine procedures, or question their discretion in ways similar to adult defendants' trial penalty—the harsher sentences imposed on those who demand a jury trial rather than plead guilty.[247]

Heavy caseloads and inadequate resources preclude effective pretrial investigations. Courtroom cultures that discourage advocacy and appointed-counsel systems that make lawyers dependent on judges for future clients impede filing of motions and factual testing of the state's case. Waivers of counsel encourage many short-sighted youths to plead guilty at arraignments or to avoid detention, even if they have valid defenses. Court practices that appoint lawyers who meet their clients for the first time on the day of trial create a system conducive to inadequate representation and wrongful convictions.[248]

Appellate Review

Gault rejected the fifteen-year-old's request for a constitutional right to appellate review because it had not found that criminal defendants enjoyed such a right.[249] However, states invariably provided adult defendants with a statutory right to appellate review. By not reaching the constitutional issue, the Court undermined the other rights that it granted delinquents. "The only possible way of enforcing the rules would have been through appellate review of juvenile court decisions, since judge who found their decisions constantly overturned on procedural grounds might eventually have begun to comply with *Gault* and its progeny."[250]

Regardless of how poorly lawyers perform, appellate courts seldom can correct juvenile courts' errors.[251] Juvenile defenders rarely, if ever, appeal adverse decisions and often lack a record with which to challenge an invalid waiver of counsel or trial errors.[252] Adult defense lawyers appeal criminal cases about ten times as frequently as do juvenile defenders.[253] Juvenile court culture, even among public defenders, may discourage appeals as an impediment to a youth assuming responsibility. Overwhelming caseloads make specialized appellate divisions a luxury few defender offices can afford. The vast majority of delinquents enter guilty pleas, which waive the right to appeal and further preclude appellate review. Moreover, juveniles who waive counsel at trial will be less aware of or able to pursue an appeal. The short length of most juvenile dispositions renders many appealed cases moot if the child is released before a court reviews the case. Against this backdrop, the Alaska Supreme Court observed, "We cannot help but notice that the children's cases appealed to this court have often shown much more extensive and fundamental error than is generally found in adult criminal cases."[254]

The lack of appeals from juvenile courts retards the development of substantive law. Appellate courts can only expand the law only if parties present issues to them. If defense counsel do not challenge judges' decisions, then appellate courts cannot develop a body of case law. The dearth of substantive law undermines attorney's views of juvenile courts as courts of law, discourages their presence, and limits the arguments available to creative advocates.[255]

Conclusions

The formal procedures of juvenile and criminal courts have converged in the decades since *Gault*.[256] Differences in age and competence would suggest that youths should receive more safeguards than adults to protect them from punitive delinquency adjudications and their own limitations. States do not provides juveniles with additional safeguards to protect them from their own immaturity—mandatory non-waivable appointment of counsel or pre-waiver consultation with a lawyer. Instead, they use adult legal standards that most youths are unlikely to meet. A justice system that recognizes youths' developmental limitations would provide, at a minimum, no pretrial waivers of *Miranda* rights or counsel without prior consultation with counsel.[257] If, as *Gault* noted, delinquency proceeding are comparable to a felony prosecution, then no youth should face the power of the state alone and unaided. The juvenile court is a system of crime control and not a welfare agency. *Gault* rejected juvenile court judges' and social workers' benevolence as inadequate safeguards and relied instead on an adversarial process. As *Michael C.* repeatedly emphasized, lawyers play a unique role in the legal process and only they can effectively invoke the procedural safeguards that are every citizens' right. A rule that requires mandatory non-waivable appointment of counsel would impose substantial costs and burdens on legal services delivery in most states. But after *Gault*, all juveniles are entitled to appointed counsel. Waiver doctrines to relieve states' fiscal or administrative burdens are scant justifications to deny fundamental rights. A protectionist stance would recognizes youths' immaturity and provide greater safeguards than adults receive to offset their developmental limitations.

States use the adult standard to gauge juveniles' waivers of counsel, even though many youths cannot meet it. High rates of waiver undermine the legitimacy of the juvenile justice system because assistance of counsel is the prerequisite to exercise of other rights.[258] Youths require safeguards that only lawyers can provide to protect against erroneous and punitive state intervention. The direct consequence of delinquency convictions—institutional confinement—and use of prior convictions to sentence recidivists more harshly, to waive youths to criminal court, and to enhance criminal sentences makes assistance of counsel imperative. Only mandatory non-waivable counsel can prevent erroneous convictions and collateral use of adjudications that compound injustice. Lawyers can only represent delinquents effectively if they have adequate support and resources and specialized training to represent children.

Jury Trial: Fact-Finding, Government Oppression, and Collateral Consequences

States treat juveniles just like adults when formal equality produces practical inequality. Conversely, they use juvenile court procedures that provide *less* effective protection when called upon to provide delinquents with adult safeguards. *Duncan v. Louisiana* gave adult defendants the right to a jury trial to assure accurate fact-finding and to prevent governmental oppression.[259] By contrast, *McKeiver v. Pennsylvania* denied delinquents protections the Court deemed fundamental to criminal trials.[260] The presence of lay citizens functions as a check on the state, provides protection against vindictive prosecutors or biased judges, upholds the criminal standard of proof, and enhances the transparency and accountability of the justice system. Despite those salutary functions, *McKeiver* insisted that "the juvenile court proceeding has not yet been held to be a 'criminal prosecution,' within the meaning and reach of the Sixth Amendment, and also has not yet been regarded as devoid of criminal aspects merely because it usually has been given the civil label."[261]

The *McKeiver* plurality reasoned that a judge could find facts as accurately as a jury, rejected concerns that informality could compromise fact-finding, invoked the imagery of a paternalistic judge, and disregarded delinquents' need for protection from state overreaching.[262]

> Concern about the inapplicability of exclusionary and other rules of evidence, about the juvenile court judges' possible awareness of the juvenile's prior record and of the contents of the social file; about repeated appearances of the same familiar witnesses in the persons of juvenile and probation officers and social workers—all to the effect that this will create the likelihood of pre-judgment—chooses to ignore, it seems to us, every aspect of fairness, of concern, of sympathy, and of paternal attention that the juvenile court system contemplates.[263]

The Court feared that jury trials would interfere with juvenile courts' informality, flexibility, and confidentiality, make juvenile and criminal courts procedurally indistinguishable, and lead to abandonment of the juvenile court.[264]

The *McKeiver* dissenters insisted that when the state charges a delinquent with a crime for which it could incarcerate her, she should enjoy the same jury right as an adult.[265] For them, *Gault*'s rationale—criminal charges and the possibility of confinement—required comparable procedural safeguards. The dissenters feared that juvenile courts' informality would contaminate fact-finding. The vast majority of delinquents, like criminal defendants, plead guilty rather than have their cases decided by juries. But the possibility of a jury trial provides an important check on prosecutorial overcharging, on judges' evidentiary rulings, and the standard of proof beyond a reasonable doubt. Despite the prevalence of guilty pleas, lawyers are supposed to evaluate cases as if they were to go to trial and practice in the shadow of the jury.[266] The possibility of a jury trial increases the visibility and accountability of justice administration and the performance of lawyers and judges. The jury's checking function may be even more important in highly discretionary, low-visibility juvenile courts that deal with poor and dependent youths who cannot effectively protect themselves.

A few states give juveniles a right to a jury trial as a matter of state law, but the vast majority do not.[267] As we saw in Chapter 5, in the decades since *McKeiver*, states adopted get tough provisions, revised their juvenile codes' purpose, opened delinquency trials to the public, fostered a punitive convergence with criminal courts, imposed collateral consequences for delinquency convictions, and eroded the rationale for fewer procedural safeguards. Despite the explicit shift from treatment to punishment, most state courts continue to deny juveniles a jury.[268]

In Chapter 2, I argued that constitutional procedural protections serve dual functions: assure accurate fact-finding *and* protect against governmental oppression. In this section, I argue that *McKeiver's* denial of a jury fails on both counts. First, judges and juries find facts differently and when they differ, judges are more likely to convict than a panel of laypeople. Second, the get tough changes reviewed in Chapter 5 increase the need to protect delinquents from direct and collateral consequences of convictions. Providing delinquents with a second-rate criminal court denies them fundamental fairness, undermines the legitimacy of the process, and increases the likelihood of wrongful convictions.

Accurate Fact-Finding

Winship reasoned that the seriousness of proceedings and the consequences for a defendant—juvenile or adult—required proof beyond a reasonable doubt. *McKeiver* assumed that judges could find facts as accurately as juries. Its rejection of jury trials undermines factual accuracy and increases the likelihood that outcomes will differ in delinquency and criminal trials. Although juries and judges agree about defendants' guilt or innocence in about four-fifths of criminal cases, when they differ, juries acquit more often than do judges.[269]

Fact-finding by judges and juries differs because juvenile court judges may preside over hundreds of cases a year while a juror may participate in only one or two cases in a lifetime.[270] The presence of jurors affects the ways in which lawyers present their cases. "Lawyers and judges accommodate juries by slowing things down and making efforts to present testimony and explain their arguments in laymen's terms. In contrast, the overtaxed judge-run juvenile system runs in high gear. Cases are whisked before the judge and presented in summary terms that make sense only to the 'regulars'—the lawyers, probation officers, and judges."[271]

Several factors contribute to jurors' greater propensity to acquit than judges. As judges hear many cases, they may become less meticulous when they weigh evidence and apply less stringently the reasonable doubt standard than do jurors.[272] Judges hear testimony from police and probation officers on a recurring basis and form settled opinions about their credibility.[273] Similarly, judges may have formed an opinion about a youth's credibility or character, or about the case itself from hearing earlier charges against her or presiding at a detention hearing.

Delinquency proceedings' informality compounds differences between judge and jury fact-finding and further disadvantages delinquents. A judge does not discuss either the law or the evidence before reaching a conclusion and lack of diverse opinions increases the variability of outcomes.[274] Judges in criminal cases instruct jurors about the applicable law. By contrast, a judge in a bench trial does not state the law, which makes it more difficult for an appellate court to determine whether she correctly understood or applied it.[275] Justice Blackmun, who wrote the plurality opinion in *McKeiver*, subsequently wrote the opinion in *Ballew v. Georgia*, which recognized the superiority of group decision making over individual judgments.[276] Some group members remember facts that others forget and the give-and-take of deliberations airs competing views and promotes more accurate decisions.[277] By contrast, the need to administer the courtroom, make evidentiary rulings, take notes, and conduct sidebars with lawyers diverts judges' attention during proceedings.

The greater flexibility and informality of closed juvenile proceedings compounds the differences between judge and jury reasonable doubt. When a judge presides at a youth's detention hearing, she receives information about the offense, criminal history, and social background, which may contaminate impartial fact-finding.[278] Exposure to non-guilt-related evidence increases the likelihood that a judge subsequently will convict and institutionalize her.

A finding of criminal guilt entails more than just a factual evaluation, but involves an assessment of culpability—the reasonableness of a response to provocation, the perceived need for self-defense, immaturity, and the like. Jurors carry the community's norms and sense of justice when they apply the law to the facts. Analysts attribute some differences between judges and juries to differences in how they evaluate evidence, jury sentiments about the law—equity and nullification—and sympathy for the defendant. "[W]hen juries differ with the result at which the judge would have arrived, it is usually because they are serving some of the very purposes for which they were created and for which they are now employed."[279] Some differences between judges and juries reflect the latter's use of a higher threshold of proof—beyond a reasonable doubt, which may require somewhat more compelling evidence.[280] "If a society wishes to be serious about convicting only when the state has been put to proof beyond a reasonable doubt, it would be well advised to have a jury system."[281]

The youthfulness of a defendant is a factor that elicits jury sympathy and accounts for some differences between judge and jury decisions.[282] By contrast, juvenile court judges may be more predisposed to find jurisdiction to help a troubled youth. As one court commented, "the real danger may come . . . from the 'kindly, fatherly or motherly judge' who sees a youngster mired in a horrendous environment and wants to rescue the juvenile before it is too late. The temptation, often irresistible, is to remove the child from those terrible circumstances even though that may require bending the reasonable doubt standard in order to find him or her guilty of the charged offense."[283] Finally, without a jury, judges adjudicate many delinquents without an attorney, which prejudices fact-finding and increases the likelihood of erroneous convictions.

Suppression Hearing and Evidentiary Contamination

In bench trials, judges typically conduct suppression hearings immediately before or during trial, a practice that exposes them to inadmissible evidence and prejudicial information.[284] A judge may know about a youth's prior delinquency from presiding at a detention hearing, prior adjudication, or trial of co-offenders. Similarly, a judge who suppresses an inadmissible confession or illegally seized evidence may still be influenced by it.[285] The presumption that exposure to inadmissible evidence will not affect a judge is especially problematic where the same judge typically handles a youth's case at several different stages. An adult defendant can avoid these risks by opting for a jury trial, but delinquents have no way to avoid the cumulative risks of prejudice in a bench trial.[286] Critics of juvenile courts' fact-finding at trial conclude that "judges often convict on evidence so scant that only the most closed-minded or misguided juror could think the evidence satisfied the standard of proof beyond a reasonable doubt."[287] As a result, states adjudicate youths as delinquent in cases in which they could not have obtained convictions with adequate procedural safeguards.

The factual and legal issues in delinquency hearings are the same as those in criminal trials—has the state proven beyond a reasonable doubt that the defendant committed a crime? Given the importance of juries, *McKeiver* made it easier to convict a youth appearing before a juvenile court judge than to convict a criminal defendant with the same evidence before a group of detached citizens.[288] The differences between the validity and reliability of delinquency adjudications and criminal convictions raises questions about the use of juveniles' records to enhance criminal sentences.

Preventing Governmental Oppression and Get Tough Policies

McKeiver uncritically assumed that juvenile courts treated delinquents rather than punished them, but it did not review any record to support that assumption. Rather, it asserted that juvenile courts conduct "an intimate, informal protective proceeding," even as it conceded that states seldom, if ever realized that ideal.[289] *McKeiver* did not analyze juvenile code purpose clauses, sentencing statutes, judges' sentencing practices, conditions of confinement, or intervention outcomes when it denied delinquents a jury.[290] In its embrace of Progressive rhetoric, the Court did not consider whether delinquents needed protection from the state.

McKeiver itself demonstrated the need to protect youths from states' abuse of the justice process. *McKeiver* decided appeals arising in two cases: one from Pennsylvania, the other from North Carolina. Although *McKeiver* involved ordinary criminal charges of robbery and assault, the North Carolina companion case, *In re Burrus et al.*, involved *en masse* delinquency prosecutions of forty-five Black children ranging in age from eleven to fifteen years, for "willfully impeding traffic," charges arising out of "a series of [civil rights] demonstrations . . . protesting school assignments and a school consolidation plan."[291] *Burrus* exemplified the use of the criminal law to punish youthful activism during the civil rights movement. "The police and courts often criminalized and punished the pro–civil rights activities of white and black youths and young adults."[292] In the South in the 1960s, judges adjudicated delinquent and institutionalized hundreds of Black youths for participating in civil rights demonstrations.[293]

The Court long has recognized that juries serve a special role to prevent governmental oppression and protect citizens facing punishment. In our system of checks and balances, lay-citizen jurors represent the ultimate restraint on abuses of governmental power, which is why the jury trial is the only procedural safeguard listed in three different places in the Constitution. The Court in *Baldwin v. New York* explained that "[t]he primary purpose of the jury is to prevent the possibility of oppression by the Government; the jury interposes between the accused and his accuser the judgment of laymen who are less tutored perhaps than a judge or panel of judges, but who at the same time are less likely to function or appear as but another arm of the Government that has proceeded against him."[294] In *Duncan v. Louisiana*, decided three years before *McKeiver*, the Court held that the Sixth Amendment guaranteed a jury right in state criminal proceedings to assure accurate fact-finding *and* to prevent governmental oppression. *Duncan* emphasized that juries inject community values into the law, increase the visibility of justice administration, and check abuses by prosecutors and judges.

Providing an accused with the right to be tried by a jury of his peers gave
him an inestimable safeguard against the corrupt or overzealous prosecutor and against the compliant, biased, or eccentric judge. If the defendant
preferred the common sense judgment of a jury to the more tutored but
perhaps less sympathetic reaction of the single judge, he was to have it.
Beyond this, the jury trial provisions . . . reflect a fundamental decision
about the exercise of official power—a reluctance to entrust plenary powers over the life and liberty of the citizen to one judge or to a group of
judges. Fear of unchecked power . . . found expression in the criminal law
in this insistence upon community participation in the determination of
guilt or innocence.[295]

The year after *Duncan*, *Baldwin v. New York* again emphasized the
jury's role to prevent government oppression by interposing lay citizens
between the state and the defendant.[296] *Baldwin* is especially critical for
juvenile justice because an adult charged with any offense that carries
a *potential* sentence of confinement of six months or longer enjoys a
right to a jury trial. Although *Scott v. Illinois* limited the right to counsel to cases in which a court *actually* incarcerated defendants, *Baldwin*
granted the right to a jury whenever the *authorized* sentence exceeded
six months.[297] States' delinquency statutes typically authorize indeterminate dispositions for the duration of minority or for a term of years,
which means that *Baldwin* would extend the jury right to most delinquency proceedings.

McKeiver feared that granting delinquents jury trials would also lead
to public trials.[298] *Gault* recognized that confidential proceedings "hide
youthful errors from the full gaze of the public and bury them in the
graveyard of the forgotten past," but acknowledged that juvenile courts
regularly provided information about youths' contacts to the military,
government agencies, the FBI, and private employers.[299] In other cases,
the Court subordinated juvenile courts' desire to protect youths' privacy to newspapers' right to publish lawfully obtained information and
to criminal defendant's right to confront and cross-examine witnesses
about their delinquency records.[300]

Justice Brennan's concurring-dissenting opinion in *McKeiver* reasoned that a public trial could provide equivalent safeguards of a
jury—preventing government oppression—by making proceedings

visible and accountable. *In re Oliver* recognized that public trials protected defendants against the abuses of secret proceedings and enabled citizens to observe justice administration. "The knowledge that every criminal trial is subject to contemporaneous review in the form of public opinion is an effective restraint on possible abuse of judicial power."[301] Greater visibility might induce juvenile court judges to appoint counsel routinely and assure the public about the fairness of proceedings.

Many get tough reforms adopted in the 1990s increased the visibility and accountability of juvenile courts. About half the states authorized public access to all delinquency proceedings or to felony prosecutions.[302] States limited confidentiality protections to hold youths accountable and put the public on notice of who poses risks to the community.[303] Punitive legislators anticipated that greater visibility might temper judges' inclination toward leniency. The newfound openness obviates *McKeiver's* concerns about public trials.

Punitive Juvenile Justice and McKeiver's Questionable Validity

Kent, Gault, and *Winship* recognized that juvenile courts often failed to rehabilitate youths. *Kent* noted that "studies and critiques in recent years raise serious questions as to whether actual performance measures well enough against theoretical purpose to make tolerable the immunity of the process from the reach of constitutional guaranties applicable to adults. . . . [J]uvenile courts . . . lack the personnel, facilities and techniques to perform adequately as representatives of the State in a *parens patriae* capacity, at least with respect to children charged with law violation."[304] *Gault* noted that "[n]either sentiment nor folklore should cause us to shut our eyes" to the stigma of a delinquency conviction, high rates of recidivism, breaches of confidentiality, and conditions of confinement.[305] *Winship* equated the risks of delinquency and criminal cases and concluded that judicial intervention "cannot take the form of subjecting the child to the stigma of a finding that he violated a criminal law and to the possibility of institutional confinement on proof insufficient to convict him were he an adult."[306] The Court recognized juvenile courts' penal character well before the Get Tough Era and states' explicit endorsement of punishment.

The vast majority of states deny delinquents the right to a jury and youths have challenged *McKeiver*'s half-century-old rationale in light of get tough changes. Most state appellate courts have rejected their claims with deeply flawed analyses.

> Some courts simply reach conclusions without even attempting to identify the presence or absence of the punitive sanction. Others fail to distinguish punishment from rehabilitation by applying overly broad definitions of rehabilitation, conflating the concept of punishment into that of rehabilitation, causing the court to state such things as "treatment is often disguised punishment" and "punishment . . . does as much to rehabilitate . . . an errant youth as does the prior philosophy of focusing upon the particular characteristics of the individual juvenile." Still others apply an overly broad definition of punishment, unduly emphasizing the significance of the conditions of a given sanction as they impact its recipient, resulting in conflating the concept of rehabilitation into that of punishment.[307]

In short, few courts engage in the careful analysis required to distinguish treatment from punishment that would trigger the right to a jury.

The Wisconsin Supreme Court in *State v. Hezzie R.* reviewed get tough changes that lengthened delinquency sentences to secure confinement for several years, expanded collateral consequences, and repealed a statutory right to a jury trial.[308] Despite numerous punitive changes, the majority concluded that the amendments attempted to "balance the rehabilitative needs for care and treatment of each juvenile, with holding the juvenile accountable for his or her acts, and protecting the public."[309] The *Hezzie R.* dissent analyzed the legislative purpose, sentencing provisions, and collateral changes, and concluded that not only has the juvenile code "shifted treatment of juvenile offenders in Wisconsin 'closer to' the criminal sphere, it has dramatically crossed the constitutional line. . . . [The juvenile code] is a criminal code in purpose and effect and cannot be deemed a civil code designed solely to rehabilitate the juvenile. . . . We must either restore the juvenile court's primary rehabilitative approach or restore the constitutional right of juveniles to trial by jury."[310]

Several other states rejected juveniles' challenges to get tough changes. The Louisiana Supreme Court considered the impact of get tough amendments—open hearings, mandatory sentences, delinquency convictions to enhance criminal sentence—but concluded that "notwithstanding the changes in the juvenile justice system . . . there remains a great disparity in the *severity of penalties* faced by a juvenile charged with delinquency and an adult defendant charged with the same crime."[311] Again, once a penalty crosses *Baldwin's* six-month *authorized sentence* threshold, further severity is constitutionally irrelevant. Juveniles in Pennsylvania requested a jury in response to get tough changes which they argued had transformed the juvenile court from a benevolent welfare institution "into a more punitive system, much more akin to the adult criminal justice system."[312] The Pennsylvania Supreme Court concluded that a delinquency trial "remains an informal protective proceeding," and uncritically asserted that "much of the reasoning of the plurality in *McKeiver*, despite the changes in society and the juvenile system . . . remains valid and compelling in reference to the juvenile court system of today."[313]

By contrast, the Kansas Supreme Court in *In re L.M.* used the analytical tools discussed in Chapter 5 to distinguish treatment from punishment and concluded, "These changes to the juvenile justice system have eroded the benevolent *parens patriae* character that distinguish it from the adult criminal system."[314] While acknowledging that other states had declined to extend delinquents a right to a jury trial, the court concluded that the Kansas juvenile code "has lost the *parens patriae* character" of earlier juvenile laws and has been "transformed into a system for prosecuting juveniles charged with committing crimes."[315]

Juvenile and criminal courts perform similar social control functions—responding to and sanctioning lawbreakers. To claim that they intervene solely to rehabilitate youths who commit crimes is disingenuous. As critical consumers of justice, juveniles readily perceive the hypocrisy of a court finding that they committed a crime, albeit obscured by euphemisms, and imposing a sanction that they experience as penal without providing them the procedural rights afforded adults. "[A]dolescents are very sensitive to perceived injustice, and unfair treatment by the legal system may accentuate antisocial tendencies, whereas fair official responses to wrongdoing may enhance respect for and obedience to law and reduce the likelihood of reoffending."[316] Youths know what a real trial involves based on courtroom dramas and publicized criminal trials. The contrast between their expectations of justice and fairness—a jury trial and a zealous defense lawyer—and a juvenile bench trial fosters a sense of injustice, delegitimates the process, and impedes rehabilitation.

Delinquency Convictions to Enhance Criminal Sentences

Apprendi v. New Jersey ruled that "any fact that increases the penalty for a crime beyond the statutory maximum, *other than the fact of a prior conviction*, must be submitted to a jury and proved beyond a reasonable doubt."[317] The Court exempted the *"fact of a prior conviction"* because criminal defendants enjoyed the right to a jury trial and proof beyond a reasonable doubt which assured validity and reliability of prior convictions.[318] *Apprendi* emphasized the jury's role to uphold *Winship's* standard of proof beyond a reasonable doubt. While *McKeiver* approved jury-free delinquency convictions to impose rehabilitative dispositions, they would *not* be adequate to punish a youth.

Criminal courts' use of delinquency convictions raises several issues. Juvenile courts historically restricted access to records to avoid stigmatizing youths.[319] But criminal courts need to know which juveniles' delinquent careers continue into adulthood to incapacitate them, punish them, or protect public safety.[320] A strong relationship exists between age and crime—the age-crime curve—and rates for most offenses peak in mid- to late adolescence.[321] Although most youths desist after one or two contacts, chronic or life-course persistent offenders continue into adulthood.[322] A record of persistent offending, whether as a juvenile or as an adult, provides the best evidentiary basis for incapacitation or enhanced punishment.[323]

Historically, criminal courts lacked access to delinquency records because of juvenile courts' confidentiality, the physical separation of juvenile and criminal court staff who maintain the records, and the difficulty of maintaining systems to track offenders and compile histories across both systems.[324] Juvenile courts' sealing or expunging delinquency records impede their use to identify young career offenders for enhanced sentences.[325]

Courts long have noted the policy conflict between confidentiality and punishing repeat offenders, but assert the importance of delinquency records to distinguish errant offenders from chronic lawbreakers. "These pubescent transgressions, when considered along with adult offenses, help the sentencing judge to determine whether the defendant has simply taken one wrong turn from the straight and narrow or is a criminal recidivist."[326] Despite a tradition of confidentiality, states have long used delinquency convictions in sentencing for subsequent crimes.[327] *United States v. Williams* reasoned that delinquency convictions could be used to enhance criminal sentences, even though they were originally obtained to treat youths using less rigorous procedures.[328] The defendant in *United States v. Johnson* challenged the U.S. Sentencing Guidelines' policy to equate juvenile confinement with adult imprisonment to calculate the criminal history score.[329] *Johnson* recognized that states confined delinquents for different reasons than they imprisoned criminals, but concluded, "It is a method, rough to be sure, of measuring relative culpability among offenders and the likelihood of their engaging in future criminal behavior."[330] The dissent in *Johnson* decried equating juvenile confinement for treatment with adult imprisonment for punishment as irrational.

> Unlike criminal punishment, which might be imposed in pursuit of retributive as well as rehabilitative objectives, the focus of juvenile confinement traditionally has been primarily, or even exclusively on reforming and treatment the offender. . . . [W]hile the purposes of confinement in the juvenile and adult sphere may occasionally converge, they have never been congruent. Two-thirds of the states continue to employ the offender-specific rehabilitation model, and in all states the initially distinct emphases of the juvenile and adult criminal systems have led to the development of a very different set of procedures and standards for confinement and incarceration.[331]

Giving youths fewer procedural safeguards to rehabilitate them and then using those less reliable convictions to punish them more severely seems contradictory and unfair.

Some states use juvenile records on a discretionary basis. Many state and federal sentencing guidelines include some delinquency convictions in defendants' criminal history score.[332] California's three-strikes law counts juvenile felony convictions as strikes for sentence enhancements.[333] Some states' guidelines weight delinquency convictions less heavily than criminal convictions because of concerns about the reliability of juvenile court procedures.[334] Other do not distinguish between juvenile and adult convictions and count both equally. Sometimes, criminal courts may not know the exact offense of which a youth was convicted because juvenile courts adjudicate youths delinquent rather than find them guilty of specific crimes.[335]

There are two reasons why states should not equate delinquency and criminal convictions for sentence enhancements. First, as we saw in Chapter 8, even though juveniles may cause the same physical injury or property loss as older actors, their choices are less blameworthy and should not be weighted the same. Even if nominally convicted of the same crime, their reduced culpability makes their crimes less serious and nonequivalent. Second, use of delinquency records to enhance criminal sentences raises questions about the procedures used to obtain those convictions. Juvenile courts in many states adjudicate half or more delinquent without counsel, including many convicted of felonies. The vast majority deny juveniles the right to a jury trial. Because judges in bench trials apply *Winship*'s reasonable doubt standard less stringently, some youths would have been acquitted with adequate safeguards.[336]

Apprendi reaffirmed the jury's role to assure the reliability of factfinding. But its exception for "the fact of prior conviction" created a conundrum for appellate courts. Although sentencing policies to incapacitate chronic offenders support using delinquency records to sentence criminals, the denial of a jury right and questionable waivers of counsel call into question the reliability of those convictions. Federal and state courts are divided whether *Apprendi* allows judges to use delinquency convictions to enhance criminal sentences.[337]

In *United States v. Tighe*, the federal trial judge imposed a mandatory minimum fifteen-year sentence rather than a ten-year maximum sentence based on a prior record that included a delinquency conviction obtained without a jury right.[338] The Court of Appeals reversed and reasoned that *Apprendi*'s exception for prior convictions "was rooted in the concept that prior convictions have been, by their very nature, subject to the fundamental triumvirate of procedural protections intended to guarantee the reliability of criminal convictions: fair notice, reasonable doubt and *the right to a jury trial*."[339] By contrast, *United States v. Smalley* considered the same facts and issues presented in *Tighe*, but reached the opposite result.[340] While *Apprendi* identified the procedural safeguards that clearly established reliable prior convictions—notice, right to a jury, and proof beyond a reasonable doubt—*Smalley* reasoned that they were not essential prerequisites to a valid conviction. "[W]e think that it is incorrect to assume that it is not only sufficient but necessary that the 'fundamental triumvirate of procedural protections' . . . underly [*sic*] an adjudication before it can qualify for the *Apprendi* exemption."[341] *Smalley* concluded that *Gault* and *Winship*'s procedural safeguards were more than adequate to ensure the reliability that *Apprendi* requires.[342] *Smalley* did not examine *McKeiver*'s reasons to provide less rigorous safeguards or the contradiction between using procedurally less rigorous convictions obtained for a benign purpose subsequently to punish. For *Tighe*, a jury distinguished criminal trials from other proceedings and non-jury delinquency convictions simply failed to ensure such reliability. *Tighe*'s understanding of the jury's role appears more consistent with *Apprendi*'s jurisprudence than *Smalley*, which relied only on *McKeiver*.[343]

Juveniles have raised *Apprendi* challenges to states' use of delinquency convictions to enhance criminal sentences.[344] State appellate court rulings reflect the *Tighe/Smalley* split of opinion about the reliability of delinquency convictions. *State v. Brown* emphasized that *McKeiver* denied a jury right because delinquents received "non-criminal treatment" and held that "because juveniles do not have a right to a jury trial in these proceedings, juvenile adjudications cannot be used to enhance adult felony convictions. . . . [J]uvenile adjudications . . . are sufficiently reliable, even without a jury trial, to support dispositions within the juvenile justice system. However, *Apprendi* has raised the issue of whether these adjudications, rendered without the right to a jury trial are sufficiently reliable to support enhanced sentencing for adults."[345] By contrast, *State v. Hitt* reasoned that because juveniles received all the procedural safeguards to which the Constitution entitled them, courts could use valid prior convictions to enhance subsequent sentences. "The *Apprendi* Court spoke in general terms of the procedural safeguards attached to a prior conviction. It did not specify *all* procedural safeguards nor did it require *certain* crucial procedural safeguards."[346] Until the Court clarifies

Apprendi, defendants in some states or federal circuits will serve longer sentences than those in other jurisdictions based on flawed delinquency convictions.

The use of delinquency convictions to enhance criminal sentences further aggravates endemic racial disparities in justice administration.[347] Recall from Chapter 5, at each stage of the juvenile justice system, racial disparities compound, cumulate, and contribute to disproportionate minority confinement. As a result, Black youths acquire more extensive prior delinquency records than do their white counterparts.[348] Those prior records contribute to racial disparities in waiver to criminal court and commitments to prison. Judges sentence more Black youths with a prior record to prison than similarly situated white youths, perhaps because judges make stereotypic assumptions based on racial stereotypes.[349] Richard Frase's magisterial analysis of racial disparities in criminal sentencing in Minnesota concludes that "seemingly legitimate sentencing factors such as criminal history scoring can have strong disparate impacts on nonwhite defendants."[350]

Collateral Consequences of Delinquency Convictions

The denial of a jury adversely affects rules of evidence, timing of suppression hearings, and appointment of counsel and raises questions about the reliability of convictions. In addition to direct penalties—institutional confinement and enhanced sentences as juveniles or as adults—extensive collateral consequences follow from delinquency convictions. Although state policies vary, they may follow youths for decades and affect future housing, education, and employment opportunities.[351] Upon arrest, states may enter juveniles' fingerprints, photographs, and DNA into databases accessible to law enforcement and other agencies.[352] Some states' get tough reforms opened delinquency trials and juvenile records to the public. Media access to court proceedings, information available to the public, and print or televised reports on the Internet can create a permanent and easily accessible record of a youth's delinquency.[353] Even if not released to the public, criminal justice agencies, schools, childcare providers, the military, and others may have access to juvenile court records automatically or by petition to the court.[354] In most jurisdictions, expungement of delinquency records is not automatic and requires a youth to file a petition, which the court may or may not grant depending on the seriousness of the offense and the time that has elapsed since the conviction.[355] Youths may have their privilege to drive suspended or revoked, which impairs their ability to attend school, get to work, and participate in court-ordered services.[356] Delinquency convictions may affect youths' ability to obtain professional licensure, to receive government aid, to join the military, to obtain or keep legal immigration status, or to live in public housing.[357]

As noted in Chapter 7, crimes committed in school or even off campus may lead to suspension or expulsion.[358] School administrators may place returning youths on probation, assign them to an alternative school, or prohibit them from participating in extracurricular activities. Youths applying to college must acknowledge arrests, suspensions, or expulsions, which may adversely affect their admission.[359] Delinquency adjudications may make youths ineligible for scholarships or federal grants. Adjudication may cause a youth—and his family—to be evicted from public housing.[360] A delinquency conviction may prevent a youth from possessing a firearm as an adult.[361] Juveniles convicted as adults suffer all the disabilities imposed on criminals; those found guilty of a felony may lose the right to serve on a jury or to vote even before they are eligible to register.[362] The erosion of juvenile courts' confidentiality labels youths as criminals and undermines *McKeiver*'s rationale to deny a jury.

Sex Offender Registration

The response to juvenile sex offenders is among the most onerous collateral consequences of delinquency adjudication.[363] In *An American Travesty*, Franklin Zimring argues that despite developmental differences between juveniles and adults, states' sex-offender laws assume that "adolescent and adult sexual behavior should be judged by the same standards of culpability, clinical significance, and indications of future danger to the community."[364] He argues that sex-offender laws assume a pathological sexual orientation, specialization in sex offenses, a fixed proclivity to commit sex offenses, and a high likelihood of future sex offending. These assumptions are of questionable validity for many adults and even more inapposite for most juveniles engaged in sexual activity.[365] "[T]he sexual behavior of juvenile sexual offenders differs from the sexual behavior of nondelinquents in its delinquent characteristics rather than its sexual characteristics."[366] Juveniles adjudicated for a sexual offense are less likely to be arrested as adults for sexual offenses than are delinquents convicted of other crimes.[367] Applying laws created to punish adults who sexually exploit children to adolescents engaged in consensual underage sex, is an instance of "the felonization of adolescent sex . . . based on an invalid analogy with adult behavior."[368]

Although adolescent sex offending is less likely to be driven by stable personality characteristics than is adult sex offending, the federal Adam Walsh Child Protection and Safety Act—also known as the Sex Offender Registration and Notification Act (SORNA)—requires states to implement registration and notification standards for individuals convicted as adults or juveniles for certain sex offenses.[369] States may subject youths convicted of a sex offense to a lifetime registration requirement including a duty to register annually and immediately following any change of address.[370] States limit where registered offenders can live, work, or attend school. Failure to register is a separate crime for which they may be imprisoned. Some jurisdiction require neighborhood notification based on the belief that potential victims and communities require protection against sexual threats.[371] They may have their DNA collected and stored in a database accessible to the FBI and other state law enforcement agencies.[372] Although the Court has deemed sex-offender registration as civil in nature, adolescents experience mental distress, community harassment, and social isolation, which impedes reintegration into the community.[373]

Reforming Court Procedures to Prevent Wrongful Convictions

Recent developmental psychological and neuroscience research has taught us much more than we previously knew about how children think, act, and differ from adults. It reinforces the recognition that youth are less competent than adults and provides rationale for a separate juvenile justice system. Progressive reformers designed juvenile courts without procedural safeguards or substantive constraints on judges' discretion to pursue the rehabilitative ideal. But a century later, get tough statutory changes have transformed them into second-rate criminal courts that provide neither therapy nor justice.

Since *Gault*, the procedural as well as substantive convergence between juvenile and criminal courts has placed greater demands on juveniles' competence to exercise rights. The increased formality reflects juvenile courts' shift from rehabilitating youths to protecting public safety and punishing offenses. Despite these changes, most states do not provide delinquents formal or functional protections comparable to those of adult criminal defendants. Juveniles waive their *Miranda* rights and right to counsel under an adult standard—knowing, intelligent, and voluntary—that is unlikely to discern whether they understand and are competent to relinquish those rights. Denial of juries calls into question the accuracy and reliability of delinquency adjudications for initial dispositions and collateral uses. Get tough changes heighten juveniles' need for protection from the state and collateral consequences that may follow them well into adulthood. Despite criminalizing juvenile justice, states do not provide procedural safeguards to protect delinquents from their own immaturity, or give them the criminal procedural safeguards that afford some protection from punishment by the state. Instead, juvenile courts assure that youths continue to "receive the worst of both worlds"—treating juveniles just like adults when formal equality redounds to their disadvantage and providing less effective juvenile procedures when they provide an advantage to the state.

I argued in Chapter 2 that juvenile courts' procedural deficiencies stem in part from the Supreme Court's decision to base delinquents' rights on the Fourteenth Amendment Due Process Clause rather than the Sixth Amendment of the Bill of Rights. Theoretically, due process analysis could allow the Court to find "special circumstances" based on youths' immaturity to provide more procedural protections for delinquents than for criminal defendants. But fundamental fairness is a vague foundation and enabled *McKeiver* to deny the right to a jury trial despite *Duncan*'s recognition of its critical importance to protect citizens.

The Constitution defines the minimum procedural baseline below which states may not fall. Most of the details of juvenile justice administration are statutory, should recognize that "children are different," and could provide greater assistance. State legislators passed get tough laws to punish delinquents and simultaneously eroded the meager protections of juvenile courts—closed and confidential proceedings, limited use of delinquency convictions, and the like. State legislators failed to appropriate adequate funds for legal services and fostered crippled public defenders incapable of providing delinquents with effective assistance of counsel. Delinquents need well-funded, well-trained attorneys to advise them, protect their interests, and defend against punitive state intervention. A half century after *Gault*, many juveniles in many states are still waiting for a lawyer to advocate on their behalf.

Epilogue

Opportunities and Obstacles

Juvenile courts emerged in response to structural changes more than a century ago and spread throughout the nation during the first decades of the twentieth century. Economic modernization and the social construction of childhood provided the context within which Progressives created new institutions to control children. Over the century, the juvenile court's diversionary mission—to protect children from the harms of the criminal justice system—explains its endurance despite its inability to achieve its interventionist goal.

Over the past half century, the politics of race has shaped juvenile courts and evoked two contradictory responses. Initially, the Warren Court's due process revolution aimed to end Southern apartheid, enhance civil rights, and protect minority citizens. *Gault* extended some procedural rights to delinquents as part of the Court's broader civil rights agenda. Thereafter, Republican politicians pursued a Southern strategy to appeal to Southern, suburban, and blue-collar white voters' negative racial attitudes. By the 1980s and 1990s, structural, economic, and racial demographic changes led to a Black underclass living in concentrated poverty and a rise in drug crime, gun violence, and murder. Politicians campaigned to get tough and crack down on "youth crime," which the public understood as code for young Black males.[1] They inverted Progressives' conception of youthful innocence and immaturity into an alternative vision of adult-like super-predators. Punitive transfer laws and delinquency sanctions transformed juvenile courts into procedurally deficient, second-class criminal courts.

During the Get Tough Era, politicians ignored that children differ from adults in competence and culpability. Although they are less able to exercise rights, states use adult legal standards, posit a fictitious equality, and place youths at a procedural disadvantage. Judges readily allow delinquents to waive counsel in an increasingly complex punitive system.

When juveniles are represented, their lawyers often fail to provide effective advocacy. Five decades after *Gault*, states have yet to put the *justice* in juvenile justice.

For the past three decades, states have transferred more and younger juveniles to criminal court for prosecution as adults. Politicians characterized them as criminally responsible and disregarded youths' reduced culpability. *Roper*, *Graham*, and *Miller* finally recognized that children's immature judgment and impaired self-control diminished their responsibility and barred the harshest punishments. Other than death or LWOP, however, criminal court judges punish transferred juveniles just like adults, ignore developmental differences, and disproportionally penalize Black youths. Despite substantial declines in youth crime, the punitive legacy of the 1980s and 1990s remains in place. Belated judicial recognition that children are different and softening of punishment in a few states marks, at best, a modest retreat from repressive policies.

For a century, juvenile courts have discriminated between "our children" and "other peoples' children." Progressive reformers had to choose between fundamental reforms to alter conditions that caused crime—poverty, inequality, and discrimination—or to apply Band-Aids to children effected by them. Impelled by class and ethnic antagonism, they avoided broad structural changes and chose to save children. A century later, we face the same choices and continue to evade our responsibilities to other peoples' children.

The prevalence of violent crime in segregated inner-city areas reflect private and public policy decisions stretching back decades that created and reinforce economic inequality, concentrated poverty, and racial isolation. Political discussions about poverty, welfare benefits, income inequality, and crime function as proxies for conversations about race. Conservative politicians exploit white voters' racial animus and Americans engage in a subterranean discourse using code words and misleading images.[2] They identify long-term poverty and associated problems—unemployment, drug abuse, crime, out-of-wedlock childbirth, school-leaving, and the like—primarily as a condition of African Americans separate from the American mainstream to avoid addressing them.[3] The perception that juvenile courts' clients are young criminals of color enables politicians to withhold resources either to improve their life conditions or to provide real justice.

Juvenile Justice Reform

This is an opportune time to adopt sensible juvenile justice policies. The dramatic drop in juvenile crime reduces its salience as terrorists and immigrants have supplanted super-predators on the political agenda. Advances in developmental psychology and neuroscience increase understanding of children's behavior. Youth advocacy groups create pressures on courts and legislatures and foundations sponsor projects to implement evidence-based programs.

The Crime Drop

Since the mid-1990s, rates of youth crime—especially violence and homicide—have declined precipitously. Despite alarmists' dire predictions that a cohort of super-predators would terrorize communities, those fears never materialized.[4] Several factors may have contributed to the youth crime drop.[5] Some point to a reduction in the size of the cohort of fifteen-to-twenty-four-year-old males.[6] Others attribute it to economic growth and low unemployment in the 1990s, although the relationship between macro-economic factors and crime rates, especially for those at the bottom, remains unclear.[7] Some attribute it to a period effect or cultural contagion. While drug markets and gun violence contributed to the rise in homicide, more youths who came of age in the 1980s and 1990s and witnessed the carnage of their older peers rejected that lifestyle.[8] Some argue that changes in police practices—shifts toward community-oriented, problem-solving, and zero-tolerance policing—or aggressive stop-and-frisk contributed to crime decline.[9] Get tough advocates claim that mass incarceration increased the justice system's deterrent and incapacitative effects, although analysts find only a modest relationship between imprisonment and crime rates.[10] Others attribute it to structural changes in cities—urban development, gentrification, new housing and businesses—although those developments seldom affect the neighborhoods of the targets of get tough policies.[11] No single factor caused the crime decline of the 1990s, which makes it equally difficult to predict whether it will endure.[12] But it has alleviated the moral panic that sparked punitive laws—most of which remain in place—and allows for more sensible policies.[13]

Developmental Psychology and Neuroscience

Roper, *Graham*, and *Miller* relied on developmental psychology and neuroscience research to affirm that "children are different" and to prohibit the most extreme sentences. They emphasized immature judgment and limited self-control to explain adolescents' impetuosity and diminished responsibility. Brain-scanning technologies enable neuroscientists to examine how brain structure and circuitry change between puberty and adulthood.[14] Although neuroscientists have not established causal connections between brain structure and behavior or the relationship between aggregate studies and individual's actions, adolescents' immature brains help explain their poor judgment and impulsive behavior.[15]

Youth Advocacy and Foundation-Sponsored Reforms

In response to get tough policies, dozens of youth advocacy and policy groups emerged to oppose punitive sentencing, litigated to reform and restrict transfer policies, and lobbied to implement the right to counsel and to raise to eighteen the age of juvenile court jurisdiction. They challenged juvenile court judges' abuses of discretion and conditions of confinement in institutions.[16] They used developmental psychology and neuroscience research to generate media coverage about how children differ from adults and the iatrogenic effects of harsh policies.[17]

The MacArthur Foundation Network on Adolescent Development and Juvenile Justice studied adolescent culpability, competence, and treatment responsivity to inform juvenile justice policies.[18] In 2004, the MacArthur Foundation initiated Models for Change reforms in sixteen states. In four states—Illinois, Louisiana, Pennsylvania, and Washington—juvenile justice stakeholders agreed to implement developmentally informed policies to serve as models for system changes elsewhere.[19] In twelve states, the foundation funded programs to reduce racial disparities, increase access to mental health services, and improve delivery of legal services. The Annie E. Casey Foundation launched the Juvenile Detention Alternatives Initiative (JDAI) in 1992 to reduce the overuse and abuse of secure detention.[20] JDAI initiatives in over one hundred sites in nineteen states have reduced total detention populations by one-third and the number of minority youths in detention by one-quarter.[21] The Robert Wood Johnson Foundation has invested in juvenile justice reform efforts through its Reclaiming Futures initiatives. The Haywood Burns Institute has focused on reducing disproportionate minority confinement and developed analytical tools to rationalize decision making.

Policy Prescriptions

The time is right to reform juvenile courts' jurisdiction, jurisprudence, and procedures. Chapters 5–9 describe policies to improve justice administration within the constraints of the current system. Judges should make waiver decisions in an adversarial hearing rather than prosecutors via charging decisions. Sentences of youths convicted as adults should be substantially reduced—a Youth Discount—to reflect diminished culpability. Risk assessment instruments and other JDAI strategies could reduce pretrial detention and disproportionate minority confinement. Juvenile court interventions should keep youths in their communities and avoid out-of-home placements and secure confinement to the greatest extent possible and use evidence-based programs to rehabilitate and reintegrate them. Gender-appropriate strategies should deal with girls in the community rather than use the pretext of minor misconduct to incarcerate them. Schools should eschew prison-like environments—with pervasive police presence, surveillance technology, and mindless rule enforcement—in favor of more restorative policies, focus on inclusion rather than exclusion, and emphasize dropout prevention and reentry programs. The procedural safeguards of juvenile courts should be greatly enhanced to compensate for adolescents' limited competence: automatic competency assessment for children younger than fourteen years of age, mandatory presence of counsel during interrogation for those younger than sixteen, and mandatory non-waivable counsel for youths in court proceedings. Delinquents should enjoy the right to a jury trial to assure reliability of convictions and to increase the visibility and accountability of judges, prosecutors, and defense lawyers. States should strengthen appellate oversight of delinquency proceedings. Records of youths should be easily sealed or expunged to reduce impediments to education and employment. Collateral consequences of delinquency convictions should be eliminated.[22]

I wrote *Bad Kids: Race and the Transformation of the Juvenile Court* (1999) at the peak of the Get Tough Era. My proposal to abolish the juvenile court reflected despair over the unalloyed punitiveness and racism of delinquency sanctions, the limited efficacy of treatment, and juvenile courts' procedural deficiencies. *The Evolution of the Juvenile Court* echoes that despondency, but with a new prescription to strengthen juvenile courts' diversionary mission. Although most states' juvenile courts' jurisdiction extends to youths under eighteen years of age, North Carolina sets the boundary at sixteen and ten states set it at seventeen.[23] Developmental psychology and neuroscience research reviewed earlier strengthen the case to raise the age of jurisdiction to eighteen in every state. Indeed, it would be appropriate to extend to young adults aged eighteen to twenty-one some of the protections associated with juvenile courts—shorter sentences like a Youth Discount, rehabilitative treatment in separate facilities, protected records, and the like. Many European countries' criminal laws provide separate young adult sentencing provisions and institutions to afford greater leniency and use of rehabilitative measures.[24]

Most youths involved with the juvenile justice system will outgrow their youthful indiscretion without heroic interventions. We can facilitate desistance by reinforcing the two-track system—one informal, one formal—proposed by the President's Crime Commission a half century ago. For youths who require services, diversion to community resources provides a more efficient and flexible alternative to adjudication and disposition. If states explicitly forgo home removal, then juvenile courts can use summary processes like noncriminal traffic courts to make dispositions. *Scott v. Illinois* prohibits incarceration without representation. *Alabama v. Shelton* prohibits probation revocation and confinement of a defendant who was not represented in the original proceeding.[25] *Baldwin v. New York* affords a jury to any person facing the prospect of six months incarceration. By foregoing home removal or incarceration, states can administer a streamlined justice system for most youths. Diversion raises its own issues because low-visibility discretionary decisions contribute to racial disparities at the front end.[26] States can adopt formal criteria, risk assessment instruments, data collection, and ongoing monitoring to rationalize decisions and reduce disparities. Finally, an ounce of prevention is worth a pound of cure. Prevention programs that target at-risk youths, families, and communities have demonstrated efficacy, provide cost/benefit returns, and would reduce the number of youths referred to juvenile courts in the first instance.

States should strengthen procedural safeguards for serious young offenders whom the state seeks to remove from home or confine. Although delinquency sanctions are shorter than those imposed by criminal courts, it is disingenuous to claim that they do not pursue deterrent, incapacitative, and retributive goals.[27] Apart from those who pose a risk of flight, states should reserve secure detention for youths whose offense and prior record indicate that they likely would be removed from home if convicted. For youths facing confinement, juvenile courts *are* criminal courts and requires criminal procedural safeguards including the right to a jury. As a result of developmental immaturity, children require greater protections than adults—counsel at interrogation and mandatory non-waivable counsel at trial. Increasing protections and costs of formal adjudication provide financial and administrative incentives to divert more youths.

For the most serious young offenders, the maximum penalties that juvenile courts can impose may fall short of the minimum sanctions serious offenders deserve or the public will tolerate. In most states, juvenile courts' disposition age jurisdiction continues until age twenty-one or older.[28] Developmental psychologists report a sharp drop-off in culpability and competence among youths fifteen years of age and younger. Sixteen should be the minimum age at which judges could transfer any youths and even then that power should be used sparingly. With an appropriately crafted Youth Discount, there would be few crimes other than murder for which juvenile courts' dispositions would be inadequate.

While local, state, and federal agencies can implement many reforms to enhance juvenile justice administration, improving the lives of juvenile courts' clients requires addressing "root causes" of crime and racial disparities. The political economy—social and economic inequality—produces profound disparities in income, health, housing, education, employment, and exposure to criminogenic conditions that no justice system reforms can overcome. Although poverty has a devastating impact on all youths, larger proportions of Black youngsters and other children of color are exposed to these disadvantages.

Impediments to Reform: Politics and Political Economy

> Today in the United States, we have essentially two childhoods. The one experienced by mostly White and Asian children is one of abundance and opportunity. It is a childhood rich with educational opportunities and excellent school systems. The other childhood experienced by almost half of all African-American and Latino children is one of low income, jobs that provide limited health care, and schools that track children to bleak futures. The schools these children attend are too often underfunded, poorly staffed, and signal failure from the start.[29]

Juvenile courts do not cause delinquency in the first instance. Given limited resources and authority, they can only marginally improve the life chances of many youths whom they serve—poor, developmentally challenged, and children of color mired in social disadvantage. Jamie Fader's *Falling Back* concludes that the "the juvenile justice system is ill equipped to restructure the labor market to create better jobs, allow young people the financial freedom to invest in higher education, dismantle racial discrimination or residential segregation, or fix families struggling with poverty or addiction," and instead it attributes youths' criminality to individual deficits and poor decisions.[30] Emphasizing youths' criminality elicits public hostility and contributes to their perceived disposability. Most of the causes of delinquency are rooted in social structure—concentrated poverty, economic inequality, hypersegregation and racial isolation, spatial mismatch between skills, jobs, and employment opportunities, failing schools, and the like. No justice system can remedy these conditions.

Child Poverty in the United States

Poverty is the biggest single risk factor for successful child development.[31] It affects every dimension of a child's life beginning in utero. Within their first few years, many African American and Hispanic babies born with similar potential as white and Asian infants begin to experience very different life courses and outcomes. Poverty affects how their parents raise them, their access to healthcare, exposure to hunger and inadequate nutrition, residential instability, the safety of their communities, the quality of schools they attend, and their like-lihood of justice system involvement.[32] It adversely affects their life trajectories—lower educational achievement, early school leaving, delinquency, unmarried childbirth, and family dysfunction.[33] It stunts cognitive development and verbal ability, adds to poor language skills, and contributes to later school failure.[34] Children from impoverished homes bring to schools higher rates of truancy, disorder, and residen-tial transience, and lower levels of English proficiency.[35] Every adverse indicator of child development—suicide, mental illness, drug abuse, homelessness, teenage pregnancy, school-leaving, crime, and violent victimization—correlates with living in poverty.[36] Youths involved in the justice system—Black, white, or Hispanic—share similar charac-teristics: impoverished childhoods, abuse or neglect, family instability, poor schools, limited social and job skills, and drug and alcohol use.[37]

Although poverty is the leading risk factor for children's positive de-velopment, it does not affect all children as equally or as intensely. Fig-ure E.1 reports rates of child poverty by race over the past four decades. Historically and currently, Black children are at much greater risk to live in poverty than their white counterparts. Although child poverty rates fluctuate somewhat with larger economic trends, over the past four decades, about one in five children in the United States has lived in poverty.[38] However, the fluctuation around 20% obscures profound differences in poverty rates by race. For white children, the poverty rates is about half the overall average and for Black and Hispanic children, it is about double the overall average. "The poverty rate for African-American and Latino children ranges between 35 and 40 percent. The majority of African American children are born to single parents (more than two-thirds) and their child poverty rates is close to 60 percent."[39] As a consequence, about one in nine white children live in poverty com-pared with four in ten Black children.

As a result of deindustrialization and changes in family struc-ture, more children live with an unmarried single parent, typically a mother.[40] In the United States, living in a single-parent female-headed household is a prescription for child poverty regardless of race.[41] How-ever, more than two-thirds of Black children were born outside of mar-riage; more than half live in a single-parent household in poverty.[42] In 2006, more than two-thirds of all Black children were born to unmarried mothers, compared with one-half for Hispanic children, and one-quarter for White children.[43] The level and intensity of poverty that Black children experience is much more severe than that of poor white children. Black children are seven times more likely than white children to live in high-poverty neighborhoods and twelve times more likely to live in racially segregated ones.[44] In addition to the direct connection between single parenthood and poverty, children from low-income households without fathers present are more likely to become school dropouts, earn less money as young adults, and more likely to form single-parent households themselves.[45]

Children growing up in segregated neighborhoods of concentrated poverty experience great trauma. They are more likely to encounter environmental hazards and exposure to toxic pollutants—e.g., the lead-contaminated water in Flint, Michigan. Poverty adversely affects brain and cognitive development and socio-emotional functioning, and causes behavioral problems and depression. Children of color living in concentrated poverty are much more likely to attend segregated, inferior schools taught by demoralized teachers in deteriorated physical facilities with large classes that will seldom overcome the disadvantages they present. The school-to-prison pipeline responds to children's misfortune and misbehavior with suspension, expulsion and referral to the juvenile justice system. Bruce Western's *Punishment and Inequality in America* describes the devastating impact of mass incarceration on Black men who do not finish high school. Arrest, a criminal record, and confinement increases unemployment and makes them more likely to commit additional crimes. Social disadvantage contributes to criminality; justice system involvement worsens offenders' life chances with direct and collateral consequences.[46]

In *Our Kids: The American Dream in Crisis*, Robert Putnam addresses the questions of whether children from different social and economic backgrounds have roughly equal life chances and how their prospects have changed in recent decades.[47] He uses parental education—college graduate versus high school degree or less—as a proxy for socioeconomic class. He compares differences in family structure, parenting practices, economic stability, school quality, and neighborhoods of children like himself reared in the prosperous post–World War II era with those of youths today. As described in Chapter 3, in those days, working

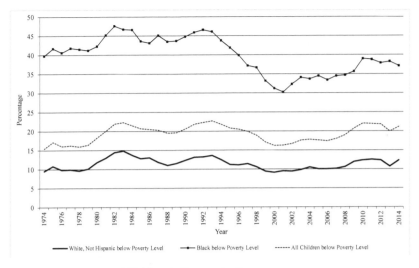

Figure E.1. Percentage of Children in Poverty, by Race
Source: U.S. Census Bureau, "Income and Poverty in the United States: 2014," www.census.gov.

men with a high school education could support a family and expect a brighter future for their children. Putnam concludes that opportunities for social and economic mobility have declined because children of affluent families today enjoy many more advantages than did affluent children of his generation, but primarily because conditions of poor children today are much worse than were their counterparts of the previous generation.[48] The top third of U.S. society invest more in family life, community networks, and civic activities than did their parents, while those in the bottom third fall further behind as families fracture, household economies decline, and adults and children disengage from mainstream society.

The decline in manufacturing jobs that began in the 1970s caused the earnings gap between high school–and college-educated workers to grow rapidly. Inequality increasingly operates through education, which correlates closely with parents' education and socioeconomic status. Over the past quarter century, the net worth of college-educated households with children increased by 47% while that of high school–educated households fell by 17%.[49] Parental wealth provides affluent children with an informal social safety net that poorer children lack.[50] Residential, educational, and class segregation create separate and unequal worlds in which to raise children. Many members of the upper middle class do not know how poor children live or recognize the growing opportunity gap between their children and other people's children.[51]

Parental education and income affect family formation and child-rearing practices. Daniel Patrick Moynihan's dire report on *The Negro Family* warned that Black male unemployment would lead to family instability, out-of-wedlock childbirth, and child poverty. Subsequent decades reveal that the relationship between employment and family formation are not race-based but class-based and affect all people. Among the college-educated upper third of Americans, women marry later, have fewer unintended pregnancies, and divorce less frequently.[52] By contrast and regardless of race, today's high school–educated women are less likely to have married their child's father, more likely to have unintended pregnancies, bear children at a younger age, and experience greatly reduced economic prospects.[53]

Class-based differences in parenting styles—a function of education and socioeconomic status—affect infants' and children's early brain development, cognitive abilities, and behavior.[54] Early interaction with caring, consistent adults fosters healthy brain development, lays the foundation for verbal and mathematical skills, and fosters socio-emotional skills—grit, sensitivity, optimism, self-control, and emotional stability.[55] By contrast, children who are physically or emotionally abused or neglected experience toxic stress, which causes biochemical and anatomical changes that harm brain development and contribute to learning, behavior, and physical and mental health problems later in life.[56] Poor parents have less time to foster their children's cognitive development than their wealthier counterparts.[57] A poor single mother working a minimum-wage job who gets to work via public transportation or in an unreliable car and comes home exhausted does not have the luxury of affluent parents to read to her child, engage in vocabulary-rich conversations, or buy books and computer learning programs.[58]

Income inequality and class-based residential segregation contribute to differences in educational outcomes. Residential segregation is deeply rooted and sustained by zoning regulations and home mortgage tax deductions; people strongly resist efforts to reduce class-based segregation. Residential segregation contributes to de facto class/race-based school segregation. Affluent parents provide their children with preschool enrichment programs and they start formal education with more school-ing than their poorer counterparts. The quality of schools that affluent children attend differ greatly from the racially and economically segre-gated urban schools.[59] As a result, children of poor, less educated par-ents are handicapped at the start and have fewer resources with which to overcome obstacles.[60]

Child Poverty Is the United States' Public Policy

Harsh as it may sound, child poverty is the United States' public policy. A much larger proportion of children in America live in poverty—one in five—than in any other Western industrialized nation. Children are the poorest Americans—one in five are below the poverty level, includ-ing one in four infants and toddlers under three, more than fifteen million in total—and more than one-third live in families with incomes half the federal poverty level.[61] Children comprise the largest age group in poverty and the macro-structural and family demographic changes of the past third of a century have exacerbated their disadvantage.

The United States' child poverty rate is double or triple that of most European countries—France (11.4%), Germany (10.5%), Ireland (10.4%), the United Kingdom (9.4%), and the Netherlands (6.3%). It is four times that experienced by children in the Nordic countries—Norway (5.0%), Denmark (4.5%), and Finland (3.7%).[62] Child poverty rates have been relatively stable in almost all advanced countries, *except* in the United States where they have increased over the past quarter century.[63] Not surprisingly, countries that spend more on social welfare and have lower levels of income and wealth inequality also have lower crime rates and levels of imprisonment.[64]

As international comparisons demonstrate, in affluent societies child poverty is not an inevitable social condition or the result of natural scar-city. It is the consequence of public policies that produce and reinforce social and economic inequalities and national priorities to prefer the elderly and wealthy over the young, the poor, and families.[65] Earned in-come is the single best antidote to child poverty and influenced by many government policies: tax code, housing subsidies, minimum wage, strat-egies to promote growth and full employment, job training and educa-tion for economically marginalized and underskilled workers.[66]

Comparative research attributes the significant differences in national child poverty rates to different levels and mixes of income packaging through government expenditures.[67] Compared with other developed nations, the United States provides fewer resources or income transfers to reduce child poverty, especially for female-headed households whose children are the most vulnerable.[68] Poor children today are comparatively poorer than poor children in the recent past, more likely to experience chronic and persistent poverty, and more likely to be isolated from non-poor children in schools and communities.[69]

What Ought to Be Done?

What do European countries do that produces such dramatically lower child poverty rates than the United States'? The root causes of child poverty in the United States are structural and political—the consequences of political-economic policies, wealth and income inequality, and racial barriers.[70] A society committed to children's welfare would assure that all children, regardless of their parents' circumstances, have a fair start and a meaningful chance to succeed. In the United States, means-tested and time-limited welfare programs for poor people effectively blame them for their own penury and put the onus on them to establish eligibility for grudging public assistance.[71] To hold young children responsible for their parents' shortcomings offends basic decency and morality.[72]

The roots of inequality and child poverty lie in political decisions to favor certain classes and interests over others. Reagan-era tax policies favored capital ownership over labor, shifted the tax burden from the very wealthy to lower-income workers, and contributed to growing wealth and income inequality.[73] A family with a $200,000 home mortgage receives a housing subsidy of more than $3,000 a year from the interest tax deduction—a tax transfer of nearly $100 billion per year—while poor people who rent receive nothing.[74] The earnings cap on Social Security income—$118,500 in 2016—exempts the wealthy from paying their proportional share and constitutes a regressive tax.[75] As a result of many wealth-skewed policy decisions, the top 1% possesses more wealth than the bottom 90% combined.[76] Public policies give much to those who have a great deal, do little for the vast majority, and are leading to a caste system of haves and have-nots exacerbated by racial disparities.

Parents shoulder a socially valuable but increasingly expensive burden to raise children and in the long run all citizens benefit from their sacrifices. Unlike in the United States, a child raised in a single-parent household in a Western European country is much less likely to live in poverty.[77] In *Poor Kids in a Rich Country*, Lee Rainwater and Timothy Smeeding compare the circumstances of low-income American children with their counterparts in other rich countries and assess the impacts of public policies to reduce child poverty and inequality. Three policies account for that difference—a children's allowance, paid parental leave, and publicly supported childcare.[78] European democracies provide a social safety net for poor children through direct income support programs to lift children out of poverty.[79] Most European countries provide a universal children's allowance—cash and tax benefits—that puts income assistance directly into the hands of families.[80] Family leave and childcare policies reduce child poverty by encouraging maternal employment. Paid parental leave allows women to take time off from work to bond with their children and yet retain their attachment to the workforce.[81] In the absence of paid leave, many women drop out of the economy, which leads to income loss and erosion of skills.[82] Public childcare subsidies and services enable women with children to reenter the labor market with confidence.[83] A $1,000 increase in public spending for childcare reduces child poverty in single-mother households by 6%.[84] A comparison of eighteen countries' policies concluded that modest increases in family income, paid parental leave, and subsidized childcare substantially reduces child poverty rates.[85]

Why What Ought to Be Done Won't Be Done

Child poverty is the root cause of many of the differences in rates of crime and violence by race. It derives from economic inequality, residential segregation, concentrated disadvantage, unemployment, and limited social capital. The historic legacy of institutional and individual racism frustrates efforts to reduce child poverty. Racial disparities "are the product of politics—of how key politicians, other public figures, interest groups, the media and social movements choose to draw from that past, reinvent that past, and discard pieces of the past as they adjust their political strategies to the political, social, and economic realities of the present."[86]

Even though white children comprise the largest number of children in poverty and would benefit most from programs to alleviate it, too many white people and public officials resist structural reforms to aid the poor because Blacks and other children of color would benefit disproportionately.[87] Progressive Era child-saving reforms—juvenile courts, child labor, and compulsory school attendance—reflect the high value we once placed on children. But they and we are more ambivalent about poor children, especially poor children of color, because of their inevitable connection with poor adults whom we expect to be self-sufficient. Welfare policies long have distinguished between the deserving and undeserving poor; racialized attitudes about welfare and the undeserving poor depict Blacks as lazy and with less commitment to work. Conservative politicians prefer to attribute poverty and crime to peoples' bad decisions and bad values, rather than to structural conditions.[88] Conservatives historically oppose childcare programs yet insist that welfare mothers work, subsidize tax cuts for the wealthy on the backs of the middle class, and regard children born into poor families simply as unfortunate, rather than as a collective responsibility to ensure society's future. While Americans invest resources, lavish affection, and want only the best for their own, they view other people's children—especially those of other races or classes—with suspicion, hostility, and as potential threats to their own children's well-being.[89]

A half century ago, the Kerner Commission warned that America was "moving toward two societies, one black, one white—separate and unequal" and predicted that failure to ameliorate income and racial inequality would "make permanent the division of our country in two societies; one largely Negro and poor, located in the central cities; the other predominantly white and affluent located in the suburbs."[90] Deindustrialization transformed cities and left an even darker legacy than that of which the Kerner Commission warned—hyper-segregation, concentrated poverty, erosion of public education, and political battles over race subsumed in cultural conflicts.

Confronting issues of political economy and racial and economic inequality requires political will and leadership, which unfortunately we greatly lack. How do we create a political environment capable of enacting child-friendly policies?[91] Conservatives in particular, but Americans in general, place greater emphases on individual behavior and cultural factors, than on structural inequality to explain differences in people's circumstances. A culture that attributes crime, poverty, and unemployment to individual deficiencies does not engender strong support for programs and policies to eradicate inequality.[92] But the only way to reduce the levels of violence in urban communities and racial disparities in justice administration is to address the profound inequality and concentrated poverty that cause them. This requires the public and politicians to make alleviating unconscionable rates of child poverty, failed urban schools, and minority unemployment a national priority. It requires changing political economy and social structure rather than applying Band-Aids to damaged individuals. It requires policies and programs to address residential segregation, inadequate housing, concentrated poverty, and unequal access to quality public education. It requires a strong commitment to alleviate child poverty through universal programs.[93] Enacting laws to alleviate the root causes of inequality requires appreciating that children are a public good and that investments in them today are necessary for society's tomorrow.[94]

After more than four decades of studying juvenile justice, I feel sadness and anger that the plight of two generations of children has worsened. The great gulf between the enormous problems our children face and our political leaders' unwillingness to address them fills me with despair. It is my fervent hope that future, more enlightened generations of Americans will look back with shame on the contemporary child abuse inflicted by the state. Although the words were spoken in a different context and addressed a different evil, the indictment is the same. "Until this moment . . . I think I have never really gauged your cruelty or your recklessness. . . . Little did I dream you could be so reckless and so cruel as to do an injury to that lad. . . . It is, I regret to say, equally true that I fear he shall always bear a scar needlessly inflicted by you. If it were in my power to forgive you for your reckless cruelty I would do so. I like to think I am a gentleman, but your forgiveness will have to come from someone other than me. . . . Have you no sense of decency, sir? At long last, have you left no sense of decency?"[95]

NOTES

INTRODUCTION

1 Rothman 1980; Feld 1999; Tanenhaus 2004; Platt 1977.
2 Platt 1977; Ryerson 1978.
3 Rothman 1980; Allen 1964.
4 Mack 1909; Allen 1964; Ryerson 1978; Tanenhaus 2004.
5 Feld 1999.
6 Rothman 1980; Feld 1999.
7 Platt 1977; Ryerson 1978; Schlossman 1977; Schlossman and Wallach 1978.
8 Feld 1999; Feld 2003a.
9 Garland 2001; Beckett and Sasson 2000; Feld 2003b.
10 Feld 1999.
11 Wilson 1987.
12 Blumstein 1995; Feld 1999; Zimring 1998.
13 Edsall and Edsall 1992:7–14; Phillips 1969:7–14.
14 Feld 1988a; Torbet et al. 1996; Snyder and Sickmund 2006; Feld and Bishop 2012.
15 Bishop 2005; Amnesty International and Human Rights Watch 2005; Juszkiewicz 2000; Bortner, Zatz, and Hawkins 2000; Poe-Yamagata and Jones 2007.
16 Kurlychek and Johnson 2004; Kurlychek and Johnson 2010; Feld and Bishop 2012.
17 Feld 1988a; Feld 1998; Torbet et al. 1996; Sheffer 1995.
18 Feld 1999; National Research Council and Institute of Medicine 2001; Hawkins and Kempf-Leonard 2005.
19 Scott and Steinberg 2008; "About the Network," MacArthur Foundation Research Network, www.adjj.org.
20 Feld 2003b.

CHAPTER 1. THE PROGRESSIVE JUVENILE COURT

1 Tanenhaus 2012:420–23; Sutton 1988; Fox 1970a; Feld 1999; Aries 1962.
2 Ward 2012:33–38; Muhammad 2010.
3 Wiebe 1967; Rothman 1980; Gilens 1999.
4 Gilens 1999:14.
5 Grubb and Lazerson 1982; Feld 1999:26.
6 Wolcott 2005:5.
7 Grubb and Lazerson 1982; Hofstadter 1955; Higham 1988.
8 Feld 1999:26–27; Hawes 1971:140; Hofstadter 1955; Wolcott 2005:5–6.
9 Massey and Denton 1993:19–20.
10 Feld 1999:27; Massey and Denton 1993:26.

11 Higham 1988; Hofstadter 1955:94–130; Lieberson 1980:20–30.
12 Feld 1999:28.
13 Kett 1977; Lasch 1977; Degler 1980.
14 Degler 1980:178–209; Kett 1977:114–16.
15 Archard 1993:16–17; Ainsworth 1991:1091–93.
16 Tanenhaus 2012:421.
17 Feld 1999:22–33; Aries 1962; Ward 2012:20.
18 Aries 1962:365–404.
19 Aries 1962.
20 Kett 1977; Lasch 1977; Degler 1980; Ward 2012:20–21.
21 Kett 1977:111–43; Degler 1980.
22 Kett 1977; Platt 1977; Feld 1999:29.
23 Kett 1977:138; Berger and Berger 1984:7; Degler 1980.
24 Degler 1980; Berger and Berger 1984:7; Feld 1999:33.
25 Platt 1977:75–83.
26 Ward 2012:23; Wolcott 2005.
27 Hofstadter 1955; Wiebe 1967; Kolko 1963 (economic regulation); Rothman 1980:5–13 (criminal and juvenile justice); Trattner 1970 (child labor); Trattner 1984:108–54 (urban welfare); Tiffin 1983:141–61 (child welfare); Muhammad 2010:27.
28 Bledstein 1976:85–92.
29 Bledstein 1976:85–92; Sutton 1988:124.
30 Garland 2001:39.
31 Ward 2012:19.
32 Rothman 1980:50.
33 Allen 1964:129–30.
34 Muhammad 2010:24–25; Ward 2009:228.
35 Lieberson 1980:135.
36 Feld 1999:33; Grubb and Lazerson 1982:49.
37 Katz 1986; Schlossman 1977:17.
38 Grubb and Lazerson 1982:27.
39 Ward 2012:25.
40 Wiebe 1967:169.
41 Scott and Steinberg 2008:64.
42 Ward 2012:26–27.
43 Cremin 1961:127–28 (compulsory school attendance laws); Tiffin 1983:141–61 (child welfare legislation); Trattner 1970:119–42 (child labor laws); Wolcott 2005:13 (policing juveniles); Nellis 2016:11–12.
44 Wolcott 2005:13.
45 Feld 1999:38–42; Hawes 1991; Katz 1968.
46 Postman 1994:39.
47 Tyack 1974; Kupchik 2010:32–33.
48 Feld 1999:40; Kupchik 2010:32–33.
49 Bowles and Gintis 1976; Feld 1999:40–42; Kupchik 2010:32–33.

50 Hirschfield 2008:80.
51 Kupchick 2010:33.
52 Fox 1970b; Weissman 1983; Walkover 1984.
53 Fox 1970b; Weissman 1983; Walkover 1984; Feld 1999:47–48.
54 Fox 1970a; Platt 1977.
55 Hawes 1971; Mennel 1973; Bernard 1992; Sutton 1988.
56 Pickett 1969; Sutton 1988.
57 Pickett 1969; Hawes 1971:52; Feld 1999:51.
58 *Ex parte Crouse* 1838:11.
59 Ward 2012:52.
60 Ward 2012:57–60.
61 Schlossman 1977; Sutton 1988.
62 Hawes 1971; Feld 1999:54–55; Schlossman 1977.
63 Kett 1977:132.
64 Ward 2012:59–60.
65 Feld 1999:55; Sutton 1988:119.
66 Wolcott 2005:18.
67 Cullen and Gilbert 1982; Garland 1990; Garland 2001.
68 Garland 1990:195.
69 Cullen and Gilbert 1982:36–42.
70 Rothman 1980:50–52.
71 Allen 1964:26; Matza 1964:6–7.
72 Allen 1981:3–7; Ward 2012:25–30.
73 Beckett 1997:8.
74 Scott and Steinberg 2008:7 (emphasis added).
75 Matza 1964:12–21; Rothman 1980:50–52; Ryerson 1978:22.
76 Feld 1999:57.
77 Feld 1999:57–59; Hawes 1971; Platt 1977; Ryerson 1978:24.
78 Feld 1999:59–60.
79 Allen 1964:26.
80 Rothman 1980:48–49.
81 Western 2006:191–92.
82 Western 2006:2.
83 Tanenhaus 2004:115–16.
84 Feld 1999:61.
85 Feld 1999:55–57; Rothman 1980:205–35.
86 National Research Council 2013:31; Scott and Steinberg 2008:7.
87 Wolcott 2005:11.
88 Ward 2012:22; Wolcott 2005:18.
89 Ward 2012:32; Wolcott 2005:17.
90 Zimring 2002:144.
91 Platt 1977:176–82; Schlossman 1977:58; Sutton 1988:232–58; Tanenhaus 2012:
    423–24.

92 Manfredi 1998:43.
93 Platt 1977:46–74; Sutton 1988:121–53; Tanenhaus 2004:22; Ward 2012:33; Wolcott 2005:77.
94 Muhammad 2010:8.
95 Feld 2013b:7–9; Wolcott 2005:104.
96 Schlossman 1977:151–53; Platt 1977:134–36.
97 Wolcott 2005:56–58.
98 Schlossman and Wallach 1978; Tanenhaus 2004:51–54.
99 Wolcott 2005:29.
100 Muhammad 2010:117–18.
101 Feld 1999:64; Tanenhaus 2004:51.
102 Ward 2012:87.
103 Ward 2012:96.
104 Tanenhaus 2004:25.
105 Tanenhaus 2004:25.
106 Scott and Steinberg 2008:65.
107 Rothman 1980; Feld 1999:68; Schlossman 1977; Ryerson 1978; Garland 1990:235; Manfredi 1998:31.
108 National Research Council and Institute of Medicine 2001:154.
109 Rothman 1980; Feld 1999:68; Schlossman 1977; Ryerson 1978; Nellis 2016:13.
110 Rothman 1980:216.
111 Manfredi 1998:20.
112 Wolcott 2005:19.
113 Rothman 1980:215; Hawes 1971:159.
114 Feld 1999:67.
115 National Research Council 2013:34.
116 Hawes 1971; Rothman 1980.
117 Allen 1964; National Research Council 2013:34.
118 Ryerson 1978:39–40; Feld 1999:70.
119 Bernard 1992:83.
120 Matza 1964:111–36.
121 Schlossman 1977; Mennel 1973.
122 Zimring 2002:146.
123 Ryerson 1978.
124 Ryerson 1978.
125 Tanenhaus 2004:35.
126 Rothman 1980; Nellis 2016:16.
127 Rothman 1980.
128 Schlossman 1977; Ryerson 1978; Brenzel 1980:205; Ferdinand 1991; Feld 1999:72–73; Rothman 1980:268.
129 Ryerson 1978:33.
130 Zimring 2002:147.
131 Schlossman and Wallach 1978:66.

132 Schlossman 1977; Hawes 1971; Platt 1977; Rothman 1980; Sutton 1988.

133 Rothman 1980:71.

134 Ward 2012:3.

135 Rothman 1980; Tanenhaus 2004:156.

136 Rothman 1980:105–6.

137 Ward 2012:11.

138 Ward 2012:38–45; Nellis 2016:10.

139 Gottschalk 2015:141.

140 Tanenhaus 2004:36–39.

141 Tanenhaus 2004:39.

142 Feld 1999:75–76; Grubb and Lazerson 1982:69; National Research Council and Institute of Medicine 2001:154–55; Rothman 1980:222.

143 Ward 2012:87.

144 Muhammad 2010:11.

145 Muhammad 2010:76.

146 Ward 2012:45.

147 Wolcott 2005:19.

148 Feld 1999:76.

149 Muhammad 2010:146.

150 Ward 2012.

CHAPTER 2. THE DUE PROCESS REVOLUTION AND THE JUVENILE COURT

1 Pound 1937:xxvii.

2 Tappan 1946:306.

3 Tappan 1946:309.

4 Tappan 1946:309.

5 Lemann 1992; Klarman 2004; Ward 2012:165.

6 Feld 1999:79–108; Powe 2000:437–39.

7 Lemann 1992:5–7; Feld 1999:81–88; Wilkerson 2010.

8 Wilkerson 2010:161.

9 Massey and Denton 1993:27–29; Wilkerson 2010:160–64.

10 Wilkerson 2010:10.

11 Lemann 1992:5–6; Wilkerson 2010:9; Mauer 1999:52; Massey and Denton 1993:27–29; Klarman 2004:106.

12 Gilens 1999:104–5.

13 Feld 1999:84; Massey and Denton 1993:28–29; Lemann 1992:14–15; Alexander 2010:30–40; Wilkerson 2010; Klarman 2004:107–8.

14 Wilkerson 2010:9–10.

15 Alexander 2010:32; Wilkerson 2010.

16 Lemann 1992:21.

17 Feld 1999:85.

18 Massey and Denton 1993:43.

19 Wilkerson 2010:187.
20 Massey and Denton 1993:18; Katz 1989:131.
21 Lieberson 1980:9; Lemann 1992:6; Wilkerson 2010:10.
22 Massey and Denton 1993:18.
23 Klarman 2004:100; Wilkerson 2010:190.
24 Feld 1999:85.
25 Massey and Denton 1993:18; Gilens 1999:104–5; Ward 2012:107.
26 Gilens 1999:105.
27 Massey and Denton 1993:45–46.
28 Hacker 1992:19; Massey and Denton 1993:30; Klarman 2004:64.
29 Massey and Denton 1993:33–35; Lieberson 1980:260.
30 Klarman 2004:64.
31 Massey and Denton 1993:30.
32 Katz 1989:133–37; Massey and Denton 1993:45–42.
33 Katz 1989:134–35.
34 Massey and Denton 1993:44–45.
35 Klarman 2004:262–64.
36 Katz 1989:134–35.
37 Katz 1989:134–35.
38 Katz 1989:135–36; Massey and Denton 1993:55–56.
39 Klarman 2004:263.
40 Omi and Winant 1994:96.
41 Powe 2000:44–49; Klarman 2004:100–3.
42 Klarman 2004:4, 101–10.
43 Beckett 1997:40; Edsall and Edsall 1992:33; Lieberson 1980:101; Omi and Winanat 1994:16; Klarman 2004:181.
44 Beckett 1997:40; Edsall and Edsall 1992:34; Powe 2000:9–10.
45 Klarman 2004:192.
46 Beckett 1997:40; Beckett and Sasson 2000:56.
47 Phillips 1969:204–8.
48 Feld 1999:86–87.
49 Feld 1999:87; Lemann 1992:111.
50 Kennedy 1997:59–60; Lopez 2014:89; Klarman 2004:174–88.
51 Powe 2000:490–92.
52 Mendelberg 2001:79–93; Powe 2000:490; Lindsey 2009:39.
53 Myrdal 1962; Lemann 1992:7; Powe 2000:44–45; Alexander 2010:35–36.
54 Klarman 2004:102.
55 Klarman 2004:113.
56 Myrdal 1962:1008–11.
57 *United States v. Carolene Products* 1938:152–53, n. 4.
58 Powe 2000:214–15; Cover 1982:1300; Klarman 2004:195–96.
59 Cover 1982:1300; Lieberson 1980:51.
60 Powe 2000:214.

61 Cover 1982:1300.
62 Gilens 1999:107; Powe 2000:486; Wilkerson 2010.
63 Hacker 1992:17.
64 Cover 1982:1303; Klarman 2004:169.
65 Gilens 1999:108.
66 *Plessy v. Ferguson* 1896; Klarman 2004:17–28.
67 Klarman 2004:10–17.
68 Klarman 2000:94.
69 *Brown v. Board of Education* 1954; Klarman 2004:292–312.
70 White 1986:280.
71 Klarman 2004:291.
72 Powe 2000:47.
73 Alexander 2010:37.
74 Klarman 2004:343.
75 Klarman 2004:350.
76 Powe 2000:162; Lopez 2014:14; Klarman 2004:399.
77 Klarman 2004:391.
78 Alexander 2010:37. See also Klarman 2004:392.
79 Edsall and Edsall 1992:76–79; Powe 2000:60–62.
80 Mendelberg 2001:18.
81 Gilens 1999:108; Powe 2000:174; Lindsey 2009:39.
82 Alexander 2010:38; Lindsey 2009:39.
83 Powe 2000:232.
84 Mendelberg 2001:19.
85 National Research Council 2014:107.
86 *Moore v. Dempsey* 1923 (state criminal conviction obtained through mob-dominated sham trials); *Powell v. Alabama* 1932 (Scottsboro Boys case using Fourteenth Amendment Due Process Clause to grant limited right to counsel); *Norris v. Alabama* 1935 (exclusion of black jurors from venire); *Brown v. Mississippi* 1936 (excluding coerced confessions extracted by torture); Kennedy 1997:94–107; Klarman 2004:117–35.
87 Kennedy 1997:92–94.
88 Klarman 2004:120, 130.
89 Klarman 2000:71.
90 Powe 2000:486.
91 Klarman 2000:75.
92 Klarman 2000:92.
93 Wilson 1975; Powe 2000:408; Hinton 2016.
94 Zimring and Hawkins 1997:66; Mauer 1999:51–52.
95 Manfredi 1998:2; Edsall and Edsall 1992:4; White 1989:282–83; Howe 2001:376–77.
96 Manfredi 1998:x.
97 Graham 1970; Edsall and Edsall 1992:110–11.
98 Garland 2001:57; Powe 2000:386; Note 1988:1488–94; Klarman 2004:155.

99 Powe 2000; Allen 1975:525–26.

100 Allen 1975:525–31.

101 Gottschalk 2015:145.

102 Graham 1970:41–66; Israel 1977:1324–25.

103 Powe 2000:412.

104 LaFave et al. 2009:48–68.

105 Feld 1999:86–88; Graham 1970:67–85.

106 *Mapp v. Ohio* 1961; *Miranda v. Arizona* 1966.

107 Edsall and Edsall 1992:111.

108 Gilens 1999:107–10; Edsall and Edsall 1992:74–77.

109 Simon 2007:18; Western 2006; Garland 2001.

110 Garland 2001.

111 Garland 2001:27.

112 Garland 2001:34–35.

113 Rothman 1980:53–61; Allen 1964:44–61.

114 Allen 1964:26–27; Allen 1981:25–41.

115 Ryerson 1978:42–43; Rothman 1980:242–43.

116 Garland 2001:39.

117 Allen 1981; Garland 2001; Gottschalk 2015:146.

118 Garland 2001:55.

119 American Friends Service Committee 1971:83–99; Mauer 1999:44.

120 Rothman 1980:82–84; Allen 1981:87–88; Garland 2001:36.

121 Edsall and Edsall 1992:49–52; Hacker 1992:22.

122 President's Commission 1967a; Paulsen 1967; Note 1966:775–76; Nellis 2016:21.

123 *Kent v. United States* 1966:553–63; Paulsen 1967:167–78.

124 *In re Gault* 1967.

125 Manfredi 1998:80–129; Tanenhaus 2011.

126 *In re Gault* 1967:4–8; Manfredi 1998:85–87; Tanenhaus 2011:24–32.

127 Tanenhaus 2011:30.

128 *In re Gault* 1967:7–8.

129 *In re Gault* 1967:29.

130 President's Commission 1967b:80.

131 Wolcott 2005:118–19.

132 Ward 2012:98–103.

133 Arnold 1971.

134 Axelrad 1952.

135 President's Commission 1967b:7.

136 President's Commission 1967b:82; Feld 1993b:54–56.

137 Manfredi 1998:39–40.

138 *In re Gault* 1967:14–17.

139 Manfredi 1998:32–33; Zimring 2000c:276; National Research Council 2013:36.

140 *In re Gault* 1967:27–28; Bartollas, Miller, and Dinitz 1976; Feld 1977.

141 *In re Gault* 1967:31–57; Rosenberg 1980:662–63; Feld 1984:154–57.

142 *In re Gault* 1967:13, 31, n. 48.

143 Manfredi 1998:21.

144 *In re Gault* 1967; Manfredi 1998:101–107.

145 U.S. Constitution, Amendment VI.

146 *In re Gault* 1967:33.

147 *In re Gault* 1967:41.

148 *In re Gault* 1967:57.

149 *In re Gault* 1967:49–50.

150 Manfredi 1998:105.

151 *Murphy v. Waterfront Commission* 1964:55.

152 Manfredi 1998:18, 124–25.

153 *Gallegos v. Colorado* 1962:54–55; *Haley v. Ohio* 1948:601.

154 *In re Gault* 1967:47.

155 Manfredi 1998:124–25.

156 *In re Gault* 1967:61.

157 National Research Council 2013:37.

158 *In re Gault* 1967:38.

159 *In re Gault* 1967:39.

160 *In re Gault* 1967:42.

161 *In re Winship* 1970:368.

162 *In re Winship* 1970:367.

163 *Breed v. Jones* 1975:541.

164 *Breed v. Jones* 1975:528–29.

165 *Breed v. Jones* 1975:531.

166 *Duncan v. Louisiana* 1968.

167 *McKeiver v. Pennsylvania* 1971:540.

168 Feld 2003a:1147–55.

169 *McKeiver v. Pennsylvania* 1971:541.

170 *McKeiver v. Pennsylvania* 1971:541.

171 *McKeiver v. Pennsylvania* 1971:545.

172 *McKeiver v. Pennsylvania* 1971:553–55.

173 *McKeiver v. Pennsylvania* 1971:550.

174 *In re Gault* 1967:39.

175 Feld 2003a:1153; Feld 1995:1107–8.

176 *McKeiver v. Pennsylvania* 1971:550.

177 Feld 1999:153–57; Feld 2003a.

178 Paulsen 1966:168–69; Paulsen 1967:237; Feld 1984.

179 Zimring 2002:149.

180 Manfredi 1998:159.

181 Zimring and Tanenhaus 2014:232.

182 Manfredi 1998:4–5.

CHAPTER 3. THE GET TOUGH ERA I

1 Beckett and Sasson 2000:10–11; Garland 2001:195; Ward 2012:201; Zimring 2014:7.
2 Zimring and Hawkins 1997:58; Edsall and Edsall 1992:111–12.
3 Feld 1999:206–7; Massey and Denton 1993:174; Blumstein 1995:34–35.
4 Beckett and Sasson 2000:33; Gottschalk 2015:277–78.
5 Beckett and Sasson 2000:34; Zimring and Hawkins 1998:34–50.
6 Sampson and Wilson 1995:38.
7 Katz 1989:128–92; Wilson 1996:25–34.
8 Lindsey 2009:3–6.
9 Lindsey 2009:35–36.
10 Garland 2001:79.
11 Hacker 1992:101.
12 Garland 2001:49.
13 Garland 2001:51; Edsall and Edsall 1992:105.
14 Edsall and Edsall 1992:105.
15 Putnam 2015:34.
16 Garland 2001:81.
17 Garland 2001:78; Katz 1989:124–28; Alexander 2010:49–51; Putnam 2015:35–37.
18 Katz 1989:128; Lemann 1992:201–2.
19 Edsall and Edsall 1992:105.
20 Katz 1989:128.
21 Wilson 2009:6–7.
22 Garland 2001:76; Omi and Winant 1994:116; Edsall and Edsall 1992:199.
23 Omi and Winant 1994:116.
24 Entman and Rojecki 2000:76.
25 Wilson 2009:40.
26 Putnam 2015:18–19.
27 Katz 1989:128–29; Putnam 2015.
28 Wilson 1996:25–34; National Research Council 1993:26.
29 National Research Council 1993:25–26.
30 Edsall and Edsall 1992:245.
31 Edsall and Edsall 1992:231–36.
32 Omi and Winant 1994:114.
33 Western 2006:56.
34 Lindsey 2009:50–54.
35 Lindsey 2009:6.
36 Hinton 2016:314.
37 Lindsey 2009:4.
38 Putnam 2015:36.
39 Lindsey 2009:45–53, 62–63.
40 Edsall and Edsall 1992:108; Garland 2001:82–84; Putnam 2015:71–72.
41 Lindsey 2009:60.

42 Garland 2001:83.
43 Edsall and Edsall 1992:27; Katz 1989:51; Lemann 1992:103; Lieberson 1980:10–11.
44 Gottschalk 2015:85.
45 Katz 1989:51; Gottschalk 2015:85–87.
46 Lieberson 1980:10–11; Massey and Denton 1993:2.
47 Garland 2001:84; Katz 1989:134; Lemann 1992:118.
48 Wilson 2009:41.
49 Wilson 2009:10.
50 Massey and Denton 1993:83; Wilson 2009:10.
51 Sampson and Wilson 1995:48; Wilson 2009:28–29.
52 Massey and Denton 1993:19–59; Beckett and Sasson 2000:39; Mauer 1999:123; Sampson and Wilson 1995:43; Wilson 2009:29.
53 Sampson and Wilson 1995:49; Wilson 2009:33.
54 Wilson 2009:35.
55 Wilson 2009:35–38.
56 Sampson and Wilson 1995:48–49; Wilson 2009:28–39.
57 National Advisory Commission 1968:1, 11–13.
58 Sampson and Lauritsen 1997:338.
59 Sampson and Lauritsen 1997:338.
60 Mauer 1999:168–69; Beckett and Sasson 2000:37; Katz 1989:207.
61 Beckett and Sasson 2000:33–34.
62 Gottschalk 2015:277. See also Sampson and Wilson 1995:41.
63 Wilson 2009:52.
64 Wilson 2009.
65 Sampson and Wilson 1995:50–52; Sampson and Lauritsen 1997:338; Massey and Denton 1993:13.
66 Kennedy 1997:14.
67 Edsall and Edsall 1992:227.
68 Orfield 2015:399–400.
69 Simon 2007:29. See *Milliken v. Bradley* 1974.
70 Edsall and Edsall 1992:227.
71 Putnam 2015:38.
72 Putnam 2015:164.
73 Edsall and Edsall 1992:228; Phillips 1969:467; Wilson 2009:31–32.
74 Hacker 1992:211.
75 Massey and Denton 1993:158; Hacker 1992:224.
76 Putnam 2015:39.
77 Edsall and Edsall 1992:85.
78 Kozol 1991.
79 Katz 1989:199; Katz 1993:4; Edsall and Edsall 1992:244; Wilson 1996:25–110.
80 Wilson 1987:72–84; Wilson 1996:87–110; Putnam 2015:73–74.
81 Wilson 1987:83–92, 145–46; Western 2006:131–33.
82 Garland 2001:83; Wilson 1987; Massey and Denton 1993; Lichter 1997:134.

83 Lindsey 2009:14–17.
84 Wilson 2009:33–34.
85 Massey and Denton 1993:7.
86 Edsall and Edsall 1992:231
87 Wilson 1987:55–56; Edsall and Edsall 1992:281; Sampson and Wilson 1995:42–43.
88 Sampson and Wilson 1995:51.
89 Feld 1999:197–218; Zimring 1998:3–10; Blumstein 1995:16–20, 24–29; Cook and Laub 1998:51–58; Cook and Laub 2002; Garland 2001:90; Zimring 2014:7.
90 Feld 1999:197–202.
91 Feld 1999:367–68.
92 Feld 1999:203–8; Feld 2003a:1523–38.
93 Beckett 1997:84–88.
94 Feld 1999:197–202; Snyder and Sickmund 1999:13; Blumstein and Wallman 2000:13.
95 Feld 1999:197–202; Zimring and Hawkins 1998:58; Cook and Laub 1998:51–58.
96 Hinton 2016:24.
97 Feld 1999:202.
98 Feld 1999:199–205; Feld 1998:192–94.
99 Zimring and Hawkins 1997:76–77; Cook and Laub 1998:42–43; Feld 1999:203.
100 Zimring and Hawkins 1997:64; Western 2006:36.
101 Zimring and Hawkins 1997:65.
102 Sampson and Wilson 1995:44.
103 Cook and Laub 1998:39–44; Mauer 1999:84; Snyder and Sickmund 1995:56.
104 Zimring and Hawkins 1997:66.
105 Feld 1999:204–5; Zimring 1996:28.
106 Zimring 1996:27; Blumstein and Wallman 2000:29–30; Zimring and Hawkins 1997:108; Zimring 1998:35.
107 Blumstein 1995:16–22; Zimring 1996:29; Zimring 1998:89; Nellis 2016:35–36.
108 Blumstein 1995:29–32; Beckett and Sasson 2000:28; Cook and Laub 1998:53–54; Nellis 2016:37–38.
109 Blumstein and Wallman 2000:39; Blumstein 1995:29–32; Cook and Laub 1998:53–54.
110 National Research Council 1993:67–68.
111 Blumstein 1995; Cook and Laub 1998:58; Nellis 2016:37–38.
112 Anderson 1999; Beckett and Sasson 2000:8, 28; National Research Council 2013:21.
113 National Research Council 1993:67–68; Wilson 2009:17–23.
114 Zimring and Hawkins 1997:78.
115 Mauer 1999:50–55; Miller 1996:149–58; Edsall and Edsall 1992:113.
116 Bennet and DiIulio 1996:25–34, 59, 117, 194; Miller 1996:149–58; Mauer 1999:50–55.
117 Zimring 1998:63.
118 Putnam 2015.

CHAPTER 4. THE GET TOUGH ERA II

1 Edsall and Edsall 1992; Lopez 2014.
2 Edsall and Edsall 1992:69–73; Mendelberg 2001:90–98; Lopez 2014.
3 Simon 2007:97.
4 Scott and Steinberg 2008:9.
5 Beckett and Sasson 2000:47; Miller 1996:2–3.
6 Beckett and Sasson 2000:47–48; Entman and Rojecki 2000:49.
7 Western 2006:53.
8 Beckett 1997:85–88; Hinton 2016.
9 Lopez 2014:48.
10 Garland 2001:94–102; Hacker 1992:209.
11 Katz 1989:53; Lieberson 1980:116.
12 Lemann 1992:200.
13 Edsall and Edsall 1992:55–110; Lopez 2014:17–22.
14 Edsall and Edsall 1992:7; Omi and Winant 1994:106.
15 Gilens 1999:205; Omi and Winant 1994:88–89.
16 Lindsey 2009.
17 Gilens 1999:104–11.
18 Gilens 1999:106.
19 Gilens 1999:104–11; Katz 1989:23.
20 Gilens 1999:5; Beckett and Sasson 2000:52; Kinder and Mendelberg 1995:406.
21 Garland 2001:15; Gilens 1999:5; Beckett and Sasson 2000:132–33.
22 Lindsey 2009:79–80.
23 Wilson 2009:43.
24 Lopez 2014:97.
25 Katz 1989; Wilkerson 2010:14.
26 Gilens 1999:205; Beckett and Sasson 2000:10; Alexander 2010:45.
27 Lindsey 2009:72–75.
28 Lopez 2014:68.
29 Gilens 1999:3.
30 Edsall and Edsall 1992:98; Beckett and Sasson 2000:10–11; Simon 2007:25–26.
31 Alexander 2010:44–45; Beckett 1997:34.
32 Lopez 2014:93.
33 Edsall and Edsall 1992:151.
34 Gottschalk 2015:147.
35 Lindsey 2009:81.
36 Putnam 2015:61–64.
37 Moynihan 1965.
38 Katz 1989:25; Lemann 1992:172–76.
39 Wilson 1987:20–62; Gilens 1999:19–22.
40 Moynihan 1965:51.
41 Wilson 2009:96–105; Lopez 2014:94–107.

42 Putnam 2015:63.

43 Putnam 2015:72.

44 Powe 2000:274–75.

45 Edsall and Edsall 1992:49–50; Hacker 1992:22; National Advisory Commission 1968:109–12, 203–6.

46 Lemann 1992:190; Powe 2000:275–76; National Advisory Commission 1968:203–6.

47 Lemann 1992:190; Powe 2000:275–76.

48 Garland 2001:97; Powe 2000:277–78; Hacker 1992:22; Gilens 1999:110.

49 National Advisory Commission 1968:203–6.

50 National Advisory Commission 1968:1.

51 National Advisory Commission 1968:22.

52 Hacker 1992:22; Gilens 1999:109–10; Western 2006:59.

53 Tonry 2011:83.

54 Powe 2000:495; Beckett and Sasson 2000:51–54.

55 Beckett 1997:10; Powe 2000:495; Beckett and Sasson 2000:52–54.

56 Mauer 1999:53; *Furman v. Georgia* 1972.

57 Western 2006:48; Simon 2007:114.

58 Western 2006:3.

59 Beckett and Sasson 2000:49; Omi and Winant 1994:98; Kennedy 1997:63.

60 Klarman 2004:385.

61 Klarman 2004:408–410.

62 Beckett and Sasson 2000:49; Beckett 1997:28; Alexander 2010:41–42; Gottschalk 2015:145–46; Lopez 2014:23–24.

63 Beckett 1997:32; Gottschalk 2015:29–30, 145.

64 Mendelberg 2001:93.

65 Edsall and Edsall 1992:57–64, 72–73; Mendelberg 2001:94.

66 Edsall and Edsall 1992:57–61; Lopez 2014:172–76.

67 Edsall and Edsall 1992:71; Lopez 2014:69–71.

68 Garland 2001:97.

69 Klarman 2004:374–76.

70 Edsall and Edsall 1992:34–36; Beckett and Sasson 2000:56.

71 Edsall and Edsall 1992:51–73; Gilens 1999:116–23; Mendelberg 2001:93–98; Simon 2007:29.

72 Lopez 2014:17–22.

73 Edsall and Edsall 1992:44; Gest 2001:5–6.

74 Western 2006:69.

75 Powe 2000:328; Edsall and Edsall 1992:44; Gest 2001:5–6.

76 Edsall and Edsall 1992:72.

77 Hacker 1992:56; Powe 2000:278; Lopez 2014:19–20.

78 Beckett 1997:11; Edsall and Edsall 1992:7; Omi and Winant 1994:106; Western 2006:59.

79 Edsall and Edsall 1992:59–61; Garland 2001:97; Lopez 2014:24; Gottschalk 2015:147.

80 Beckett and Sasson 2000:10; Beckett 1997:87; Hacker 1992:210; Gottschalk
2015:143.
81 Simon 2007:25.
82 Beckett 1997:11; Entman and Rojecki 2000:43; Murray 1984:38–40; Alexander
2010:44–45.
83 Gottschalk 2015:147–48.
84 Edsall and Edsall 1992:8.
85 Edsall and Edsall 1992:46.
86 Edsall and Edsall 1992:11; Garland 2001:96–97.
87 Edsall and Edsall 1992:11; Garland 2001:96–97; Lopez 2014:13–17.
88 Edsall and Edsall 1992:77; Omi and Winant 1994:124.
89 Edsall and Edsall 1992:79; Phillips 1969:463.
90 Powe 2000:399; Gest 2001:14; Beckett 1997:38; Lopez 2014:24–25.
91 Beckett and Sasson 2000:51; Alexander 2010:42–43.
92 National Research Council 2014:113.
93 Garland 2001:96–97; Lemann 1992:201; Edsall and Edsall 1992:4; Alexander
2010:43–44; Tonry 2011:81–83; Lopez 2014:1–5; Gottschalk 2015:148–49.
94 Lopez 2014:6.
95 Garland 2001:96–97; Edsall and Edsall 1992:98.
96 Lemann 1992:201.
97 Phillips 1969:22–23; Kinder and Mendelberg 1995:403; Omi and Winant 1994:124;
Tonry 2011:110.
98 Edsall and Edsall 1992:74–80; Mendelberg 2001:95–96; Lopez 2014:22–27.
99 Mendelberg 2001:97.
100 Edsall and Edsall 1992:74–75; Entman and Rojecki 2000:46–47.
101 Alexander 2010:42–43; Tonry 2011:106–14.
102 Edsall and Edsall 1992:98.
103 Edsall and Edsall 1992:5–6; Alexander 2010:43; Lopez 2014:26.
104 Edsall and Edsall 1992:5, 14, 80.
105 Edsall and Edsall 1992:89–98; Beckett and Sasson 2000:52–58.
106 Phillips 1969:32–33; Edsall and Edsall 1992:5–6; Western 2006:4; Lopez 2014:30–31;
Alexander 2010:54.
107 Edsall and Edsall 1992:87.
108 Tonry 1995:10; Garland 2001:153; Valentino 1999:298.
109 Edsall and Edsall 1992:52–53, 258–59.
110 Garland 2001:13, 143, 172.
111 Feld 1999; Beckett 1997:80; Tonry 1994:489.
112 Garland 2001:13–14; Kennedy 1997:3–4; Beckett 1997:45; Beckett and Sasson
2000:69.
113 Entman 1990:332–33; Gilliam and Iyengar 2000:566.
114 Kinder and Mendelberg 1995:403; Mendelberg 2001:95–106.
115 Beckett 1997:8–9; Miller 1996:149; Gilens 1996:602.
116 Lopez 2014:4–5.

117 Lopez 2014:16; Edsall and Edsall 1992:138; Omi and Winant 1994:123; Gilens 1999:67.
118 Omi and Winant 1994:123; Gilens 1996:593; Entman and Rojecki 2000:20.
119 Lopez 2014:36.
120 Garland 2001:135. See also Edsall and Edsall 1992:138; Gilens 1996:593.
121 Gilens 1999:3; Garland 2001:196.
122 Entman and Rojecki 2000:19.
123 Lopez 2014:58. See also Lindsey 2009:81.
124 Edsall and Edsall 1992:198–216; Omi and Winant 1994:117.
125 Beckett 1997:8–9; Miller 1996:149; Feld 1999; Feld 2003b:1552–58; Kinder and Mendelberg 1995:413.
126 Oliver and Mendelberg 2000:575; Entman and Rojecki 2000:2; Massey and Denton 1993.
127 Edsall and Edsall 1992:236; Dorfman and Schiraldi 2001:4; Nellis 2016:43–44; Kang 2005.
128 Entman and Rojecki 2000:60; Gilens 1999:160; Hurwitz and Peffley 1997:377–78; Peffley, Hurwitz, and Sniderman 1997:31.
129 Entman and Rojecki 2000:57–58; Mendelberg 2001:117–21; Gilens 1999:161; Kang 2005:1500.
130 Wilson 2009:15; Muhammad 2010.
131 Edsall and Edsall 1992:232; Entman and Rojecki 2000:61–62; Gilens 1999:159; Tonry 2011:79.
132 Entman and Rojecki 2000:73; Gilens 1999:140–42; Kennedy 1997:378; Valentino 1999:297.
133 Gilliam et al. 1996:7; Entman and Rojecki 2000:80.
134 Gilliam et al. 1996:8; Gilliam and Iyengar 2000:561; Gest 2001:266; Entman and Rojecki 2000:78.
135 Beckett and Sasson 2000:89–97; Tonry 2011:x; Dorfman and Schiraldi 2001:3–4; Gilens 1999:149; Gilliam et al. 1996:8–10; Iyengar 2010; Nellis 2016:44; Entman and Rojecki 2000:81; Garland 2001:146; Gilens 1999:137; Gilliam and Iyengar 2000:561; Peffley, Hurwitz, and Sniderman 1997:310; Dorfman and Schiraldi 2001:7; Entman and Rojecki 2000:80; Beckett and Sasson 2000:77; Mauer 1999:172–73; Scott and Steinberg 2008:106.
136 Beckett and Sasson 2000:79; Dorfman and Schiraldi 2001:13–14; Entman and Rojecki 2000:81–84; Simon 2007:76.
137 Beckett and Sasson 2000:79; Dorfman and Schiraldi 2001:15; Entman 1990:337; Miller 1996:174–75; Entman 1992:349–53; Entman and Rojecki 2000:82–84; Peffley, Hurwitz, and Sniderman 1997:310.
138 Lopez 2014:182; Entman and Rojecki 2000:94; Gilliam et al. 1996:15; Gilliam and Iyengar 2000:570; Muhammad 2010.
139 Tonry 2011:7; Gottschalk 2015:28; Garland 2001:133.
140 Mendelberg 2001:120–25; Gilliam and Iyengar 2000:571; Dorfman and Schiraldi 2001:23; Gilliam and Iyengar 1998:46; Gilens 1999:140–53; Kennedy 1997:4–5.

141 Gilliam et al. 1996:8; Oliver 1999:46–47; Entman and Rojecki 2000:82; Scott and Steinberg 2008:110; Tonry 1995:11–12; Tonry 1994:475; Edsall and Edsall 1992:224; Beckett 1997:62–78; Beckett and Sasson 2000:75–98; Alexander 2010:104–5; Garland 2001:13.

142 Mendelberg 2001:134–64; Entman and Rojecki 2000:78–93; Garland 2001:157–58; Scott and Steinberg 2008:111; Valentino 1999:294; Beckett 1997:84; Beckett and Sasson 2000:120; Gilliam et al. 1996:7; Gilliam and Iyengar 2000:564; Gilens 1999:133–34; Peffley, Hurwitz, and Sniderman 1997:321.

143 Beckett and Sasson 2000:88–98; Tonry 1995:83–104; Tonry 2011:146–49; Mauer 1999:60–63; Garland 2001:132; Alexander 2010:48–49; Hurwitz and Peffley 1997:395.

144 Alexander 2010:5.

145 Tonry 1995:104–23. See also Garland 2001:132.

146 Western 2006; Beckett and Sasson 2000:88; Kennedy 1997:364–86; Miller 1996:82–83.

147 Beckett and Sasson 2000:135.

148 National Research Council 2014:123.

149 Tonry 2011:9.

150 Mendelberg 1997:152.

151 Western 2006:11–32.

152 Tonry 2011:9–10.

153 Wacquant 2008:65.

154 Alexander 2010:17.

CHAPTER 5. THE KID IS A CRIMINAL

1 Garland 2001:27–28; National Research Council and Institute of Medicine 2001:154.

2 Feld 1999:294–96.

3 Feld 1999:295; Garland 1990:237.

4 Garland 2001:10; Ward 2012:238; DiIulio 1995; Bennet and DiIulio 1996.

5 Fox 1996; Zimring 1998; Zimring 2014.

6 Scott and Steinberg 2008:109.

7 Cullen and Gilbert 1982:39–40; Garland 2001:55.

8 Bernard 1992:3–5; Garland 2001:108; National Research Council and Institute of Medicine 2001:223.

9 National Research Council and Institute of Medicine 2001:210; Mauer 1999:37–38; Ward 2012:234–35.

10 Garland 2001:140.

11 Garland 2001:53–60.

12 Martinson 1974:25.

13 Martinson 1974:25; Allen 1981:57–58; Mauer 1999:48–49.

14 Western 2006:2, 68.

15 Garland 2001; Simon 2007.

16 Tonry 1996:6–13.
17 Von Hirsch 1985:31–39.
18 American Friends Service Committee 1971:83–96, 124; Gottschalk 2015:123; National Research Council 2014:72–73; Garland 2001:59; Feld 1988b:835–36.
19 Garland 2001:9.
20 Garland 2001:60; American Friends Service Committee 1971; Mauer 1999:45.
21 Nellis 2016:49–50; Beckett and Sasson 2000:4.
22 Garland 2001:61; Hinton 2016.
23 Beckett 1997:42–43; Omi and Winant 1994:5; Hinton 2016.
24 Garland 2001:193; Simon 2007:23.
25 Simon 2007:6; Western 2006; Tonry 1995; Tonry 2011; Alexander 2010; National Research Council 2014.
26 Torbet et al. 1996:59–61; Feld 1998:189–261.
27 Podkopacz and Feld 1995; Podkopacz and Feld 1996; U.S. General Accounting Office 1995; Mulvey and Schubert 2012:844.
28 Zimring and Fagan 2000.
29 Feld and Bishop 2012:802–22; Snyder and Sickmund 2006:85–89; Griffin 2012.
30 Bishop and Frazier 2000; Feld 1998:195–98.
31 *Kent v. United States* 1966:553; Feld 1987:487–94; Fagan 2008; Feld and Bishop 2012:803–5.
32 Snyder and Sickmund 2006:88; Feld 1987:494–99.
33 Griffin 2012; Feld 2008.
34 Snyder and Sickmund 2006:87; Feld 2000a:98–101.
35 Snyder and Sickmund 2006:87; Feld 2000a:98–101; Feld and Bishop 2012:811.
36 Feld 2000a:98–101; Snyder and Sickmund 2006:87; Griffin 2012.
37 Feld and Bishop 2012:806; Snyder and Sickmund 2006.
38 Feld 1995; Podkopacz and Feld 2001.
39 Feld and Bishop 2012:815; Poe-Yamagata and Jones 2007:5.
40 Amnesty International and Human Rights Watch 2005:19, n. 30; Feld 2013d:265.
41 Campaign for Youth Justice 2006; Griffin et al. 2011.
42 Griffin et al. 2011.
43 Bennet and Dilulio 1996:21–34; Zimring 1998; Moriearty 2011:850–51; National Research Council and Institute of Medicine 2001:204–9, 214–18; Feld 1998:194; Feld 1995:966–97; Feld 2003b:1556–58.
44 Simon 2007:112–13.
45 National Research Council 2013:38; Ward 2012:233.
46 Feld 2000:124–29; Feld 2013c:267; Amnesty International and Human Rights Watch 2005:3.
47 Griffin et al. 2011; Griffin 2012; Feld and Bishop 2012:807–11; Campaign for Youth Justice 2006:71; Snyder and Sickmund 2006:12–14.
48 Feld 2003b:15–23; Feld 2013d:267; Griffin et al. 2011.
49 Juszkiewicz 2000:5; Amnesty International and Human Rights Watch 2005:19; Schiraldi and Ziedenberg 2000:47; Frazier et al. 1999:579.

50 Rothman 1980; Tanenhaus 2000.
51 *Kent v. United States* 1966; Feld 1978; Feld 1987.
52 *Breed v. Jones* 1975.
53 *Kent v. United States* 1966:566–67.
54 Fagan and Deschenes 1990:336–42; Podkopacz and Feld 1995:121–23; Podkopacz and Feld 1996:479–80; U.S. General Accounting Office 1995; Snyder and Sickmund 2006.
55 Podkopacz and Feld 1995; Podkopacz and Feld 1996.
56 Fagan and Deschenes 1990; Podkopacz and Feld 1995:121–31; Podkopacz and Feld 1996:467–71; Howell 1996; Lanza-Kaduce et al. 2006.
57 Zimring 1981a:195; *Furman v. Georgia* 1972.
58 Feld 1978; Feld 1990.
59 Fagan 2008; Simon 2007:113–14.
60 Hamparian et al. 1982.
61 Dawson 1992; Bishop, Frazier, and Henretta 1989.
62 Hamparian et al. 1982; Feld 1990; Poulos and Orchowsky 1994; U.S. General Accounting Office 1995:59.
63 Podkopacz and Feld 1995; Podkopacz and Feld 1996.
64 Hamparian et al. 1982:104–5; Fagan, Forst, and Vivona 1987:276; U.S. General Accounting Office 1995:59; Bortner, Zatz, and Hawkins 2000; Amnesty International and Human Rights Watch 2005.
65 National Research Council and Institute of Medicine 2001:216; Poe-Yamagata and Jones 2007:12–14.
66 Poe-Yamagata and Jones 2000:17.
67 Males and Macallair 2000:7–8.
68 Bureau of Justice Statistics 1998; National Research Council and Institute of Medicine 2001:220.
69 Feld 1987; White et al. 1999; Feld 2000a; Fagan 2008.
70 American Friends Service Committee 1971; Von Hirsch 1976.
71 Cullen and Gilbert 1982; Tonry 1996; Garland 2001; National Research Council 2014.
72 Feld 1978; Feld 1987; Feld 1988b; Feld 1998; Feld 2003a; Von Hirsch 1976; Tonry 1995; Garland 2001.
73 Feld 1978; Feld 1995.
74 Feld and Bishop 2012:809–10; Griffin et al. 2011.
75 Feld and Bishop 2012; Griffin 2012.
76 Wolfgang, Figlio, and Sellin 1972; Blumstein, Farrington, and Moitra 1985; Piquero, Hawkins, and Kazemian 2012.
77 Wolfgang, Figlio, and Sellin 1972; Blumstein, Farrington, and Moitra 1985; Greenwood 1986.
78 Blumstein, Farrington, and Moitra 1985; Farrington 1998.
79 Wolfgang, Figlio, and Sellin, 1972; Petersilia 1980; Greenwood 1986; Piquero, Hawkins, and Kazemian 2012.

80 Moffitt 1993; Moffitt 2003; Piquero, Hawkins, and Kazemian 2012.
81 Fox, Jennings, and Piquero 2014:555–64; Greenwood 1986:164–67.
82 Wolfgang, Figlio, and Sellin 1972:159–60; National Research Council 2013:23.
83 National Research Council 2013:143.
84 Wolfgang, Figlio, and Sellin 1972:163.
85 Tracy, Wolfgang, and Figlio 1990:15–17; Petersilia 1980; Blumstein, Farrington, and Moitra 1985; National Research Council 2013:24–25; Piquero, Hawkins, and Kazemian2012.
86 Fox, Jennings, and Piquero 2014:555–64; Loeber and Farrington 1998.
87 Farrington 1986; Loeber and Farrington 1998; Fox, Jennings, and Piquero 2014:559.
88 Blumstein, Farrington, and Moitra 1985; Piquero, Hawkins, and Kazemian 2012.
89 Snyder and Sickmund 2006; Torbet et a1. 1996.
90 Feld 1987; Feld 2003a; Feld 2003b.
91 *United States v. Bland* 1972:1330.
92 *United States v. Bland* 1972:1335–37.
93 Feld and Bishop 2012:811–12; Griffin 2012; Feld 2000a.
94 Zimring 2014:44; Simon 2007:35; Ward 2012:252.
95 Feld 2000a.
96 Bishop and Frazier 1991.
97 Bishop and Frazier 1991; Kupchik 2006.
98 Sridharan, Greenfield, and Blakley 2004.
99 Bishop 2004.
100 Bishop, Frazier, and Henretta 1989; Bishop and Frazier 1991; Sridharan, Greenfield, and Blakley 2004; Simon 2007:37–40.
101 Simon 2007:39–40.
102 Kupchik 2006.
103 *Manduley v. Superior Court of San Diego County* 2002.
104 *Manduley v. Superior Court of San Diego County* 2002:562–63.
105 *Manduley v. Superior Court of San Diego County* 2002:567–71.
106 Amnesty International and Human Rights Watch 2005; Snyder and Sickmund 2006; Simon 2007:43.
107 U.S. General Accounting Office 1995a; Feld 1998; Bishop and Frazier 1991; Frazier et al. 1999; Schiraldi and Zeidenberg 2000.
108 Juszkiewicz 2000; Simon 2007:40.
109 National Research Council 2013:135.
110 Allen 2000.
111 Redding and Howell 2000.
112 Snyder and Sickmund 2006; Torbet et al. 1996; Griffin 2012.
113 Torbet et al. 1996; Redding and Howell 2000.
114 Snyder and Sickmund 2006.
115 Zimring 1998; Redding and Howell 2000.
116 Redding and Howell 2000; Podkopacz and Feld 2001.

117 Podkopacz and Feld 2001.

118 Podkopacz and Feld 2001.

119 Podkopacz and Feld 2001; Zimring 2014:49.

120 Zimring 2014:49.

121 Fagan, Forst, and Vivona 1989; Mulvey and Schubert 2012:851.

122 Snyder and Sickmund 2006; Feld and Bishop 2012.

123 Feld 2000a.

124 Kupchik 2006.

125 Mulvey and Schubert 2012:845–46.

126 Mulvey and Schuberg 2012:846–48.

127 Feld 1977; Forst, Fagan, and Vivona 1989; Beyer 1997; Mulvey and Schubert 2012:847; Deitch and Arya 2014:252.

128 Mulvey and Schubert 2012:848.

129 Deitch and Arya 2014:252–53.

130 Loeber and Farrington 2012.

131 Mulvey and Schubert 2012:849.

132 National Research Council 2013:134.

133 National Research Council 2013:135.

134 Sampson and Laub 1993; Western 2006:5–6; Mulvey and Schubert 2012:851.

135 Western 2006:20.

136 Mulvey and Schubert 2012:845.

137 Mulvey and Schubert 2012:855–56.

138 Western 2006:21; Mulvey and Schubert 2012:852; National Research Council 2013:135.

139 Western 2006:6.

140 Howell, Feld , and Mears 2012.

141 Feld 1987; Feld 1995; Podkopacz and Feld 1995; Podkopacz and Feld 1996.

142 Feld 1987; Feld 1999:230–33.

143 Hamparian et a1. 1982; Steiner 2005; Mulvey and Schubert 2012:854.

144 Bishop and Frazier 1996; Kupchik, Fagan, and Liberman 2003.

145 Schubert et al. 2010:467–468.

146 Deitch and Arya 2014:251.

147 Deitch and Arya 2014:251.

148 *Roper v. Simmons* 2005:571.

149 Singer and McDowall 1988.

150 Jensen and Metsger 1994.

151 Barnowski 2003.

152 Levitt 1998.

153 Steiner, Hemmens, and Bell 2006; Steiner and Wright 2006; National Research Council 2013:122.

154 Redding 2008; Podkopacz and Feld 1995; Podkopacz and Feld 1996; Myers 2003.

155 Fagan 1995.

156 Fagan, Kupchik, and Liberman 2003.

157 Bishop and Frazier 1996; Winner et al. 1997; Bishop and Frazier 2000:261.

158 Lanza-Kaduce et al. 2006.

159 Centers for Disease Control 2007; National Research Council 2013:175–76.

160 Centers for Disease Control 2007:13.

161 National Research Council 2013:123.

162 Snyder and Sickmund 2006; Levin, Langan and Brown 1996; Tanenhaus and Drizin 2004; Kurlychek and Johnson 2004; Kurlychek and Johnson 2010.

163 Tonry 2004:155.

164 Bishop and Frazier 1991.

165 Snyder and Sickmund 2006; Feld 2008.

166 Rainville and Smith 2003; Steiner 2009.

167 Kurlychek and Johnson 2004; 2010.

168 National Research Council and Institute of Medicine 2001:204–9, 214–18; Torbet et al. 1996:3–8; Feld 1995:966–97.

169 Garland 2001:10.

170 Gest 2001:89.

171 Feld 1997:97–107; Scott and Grisso 1997; Garland 2001:128–29.

172 Garland 2001:130; Ward 2012:257.

173 National Research Council and Institute of Medicine 2001:216; Poe-Yamagata and Jones 2007:12–14.

174 Hamparian et al. 1982:104–5; Fagan, Forst, and Vivona 1987:276.

175 National Research Council and Institute of Medicine 2001:204–9, 214–18; Torbet et al. 1996:3–8; Feld 1998:194; Feld 1995:966–97; U.S. General Accounting Office 1995a:59; Poe-Yamagata and Jones 2007:17.

176 Males and Macallair 2000:7–8; National Research Council and Institute of Medicine 2001:220; Ward 2012:253.

177 Zimring 1998; Feld 1999; Bishop 2004; Fagan 2008; Scott and Steinberg 2008

178 Zimring 1981a; Zimring 1991; Zimring 1998; Feld 1987; Feld 1995; Feld 1999; Bishop 2004; Fagan 2008; Scott and Steinberg 2008.

179 Langan and Levin 2002.

180 Moffitt 1993; Moffitt 2003; Patterson and Yoerger 2004; Blumstein, Farrington, and Moitra 1985; Farrington 1998.

181 Feld 1998; Feld 1999; Feld 2003a; Zimring 1998; Zimring 2000b; Bishop 2004; Kupchik 2006; Tonry 2007; Scott and Steinberg 2008.

182 Feld 2013b:441–43.

183 Snyder and Sickmund 2006:168; Sickmund, Sladky, and Kang 2014.

184 Sickmund, Sladky, and Kang 2014.

185 Snyder and Sickmund 2006:169–70.

186 *Schall v. Martin* 1984:255.

187 *Schall v. Martin* 1984:256–57.

188 *Schall v. Martin* 1984:265–65.

189 *Schall v. Martin* 1984:265.

190 *Schall v. Martin* 1984:266.

191 Tanenhaus 2011:117–21.
192 *Schall v. Martin* 1984:290, n. 13; *Martarella v. Kelley* 1972.
193 *Martarella v. Kelley* 1972:580–83.
194 *Schall v. Martin* 1984:269.
195 *Schall v. Martin* 1984:265–75; *Gerstein v. Pugh* 1975.
196 *Schall v. Martin* 1984:288, nn. 5–6.
197 *Schall v. Martin* 1984:278–79.
198 *Schall v. Martin* 1984:278, n. 30.
199 Feld 1999:140–45.
200 Feld 1999:143.
201 Feld 1999:143.
202 Monohan 1981:77; Gottfredson 1987; Fagan and Guggenheim 1996.
203 Feld 1999:140–45.
204 *Barefoot v. Estelle* 1983:899–902; Feld 1999:143.
205 Fagan and Guggenheim 1996.
206 *Schall v. Martin* 1984:296–98.
207 *Martarella v. Kelley* 1973:580–83.
208 Dale 1998:696.
209 Dale 1998:696–98.
210 Barton 2012:646.
211 Parent et al. 1994.
212 *Schall v. Martin* 1984:265; *N.G. v. Connecticut* 2004; *Smook v. Minnehaha County Juvenile Detention Center* 2006.
213 Barton 2012:645.
214 Moriearty 2008:305.
215 *Schall v. Martin* 1984:306–7.
216 Poe-Yamagata and Jones 2000:9.
217 Hartney and Vuong 2009:30.
218 Bishop 2005:23; Piquero 2008:59; Kempf-Leonard 2007; Hartney and Vuong:2009:31.
219 Leiber 2013.
220 Rodriguez 2010:391–92.
221 National Research Council 2014:50; Tonry 2011; Hinton 2016:318; Alexander 2010:54–60; Western 2006:47.
222 National Research Council 2014:97.
223 Annie E. Casey Foundation.
224 Annie E. Casey Foundation; Barton 2012:652–54; National Research Council 2013:5.
225 Barton 2012:653; Ward 2012:251.
226 Feyerherm 2000.
227 *Schall v. Martin* 1984:277.
228 *State ex rel. D.D.H. v. Dostert* 1980.
229 Rothman 1980; Wolcott 2005; Tanenhaus 2004.

230 Feld 1988b.
231 Gardner 1982; Feld 1988b.
232 Hart 1968:4–6.
233 Hart 1968; von Hirsch 1976:49; Matza 1964:5.
234 Feld 1978:530–40; Gardner 1982:791; Twentieth Century Fund 1976:11–14.
235 Packer 1968:23–28; Allen 1964:25; Allen 1981:2–3.
236 *Smith v. State* 1969; *In re Eric J.* 1979; Gardner 1982.
237 *Nelson v. Heyne* 1974; *Santana v. Collazo* 1983; *Alexander S. v. Boyd* 1995.
238 Gardner 1982; Feld 1988b.
239 *Kennedy v. Mendoza-Martinez* 1963:168–69.
240 *Allen v. Illinois* 1986:367.
241 *Allen v. Illinois* 1986:369–70.
242 *Allen v. Illinois* 1986:373–74.
243 *Allen v. Illinois* 1986:373.
244 *McKeiver v. Pennsylvania* 1971:551–52.
245 *McKevier v. Pennsylvania* 1971:551–52.
246 Feld 1988b; Feld 1999:251–83; Gardner 1982.
247 Ill. Rev. Stat. ch. X, §21 (1899).
248 Ill. Ann. Stat. ch 37, ¶ 701–2 (Smith-Hurd 1972).
249 Feld 1988b:841–45.
250 Feld 1998:222–23; Feld 1999; Torbet et al. 1996; Giardino 1997; McNeece and Ryan 2014:44.
251 Feld 1988b:833–47; Feld 1998:222–23; Giardino 1997:238–46; Ward 2012:240.
252 Ward 2012:241.
253 Feld 1988b:844–47; Feld 1998; Feld 1999:252–53; Nellis 2016:47–48.
254 *In re Seven Minors* 1983:950.
255 *State v. Lawley* 1979:773.
256 Twentieth Century Fund 1978:15–17.
257 American Bar Association and Institute of Judicial Administration 1980:37.
258 Torbet et al. 1996:11–16; Feld 1998:220–28; Sheffer 1995:489–91.
259 Feld 1988b:850–79; Feld 1998:224–28; Sheffer 1995:489–91.
260 Torbet et al. 1996:14; Sheffer 1995:491–92.
261 Feld 1998:227–28; Feld 1999:259–60.
262 National Research Council and Institute of Medicine 2001:210.
263 Bishop and Frazier 1996:401; Feld 1999:264–67; Scott and Steinberg 2008:229–31.
264 Matza 1964; Feld 1999:266–67.
265 Feld 1999:267–72; Frazier and Bishop 1995:23–27; National Research Council and Institute of Medicine 2001:228; Bishop and Leiber 2012.
266 Bishop and Leiber 2012:453–61.
267 Gottschalk 2015:124.
268 Bishop and Leiber 2012:446–53; National Research Council and Institute of Medicine 2001:231; Poe-Yamagata and Jones 2000:9.
269 Miller 1996:69–72; Poe-Yamagata and Jones 2007:16.

270 National Research Council 2013:214–21; Gottschalk 2015:125–26.

271 Lauritsen 2005:95–100; National Research Council 2013:219–20.

272 Piquero 2008:64; National Research Council 2013:223–24.

273 Sampson and Lauritsen1997:363.

274 Fox, Jennings, and Piquero 2014:559–60; Loeber and Farrington 1998.

275 Massey and Denton 1993; Wilson 1987; 1995; Fox, Jennings, and Piquero 2014:559; National Research Council 2014:96–97; Sampson and Wilson 1995; Tonry 2011:30.

276 Anderson 1999; Fagan 2000:382.

277 Bishop and Leiber 2012:461; Bishop 2005; Hartney and Vuong 2009:30.

278 Bishop and Leiber 2012:461; Bishop 2005.

279 National Research Council and Institute of Medicine 2001:257; National Research Council 2013:77.

280 Bridges and Steen 1998:554; National Research Council and Institute of Medicine 2001:251.

281 National Research Council and Institute of Medicine 2001:251.

282 Graham and Lowery 2004.

283 Ward 2012:244.

284 National Research Council and Institute of Medicine 2011:25.

285 Feld 1993:158–62; Feld 1991:185–90.

286 Clarke and Koch 1980:294; Feld 1989:1337–39; Rodriguez 2010.

287 Feld 1999:271–72; Snyder and Sickmund 2006; Sampson and Laub 1993; Bray, Sample, and Kempf-Leonard 2005.

288 Sickmund et al. 2015.

289 National Research Council and Institute of Medicine 2001:228–29; 42 U.S.C. §5633(a)(16)(2000).

290 National Research Council 2013:211–12.

291 Feld 1999:268; National Research Council 2013:221.

292 Poe-Yamagata and Jones 2007.

293 Hartney and Vuong 2009:32; Sickmund et al. 2013.

294 Poe-Yamagata and Jones 2007:18–21; National Research Council 2013:221–22.

295 Parent et al. 1994; Krisberg 2012:757–58; Snyder and Sickmund 2006:218–24.

296 Sickmund, Sladky, and Kang 2014.

297 Sickmund et al. 2015; Snyder and Sickmund 2006:222–23.

298 Greenwood and Turner 2012:725; MacKenzie and Freeland 2012:773.

299 E.g., Lipsey 2009.

300 Greenwood and Turner 2012:726–28; MacKenzie and Freeland 2012:790.

301 See, e.g., Greenwood and Turner 2012; MacKenzie and Freeland 2012.

302 Greenwood and Turner 2012:725; Greenwood 2006.

303 MacKenzie and Freeland 2012:790–91; Nellis 2016:83–86.

304 Greenwood and Turner 2012:728.

305 Lipsey 2009.

306 Garrido and Morales 2007; MacKenzie and Freeland 2012:771.

307 Welsh et al. 2012:262–68.

308 Welsh et al. 2012:267–70.

309 MacKenzie and Freeland 2012:771.

310 Greenwood and Turner 2012:738–40; Grisso 2004:91–94; Nellis 2016:84.

311 Greenwood and Turner 2012:744.

312 *Allen v. Illinois* 1986:373–74.

313 *In re Gault* 1967:27.

314 Schlossman 1977; Rothman 1980.

315 Krisberg 2012:751–52.

316 Krisberg 2012:754–57.

317 MacKenzie and Freeland 2012:775.

318 Bartollas, Miller, and Dinitz 1976; Feld 1977; Lerner 1986.

319 Parent et al. 1994; Snyder and Sickmund 2006; MacKenzie and Freeland 2012:774.

320 Gottschalk 2015:175.

321 Feld 1977.

322 Miller 1991; Feld 1977; Krisberg, Austin, and Steele 1991; Krisberg 2012:753; Nellis 2016:27–30.

323 Coates, Miler, and Ohlin 1978; Krisberg, Austin, and Steele 1991; MacKenzie and Freeland 20112:775–76.

324 Feld 1999:274–77; Krisberg 2012:753–54; Holland and Mlyniec 1995; Nellis 2016:113–15.

325 Feld 1999:275–76; Krisberg 2012:754–55.

326 Feld 2013b:969–81.

327 *Youngberg v. Romeo* 1982.

328 *Youngberg v. Romeo* 1982; *Alexander S. v. Boyd* 1995.

329 Prison Litigation Reform Act 1999.

330 Krisberg 2012:761–62; Greenwood and Turner 2012:743–44.

331 Feld 1999:279–83; Krisberg 2012:762–64; MacKenzie and Freeland 2012.

332 MacKenzie and Freeland 2012:794,

333 MacKenzie and Freeland 2012:784; Nellis 2016:57–58, 84–85.

334 Krisberg 2012:763; Snyder and Sickmund 2006; McKenzie and Freeland 2012:729.

335 Krisberg 2012:763–64.

336 Nellis 2011:22.

337 Western 2006.

338 Fader 2013:108.

339 Fader 2013:97.

340 Zimring 2014:169.

341 Zimring 2014:174.

342 Zimring and Tanenhaus 2014:228.

343 Miller 1991:177–90.

344 Krisberg, Austin, and Steele 1989; Miller 1991:218–26.

345 National Research Council 2013:416; Roush, Brazeal, and Church 2014:208–9.

346 National Research Council 2013:422–24; Nellis 2016:86–87.

347 Krisberg 2012:748.

348 Garland 2001:176.
349 Welsh 2012:395; Farrington and Welsh 2007; Greenwood 2006.
350 Welsh 2012:398–99.
351 Welsh 2012:398.
352 Welsh et al. 2012:248–51; Greenwood 2006.
353 Welsh et al. 2012:249–50; Greenwood 2006.
354 Farrington and Welsh 2007.
355 Greenwood 2006:90–96.
356 Greenwood 2006:167.
357 Welsh 2012:409.
358 Western 2006; Alexander 2010; Tonry 2011; Gottschalk 2015.
359 Zimring 2002:153–54.
360 Zimring 2002:154–55.
361 *In re Gault* 1967:26–27.

CHAPTER 6. THE GIRL IS A CRIMINAL

1 Steffensmeier et al. 2005; Feld 2009a; Feld 2009b; Snyder 2012:17–19.
2 Scelfo 2005; Sanders 2005; Kluger 2006.
3 Garland 2001; Steffensmeier et al. 2005; Kempf-Leonard and Johansson 2007; Strom et al. 2014.
4 Steffensmeier et al. 2005:397.
5 Steffensmeier et al. 2005; Garland 2001; Feld 2009a; Feld 2009b.
6 Bishop and Frazier 1992; Feld 1999.
7 Zimring 2002.
8 Rothman 1980; Ryerson 1978; Platt 1977; Tanenhaus 2004.
9 Feld 2013b:7.
10 Feld 1999:167.
11 Zimring 2002:148.
12 Schlossman 1977; Sutton 1988; Tanenhaus 2004:51–52; Wolcott 2005:46–52, 181–84.
13 Sutton 1988; Tanenhaus 2004; Schlossman and Wallach 1978; Kempf-Leonard and Johansson 2007.
14 Wolcott 2005:182.
15 Platt 1977; Schlossman 1977; Tannenhaus 2004.
16 Schwartz, Steketee, and Schneider 1990.
17 Schwartz, Steketee, and Schneider 1990; Feld 1999:169–73.
18 42 U.S. C. § 223 (a)(12)(1974); Schwartz 1989.
19 Schwartz 1989.
20 Bishop and Frazier 1992; Hoyt and Scherer 1998.
21 Bloom et al. 2002; MacDonald and Chesney-Lind 2001; Community Research Associates 1998; Kempf-Leonard and Sample 2000.
22 Handler and Zatz 1982; Chesney-Lind 1988; Maxson and Klein 1997.
23 Handler and Zatz 1982.
24 U.S. General Accounting Office 1991.

25 McNeece and Ryan 2014:39–40; Weithorn 1988.
26 Bishop and Frazier 1992.
27 Handler and Zatz 1982; Costello and Worthington 1981; Kempf-Leonard and Sample 2000; Federle and Chesney-Lind 1992.
28 Maxson and Klein 1997; Hoyt and Scherer 1998.
29 Zimring 1998; Feld 1999.
30 Poulin 1996; Chesney-Lind and Belknap 2004.
31 Sickmund and Puzzanchera 2014:118.
32 Federal Bureau of Investigation 2013:Tables 39, 40.
33 Girls Inc. 1996; Strom et al. 2014.
34 Steffensmeier 1993.
35 Sickmund and Puzzanchera 2014:120.
36 Sickmund and Puzzanchera 2014:120.
37 Steffensmeier et al. 2005.
38 Blumstein and Wallman 2000.
39 Wolcott 2005:50.
40 Zimring 1998:39–40, 46.
41 Zimring 1998; Zimring and Hawkins 1997; Snyder and Sickmund 2006.
42 Steffensmeier et al. 2005.
43 Steffensmeier et al. 2005:387.
44 Steffensmeier et al. 2005:357.
45 Chesney-Lind, Morash, and Irwin 2007.
46 Steffensmeier et al. 2005:363.
47 Sherman and Berk 1984.
48 Blumstein and Wallman 2000; Miller 2005; Strom et al. 2014; Snyder 2012:19.
49 Chesney-Lind 2002; Miller 2005.
50 Strom et al. 2014:431.
51 Schneider 1984; Mahoney and Fenster 1982; Chesney-Lind and Belknap 2004; Girls Inc. 1996; Snyder 2000:4.
52 Strom et al. 2014:444–45.
53 Bloom et al. 2002; Hoyt and Scherer 1998.
54 Franke, Huynh-Hohnbaum, and Chung 2002.
55 Strom et al. 2014:432.
56 Bureau of Criminal Information and Analysis 1999.
57 American Bar Association and National Bar Association 2001:3.
58 Strom et al. 2014:444.
59 Acoca and Dedel 1998; Acoca 1999.
60 Gaarder, Rodriguez, and Zatz 2004.
61 Gaarder, Rodriguez, and Zatz 2004:565.
62 Chesney-Lind and Pasko 2004.
63 Artz 1998; Bond-Maupin, Maupin, and Leisenring 2002; Gaarder, Rodriguez, and Zatz 2004.
64 Sickmund and Puzzanchera 2014:77.

65 Snyder and Sickmund 2006.
66 Sickmund and Puzzanchera 2014:122.
67 Kupchik 2010:188.
68 Curran 1984.
69 Schwartz, Steketee, and Schneider 1990.
70 Schwartz, Steketee, and Schneider 1990.
71 National Research Council 2013:295.
72 Feld 1999; National Research Council and Institute of Medicine 2001.
73 Hoyt and Scherer 1998.
74 Schlossman 1977; Schlossman and Wallach 1978; Chesney-Lind 1988; Johnson and Scheuble 1991.
75 Bishop and Frazier 1992.
76 Corley, Cernkovich, and Giordano 1989; U.S. General Accounting Office 1991; Hoyt and Scherer 1998.
77 Alder 1984.
78 Bishop and Frazier 1992.
79 Johnson and Scheuble 1991:680.
80 Snyder and Sickmund 2006; Feld 2009b.
81 Sickmund et al. 2015.
82 Schaffner 1998.
83 Sutton 1988; Schwartz, Weiner, and Enosh 1998.
84 Federle 2000; Sutton 1988.
85 Garland 2001; Steffensmeier et al. 2005:363.
86 Schneider 1984:367.
87 Mahoney and Fenster 1982.
88 Castellano 1986; Schneider 1984.
89 American Bar Association and National Bar Association 2001:14.

CHAPTER 7. THE STUDENT IS A CRIMINAL

1   Feld 1999:38–42.
2   Coleman et al. 1974:18.
3   *Brown v. Board of Education* 1954:493.
4   Kupchik 2010:24–25.
5   Nance 2014:82; Orfield and Frankenberg 2008; Orfield, Kuscera, and Siegel-Hawley 2012.
6   Hirschfield 2008:80.
7   Kupchik 2014:95.
8   Kupchik 2014:95.
9   Hirschfield 2008:81.
10 *T.L.O. v. New Jersey* 1985.
11 *T.L.O. v. New Jersey* 1985:335–38.
12 *T.L.O. v. New Jersey* 1985:337.
13 *T.L.O. v. New Jersey* 1985:338.

14 *T.L.O. v. New Jersey* 1985:339.

15 *T.L.O. v. New Jersey* 1985:352–53.

16 *T.L.O. v. New Jersey* 1985:341.

17 *T.L.O. v. New Jersey* 1985:341.

18 *T.L.O. v. New Jersey* 1985:342.

19 Zane 1987:386–90; Gardner 1988:923–24; Feld 2011.

20 *T.L.O. v. New Jersey* 1985:354.

21 *T.L.O. v. New Jersey* 1985:354, 371.

22 *T.L.O. v. New Jersey* 1985:358.

23 *Illinois v. Gates* 1983.

24 *T.L.O. v. New Jersey* 1985:364.

25 LaFave et al. 2009:165–81; *Illinois v. Gates* 1983.

26 *Terry v. Ohio* 1968.

27 *Illinois v. Gates* 1983:238.

28 *Adams v. Williams* 1972.

29 *Illinois v. Gates* 1983:232.

30 *United States v. Cortez* 1981:417.

31 *Ornelas v. United States* 1996:695.

32 *United States v. Sokolow* 1989:7.

33 *Safford Unified School District #1 v. Redding* 2009:2639.

34 *Safford Unified School District #1 v. Redding* 2009:2638.

35 *Safford Unified School District #1 v. Redding* 2009:2643.

36 *Safford Unified School District #1 v. Redding* 2009:2644.

37 *Harlow v. Fitzgerald* 1982:807.

38 *B.C. v. Plumas Unified School District* 1999:1268.

39 *Monell v. N.Y. Dep't of Soc. Servs.* 1978:694.

40 Tanenhaus 2011:124–28.

41 *T.L.O. v. New Jersey* 1985:341, n. 7.

42 Redding and Shalf 2001:298–302; Pinard 2003:1068–69; Advancement Project 2005:7.

43 Kupchik 2010:30.

44 Feld 2011:892; Blumenson and Nilsen 2003:69; Advancement Project 2005:15; Advancement Project and Civil Rights Project 2000; National Research Council 2013:111.

45 Wald and Thurau 2010.

46 Nance 2014:98.

47 Theriot 2009:281; Lawrence 2007; National Research Council 2013:82; Kupchik 2010:3.

48 Pinard 2003:1075–76; Redding and Shalf 2001:319–20; Theriot 2009; Kupchik 2010:14–15.

49 Dohrn 2002:283.

50 Theriot 2009; Nance 2015; Jaggers, Young, and Church 2014:160.

51 Kupchik 2010:211.

52 Simon 2007:211.
53 Kupchik 2010:11; Blue Ribbon Commission 2007; Pinard 2003:1079.
54 Pinard 2003:1106.
55 Kupchik 2014:103; Theriot 2009; Nance 2015.
56 *People v. Dilworth* 1996:318.
57 *People v. Dilworth* 1996:321.
58 Kim, Losen, and Hewitt 2010:120–22; *J.A.R. v. State* 1997:1244.
59 Pinard 2003:1070.
60 Simon 2007:210; Kupchik 2010:14.
61 Kupchik 2014:103.
62 Nellis 2016:101–2.
63 Garcia and Kennedy 2003:274; Rossow and Stefkovich 1995:34.
64 Advancement Project 2005:11; Hirschfield 2008:82–83.
65 *In re F.B.* 1995; *People v. Pruitt* 1996.
66 Feld 2011:904–5.
67 Kupchik 2010:168.
68 Nellis 2016:102.
69 Kupchik 2010:36–37; Nance 2014:82–83.
70 *Illinois v. Caballes* 2005:409.
71 *Illinois v. Caballes* 2005:409.
72 *Illinois v. Caballes* 2005:410.
73 *Illinois v. Caballes* 2005:421–22.
74 *Illinois v. Caballes* 2005:422.
75 *Myers v. State* 2005.
76 Feld 2011:937–41; *State v. Best* 2010:607.
77 *State v. Best* 2010:613.
78 *B.C. v. Plumas Unified School District* 1999; Feld 2011:907–13.
79 LaFave 1987:373–74.
80 *Doe v. Renfrow* 1979.
81 *B.C. v. Plumas Unified School District* 1999; *Commonwealth v. Martin* 1993; Feld
    2011:907–13; *Horton v. Goose Creek Ind. Sch. Dist.* 1982:478–79; Gardner 1980.
82 Wilson and Kelling 1982:31.
83 Blumenson and Nilsen 2003:79–81.
84 Kupchik 2010:2, 15.
85 Hirschfield 2008:82; Nellis 2016:94.
86 20 U.S.C.A. § 7151; Pinard 2003:1109; National Research Council 2013:111–12; Nellis
    2016:94–97.
87 Dohrn 2002:283.
88 Simon 2007:216; Kim, Losen, and Hewitt 2010:79–80; Nellis 2016:95–96.
89 Simon 2007:215.
90 Kupchik 2010:79–80; National Research Council 2013:111.
91 National Research Council 2013:112.
92 Krezmien, Leone, and Wilson 2014.

93 Krezmien, Leone, and Wilson 2014:268–69.

94 Krezmien, Leone, and Wilson 2014:272.

95 Kim, Losen, and Hewitt 2010:78; Nance 2014:103; Nellis 2011:4–6.

96 Skiba et al. 2006; Dohrn 2002:283; Theriot 2009; Nance 2015.

97 Blumenson and Nilsen 2003:66.

98 Simon 2007:222; Kupchik 2010:200.

99 Kupchik 2010:9.

100 Blumenson and Nilsen 2003:66; Dohrn 2002:283; Pinard 2003:1108–19; Krezmien, Leone, and Wilson 20014:275; Wald and Losen 2003:10; Kupchik 2014:96–97.

101 Nance 2014:94–95.

102 "No Child Left Behind," U.S. Department of Education, www.ed.gov.

103 Kozol 2005:53; Lindsey 2009:21–22.

104 Kupchik 2010:28.

105 Nance 2014:83; Nellis 2016:65–66.

106 Kupchik 2010:172.

107 Kim, Losen, and Hewitt 2010:1–2.

108 Nellis 2016:98.

109 Krezmien, Leone, and Wilson 2014:276–79.

110 Orfield 2015.

111 *Milliken v. Bradley* 1974; Orfield 2015; Orfield and Frankenberg 2008.

112 Putnam 2015:253.

113 *Parents Involved in Community Schools v. Seattle School District No. 1*, 127 S. Ct. 2738.

114 Orfield and Frankenberg 2008:7.

115 Orfield and Frankenberg 2008:6.

116 Orfield 2015:432–36.

117 Orfield, Kuscera, and Siegel-Hawley 2012:9.

118 Mickelson 2008; Mickelson 2015.

119 Putnam 2015:253.

120 Kozol 1991; Kozol 2005.

121 Fenning and Rose 2007:539–42; Smith 2009:1013; Fabelo et al. 2011; Kupchik 2010:19, 159; Skiba et al. 2002; Kim, Losen, and Hewitt 2010:43–54; Nance 2014:84; Krezmien, Leone, and Wilson:268–69.

122 Kupchik 2010:25; Kim, Losen, and Hewitt 2010:1.

123 Kupchik 2014:94.

124 Sweeten, Bushway, and Paternoster 2009:50.

125 Kupchik 2010:18.

126 Kupchik 2010:165; Hirschfield 2008:86–87.

127 Fabelo et al. 2011.

128 Kim, Losen, and Hewitt 2010:2; Nellis 2016:96–97.

129 National Research Council 2013:112.

130 Nance 2014:86.

131 Nance 2013:37–43; Nance 2014:82.

132 Nance 2014:90.
133 Fenning and Rose 2007:539–40.
134 Nance 2014:86.
135 Sampson and Laub 1993; Bridges and Steen 1998; Kupchik 2010:160; Kupchik 2014:97.
136 Kupchik 2010:185.
137 Kupchik 2014:101, 163.
138 Fenning and Rose 2007:537; Blumenson and Nilsen 2003:71–72.
139 Kupchik 2010:173–87; Advancement Project 2005:12.
140 Blumenson and Nilsen 2003:83–85; Theriot 2009:280–81.
141 Sweeten, Bushway, and Paternoster 2009.
142 Wilson 2009:66; Western 2006.
143 Western 2006:24–28.
144 Hirschfield 2008:92.
145 Wacquant 2001:108.
146 Blumenson and Nilsen 2003:173.
147 *West Virginia State Bd. of Educ. v. Barnette* 1943:637.
148 Kupchik 2010:6–7.
149 *Tinker v. Des Moines Sch. Dist.*1969:506.
150 Kupchik 2014:16–17, 98–99.
151 Kupchik 2010:35.
152 Kupchik 2014:105.
153 Nance 2014:105–6.
154 Nance 2013:25.

CHAPTER 8. THE CRIMINAL IS A KID
1 Feld 2008; Feld 2013d; Feld 2013e.
2 *Harris v. Wright* 1996:585.
3 *Rice v. Cooper* 1998; *Tate v. State* 2003.
4 Feld and Bishop 2012:815; Poe-Yamagata and Jones 2007:5; Campaign for Youth Justice 2006:6; Snyder and Sickmund 2006; Amnesty International and Human Rights Watch 2005:19, n. 30; Griffin 2012; Steiner, Hemmens, and Bell 2006:49–50; Steiner and Wright 2006:191–95.
5 Bennet and DiIulio 1996:21–34; Zimring 1998; Moriearty 2011:850–51.
6 National Research Council and Institute of Medicine 2001:204–9; 214–18; Feld 2003b:1556–58; Feld 2007b:31–38; Juszkiewicz 2000:1; Feld 2000a:124–29; Feld and Bishop 2012.
7 Amnesty International and Human Rights Watch 2005:15–16; Fagan, Forst, and Vivona 1987:276; Bortner, Zatz, and Hawkins 2000:277; Juszkiewicz 2000:6; Campaign for Youth Justice 2006:11; Males and Macallair 2000:7–8; National Research Council and Institute of Medicine 2001.
8 Feld 2003b:1552–58; Moriearty 2011:850–51; Graham and Lowery 2004:488–95; Bridges and Steen 1998:561.

9 Poe-Yamagata and Jones 2007:34; Males and Macallair 2000:9; Juszkeweicz 2000:18; Amnesty International and Human Rights Watch 2005:6; Human Rights Watch 2009:6.

10 Ward 2012:115–18.

11 Tonry 1996; Tonry 2011.

12 Austin, Johnson, and Gregoriou 2000; Massey 2006:1089; Streib and Schrempp 2007:7; Campaign for Youth Justice 2006:13; Mauer, King, and Young 2004:17.

13 *Roper v. Simmons* 2005.

14 *Graham v. Florida* 2010:2026; Maroney 2011.

15 *Graham v. Florida* 2010:2030 (majority); id.:2046 (dissent).

16 *Miller v. Alabama* 2012; *Jackson v. Hobbs* 2012.

17 U.S. Constitution, Amendment VIII.

18 *Eddings v. Oklahoma* 1982.

19 *Thompson v. Oklahoma* 1988:835.

20 *Stanford v. Kentucky* 1989.

21 *Roper v. Simmons* 2005.

22 *Atkins v. Virginia* 2002.

23 Feld 2008.

24 *Roper v. Simmons* 2005:569.

25 *Roper v. Simmons* 2005:569–70.

26 *Roper v. Simmons* 2005:570.

27 *Roper v. Simmons* 2005:570.

28 *Roper v. Simmons* 2005:571.

29 *Roper v. Simmons* 2005:571.

30 Feld 2013d; Feld 2013e.

31 *Roper v. Simmons* 2005:572–73.

32 *Roper v. Simmons* 2005:569; Denno 2006:396.

33 Sullivan and Frase 2009:161; Frase 2005:589–91; von Hirsch 1976:48.

34 Logan 1998:707; Scott and Steinberg 2003:822; Scott and Steinberg 2008:123–24; Zimring 2000c:271.

35 Amnesty International and Human Rights Watch 2005:113.

36 Brink 2004:1557; Scott and Grisso 1997:176; Steinberg and Cauffman 1999:407–9; Zimring 2000c:273.

37 Zimring 2000c:278; Scott and Steinberg 2008:121–22.

38 Scott and Steinberg 2008:129.

39 National Research Council and Institute of Medicine 2011:48–49.

40 National Research Council and Institute of Medicine 2011:52.

41 National Research Council 2013:1–2, 90.

42 National Research Council 2013:91.

43 Cauffman, Woolard, and Repucci 1999:406–7; Scott 1992:1609; National Research Council 2013:95.

44 Morse 1998:52–53.

45 Cauffman and Steinberg 1995:1770; Steinberg and Cauffman 1996:250; Spear 2000:423; Steinberg 2014:76–78.
46 Dahl 2001:61; Aronson 2007:119; National Research Council 2013:91; National Research Council and Institute of Medicine 2011:39; Spear 2010:139–40; Monahan, Steinberg, and Piquero 2015:588.
47 Aronson 2007:119.
48 National Research Council 2013:93; Spear 2010:139–40.
49 National Research Council and Institute of Medicine 2011:40.
50 Figner et al. 2009:726–28; Dahl 2001:62.
51 "About the Network," MacArthur Foundation Research Network, www.adjj.org; Monahan, Steinberg, and Piquero 2015:603–4; Nellis 2016:79–82.
52 Scott and Steinberg 2008:131–39; Woolard 2012:107–8.
53 Woolard 2012:108.
54 Scott and Steinberg 2008:36–37; Scott and Steinberg 2003:813; Taylor-Thompson 2003:152; Steinberg 2014:69.
55 "The Immaturity Gap," MacArthur Foundation Research Network, www.adjj.org.
56 Scott and Steinberg 2008:37–44; National Research Council 2013:2.
57 Scott and Steinberg 2008:48.
58 National Research Council and Institute of Medicine 2011:2; Spear 2000:421; Gardner 1993; Steinberg 2014:68–69; Spear 2010:130–44.
59 Furby and Beyth-Marom 1992:3–4; Grisso 1996:241; National Research Council 2011:52–56.
60 Furby and Beyth-Marom 1992:19; Grisso 2000:139; Woolard 2012:109–10; Spear 2010:136.
61 Scott 2000:304–5; Taylor-Thompson 2003:153; Spear 2010:137–39.
62 "With Age, Longer Time Spent Thinking before Acting," MacArthur Foundation Research Network, www.adjj.org.
63 "Risk Perception Declines and Then Increases after Mid-Adolescence," MacArthur Foundation Research Network, www.adjj.org.
64 Scott 1992:1645–57; Taylor-Thompson 2003:154; National Research Council and Institute of Medicine 2011:54–56; "Future Orientation Increases with Age," MacArthur Foundation Research Network, www.adjj.org.
65 National Research Council 2013:95.
66 "Older Individuals Are More Willing to Delay Gratification," MacArthur Foundation Research Network, www.adjj.org; National Research Council 2013:91, 93.
67 Scott and Steinberg 2003; Scott and Steinberg 2008; National Research Council and Institute of Medicine 2011:50.
68 Spear 2010:135–36.
69 Scott and Grisso 1997:163; Spear 2000:422; National Research Council and Institute of Medicine 2011:42.
70 Woolard 2012:114.
71 Scott and Steinberg 2008:44–50; Spear 2010:140–41; "Preference for Risk Peaks in Mid-Adolescence" and "Sensation-Seeking Declines with Age," MacArthur

Foundation Research Network, www.adjj.org; Steinberg, et al. 2008; National Research Council 2013:91–92.

72 Cohn et al. 1995:221; Furby and Beyth-Marom 1992:19–21.

73 Sowell et al. 1999:859; Sowell et al. 2001:8819; Paus et al. 1999:1908; Spear 2000:438; Spear 2010; National Research Council 2013:96–100; Monahan, Steinberg, and Piquero 2015; Gruber and Yurgelin-Todd 2006:330; Casey 2008.

74 Steinberg 2008; Steinberg 2010:217.

75 Scott and Steinberg 2003:816; Feld, Casey, and Hurd 2013.

76 Gruber and Yurgelun-Todd 2006:323; Sowell et al. 2001:8819; Casey 2008:63; Spear 2010:102–9; Casey, Giedd, and Thomas 2000:244.

77 National Research Council and Institute of Medicine 2011:37.

78 Gruber and Yurgelun-Todd 2006:325; Paus et al. 1999:1908; Sowell et al. 2001:8828; Steinberg 2014:31–33.

79 Nagy, Westerberg, and Klingberg 2004:1231; Goldberg 2001:144; Spear 2010:64.

80 Paus et al. 1999:1908.

81 National Research Council and Institute of Medicine 2011:37; Steinberg 2014:26; Spear 2010:75–76.

82 Casey, Giedd, and Thomas 2000:241; Gogtay et al. 2004:8175; National Research Council 2013:96; National Research Council and Institute of Medicine 2011:37.

83 Gruber and Yurgelun-Todd 2006:325; Feld, Casey, and Hurd 2013:189–91.

84 Baird et al. 1999:195; Spear 2010:68–69.

85 Steinberg 2014:72–74.

86 Spear 2010:180; Baird et al. 1999:198; Burnett et al. 2009:173; Blakemore 2007:130; Feld, Casey, and Hurd 2013:191–93.

87 Dahl 2001:64; Steinberg 2014:74; Steinberg 2008; Steinberg 2010:161–62; National Research Council and Institute of Medicine 2011:38.

88 Steinberg 2008; Steinberg 2010; Scott and Steinberg 2008:48; Feld, Casey, and Hurd 2013:193–94.

89 Johnson, Riss, and Noble 2016:1.

90 Steinberg 2014:23–24; Putnam 2015:110.

91 Steinberg 2014:9–10; Hanson et al. 2012; Feld, Casey, and Hurd 2013:203–4.

92 Steinberg 2014:166.

93 Noble et al. 2015:774.

94 Hanson and Hackman 2012:174–78; Johnson, Riss, and Noble 2016; Noble et al. 2015:777.

95 Johnson, Riss, and Noble 2016:9.

96 Hanson and Hackman 2012:175; Johnson, Riss, and Noble 2016:9.

97 National Research Council and Institute of Medicine 2011:59.

98 Putnam 2015:112.

99 Steinberg 2014:165–66.

100 Putnam 2015:109–44; Johnson, Riss, and Noble 2016:9–10.

101 Hanson and Hackman 2012:175.

102 Hanson and Hackman 2012; Hanson et al. 2012.

103 Steinberg 2014:171–72; Putnam 2015:121–22.

104 Putnam 2015:115.

105 Noble et al. 2015:778.

106 Monahan, Steinberg, and Piquero 2015:586–87.

107 Maroney 2009; Maroney 2011:769; Morse 2004:157; Morse 2006:405–6; Aronson 2007:136; Scott and Steinberg 2008:46; Steinberg 2014:4; Monahan, Steinberg, and Piquero 2015:605–6.

108 Scott et al. 2015:18–19. See also Maroney 2011:769.

109 Scott and Steinberg 2008:35, 50; Zimring 2000c:280–81; Spear 2010:155–57.

110 National Research Council and Institute of Medicine 2011:36; National Research Council 2013:94; Spear 2010:15–17.

111 National Research Council and Institute of Medicine 2011:50; Scott and Steinberg 2008:51.

112 Scott and Steinberg 2008:38.

113 Woolard 2012:112; Scott and Steinberg 2008:22.

114 Zimring 2000c:281–82.

115 Scott and Steinberg 2003:815; Gardner and Steinberg 2005:625–26; Monahan, Steinberg, and Piquero 2015:587.

116 Chein et al. 2011:F1, F8; Steinberg 2014:77, 98.

117 Snyder and Sickmund 1999; Zimring 1981b:870; Zimring 1998:152; Steinberg 2014:93; Zimring 2000c:282.

118 "With Age, Individuals Become More Resistant to Peer Influence," MacArthur Foundation Research Network, www.adjj.org; Zimring 2000c:280; Steinberg and Monahan 2007:1531; Gardner and Steinberg 2005:626.

119 Scott and Steinberg 2008:35.

120 Zimring 1998:152.

121 *Roper v. Simmons* 2005:569.

122 Arredondo 2003:16–17; Fagan 1998:535–39; Scott 2000b:547.

123 Anderson 1990; Anderson 1998:82–88; Anderson 1999; Fagan 1998:535–39.

124 *Rummel v. Estelle* 1980:272; Stinneford 2011.

125 Feld 2008; Feld 2013c.

126 *Atkins v. Virginia* 2002 (mental retardation); *Roper v. Simmons* 2005 (juveniles); *Kennedy v. Louisiana* 2008 (rape of a child); *Lockett v. Ohio* 1978 (felony murder).

127 *Rummel v. Estelle* 1980.

128 *Solem v. Helms* 1983.

129 *Solem v. Helms* 1983:292.

130 *Harmelin v. Michigan* 1991; Frase 2005.

131 *Ewing v. California* 2003; Frase 2005.

132 *Kennedy v. Louisiana* 2008 (rape of a child); *Enmund v. Florida* 1982 (felony murderer who did not kill or intend to kill); *Coker v. Georgia* 1977 (rape of an adult woman).

133 *Roper v. Simmons* 2005; *Atkins v. Virginia* 2002.

134 *Graham v. Florida* 2010:2022–23.

135 *Graham v. Florida* 2010:2046.

136 *Graham v. Florida* 2010:2026.

137 *Graham v. Florida* 2010:2027; *Kennedy v. Louisiana* 2008; *Coker v. Georgia* 1977.

138 *Graham v. Florida* 2010:2027.

139 *Graham v. Florida* 2010:2027.

140 Nellis 2012:4.

141 *Graham v. Florida* 2010:2032.

142 Grisso et al. 2003:356; Steinberg 2009:63; Bonnie and Grisso 2000:87–88.

143 *Graham v. Florida* 2010:2030.

144 *Graham v. Florida* 2010:2034.

145 *Graham v. Florida* 2010:2046.

146 *Graham v. Florida* 2010:2057.

147 Amnesty International and Human Rights Watch 2005:25, n. 44.

148 Amnesty International and Human Rights Watch 2005:1; Feld 2013d.

149 Amnesty International and Human Rights Watch 2005:1–6; Gottschalk 2015:180.

150 LaBelle 2004:4; Amnesty International and Human Rights Watch 2005:27–28; Human Rights Watch 2012:4.

151 Bishop and Frazier 2000:236–37; Kurlychek and Johnson 2010; Tanenhaus and Drizin 2003:665; Amnesty International and Human Rights Watch 2005:33; Human Rights Watch 2012:4.

152 Mauer, King, and Young 2004:5–8; Tonry 1996:6–13; Nellis 2013.

153 Nellis and King 2009:5–11; Gottschalk 2015:192–93.

154 Mauer, King, and Young 2004:1; Tonry 1996:6–13.

155 Note 2006:1842; Nellis 2013:447–48.

156 Note 2006:1851–52.

157 Nellis 2013:441–42.

158 Amnesty International and Human Rights Watch 2005:1; Human Rights Watch 2009; Human Rights Watch 2012:2; Nellis and King 2009:17–25.

159 Amnesty International and Human Rights Watch 2005:2.

160 Amnesty International and Human Rights Watch 2005:25; Feld 2013d; Feld 2013e.

161 Amnesty International and Human Rights Watch 2005:39; LaBelle 2004:6; Nellis 2012:3.

162 Nellis 2012:3, 16.

163 *Miller v. Alabama* 2012:2460.

164 *Miller v. Alabama* 2012:2465.

165 *Miller v. Alabama* 2012:2463.

166 *Woodson v. North Carolina* 1976:280; *Sumner v. Shuman* 1987:77; Feld 2013d; Feld 2013e.

167 *Miller v. Alabama* 2012:2464, 2467.

168 *Miller v. Alabama* 2012:2469.

169 *Miller v. Alabama* 2012:2485–86.

170 *Miller v. Alabama* 2012:2465.

171 *Miller v. Alabama* 2012:2479.

172 *Miller v. Alabama* 2012:2471.

173 Feld and Bishop 2012.

174 Nellis 2012.

175 Moriearty 2015:957–65.

176 *State v. Ragland* 2013:114.

177 Moriearty 2015:962–67.

178 Moriearty 2015:967–73.

179 Moriearty 2015:974.

180 *Montgomery v. Louisiana* 2016:732–34, 736.

181 *Montgomery v. Louisiana* 2016:732–33.

182 *Montgomery v. Louisiana* 2016:736.

183 *Miller v. Alabama* 2012:2468–69.

184 *Commonwealth v. Knox* 2012:769; *People v. Carp* 2014; *Bear Cloud v. State* 2013:47; Drinan 2016:1816–24.

185 *People v. Gutierrez* 2014.

186 *People v. Chavez* 2014:34.

187 Holt 2015:1419, n. 202.

188 Sentencing Project 2014:2–3.

189 Drinan 2016:1816–19.

190 Fl. Stat. Ann. § 921.1401 (2014).

191 Moriearty 2015:975–76; Scott et al. 2015:11–12; Sentencing Project 2014; 18 Pa. Stat. and Cons. Stat. Ann. §1102.1(a)(1–2); Gottschalk 2015:176; Drinan 2016:1816–24.

192 *State v. Sweet* 2016:838–39.

193 Sentencing Project 2014.

194 Gottschalk 2015:176.

195 Nellis and King 2009:3, 17.

196 *People v. Caballero* 2012:295–96.

197 *State v. Null* 2013:72.

198 *State v. Null* 2013:71.

199 *Bunch v. Smith* 2012:550.

200 *Miller v. Alabama* 2012:2482.

201 *State v. Lyle* 2014:409–10; Drinan 2016.

202 *State v. Lyle* 2014:400.

203 *State v. Lyle* 2014:386; Drinan 2016:1822–24.

204 *Miller v. Alabama* 2012:2466; Drinan 2016:1825–26.

205 Hoeffel 2013:54.

206 *Graham v. Florida* 2010:2030; Drinan 2016:1828–31.

207 Drinan 2012:76.

208 *Miller v. Alabama* 2012:2482.

209 Zimring 1998; Feld 2000a.

210 Scott 1992; Zimring 1998; Feld 1999; Feld 2013d; Feld 2013e; Scott and Grisso 1997; Scott 2000; Zimring 2000c; *State v. Lyle* 2014:398; *State v. Null* 2013:75; *Thomson v. Oklahoma* 1988:834; Amnesty International and Human Rights Watch 2005:113.

211 *R. v. D.B.* 2008.

212 *Roper v. Simmons* 2005:573.

213 *Roper v. Simmons* 2005:574; Feld 2007b; Feld 2008.

214 *Roper v. Simmons* 2005:573.

215 Scott and Steinberg 2003; Duff 1993; Moore 1997.

216 Fagan 2003; Emens 2005:87; Scott and Steinberg 2008:30–31.

217 Feld 2013c; Feld 2013d; Howell, Feld, and Mears 2012.

218 Feld 2007; Feld 2008.

219 Brink 2004; Fagan 2003; Zimring 1998.

220 Scott and Steinberg 2008:140.

221 Fagan 2003:248; Howell, Feld, and Mears 2012:229.

222 Scott and Steinberg 2003; Scott and Steinberg 2008; Von Hirsch 2001:227.

223 Zimring 1982; Scott 1992.

224 *Roper v. Simmons* 2005:553–54; Emens 2005.

225 Ghetti and Redlich 2001.

226 Scott and Steinberg 2008:141.

227 Scott and Steinberg 2008:140.

228 Feld 1987; Feld 1997; Feld 1999; Feld 2008; Feld 2013d; Feld 2013e; Howell, Feld, and Mears 2012; Scott and Steinberg 2008:139.

229 Zimring 1998; von Hirsch 2001; Howell, Feld and Mears 2012.

230 *Miller v. Alabama* 2012:2455.

231 von Hirsch 2001:227; Feld 1997.

232 Feld 1997; Scott and Steinberg 2003; Scott and Steinberg 2008.

233 Amnesty International and Human Rights Watch 2005; Scott and Steinberg 2008; Mauer, King, and Young 2004; Howell, Feld, and Mears 2012.

234 Arias 2006; Feld 2008; *Bear Cloud v. State* 2014:142.

235 Amnesty International and Human Rights Watch 2005; LaBelle 2004; Nellis 2012.

236 American Law Institute Model Penal Code, § 6.11A (g).

237 Tanenhaus and Drizin 2002:697–98.

238 Scott and Steinberg 2008:246.

239 Howell, Feld, and Mears 2012:213.

240 American Bar Association 2008.

241 American Law Institute Model Penal Code, § 6.11A (a).

242 *Roper v. Simmons* 2005:573.

243 Stinneford 2011.

244 *Roper v. Simmons* 2005:570; *Graham v. Florida* 2010:2026; *Miller v. Alabama* 2012:2475.

245 Zimring 1998; Scott and Steinberg 2008:136–37; Zimring 2000c:284–85.

246 Wolfgang, Figlio, and Sellin 1972; Snyder and Sickmund 2006; Scott and Steinberg 2008; Zimring 2000c:284.

247 Zimring 1978; Zimring 1998; Feld 1997.

248 National Research Council 2013:5.

CHAPTER 9. THE DEFENDANT IS A KID

1 *Kent v. United States* 1966:556.
2 Feld 1999; Tanenhaus 2004.
3 Feld 1984; Feld 1988a; Feld 1999; Scott and Steinberg 2008.
4 *In re Winship* 1970:364–68.
5 *Breed v. Jones* 1975:341.
6 *McKeiver v. Pennsylvania* 1971:545–62.
7 Feld 2003a; Drizin and Luloff 2007.
8 Zimring 2002:150.
9 President's Commission 1967b:2.
10 President's Commission 1967b:91; Schur 1973.
11 President's Commission 1967a:81–85; President's Commission 1967b:2.
12 Snyder and Sickmund 2006; Mears 2012.
13 Mears 2012:587; Bishop 2005:39–40.
14 Fagan and Tyler 2005:218.
15 Kupchik 2010:17; Fagan and Tyler 2005:221.
16 Fagan and Tyler 2005:231.
17 Ainsworth 1991; Feld 1999:163; Fagan and Tyler 2005; National Research Council 2013:193.
18 Fagan and Tyler 2005:236; National Research Council 2013:192; Grisso and Schwartz 2000:70.
19 *Haley v. Ohio* 1948; *Gallegos v. Colorado* 1962; *In re Gault* 1967; *Fare v. Michael C.* 1979; *Yarborough v. Alvarado* 2004; *J.D.B. v. North Carolina* 2011.
20 *Fare v. Michael C.* 1979:725.
21 Feld 1999:106–8; Owen-Kostelnik et al. 2006.
22 *Haley v. Ohio* 1948:599–601.
23 *Gallegos v. Colorado* 1962:54.
24 *In re Gault* 1967:45, 55.
25 *In re Gault* 1967:49–50.
26 *In re Gault* 1967:47 (emphasis supplied).
27 *Fare v. Michael C.* 1979; King 2006:449.
28 Rosenberg 1980:686–90.
29 *Miranda v. Arizona* 1966:444.
30 *J.D.B. v. North Carolina* 2011:2394.
31 *J.D.B. v. North Carolina* 2011:2403.
32 *J.D.B. v. North Carolina* 2011:2404.
33 *J.D.B. v. North Carolina* 2011:2404, 2407.
34 *J.D.B. v. North Carolina* 2011:2403.
35 *Haley v. Ohio* 1948; *Gallegos v. Colorado* 1962.
36 Larson 2003:645, n. 91; King 2006:456.
37 *West v. United States* 1968:469; *Fare v. Michael C.* 1979.
38 Feld 1984; Feld 2000b:113; Feld 2006a:112–13.

39 Kassin et al. 2010:11.
40 Bishop and Farber 2007.
41 Garrett 2008:88–91.
42 King 2006:456–57; Feld 2000b; Feld 2006a.
43 Farber 2004:1287, n. 65; Feld 2006a; Krzewinski 2002:374–77; King 2006:451–52.
44 *In re BMB* 1998:1312–13; *Commonwealth v. A Juvenile* 1983:657; *State v. Presha* 2000:114, 117.
45 Krzewinksi 2002:374–77; Drizin and Colgan 2004:153–55; Reba, Waldman, and Woodhouse 2011.
46 Feld 2000b:117–18; Farber 2004.
47 *In re Dino* 1978.
48 *State v. Presha* 2000.
49 Farber 2004.
50 Reba, Waldman, and Woodhouse 2011.
51 Grisso 1981:180–81; Farber 2004; Reba, Waldman, and Woodhouse 2011.
52 Larson 2003; Grisso 1981; Kaban and Tobey 1999; Woolard et al. 2008; Reba, Waldman, and Woodhouse 2011.
53 *Duckworth v. Eagan* 1988; Rogers et al. 2007:181.
54 Rogers et al. 2008b:72–85; 2008a:135.
55 Rogers et al. 2008b:74, tbl. 3.
56 Goldstein and Goldstein 2010.
57 Rogers et al. 2008b:71.
58 Rogers et al. 2008b:71.
59 Grisso 1980:1152–54; Grisso 1981:106–07; Grisso 1997a:11; Grisso 1997b; Grisso et al. 2003:35.
60 Grisso 1980:1152–54; Grisso 1981.
61 Grisso 1980:1160; Viljoen, Klaver, and Roesch 2005:256.
62 Beyer 2000:28; Abramovitch, Higgins-Biss, and Biss 1993:320; Abramovitch, Peterson-Badali, and Rohan 1995:10–11; Redlich, Silverman, and Steiner 2003:405; Viljoen and Roesch 2005:256; Goldstein and Goldstein 2010.
63 Grisso 1998.
64 Grisso 1998; Bishop and Farber 2007.
65 Grisso 1980; 1981.
66 Grisso 1997:11.
67 Viljoen and Roesch 2005:736.
68 Kassin et al. 2010:8.
69 Viljoen, Zapf, and Roesch 2007:9.
70 Viljoen, Zapf, and Roesch 2007.
71 Viljoen and Roesch 2005:736.
72 Grisso 2004.
73 Grisso 2004:164–67.
74 Grisso 1981:130; Grisso 1997a:11; Larson 2003:649–53.
75 Grisso 1997a:10–11.

76 Grisso 1981; Grisso 2000:148–49.

77 Viljoen and Roesch 2005:738.

78 Viljoen, Klaver, and Roesch 2005:256.

79 *Miranda v. Arizona* 1965:455–58.

80 Larson 2003; Owen-Kostelnik, Reppucci, and Meyer 2006:764.

81 Kassin et al. 2010:8.

82 Meyer and Reppucci 2007:764; Billings et al. 2007:126; Ainsworth 1993; Kaban and Tobey 1999; Owen-Kostelnik, Reppucci, and Meyer 2006:292.

83 Billings et al. 2007; Meyer and Reppucci 2007:764.

84 Steinberg and Cauffman 1996:261; Grisso 1981:158–59; Grisso et al. 2003:357.

85 Grisso et al. 2003.

86 *Berghuis v. Thompkins* 2010:2260; *Davis v. United States* 1994:459.

87 Ainsworth 1993a:318; Beyer 2000.

88 *Davis v. United States* 1994:460.

89 Leo 2008; Feld 2013a:93–98; Feld 2013c; Goldstein and Goldstein 2010:50; Grisso 1980; Grisso and Pomiciter 1977:333–34.

90 Feld 2013a:93–98; Feld 2013c.

91 Feld 2013a:93–98.

92 Feld 2013a; Feld 2013c.

93 Feld 2013a:110; Kassin 2005:218; Kassin and Gudjonsson 2004:42–44; Kassin et al. 2010:12.

94 Kassin 2005:223; Leo 2008; Feld 2013a:110.

95 Owen-Kostelnik, Reppucci, and Meyer 2006:291; Feld 2013a.

96 Feld 2006b; Feld 2013a; Leo 1996b.

97 Redlich and Drizin 2007:210; Tanenhaus and Drizin 2002:671–77.

98 Grisso 1981; Feld 2013a; Woolard et al. 2008.

99 Woolard et al. 2008.

100 Woolard et al. 2008.

101 Feld 2013a.

102 Feld 2013a:195–200.

103 Feld 2013a:190–95.

104 Feld 2013a:200–3.

105 Feld 2013a:203–6.

106 Drizin and Leo 2004:945; Garrett 2011; Gross et al. 2005:545.

107 Tepfer, Nirider, and Tricarico 2010:904.

108 Drizin and Leo 2004:945.

109 Gross et al. 2005:545.

110 Bonnie and Grisso 2000; Redlich et al. 2004:114.

111 Redlich et al. 2004.

112 Gudjonsson 2003:381.

113 Grisso 1980; Grisso et al. 2003.

114 Goldstein and Goldstein 2010:63; Owen-Kostelnik, Reppucci, and Meyer 2006:295.

115 Gruber and Yurglin-Todd 2006; Maroney 2009.

116 Weisselberg 2008; Slobogin 2007.

117 Weisselberg 2008; Leo 2008.

118 *Missouri v. Seibert* 2004.

119 Drizin and Leo 2004; Gross et al. 2005; Garrett 2011.

120 Drizin and Leo 2004; Tepfer, Nirider, and Tricarico 2010.

121 Grisso 1980; Grisso et al. 2003.

122 Kassin et al. 2010:28.

123 American Bar Association and Institute of Judicial Administration 1980:92.

124 Bishop and Farber 2007; Farber 2004; American Bar Association and Institute of Judicial Administration 1980.

125 Feld 2013a; Feld 2013c.

126 Drizin and Leo 2004.

127 Leo et al. 2006.

128 Feld 2013a; Feld 2013c; Garrett 2010; Garrett 2011; Gudjonsson 2003; Milne and Bull 1999.

129 *In the Interest of Jerrell C.J.* 2005.

130 Garrett 2011; Leo 2008.

131 Slobogin 2003.

132 Garrett 2010; Garrett 2011.

133 Garrett 2011; Gudjonsson 2003.

134 Garrett 2011; Kassin 1997.

135 Scott and Grisso 2005:800.

136 *Dusky v. United States* 1960:402.

137 *Drope v. Missouri* 1975:171.

138 *Godinez v. Moran* 1993:402.

139 Sanborn 2009:137.

140 Grisso et al. 2003:335; Grisso 2004:102–4.

141 Sanborn 2009:138.

142 Viljoen et al. 2012:530.

143 Viljoen et al. 2012:530; American Psychiatric Association 2000.

144 Grisso 2004; Viljoen et al. 2012; Weaver et al. 2014:415–18.

145 Redding and Frost 2001:374–78; Scott and Grisso 2005:796; Grisso 1997a:6; Grisso 2004:105; Scott and Steinberg 2008:151–52.

146 Grisso 1997a; Scott and Grisso 2005; Scott and Steinberg 2008:158–60.

147 Grisso et al. 2003:344.

148 Bonnie and Grisso 2000; Redding and Frost 2001; Cowden and McKee 1995; Scott and Steinberg 2008:162–65.

149 Grisso et al. 2003:356.

150 Grisso et al. 2003:344.

151 Sanborn 2009:171.

152 Grisso et al. 2003:356.

153 Viljoen et al. 2012:530.

154 Grisso et al. 2003:356.

155 Viljoen et al. 2012:535; Viljoen and Grisso 2007.

156 Scott and Grisso 2005:797.

157 Woolard 2012:110; Viljoen et al. 2007; Viljoen et al. 2012:530; Sanborn 2009:145–47.

158 *Graham v. Florida* 2010:2032.

159 Grisso 2004:5.

160 Viljoen et al. 2012:529; Kazdin 2000:38–42; Grisso 2000:145; Grisso 2004:6–13.

161 Viljoen et al. 2012:530; Viljoen and Roesch 2005.

162 Scott and Grisso 2005:804–5; Sanborn 2009:147–49.

163 Scott and Grisso 2005; Sanborn 2009:140–42; Feld 2013b.

164 Viljoen et al. 2012:532; Sanborn 2009:141–42.

165 *In re W.A.F.* 1990:1267; *In re D.D.N.* 1998.

166 *In re D.D.N.* 1998:281.

167 *In re K.G.* 2004; *In re Bailey* 2002; Scott and Grisso 2005; Sanborn 2009:141–42.

168 Scott and Grisso 2005:831–38; Scott and Steinberg 2008:168–77; Viljoen, Zapf, and Roesch 2007.

169 Scott and Grisso 2005:840–43.

170 Scott and Steinberg 2008:174 (emphasis added).

171 *Breed v. Jones* 1975.

172 Sanborn 2009:207.

173 Sanborn 2009:190; Grisso 2000:141.

174 Sanborn 2009:185–86.

175 Scott and Steinberg 2008:173.

176 Grisso 2004:21.

177 Sanborn 2009:207.

178 *In re W.A.F.* 1990:1267.

179 Feld 2013b.

180 Viljoen et al. 2012:533–34.

181 Grisso 2004:168–70.

182 Grisso 2004:77–80.

183 *In re Gault* 1967:36.

184 *In re Gault* 1967:27–30; *Gideon v. Wainwright* 1961:344.

185 *In re Gault* 1967:42; Feld 1984; Feld 1993.

186 Feld 1988a; Feld 1993; Harlow 2000; Jones 2000; Burruss and Kempf-Leonard 2002

187 Feld 1991:157–58; Feld 1993; Burruss and Kempf-Leonard 2002; Bray et al. 2005; Guevara et al. 2008; Feld and Schaefer 2010a; Feld and Schaefer 2010b.

188 Feld 1991; Feld 1993; Burruss and Kempf-Leonard 2002.

189 Feld 1988b; Feld 1991; Burruss and Kempf-Leonard 2002; Feld and Schaefer 2010a.

190 Feld 1989; Feld 1993; Feld and Schaefer 2010a.

191 Note 1966:796–99; Manfredi 1998:40–41.

192 Manfredi 1998:41.

193 Lefstein, Stapleton, and Teitelbaum 1969:517–24, 530–37; Canon and Kolson 1971; Ferster, Courtless, and Snethen 1971; Stapleton and Teitelbaum 1972.

194 Lefstein, Stapleton, and Teitelbaum 1969.

195 Clarke and Koch 1980:297; Bortner 1982:139; Aday 1986:114.

196 Feld 1988a; Feld 1989:1200; Feld 1991; Feld 1993.

197 Feld and Schaefer 2010a; Feld and Schaefer 2010b.

198 Feld 1988a.

199 U.S. General Accounting Office 1995b; Burruss and Kempf-Leonard 2002.

200 U.S. General Accounting Office 1995b.

201 Burruss and Kempf-Leonard 2002.

202 Guevara et al. 2008.

203 American Bar Association 1993:60; Bishop and Farber 2007.

204 American Bar Association 1995:52–56.

205 Celeste and Puritz 2001:59–62; Puritz and Brooks 2002:29; Puritz et al. 2002:24–25; Brooks and Kamine 2004; Bookser 2004; Drizin and Luloff 2007.

206 American Bar Association 1995:52–56.

207 American Bar Association 1995:44–45; Cooper et al. 1998:654–60; Berkheiser 2002; Bookser 2004; National Research Council 2013:1999.

208 Lefstein, Stapleton, and Teitelbaum 1969; Feld 1984; Feld 1989; Burruss and Kempf-Leonard 2002.

209 National Research Council 2013:1999.

210 Feld 1989; Feld 1999:127–28; National Research Council 2013:199.

211 American Bar Association 1995; Feld 1993:190; Cooper et al. 1998; Berkheiser 2002:649–50.

212 National Research Council 2013:199–200.

213 *Johnson v. Zerbst* 1938; *Fare v. Michael C.* 1979; Berkheiser 2002.

214 Feld 1984; Feld 1989; Feld 2006a.

215 Grisso 2000:247; Berkheiser 2002

216 *In re Manuel R.* 1988; *In re Christopher H.* 2004; Berkheiser 2002; Drizin and Luloff 2007.

217 Feld 2003a:1175; Celeste and Puritz 2001:59–60.

218 Grisso 1980; Grisso 1997; Grisso et al. 2003; American Bar Association 1995.

219 Feld 1988b; Harlow 2000.

220 Feld 1993; Feld 2013a; National Research Council 2013:201–2.

221 Rosenberg 1993.

222 Sanborn 1993a.

223 Sanborn 1992; Sanborn 1993a; Singleton 2007.

224 National Research Council 2013:201–2.

225 Singleton 2007.

226 Berkheiser 2002; Harris 1994; Sanborn 1992; Sanborn 1993a.

227 Drizin and Luloff 2007.

228 Stapleton and Teitelbaum 1972:102–6; Clarke and Koch 1980:305; Bortner 1982:136–39; Feld 1984.

229 Bortner 1982:139–40; Feld 1988b:418–19; Feld 1989:1330; Burruss and Kempf-Leonard 2002; Feld and Schaefer 2010a.

230 Duffee and Siegel 1971:552; Clarke and Koch 1980; Bortner 1982:139–40; Feld 1989; Feld 1993:98; Burruss and Kempf-Leonard 2002; Guevara et al. 2004; Feld and Schaefer 2010a.

231 Feld and Schaefer 2010a; Feld and Schaefer 2010b.

232 Buss 2000:248.

233 Lefstein, Stapleton, and Teitelbaum 1969; Stapleton and Teitelbaum 1972:102–6; Cooper et al. 1998.

234 Handler 1965; Flicker 1983.

235 Drizin and Luloff 2007.

236 National Research Council 2013:200.

237 Flicker 1983; Feld 1989.

238 Drizin and Luloff 2007; Ainsworth 1991; National Research Council 2013:201.

239 American Bar Association 1995; Cooper et al. 1998; Jones 2004.

240 Celeste and Puritz 2001; Puritz and Brooks 2002; Puritz, Scali, and Picou 2002; Brooks and Kamine 2004; Jones 2004; National Research Council 2013:58.

241 Drizin and Luloff 2007; Garrett 2011P:165–66.

242 Canon and Kolson 1971; Aday 1986.

243 *Scott v. Illinois* 1979:373–74; Feld and Schaefer 2010a.

244 Feld 1984.

245 Burruss and Kempf-Leonard 2002; Guevara, Spohn, and Herz 2008; Feld and Schaefer 2010a.

246 Burruss and Kempf-Leonard 2002; Guevara, Spohn, and Herz 2004.

247 Engen and Steen 2000.

248 Drizin and Luloff 2007; National Research Council 2013:198–99.

249 *In re Gault* 1967:58.

250 Manfredi 1998:158.

251 Berkheiser 2002.

252 Harris 1998; Crippen 2000; Puritz and Shang 2000; Berkheiser 2002; Bookser 2004.

253 Harris 1998.

254 *R.L.R. v. State* 1971:38.

255 Feld 1999:136.

256 Feld 1984; Feld 1993b; Feld 1999.

257 American Bar Association and Institute of Judicial Administration 1980; Feld 1993b:291.

258 Drizin and Luloff 2007; Guggenheim and Hertz 1998.

259 *Duncan v. Louisiana* 1968:156.

260 *McKeiver v. Pennsylvania* 1971:545.

261 *McKeiver v. Pennsylvania* 1971:541; *Duncan v. Louisiana* 1968.

262 Feld 2003a; Poe-Yamagata and Jones 2000; National Research Council and Institute of Medicine 2001.

263 *McKeiver v. Pennsylvania* 1971:550.

264 Feld 2003a.

265 *McKeiver v. Pennsylvania* 1971:559; Feld 2003a:1145.

266 Ainsworth 1995:943.

267 Feld 2003a; *In re L.M.* 2008.

268 *In re. D.J.* 2002; *State v. Hezzie R.* 1998; *In re. J.F. and G.G.* 1998.

269 Kalven and Zeisel 1966:185–90, 209–13; Greenwood et al. 1983:30–31.

270 Kalven and Zeisel 1966:58–59; Ainsworth 1991:1123; Saks 1997:42–43.

271 Buss 2000:252.

272 Guggenheim and Hertz 1998:564.

273 Guggenheim and Hertz 1998:568–74; Feld 1984.

274 Saks 1997:14.

275 Ainsworth 1991.

276 *Ballew v. Georgia* 1978:232–39.

277 Guggenheim and Hertz 1998:578.

278 Sanborn 1998:212.

279 *Duncan v. Louisiana* 1968:157.

280 Kalven and Zeisel 1966:185–90.

281 Kalven and Zeisel 1966:189–90.

282 Kalven and Zeisel 1966:210.

283 *People v. Smith* 2003:926.

284 Feld 1984:231–41; Guggenheim and Hertz 1998:571.

285 Guggenheim and Hertz 1998:571.

286 Feld 1984; Drizin and Luloff 2007.

287 Guggenheim and Hertz 1998:564.

288 Greenwood et al. 1983:30–31; Drizin and Luloff 2007.

289 *McKeiver v. Pennsylvania* 1971:545.

290 Feld 1988b:838–47; Feld 1995:1087–94; Feld 1998:223–29; Giardino 1996:232–37; *State v. Lawley* 1979; Torbet et al. 1996:15–16.

291 *McKeiver v. Pennsylvania* 1971:536.

292 Ward 2012:203.

293 Ward 2012:207.

294 *Baldwin v. New York* 1969:72.

295 *Duncan v. Louisiana* 1968:156.

296 *Baldwin v. New York* 1969:72.

297 *Scott v. Illinois* 1979.

298 *McKeiver v. Pennsylvania* 1971:550.

299 *In re Gault* 1967:24.

300 *Smith v. Daily Mail Publishing Co.* 1978; *Davis v. Alaska* 1974.

301 *In re Oliver* 1948:270.

302 Sanborn 1993b; Torbet et al. 1996.

303 National Research Council 2013:81.

304 *Kent v. United States*, 1966:555–56.

305 *In re Gault* 1967:18, 21–24.

306 *In re Winship* 1970:367.

307 Gardner 2012:50–51.

308 *State v. Hezzie R.* 1998.

309 *State v. Hezzie R.* 1998:675.

310 *State v. Hezzie R.* 1998:682, 687.

311 *In re D.J.* 2002:33 (emphasis supplied).

312 *In re J.F. and G.G.* 1998:469.

313 *In re J.F. and G.G.* 1998:473.

314 *In re L.M.* 2008:170.

315 *In re L.M.* 2008:171.

316 National Research Council 2013:128.

317 *Apprendi v. New Jersey* 2000:490.

318 Feld 2003a:1132–34.

319 Jacobs 2014:150–51.

320 Feld 1999:233–35; Sanborn 1998:206; Blumstein Farrington, and Moitra 1985:197; Jacobs 2014:155.

321 Blumstein et al. 1986:22–23; Farrington 1986:189.

322 Blumstein et al. 1986:75–76; Farrington 1986:189.

323 Roberts 1996:327.

324 Greenwood 1986; Petersilia 1981:1747–49.

325 Funk 1996:890–91; Funk 1998:289; Funk and Polsby 1997:161–62.

326 *United States v. Davis* 1995:280; *United States v. McDonald* 1993:872.

327 Miller 1995; Torbet et al. 1996.

328 *United States v. Williams* 1989:212.

329 *United States v. Johnson* 1994:155.

330 *United States v. Johnson* 1994:155.

331 *United States v. Johnson* 1994:159.

332 Feld 2003a:1187–88; Miller 1995:3.

333 Feld 2003a:1187–88.

334 Feld 1995:1059–61; Minnesota Sentencing Guidelines Commission 1980:cmt. II.B.406.

335 Feld 2003a:1186.

336 Dormont 1991:1798–99.

337 Feld 2003a:1196–222.

338 *United States v. Tighe* 2001:1189.

339 *United States v. Tighe* 2001:1193 (emphasis supplied).

340 *United States v. Smalley* 2002:1032.

341 *United States v. Smalley* 2002:1033.

342 *United States v. Smalley* 2002:1033.

343 Feld 2003a:1116–34.

344 Feld 2003a:1203–14.

345 *State v. Brown* 2004:1288.

346 *State v. Hitt* 2002:740.

347 Frase 2009.

348 National Research Council and Institute of Medicine 2001.

349 Nellis 2011:7.

350 Frase 2009:265.

351 National Research Council 2013:3; Burrell and Stacy 2011; Nellis 2016:61.

352 Feld 2013b:369–76.

353 Burrell and Stacy 2011:15; Nellis 2011:22.

354 Jacobs 2014:161; Nellis 2016:63–65.

355 Nellis 2011:22–23, 64.

356 Burrell and Stacy 2011:45.

357 National Research Council 2013:127; Nellis 2016:61.

358 Burrell and Stacy 2011:93–107; Nellis 2011:22.

359 Nellis 2011:22; Jacobs 2014:157.

360 Burrell and Stacy 2011:123–27; Nellis 2011:23.

361 Jacobs 2014:156–57.

362 Nellis 2011:21.

363 Nellis 2011:25; Zimring 2004; Caldwell 2014; Nellis 2016:69–73.

364 Zimring 2004:14.

365 Zimring 2004:27–32; Caldwell 2014:58–72.

366 Caldwell 2014:57.

367 Caldwell 2014:61.

368 Zimring 2004:125.

369 42 U.S.C. § 16901 et seq.; Gottschalk 2015:204–6; Nellis 2016:70–71.

370 Burrell and Stacy 2011:33; Zimring 2004.

371 Zimring 2004:144–50.

372 Burrell and Stacy 2011:24.

373 *Smith v. Doe* 2003; Caldwell 2014:80.

EPILOGUE

1 Garland 1990:198; Beckett 1997:107; Hacker 1995:25.

2 Edsall and Edsall 1990:281; Hurwitz and Peffley 1997:396; Gilens 1996:595; Mendelberg 2001:268.

3 Edsall and Edsall 1991:243; Hacker 1995:228–29.

4 Zimring 1998; Cook and Laub 2002.

5 Blumstein and Wallman 2000; Cook and Laub 2002; Zimring 2007.

6 Zimring 2007:56–62.

7 Zimring 2007:63–69.

8 Blumstein 1995; Butts and Evans 2014:64; Cook and Laub 2002; Zimring 2007:81–85.

9 Zimring 2007:73–81.

10 Butts and Evans 2014:64; Zimring 2007:45–56.

11 Butts and Evans 2014:65; Zimring 2007:136–46.

12 Zimring 2007:195–209.

13 Scott and Steinberg 2008:267.

14 Feld, Casey, and Hurd 2013.
15 Aronson 2007; Maroney 2009.
16 Bishop and Feld 2012; National Research Council 2013:247–50.
17 Scott and Steinberg 2008:268–69.
18 "About the Network," MacArthur Foundation Research Network, www.adjj.org; National Research Council 2013:257–61.
19 Nellis 2016:90–91.
20 Nellis 2016:91–92.
21 National Research Council 2013:254–56.
22 Zimring and Tanenhaus 2014:217.
23 Griffin 2012:184–86.
24 Loeber et al. 2012:350–51.
25 *Alabama v. Shelton* 2002.
26 Mears 2012.
27 Zimring 2000:210.
28 Griffin 2012:185–86.
29 Lindsey 2009:155.
30 Fader 2013:101.
31 Feld 1999:333–39; National Research Council 1993:236; Lindsey 2009.
32 Putnam 2015; Lindsey 2009:4, 12–17.
33 Wilson 2009:46–56; Loeber and Farrington 1998; Fox, Jennings, and Piquero 2014:517.
34 Wilson 2009:53–56; Steinberg 2014:165.
35 Putnam 2015:169–70.
36 National Commission on Children 1991.
37 Tonry 2011:ix.
38 Lindsey 2009:11–17; Rainwater and Smeeding 2005.
39 Lindsey 2009:4.
40 Lichter 1997:121.
41 Lindsey 2009:13–17.
42 Wilson 2009:100–5.
43 Lindsey 2009:74–75.
44 Drake and Rank 2009:1268.
45 Wilson 2009:102–3.
46 Frase 2009:263.
47 Putnam 2015:31–32.
48 Putnam 2015:29.
49 Putnam 2015:36.
50 Putnam 2015:36.
51 Putnam 2015:41.
52 Putnam 2015:61–71.
53 Putnam 2015:73.
54 Lindsey 2009:21; Steinberg 2014:124–40; Putnam 2015:122.
55 Putnam 2015:109–17.

56 Putnam 2015:111–15.

57 Steinberg 2014:171–72; Putnam 2015:121–22; Lindsey 2009:15–16.

58 Lindsey 2009:15–17.

59 Putnam 2015:170.

60 Putnam 2015:18–19.

61 National Commission on Children 1991:24; Rainwater and Smeeding 2005.

62 "LIS Inequality and Poverty Key Figures," LIS, www.lisdatacenter.org.

63 Rainwater and Smeeding 2005:29.

64 Gottschalk 2015:279.

65 Engster 2012:121; Rainwater and Smeeding 2005.

66 Wilson 1996; Wilson 2009; Wilson 1987:140–64; Jencks 1992:87–91; Katz 1989:205–15.

67 Rainwater and Smeeding 2005.

68 Lichter 1997:126.

69 Lichter 1997:129; Rainwater and Smeeding 2005:48.

70 Rainwater and Smeeding 2005.

71 Lindsey 2009:141.

72 Putnam 2015:242; Lindsey 2009:33.

73 Lindsey 2009:42–63.

74 Lindsey 2009:110–12.

75 Lindsey 2009:47–48.

76 Lindsey 2009:161.

77 Rainwater and Smeeding 2005:109–31.

78 Engster 2012:134–36.

79 Lindsey 2009:108 Rainwater and Smeeding 2005:123–24.

80 Engster 2012:122; Lindsey 2009:112; Putnam 2015:246.

81 Engster 2012:122; Rainwater and Smeeding 2005:134–37.

82 Putnam 2015:248.

83 Engster 2012:122.

84 Engster 2012:132.

85 Engster 2012:130–31.

86 Gottschalk 2015:4.

87 Lindsey 2009:20.

88 Gottschalk 2015:15.

89 Grubb and Lazerson 1982:85.

90 National Advisory Commission 1968:1.

91 Gottschalk 2015:2.

92 Wilson 2009:136.

93 Gottschalk 2015:278.

94 Gottschalk 2015:260.

95 Joseph N. Welch, addressing Senator Joseph McCarthy, Hearing of the Senate Permanent Subcommittee on Investigations, June 9, 1954. See, e.g., "McCarthy-Welch Exchange," American Rhetoric, www.americanrhetoric.com.

REFERENCES

Abramovitch, Rona, Karen L. Higgins-Biss, and Stephen R. Biss. 1993. "Young Persons' Comprehension of Waivers in Criminal Proceedings." *Canadian Journal of Criminology* 35: 309–22.

Abramovitch, Rona, Michele Peterson-Badali, and Meg Rohan. 1995. "Young People's Understanding Assertion of Their Rights to Silence and Legal Counsel." *Canadian Journal of Criminology* 37: 1–18.

Acoca, Leslie. 1999. "Investing in Girls: A 21st-Century Strategy." *Juvenile Justice* 6: 3–13.

Acoca, Leslie, and Kelly Dedel. 1998. *No Place to Hide: Understanding and Meeting the Needs of Girls in the California Juvenile Justice System.* San Francisco: National Council on Crime and Delinquency.

Adams v. Williams, 407 U.S. 143 (1972).

Aday, David P., Jr. 1986. "Court Structure, Defense Attorney Use, and Juvenile Court Decisions." *Sociological Quarterly* 27: 107–19.

Advancement Project. 2005. *Education on Lockdown: The Schoolhouse to Jailhouse Track.* www.advancementproject.org.

Advancement Project and Civil Rights Project. 2000. *Opportunities Suspended: The Devastating Consequences of Zero Tolerance and School Discipline Polices.* www.civilrightsproject.harvard.edu.

Ainsworth, Janet E. 1991. "Re-imagining Childhood and Re-constructing the Legal Order: The Case for Abolishing the Juvenile Court." *North Carolina Law Review* 69: 1083–133.

———. 1993. "In a Different Register: The Pragmatics of Powerlessness in Police Interrogation." *Yale Law Journal* 103: 259–322.

Alabama v. Shelton, 535 U.S. 654 (2002).

Alder, Christine. 1984. "Gender Bias in Juvenile Diversion." *Crime and Delinquency* 30: 400–14.

Alexander, Michelle. 2010. *The New Jim Crow: Mass Incarceration in the Age of Colorblindness.* New York: New Press.

Alexander S. v. Boyd, 876 F. Supp. 773 (D.S.C. 1995).

Allen, Francis A. 1964. "Legal Values and the Rehabilitative Ideal." In *The Borderland of the Criminal Law: Essays in Law and Criminology*, 25–27. Chicago: University of Chicago Press.

———. 1981. *The Decline of the Rehabilitative Ideal: Penal Policy and Social Purpose.* New Haven, CT: Yale University Press.

———. 2000. Forward to *The Changing Borders of Juvenile Justice: Transfer of Ado-lescents to Criminal Court*, edited by Jeffrey Fagan and Franklin Zimring, ix–xvii. Chicago: University of Chicago Press.

Allen v. Illinois, 478 U.S. 364 (1986).

American Bar Association. 1993. *America's Children at Risk: A National Agenda for Legal Action*. Washington, DC: American Bar Association.

———. 1995. *A Call for Justice: An Assessment of Access to Counsel and Quality of Representation in Delinquency Proceedings*. Washington, DC: ABA Juvenile Justice Center.

American Bar Association and Institute of Judicial Administration. 1980. *Juvenile Justice Standards Relating to Pretrial Court Proceedings*. Cambridge, MA: Balllinger.

American Bar Association and National Bar Association. 2001. *Justice by Gender: The Lack of Appropriate Prevention, Diversion and Treatment Alternatives for Girls in the Justice System*. Washington, DC: American Bar Association.

American Friends Service Committee. 1971. *Struggle for Justice*. New York: Hill and Wang.

American Law Institute. Model Penal Code, § 6.11A.

American Psychiatric Association. 2013. *Diagnostic and Statistical Manual of Mental Disorders*. 5th ed. Washington, DC: American Psychiatric Association.

Amnesty International and Human Rights Watch. 2005. *The Rest of Their Lives: Life without Parole for Child Offenders in the United States*. www.amnestyusa.org/www.hrw.org.

Anderson, Elijah. 1990. *Streetwise: Race, Class and Change in an Urban Community*. Chicago: University of Chicago Press.

———. 1998. "The Social Ecology of Youth Violence." *Crime and Justice* 24: 65–104.

———. 1999. *The Code of the Street: Decency, Violence, and the Moral Life of the Inner City*. New York: W. W. Norton & Co.

Annie E. Casey Foundation. n.d. *Juvenile Detention Alternatives Initiative*. www.aecf.org.

Apprendi v. New Jersey, 530 U.S. 466 (2000).

Archard, David. 1993. *Children: Rights and Childhood*. London: Routledge.

Arenella, Peter. 1990. "Character, Choice and Moral Agency: The Relevance of Character to Our Moral Culpability Judgments." *Social Philosophy and Policy* 7: 59–83.

Arias, Elizabeth. 2006. *National Vital Statistics Report*: "United States Life Tables, 2003." *National Vital Statistics Report* 54. Centers for Disease Control, www.cdc.gov.

Aries, Philippe. 1962. *Centuries of Childhood: A Social History of Family Life*. New York: Vintage Books.

Arnold, William R. 1971. "Race and Ethnicity Relative to Other Factors in Juvenile Court Dispositions." *American Journal of Sociology* 77: 211–27.

Aronson, Jay D. 2007. "Brain Imaging, Culpability and the Juvenile Death Penalty." *Psychology Public Policy and Law* 13: 115–42.

Arredondo, David E. 2003. "Child Development, Children's Mental Health and the Juvenile Justice System." *Stanford Law and Policy Review* 14: 13–28.

Artz, Sibylle. 1998. *Sex, Power, and the Violent School Girl*. Toronto: Trifolium Books.

Atkins v. Virginia, 536 U.S. 304 (2002).

Austin, James, Kelly Dedel Johnson, and Maria Gregoriou. 2000. *Juveniles in Adult Prisons*. Washington, DC: Bureau of Justice Assistance, U.S. Department of Justice.

Axelrad, Sidney. 1952. "Negro and White Male Institutionalized Delinquents." *American Journal of Sociology* 57: 569–74.

Baird, Abigail A., Staci Gruber, Deborah A. Fein, Luis C. Maas, Ronald J. Steingard, Perry F. Renshaw, Bruce M. Cohen, and Deborah A. Yurgelun-Todd. 1999. "Functional Magnetic Resonance Imaging of Facial Affect Recognition in Children and Adolescents." *Journal American Academy of Child and Adolescent Psychiatry* 38: 195–99.

Baldwin v. New York, 399 U.S. 66 (1969).

Ballew v. Georgia, 435 U.S. 223 (1978).

Barefoot v. Estelle, 463 U.S. 880 (1983).

Barnowski, Robert. 2003. "Changes in Washington State's Jurisdiction of Juvenile Offenders: Examining the Impact." Washington State Institute for Public Policy, http://wsipp.wa.gov.

Bartollas, Clemens, Stuart J. Miller, and Simon Dinitz. 1976. *Juvenile Victimization: The Institutional Paradox*. New York: Wiley.

Barton, William. 2012. "Detention." In *Oxford Handbook of Juvenile Crime and Juvenile Justice*, edited by Barry C. Feld and Donna M. Bishop, 636–63. New York: Oxford University Press.

B.C. v. Plumas Unified School District, 192 F.3d 1260 (9th Cir. 1999).

Bear Cloud v. State, 334 P.3d 132 (Wyo. 2014).

Beckett, Katherine. 1997. *Making Crime Pay: Law and Order in Contemporary American Politics*. New York: Oxford University Press.

Beckett, Katherine, and Theodore Sasson. 2000. *The Politics of Injustice: Crime and Punishment in America*. Thousand Oaks, CA: Pine Forge Press.

Bennet, William, and John DiIulio. 1996. *Body Count: Moral Poverty and How to Win America's War against Crime and Drugs*. New York: Simon & Schuster.

Berger, Brigitte, and Peter L. Berger. 1984. *The War over the Family: Capturing the Middle Ground*. New York: Anchor Books.

Berghuis v. Thompkins, 560 U.S. 370 (2010).

Berkheiser, Mary. 2002. "The Fiction of Juvenile Right to Counsel: Waiver in the Juvenile Courts." *Florida Law Review* 54: 577–686.

Bernard, Thomas J. 1992. *The Cycle of Juvenile Justice*. New York: Oxford University Press.

Beyer, Marty. 1997. "Experts for Juveniles at Risk of Adult Sentences." In *More than Meets the Eye: Rethinking Assessment, Competence and Sentencing for a Harsher Era of Juvenile Justice.*, edited by P. Puritz, A. Capozello, and W. Shang, 1–21. Washington, DC: American Bar Association Juvenile Justice Center.

Billings, F. James, Tanya Taylor, James Burns, Deb L. Corey, Sena Garven, and James M. Wood. 2007. "Can Reinforcement Induce Children to Falsely Incriminate Themselves?" *Law and Human Behavior* 31:125–30.

Bishop, Donna. 2004. "Injustice and Irrationality in Contemporary Youth Policy."
  Criminology and Public Policy 3: 633–44.

———. 2005. "The Role of Race and Ethnicity in Juvenile Justice Process," In *Our Chil-
  dren, Their Children: Confronting Racial and Ethnic Differences in American Juvenile
  Justice*, edited by Darnell Hawkins and Kimberly Kempf-Leonard, 23–82. Chicago:
  University of Chicago Press.

Bishop, Donna, and Hillary B. Farber. 2007. "Joining the Legal Significance of Adolescent Developmental Capacities with the Legal Rights Provided by *In re Gault*."
  Rutgers Law Review 60: 125–73.

Bishop, Donna, and Barry C. Feld. 2012. "Trends in Juvenile Justice Policy and Practice." In *Oxford Handbook of Juvenile Crime and Juvenile Justice*, edited by Barry
  C. Feld and Donna M. Bishop, 898–926. New York: Oxford University Press.

Bishop, Donna, and Charles S. Frazier. 1991. "Transfer of Juveniles to Criminal Court:
  A Case Study and Analysis of Prosecutorial Waiver." *Notre Dame Journal of Law,
  Ethics and Public Policy* 5: 281–302.

———. 1992. "Gender Bias in Juvenile Justice Processing: Implications of the JJDP Act."
  Journal of Criminal Law and Criminology 82: 1162–86.

———. 1996. "Race Effects in Juvenile Justice Decision-Making: Findings of a Statewide
  Analysis." *Journal of Criminal Law and Criminology* 86: 392–413.

———. 2000. "Consequences of Transfer." In *Changing Borders of Juvenile Justice*,
  edited by Jeffrey Fagan and Franklin E. Zimring, 227–76. Chicago: University of
  Chicago Press.

Bishop, Donna, Charles Frazier, and John Henretta. 1989. "Prosecutorial Waiver: Case
  Study of a Questionable Reform." *Crime and Delinquency* 35: 179–201.

Bishop, Donna, and Michael Leiber. 2012. "Racial and Ethnic Differences in Delinquency and Justice System Responses." In *The Oxford Handbook of Juvenile Crime
  and Juvenile Justice*, edited by Barry C. Feld and Donna M. Bishop, 445–84. New
  York: Oxford University Press.

Blakemore, S. J. 2007. "Adolescent Development of the Neural Circuitry for Thinking
  about Intentions." *Society Cognitive and Affective Neuroscience* 2: 130–39.

Bledstein, Burton J. 1976. *The Culture of Professionalism: The Middle Class and the
  Development of Higher Education in America*. New York: W. W. Norton & Co.

Bloom, Barbara, Barabara Owne, Elizabeth Piper Deschenes, and Jill Rosenbaum.
  2002. "Improving Juvenile Justice for Females: A Statewide Assessment in California." *Crime and Delinquency* 4: 526–52.

Blue Ribbon Commission on School Discipline. 2007. *A Written Report Presented
  to the Superintendent and Board of Education, Clayton County Public Schools*.
  www.clayton.k12.ga.us.

Blumenson, Eric, and Eva S. Nilsen. 2003. "One Strike and You're Out? Constitutional
  Constraints on Zero Tolerance in Public Education." *Washington University Law
  Quarterly* 81: 65–117.

Blumstein, Alfred. 1995. "Youth Violence, Guns, and the Illicit-Drug Industry."
  Journal of Criminal Law and Criminology 86: 10–36.

Blumstein, Alfred, Jacqueline Cohen, Jeffrey A. Roth, and Christy A. Visher, eds. 1986. *Criminal Careers and "Career Criminals."* Washington, DC: National Academy Press.

Blumstein, Alfred, and Daniel Cork. 1996. "Linking Gun Availability to Youth Gun Violence." *Law and Contemporary Problems* 59: 5–24.

Blumstein, Alfred, David P. Farrington, and Soumyo Moitra. 1985. "Delinquency Careers: Innocents, Desisters, and Persisters." In *Crime and Justice: An Annual Review* 6, edited by Michael Tonry and Norval Morris, 187–219. Chicago: University of Chicago.

Blumstein, Alfred, and Joel Wallman. 2000. "The Recent Rise and Fall of American Violence." In *The Crime Drop in America*, edited by Alfred Blumstein and Joel Wallman, 1–12. New York: Cambridge University Press.

Bond-Maupin, L., J. R. Maupin, and A. Leisenring. 2002. "Girls' Delinquency and the Justice Implications of Intake Workers' Perspectives." *Women and Criminal Justice* 13:51–77.

Bonnie, Richard J., and Thomas Grisso. 2000. "Adjudicative Competence and Youthful Offenders." In *Youth on Trial: A Developmental Perspective on Juvenile Justice*, edited by Thomas Grisso and Robert G. Schwartz, 73–104. Chicago: University of Chicago Press.

Bortner, M. A. 1982. *Inside a Juvenile Court.* New York: New York University Press.

Bortner, M. A., Marjorie Zatz, and Darnell Hawkins. 2000. "Race and Transfer: Empirical Research and Social Context." In *The Changing Borders of Juvenile Justice*, edited by Jeffrey Fagan and Franklin E. Zimring, 277–320. Chicago: University of Chicago Press.

Bowles, Samuel, and Herbert Gintis. 1976. *Schooling in Capitalist America: Educational Reform and the Contradictions of Economic Life.* New York: Basic Books.

Bray, Timothy, Lisa L. Sample, and Kimberly Kempf-Leonard. 2005. "Justice by Geography: Racial Disparity and Juvenile Courts." In *Our Children, Their Children: Confronting Racial and Ethnic Differences in American Juvenile Justice*, edited by Darnell Hawkins and Kimberly Kempf-Leonard, 270–99. Chicago: University of Chicago Press.

Breed v. Jones, 421 U.S. 519 (1975).

Brenzel, Barbara. 1980. "Domestication as Reform: A Study of the Socialization of Wayward Girls, 1856–1905." *Harvard Education Review* 50: 196–213.

Bridges, George S., and Sara Steen. 1998. "Racial Disparities in Official Assessments in Juveniles Offenders: Attributional Stereotypes as Mediating Mechanisms." *American Sociology Review* 63: 554–70.

Brink, David O. 2004. "Immaturity, Normative Competence, and Juvenile Transfer: How (Not) to Punish Minors for Major Crimes." *Texas Law Review* 82: 1555–85.

Brooks, Kim, and Darlene Kamine. 2003. *Justice Cut Short: An Assessment of Access to Counsel and Quality of Representation in Delinquency Proceedings in Ohio.* Washington, DC: American Bar Association Juvenile Justice Center.

Brown v. Board of Education, 347 U.S. 483 (1954).

Brown v. Mississippi, 297 U.S. 278 (1936).

Bunch v. Smith, 685 F.3d 546 (6th Cir. 2012).

Bureau of Criminal Information and Analysis. 1999. *Report on Arrests for Domestic Violence in California, 1998.* Criminal Justice Statistic Center Report Series, Vol. 1, No. 2, 5–6. Sacramento, CA: Office of the Attorney General.

Bureau of Justice Statistics. 1998. *Juvenile Felony Defendants in Criminal Courts.* Washington, DC: U.S. Department of Justice.

Burnett, Stephanie, Geoffrey Bird, Jorge Moll, Chris Frith, and Sarah-Jayne Blakemore. 2009. "Development during Adolescence of the Neural Process of Social Emotion." *Journal Cognitive Neuroscience* 21: 1736–50.

Burrell, Sue, and Rourke F. Stacy. 2011. *Collateral Consequences of Juvenile Delinquency Proceedings in California: A Handbook for Juvenile Law Professionals.* San Francisco: Pacific Juvenile Defender Center.

Burruss, George W., Jr., and Kimberly Kempf-Leonard. 2002. "The Questionable Advantage of Defense Counsel in Juvenile Court." *Justice Quarterly* 19: 37–68.

Buss, Emily. 2000. "The Role of Lawyers in Promoting Juveniles' Competence as Defendants," In *Youth on Trial: A Developmental Perspective on Juvenile Justice*, edited by Thomas Grisso and Robert Schwartz, 243–66. Chicago: University of Chicago Press.

Butts, Jeffrey A., and Douglas N. Evans. 2014. "The Second American Crime Drop: Trends in Juvenile and Youth Violence." In *Juvenile Justice Sourcebook.* 2nd ed., edited by Wesley T. Church II, David W Springer, and Albert R. Roberts, 61–78. New York: Oxford University Press.

Caldwell, Michael F. 2014. "Juvenile Sexual Offenders," In *Choosing the Future for American Juvenile Justice*, edited by Franklin E. Zimring and David S. Tanenhaus, 55–93. New York: New York University Press.

Campaign for Youth Justice. 2006. *The Consequences Aren't Minor.* www.campaignforyouthjustice.org.

Canon, Bradley C., and Kenneth Kolson. 1971. "Rural Compliance with *Gault*: Kentucky, a Case Study." *Journal of Family Law* 10: 300–26.

Casey, B. J. 2008. "The Adolescent Brain." *Developmental Review* 28: 62–77.

Casey, B. J., Jay N. Giedd, and Kathleen M. Thomas. 2000. "Structural and Functional Brain Development and Its Relation to Cognitive Development." *Biological Psychology* 54: 241–57.

Castellano, Thomas C. 1986. "The Justice Model in the Juvenile Justice System: Washington State's Experience." *Law and Policy* 8: 397–418.

Cauffman, Elizabeth, Jennifer Woolard, and N. Dickon Repucci. 1999. "Justice for Juveniles: New Perspectives on Adolescents' Competence and Culpability." *Quinnipiac Law Review* 18: 403–19.

Cauffman, Elizabeth, and Laurence Steinberg. 1995. "The Cognitive and Affective Influences on Adolescent Decision-Making." *Temple Law Review* 68: 1763–89.

Celeste, Gabriella, and Patricia Puritz. 2001. *The Children Left Behind: An Assessment of Access to Counsel and Quality of Legal Presentation in Delinquency Proceedings in Louisiana.* Washington, DC: American Bar Association Juvenile Justice Center.

Centers for Disease Control. 2007. *Effects on Violence of Laws and Policies Facilitating the Transfer of Youth from the Juvenile to the Adult Justice System*. www.cdc.gov.

Chein, Jason, Dustin Albert, Lia O'Brien, Kaitlyn Uckert, and Laurence Steinberg. 2011. "Peers Increase Adolescent Risk Taking by Enhancing Activity in the Brain's Reward Circuitry." *Developmental Science* 14: F1–F20.

Chesney-Lind, Meda. 1988. "Girls and Status Offenses: Is Juvenile Justice Still Sexist?" *Criminal Justice Abstracts* 20: 144–65.

———. 2002. "Criminalizing Victimization: The Unintended Consequences of Pro-Arrest Policies for Girls and Women." *Criminology and Public Policy* 1: 81–90.

Chesney-Lind, Meda, and Joanne Belknap. 2004. "Trends in Delinquent Girls' Aggression and Violent Behavior: A Review of the Evidence." In *Aggression, Antisocial Behavior and Violence among Girls: A Developmental Perspective*, edited by M. Puytallaz and P. Bierman, 203–22. New York: Guilford.

Chesney-Lind, Meda, Merry Morash, and Katherine Irwin. 2007. "Policing Girlhood? Relational Aggression and Violence Prevention." *Youth Violence and Juvenile Justice* 5: 328–45.

Chesney-Lind, Meda, and Lisa Pasko. 2004. *The Female Offender: Girls, Women, and Crime*. 2nd ed. Thousand Oaks, CA: Sage Publication.

Clarke, Stevens H., and Gary G. Koch. 1980. "Juvenile Court: Therapy or Crime Control, and Do Lawyers Make a Difference?" *Law and Society Review* 14: 263–308.

Coates, Robert B., Alden D. Miller, and Lloyd E. Ohlin. 1978. *Diversity in a Youth Correctional System: Handling Delinquents in Massachusetts*. Cambridge, MA: Ballinger.

Cohn, Lawrence D., Susan Macfarlane, Claudia Yanez, and Walter K. Imai. 1995. "Risk-Perception: Differences between Adolescents and Adults." *Health Psychology* 14: 217–22.

Coker v. Georgia, 433 U.S. 584 (1977).

Coleman, James S., Robert H. Bremner, Burton R. Clark, Joseph F. Kett, and John M. Mays. 1974. *Youth: Transition to Adulthood*. Chicago: University of Chicago Press.

Commonwealth v. A Juvenile, 449 N.E.2nd 654 (Mass 1983).

Commonwealth v. Knox, 50 A.3d 749, 769 (Pa. Super 2012).

Commonwealth v. Martin, 534 Pa. 136, 626 A.2d 556 (Pa. 1993).

Community Research Associates. 1998. *Juvenile Female Offenders: A Status of the States Report*. Washington, DC: ODDJP.

Cook, Phillip J., and John H. Laub. 1998. "The Unprecedented Epidemic in Youth Violence." *Crime and Justice* 24: 27–64.

———. 2002. "After the Epidemic: Recent Trends in Youth Violence in the United States." *Crime and Justice* 29: 1–37.

Cooper, N. Lee, Patricia Puritz, and Wendy Shang. 1998. "Fulfilling the Promise of *In re Gault*: Advancing the Role of Lawyers for Children." *Wake Forest Law Review* 33: 651–79.

Corley, Charles J., Stephen Cernkovich, and Peggy Giordano. 1989. "Sex and the Likelihood of Sanction." *Journal of Criminal Law and Criminology* 80: 540–56.

Costello, Jan C., and Nancy L. Worthington. 1981. "Incarcerating Status Offenders: Attempts to Circumvent the Juvenile Justice and Delinquency Prevention Act." *Harvard Civil Rights—Civil Liberties Law Review* 16: 41–81.

Cover, Robert M. 1982. "The Origins of Judicial Activism in the Protection of Minorities." *Yale Law Journal* 91: 1287–316.

Cowden, Vance L., and Geoffrey R. McKee. 1995. "Competency to Stand Trial in Juvenile Delinquency Proceedings: Cognitive Maturity and the Attorney-Client Relationships." *University of Louisville Journal of Family Law* 33: 629–60.

Cremin, Lawrence. 1961. *The Transformation of the School: Progressivism in American Education, 1876–1957*. New York: Vintage Books.

Crippen, Gary L. 2000. "Can the Courts Fairly Account for the Diminished Competence and Culpability of Juveniles? A Judge's Perspective." In *Youth on Trial: A Developmental Perspective on Juvenile Justice*, edited by Thomas Grisso and Robert Schwartz, 403–34. Chicago: University of Chicago Press.

Cullen, Francis T., and Karen E. Gilbert. 1982. *Reaffirming Rehabilitation*. Cincinnati: Anderson Publishing Co.

Curran, Daniel J. 1984. "The Myth of the 'New' Female Delinquent." *Crime and Delinquency* 30: 386–99.

Dahl, Ronald E. 2001. "Affect Regulation, Brain Development, and Behavioral/Emotional Health in Adolescence." *CNS Spectrums* 6: 60–72.

———. 2004. "Adolescent Brain Development: A Period of Vulnerabilities and Opportunities." *Annals of the New York Academy of Sciences* 1021: 1–22.

Dale, Michael J. 1998. "Lawsuits and Public Policy: The Role of Litigation in Correcting Conditions of Confinement in Juvenile Detention Centers." *University of San Francisco Law Review* 32: 675–733.

Davis v. Alaska, 415 U.S. 308 (1974).

Davis v. United States, 512 U.S. 452 (1994).

Dawson, Robert O. 1992. "An Empirical Study of *Kent* Style Juvenile Transfers to Criminal Court." *St. Mary's Law Journal* 23: 975–1054.

Degler, Carl. 1980. *At Odds: Women and the Family in America from the Revolution to the Present*. New York: Oxford University Press.

Deitch, Michele, and Neelum Arya. 2014. "Waivers and Transfers of Juveniles to Adult Court: Treating Juveniles Like Adult Criminals." In *Juvenile Justice Sourcebook*. 2nd ed., edited by Wesley T. Church II, David W. Springer, and Albert R. Roberts, 241–66. New York: Oxford University Press.

Denno, Deborah W. 2006. "The Scientific Shortcomings of *Roper v. Simmons*." *Ohio State Journal of Criminal Law* 3: 379–96.

DiIulio, John. 1995. "The Coming of the Super-Predators." *Weekly Standard*, Nov. 27, 23–29.

Disability Insurance Benefits Payments, 42 U.S.C. § 223 (a)(12) (2015).

Doe v. Renfrow, 475 F. Supp. 1012 (N.D. Ind. 1979).

Dohrn, Bernardine. 2002. "The School, the Child, and the Court." In *A Century of Juvenile Justice*, edited by Margaret K. Rosenheim, Franklin E. Zimring, David S. Tanenhaus, and Bernardine Dohrn, 267–310. Chicago: University of Chicago Press.

Dorfman, Lori, and Vincent Schiraldi. 2001. *Off Balance: Youth, Race & Crime in the News.* Building Blocks for Youth. Center on Juvenile and Criminal Justice, www.cjcj.org.

Drake, Brett, and Mark R. Rank. 2009. "The Racial Divide among American Children in Poverty: Reassessing the Importance of Neighborhood." *Children and Youth Services Review* 31: 1264–71.

Drinan, Cara H. 2012. "*Graham* on the Ground." *Washington Law Review* 87: 51–91.

———. 2016. "The *Miller* Revolution." *Iowa Law Review* 101: 1787–1832.

Drizin, Steven A., and Beth A. Colgan. 2004. "Tales from the Juvenile Confession Front: A Guide to How Standard Police Interrogation Tactics Can Produce Coerced and False Confessions from Juvenile Suspects." In *Interrogations, Confessions, and Entrapment*, edited by G. Daniel Lassiter, 127–62. New York: Kluwer Academic.

Drizin, Steven A., and Richard A. Leo. 2004. "The Problem of False Confessions in the Post-DNA World." *North Carolina Law Review* 82: 891–1008.

Drizin, Steven A. and Greg Luloff. 2007. "Are Juvenile Courts a Breeding Ground for Wrongful Convictions?" *Northern Kentucky Law Review* 34: 275–322.

Drope v. Missouri, 420 U.S. 162 (1975).

Duckworth v. Eagan, 492 U.S. 195 (1988).

Duff, R. A. 1993. "Choice, Character, and Criminal Liability." *Law and Philosophy* 12: 345–83.

Duncan v. Louisiana, 391 U.S. 145 (1968).

Dusky v. United States, 362 U.S. 402 (1960).

Eddings v. Oklahoma, 455 U.S. 104 (1982).

Edsall, Thomas Byrne, and Mary D. Edsall. 1992. *Chain Reaction: The Impact of Race, Rights, and Taxes on American Politics.* New York: W. W. Norton & Co.

Emens, Elizabeth F. 2005. "Aggravating Youth: *Roper v. Simmons* and Age Discrimination." *Supreme Court Review* 2006: 51–102.

Enmund v. Florida, 458 U.S. 782 (1982).

Engen, Rodney L., and Sara Steen. 2000. "The Power to Punish: Discretion and Sentencing Reform in the War on Drugs." *American Journal of Sociology* 10: 1357–95.

Engster, Daniel. 2012. "Child Poverty and Family Policies across Eighteen Wealthy Western Democracies." *Journal of Children and Poverty* 18: 121–39.

Entman, Robert M. 1990. "Modern Racism and the Images of Blacks in Local Television News." *Critical Studies in Mass Communication* 7: 332–45.

———. 1992. "Blacks in the News: Television, Modern Racism and Cultural Change." *Journalism Quarterly* 69: 341–61.

Entman, Robert M., and Andrew Rojecki. 2000. *The Black Image in the White Mind.* Chicago: University of Chicago Press.

Ewing v. California, 538 U.S. 11 (2003).

Ex parte Crouse, 4 Whart. 9 (Pa. 1838).

Fabelo, Tony, M. D. Thompson, M. Plotkin, D. Carmichael, M. P. Marchbanks, and E. A. Booth. 2011. *Breaking Schools' Rules: A Statewide Study of How School Discipline Relates to Students Success and Juvenile Justice Involvement.* New York: Council of State Governments Justice Center.

Fader, Jamie. 2013. *Falling Back: Incarceration and Transitions to Adulthood among Urban Youth*. New Brunswick, NJ: Rutgers University Press.

Fagan, Jeffrey. 1990. "Social and Legal Policy Dimensions of Violent Juvenile Crime." *Criminal Justice and Behavior* 17: 93–133.

———. 1995. "Separating the Men from the Boys: The Comparative Advantage of Juvenile versus Criminal Court Sanctions on Recidivism among Adolescent Felony Offenders." In *A Sourcebook of Serious, Violent, and Chronic Juvenile Offenders*, edited by James C. Howell, Barry Krisberg, J. David Hawkins, and John J. Wilson, 238–60. Thousand Oaks, CA: Sage Publications.

———. 1998. "Context and Culpability in Adolescent Crime." *Virginia Journal Social Policy and Law* 6: 507–81.

———. 2000. "Contexts of Choice by Adolescents in Criminal Events." In *Youth on Trial: A Developmental Perspective on Juvenile Justice*, edited by Thomas Grisso and Robert Schwartz, 371–402. Chicago: University of Chicago Press.

———. 2003. "*Atkins*, Adolescence, and the Maturity Heuristic: Rational for a Categorical Exemption for Juveniles from Capital Punishment." *New Mexico Law Review* 33: 207–54.

———. 2008. "Juvenile Crime and Criminal Justice: Resolving Border Disputes." *Future of Children* 18: 81–118.

Fagan, Jeffrey, and Elizabeth Piper Deschenes. 1990. "Determinants of Judicial Waiver Decisions for Violent Juvenile Offenders." *Journal of Criminal Law and Criminology* 81: 314–47.

Fagan, Jeffrey, Martin Forst, and Scott Vivona. 1987. "Racial Determinants of the Judicial Transfer Decision: Prosecuting Violent Youth in Criminal Court." *Crime and Delinquency* 33: 259–86.

Fagan, Jeffrey, Aaron Kupchik, and Akiva Lieberman. 2003. "Be Careful What You Wish For: The Comparative Impacts of Juvenile versus Criminal Court Sanctions on Recidivism among Adolescent Felony Offenders." Columbia Law School Working Paper No. 03–62, http://ssrn.com.

Fagan, Jeffrey, Ellen Slaughter, and Eliot Hartstone. 1987. "Blind Justice? The Impact of Race on the Juvenile Justice Process." *Crime and Delinquency* 33: 224–58.

Fagan, Jeffrey, and Tom Tyler. 2005. "Legal Socialization of Children and Adolescents." *Social Justice Research* 18: 217–41.

Farber, Hillary B. 2004. "The Role of the Parent/Guardian in Juvenile Custodial Interrogations: Friend or Foe?" *American Criminal Law Review* 41: 1277–312.

Fare v. Michael C., 442 U.S. 707 (1979).

Farrington, David P. 1986. "Age and Crime." In *Crime & Justice: An Annual Review* 7, edited by Michael Tonry and Norval Morris, 189–250. Chicago: University of Chicago Press.

Farrington, David P., and Brandon C. Welsh. 2007. *Saving Children from a Life of Crime: Early Risk Factors and Effective Interventions*. New York: Oxford University Press.

Federal Bureau of Investigation. 2013. *Crime in the United States, 2012: Uniform Crime Reports*. Washington, DC: U.S. Government Printing Office.

Federle, Katherine H. 2000. "The Institutionalization of Female Delinquency." *Buffalo Law Review* 48: 881–908.

Federle, Katherine H., and Meda Chesney-Lind. 1992. "Special Issues in Juvenile Justice: Gender, Race, and Ethnicity." In *Juvenile Justice and Public Policy: Toward a National Agenda*, edited by Ira Schwartz, 165–95. New York: Lexington Books.

Feld, Barry C. 1976. *Neutralizing Inmate Violence: Juvenile Offenders in Institutions.* Cambridge, MA: Ballinger.

———. 1978. "Reference of Juvenile Offenders for Adult Prosecution: The Legislative Alternative to Asking Unanswerable Questions." *Minnesota Law Review* 62: 515–618.

———. 1984. "Criminalizing Juvenile Justice: Rules of Procedure for Juvenile Court." *Minnesota Law Review* 69: 141–276.

———. 1987. "Juvenile Court Meets the Principle of Offense: Legislative Changes in Juvenile Waiver Statutes." *Journal of Criminal Law and Criminology* 78: 471–533.

———. 1988a. "*In re Gault* Revisited: A Cross-State Comparison of the Right to Counsel in Juvenile Court." *Crime and Delinquency* 34: 393–424.

———. 1988b. "Juvenile Court Meets the Principle of Offense: Punishment, Treatment, and the Difference It Makes." *Boston University Law Review* 68: 821–915.

———. 1989. "The Right to Counsel in Juvenile Court: An Empirical Study of When Lawyers Appear and the Difference They Make." *Journal of Criminal Law and Criminology* 79: 1185–346.

———. 1990. "Bad Law Makes Hard Cases: Reflections on Teen-Aged Axe-Murderers, Judicial Activism, and Legislative Default." *Journal of Law and Inequality* 8: 1–101.

———. 1991. "Justice by Geography: Urban, Suburban, and Rural Variations in Juvenile Justice Administration." *Journal of Criminal Law and Criminology* 82: 156–210.

———. 1993. *Justice for Children: The Right to Counsel and the Juvenile Court.* Boston: Northeastern University Press.

———. 1995. "Violent Youth and Public Policy: A Case Study of Juvenile Justice Law Reform." *Minnesota Law Review* 79: 965–1128.

———. 1997. "Abolish the Juvenile Court: Youthfulness, Criminal Responsibility and Sentencing Policy." *Journal of Criminal Law and Criminology* 88: 68–136.

———. 1998. "Juvenile and Criminal Justice Systems' Responses to Youth Violence." *Crime and Justice* 24: 189–261.

———. 1999. *Bad Kids: Race and the Transformation of the Juvenile Court.* New York: Oxford University Press.

———. 2000a. "Legislative Exclusion of Offenses from Juvenile Court Jurisdiction." In *The Changing Borders of Juvenile Justice*, edited by Jeffrey Fagan and Franklin E. Zimring, 93–144. Chicago: University of Chicago Press.

———. 2000b. "Juveniles' Waiver of Legal Rights: Confessions, *Miranda*, and the Right to Counsel." In *Youth on Trial: A Developmental Perspective on Juvenile Justice*, edited by Thomas Grisso and Robert Schwartz, 105–38. Chicago: University of Chicago Press.

———. 2003a. "The Constitutional Tension between *Apprendi* and *McKeiver*: Sentence Enhancements Based on Delinquency Convictions and the Quality of Justice in Juvenile Courts." *Wake Forest Law Review* 38: 1111–224.

———. 2003b. "Race, Politics, and Juvenile Justice: The Warren Court and the Conservative 'Backlash.'" *Minnesota Law Review* 87: 1447–577.

———. 2006a. "Juveniles' Competence to Exercise Miranda Rights: An Empirical Study of Policy and Practice." *Minnesota Law Review* 91: 26–100.

———. 2006b. "Police Interrogation of Juveniles: An Empirical Study of Policy and Practice." *Journal of Criminal Law and Criminology* 97: 219–316.

———. 2008. "A Slower Form of Death: Implications of *Roper v. Simmons* for Juveniles Sentenced to Life without Parole." *Notre Dame Journal of Law, Ethics, and Public Policy* 22: 9–65.

———. 2009a. "Violent Girls or Relabeled Status Offenders? An Alternative Interpretation of the Data." *Crime and Delinquency* 55: 241–65.

———. 2009b. "Girls in the Juvenile Justice System." In *The Delinquent Girl*, edited by Margaret Zahn, 225–64. Philadelphia: Temple University Press.

———. 2011. "*T.L.O.* and *Redding*'s Unanswered (Misanswered) Fourth Amendment Questions: Few Rights and Fewer Remedies," *Mississippi Law Journal* 80: 847–954.

———. 2013a. *Kids, Cops, and Confessions: Inside the Interrogation Room*. New York: New York University Press.

———. 2013b. *Cases and Materials on Juvenile Justice Administration*. 4th ed. St. Paul, MN: West Publishing.

———. 2013c. "Real Interrogation: What Happens When Cops Question Kids." *Law and Society Review* 47: 1–35.

———. 2013d. "Adolescent Criminal Responsibility, Proportionality, and Sentencing Policy: *Roper, Graham, Miller/Jackson*, and the Youth Discount." *Law and Inequality Journal* 31: 263–330.

———. 2013e. "The Youth Discount: Old Enough to Do the Crime, Too Young to Do the Time." *Ohio State Journal of Criminal Law* 11: 107–48.

Feld, Barry C., and Donna M. Bishop. 2012. "Transfer of Juveniles to Criminal Court." In *Oxford Handbook of Juvenile Crime and Juvenile Justice*, edited by Barry C. Feld and Donna M. Bishop, 801–42. New York: Oxford University Press.

Feld, Barry C., B. J. Casey, and Yasmin Hurd. 2013. "Adolescent Competence and Culpability: Implications of Neuroscience for Juvenile Justice Administration." In *A Primer on Criminal Law and Neuroscience*, edited by Stephen J. Morse and Adina L. Roskies, 179–215. New York: Oxford University Press.

Feld, Barry C., and Shelly Schaefer. 2010a. "The Right to Counsel in Juvenile Court: The Conundrum of Attorneys as an Aggravating Factor in Dispositions." *Justice Quarterly* 27: 713–41.

———. and Shelly Schaefer. 2010b. "The Right to Counsel in Juvenile Court: Law Reform to Deliver Legal Services and Reduce Justice by Geography." *Criminology and Public Policy* 9: 327–56.

Fenning, Pamela, and Jennifer Rose. 2007. "Overrepresentation of African American Students in Exclusionary Discipline: The Role of School Policy." *Urban Education* 42: 536–59.

Ferster, Elyce Zenoff, Thomas F. Courtless, and Edith N. Snethen. 1971. "The Juvenile Justice System: In Search of the Role of Counsel." *Fordham Law Review* 39: 375–412.

Feyerherm, William H. 2000. "Detention Reform and Overrepresentation: A Successful Synergy." *Corrections Management Quarterly* 4: 44–51.

Figner, Bernd, Rachael J. Mackinlay, Friedrich Wilkening, and Elke U. Weber. 2009. "Affective and Deliberative Processes in Risky Choice." *Journal of Experimental Psychology* 35: 709–28.

Fox, Bryanna Hahn, Wesley G. Jennings, and Alex R. Piquero. 2014. "Serious, Chronic, and Violent Offenders." In *Juvenile Justice Sourcebook*. 2nd ed., edited by Wesley T. Church II, David W. Springer, and Albert R. Roberts, 553–80. New York: Oxford University Press.

Fox, James Alan. 1996. *Trends in Juvenile Violence: A Report to the United States Attorney General on Current and Future Rates of Juvenile Offending*. Washington, DC: U.S. Department of Justice.

Fox, Sanford J. 1970a. "Juvenile Justice Reform: An Historical Perspective." *Stanford Law Review* 22: 1187–239.

———. 1970b. "Responsibility in the Juvenile Court." *William & Mary Law Review* 11: 659–84.

Franke, Todd Michael, Anh-Luu T. Huynh-Hohnbaum, and Yunah Chung. 2002. "Adolescent Violence: With Whom They Fight and Where." *Journal of Ethnic and Cultural Diversity in Social Work* 11: 133–58.

Frase, Richard. 2005. "Excessive Prison Sentences, Punishment Goals, and the Eighth Amendment: 'Proportionality' Relative to What?" *Minnesota Law Review* 89: 571–651.

———. 2009. "What Explains Persistent Racial Disproportionality in Minnesota's Prison and Jail Populations." *Crime and Justice* 38: 201–80.

Frazier, Charles E., Donna M. Bishop, Lonn Lanza-Kaduce, and Amir Marvast. 1999. "Juveniles in Criminal Court: Past and Current Research in Florida." *Quinnipiac Law Review* 18: 573–96.

Furby, Lita, and Ruth Beyth-Marom. 1992. "Risk Taking in Adolescence: A Decision-Making Perspective." *Developmental Review* 12: 1–44.

Furman v. Georgia, 408 U.S. 238 (1972).

Gaarder, Emily, Nancy Rodriguez, and Marjorie S. Zatz. 2004. "Criers, Liars, and Manipulators: Probation Officers' Views of Girls." *Justice Quarterly* 21: 547–78.

Gallegos v. Colorado, 370 U.S. 49 (1962).

Garcia, Crystal A., and Sheila Suess Kennedy. 2003. "Back to School: Technology, School Safety and the Disappearing Fourth Amendment." *Kansas Journal of Law and Public Policy* 12: 273–88.

Gardner, Margo, and Laurence Steinberg. 2005. "Peer Influence on Risk-Taking, Risk Preference, and Risky Decision Making in Adolescence and Adulthood." *Developmental Psychology* 41: 625–35.

Gardner, Martin R. 1980. "Sniffing for Drugs in the Classroom—Perspectives on Fourth Amendment Scope." *Northwestern University Law Review* 74: 803–53.

———. 1982. "Punishment and Juvenile Justice: A Conceptual Framework for Assessing Constitutional Rights of Youthful Offenders." *Vanderbilt Law Review* 35: 791–847.

———. 1988. "Student Privacy in the Wake of *T.L.O.*: An Appeal for an Individualized Suspicion Requirement for Valid Searches and Seizures in the Schools." *Georgia Law Review* 22: 897–948.

———. 2012. "Punitive Juvenile Justice and Public Trials by Jury: Sixth Amendment Applications in a Post-*McKeiver* World." *Nebraska Law Review* 91: 1–71.

Gardner, William. 1993. "A Life-Span Rational Choice Theory of Risk Taking." In *Adolescent Risk Taking*, edited by N. Bell and R. Bell, 66–83. Newbury Park, CA: Sage Publications.

Garland, David. 1990. *Punishment and Modern Society: A Study in Social Theory.* Chicago: University of Chicago Press.

———. 2001. *The Culture of Control: Crime and Social Order in Contemporary Society.* Chicago: University of Chicago Press.

Garrett, Brandon L. 2011. *Convicting the Innocent: Where Criminal Prosecutions Go Wrong.* Cambridge, MA: Harvard University Press.

Garrido, Vincente, and Luz Anyela Morales. 2007. "Serious (Violent and Chronic) Juvenile Offenders: A Systematic Review of Treatment Effectiveness in Secure Corrections." In Campbell Collaboration Reviews of Intervention and Policy Evaluations (C2-RIPE), July 2007. Philadelphia: Campbell Collaboration.

Gerstein v. Pugh, 420 U.S. 103 (1975).

Gest, Ted. 2001. *Crime and Politics: Big Government's Erratic Campaign for Law and Order.* New York: Oxford University Press.

Ghetti, Simona, and Allison D. Redlich. 2001. "Reactions to Youth Crime: Perceptions of Accountability and Competency." *Behavioral Sciences and the Law* 19: 33–52.

Giardino, Linda F. 1997. "Statutory Rhetoric: The Reality behind Juvenile Justice Policies in America." *Brooklyn Journal of Law and Policy* 5: 223–76.

Gideon v. Wainwright, 372 U.S. 335 (1963).

Gilens, Martin. 1996. "Race Coding and White Opposition to Welfare." *American Political Science Review* 90: 593–604.

———. 1999. *Why Americans Hate Welfare: Race, Media, and the Politics of Anti-Poverty Policy.* Chicago: University of Chicago Press.

Gillespie, L. Kay, and Michael D. Norman. 1984. "Does Certification Mean Prison: Some Preliminary Findings from Utah." *Juvenile and Family Court Journal* 35: 23–34.

Gilliam, Franklin D., and Shanto Iyengar. 1998. "The Superpredator Script." *Nieman Reports* 51: 44–51.

———. 2000. "Prime Suspects: The Influence of Local Television News on the Viewing Public." *American Journal of Political Science* 44: 560–73.

Gilliam, Franklin D., Jr., Shanto Iyengar, Adam Simon, and Oliver Wright. 1996. "Crime in Black and White: The Violent, Scary World of Local News." *Harvard International Journal of Press/Politics* 1: 6–23.

Girls Inc. 1996. *Prevention and Parity: Girls in Juvenile Justice.* Indianapolis: Girls Incorporated.

Godinez v. Moran, 509 U.S. 389 (1993).

Gogtay, Nitin, Jay N. Giedd, Leslie Lusk, Kiralee M. Hayashi, Deanna Greenstein, A. Catherine Vaituzis, Tom F. Nugent III, David H. Herman, Liv S. Clasen, Arthur W. Toga, Judith L. Rapoport, and Paul M. Thompson. 2004. "Dynamic Mapping of Human Cortical Development during Childhood through Early Adulthood." *Proceedings of National Academy of Science* 101: 8174–79.

Goldberg, Elkhonon. 2001. *The Executive Brain: Frontal Lobes and the Civilized Mind.* New York: Oxford University Press.

Goldstein, Alan, and Naomi E. Sevin Goldstein. 2010. *Evaluating Capacity to Waive Miranda.* New York: Oxford University Press.

Gottschalk, Marie. 2015. *Caught: The Prison State and the Lockdown of American Politics.* Princeton, NJ: Princeton University Press.

Graham, Fred. 1970. *The Self-Inflicted Wound.* New York: Free Press.

Graham v. Florida, 130 S. Ct. 2011 (2010).

Graham, Sandra, and Brian S. Lowery. 2004. "Priming Unconscious Racial Stereotypes about Adolescent Offenders." *Law and Human Behavior* 28: 483–504.

Greenwood, Peter W. 1986. "Differences in Criminal Behavior and Court Responses among Juvenile and Young Adult Defendants." In *Crime and Justice 7,* edited by Michael Tonry and Norval Morris, 151–187. Chicago: University of Chicago Press.

———. 2006. *Changing Lives: Delinquency Prevention as Crime-Control Policy.* Chicago: University of Chicago Press.

Greenwood, Peter W., Allan Abrahamse, and Franklin Zimring. 1984. *Factors Affecting Sentence Severity for Young Adult Offenders.* Santa Monica, CA: RAND.

Greenwood, Peter W., Albert J. Lipson, Allan Abrahamse, and Franklin Zimring. 1983. *Youth Crime and Juvenile Justice in California.* Santa Monica, CA: RAND.

Greenwood, Peter W., and Susan Turner. 2012. "Probation and Other Noninstitutional Treatment: The Evidence Is In." In *Oxford Handbook of Juvenile Crime and Juvenile Justice,* edited by Barry C. Feld and Donna M. Bishop, 723–47. New York: Oxford University Press.

Griffin, Patrick. 2012. "Legal Boundaries between Juvenile and Criminal Justice Systems in the United States." In *From Juvenile Delinquency to Adult Crime,* edited by Rolf Loeber and David P. Farrington, 184–99. New York: Oxford University Press.

Griffin, Patrick, Sean Addie, Benjamin Adams, and Kathy Firestine. 2011. *Trying Juveniles as Adults: An Analysis of State Transfer Laws and Reporting.* Washington, DC: Office of Juvenile Justice and Delinquency Prevention.

Grisso, Thomas. 1980. "Juveniles' Capacities to Waive *Miranda* Rights: An Empirical Analysis." *California Law Review* 68: 1134–66.

———. 1981. *Juveniles' Waiver of Rights: Legal and Psychological Competence.* New York: Plenum Press.

———. 1996. "Society's Retributive Response to Juvenile Violence: A Developmental Perspective." *Law and Human Behavior* 20: 229–47.

———. 1997a. "The Competence of Adolescents as Trial Defendants." *Psychology, Public Policy, and Law* 3: 3–11.

———. 1997b. "Juvenile Competency to Stand Trial: Questions in an Era of Punitive Reform." *Criminal Justice* 12: 5–11.

———. 1998. *Instruments for Assessing Understanding and Appreciation of Miranda Rights.* Sarasota, FL: Professional Resources Press.

———. 2000. "What We Know about Youths' Capacities as Trial Defendants." In *Youth on Trial: A Developmental Perspective on Juvenile Justice,* edited by Thomas Grisso and Robert G. Schwartz, 139–72. Chicago: University of Chicago Press.

———. 2004. *Double Jeopardy: Adolescent Offenders with Mental Disorders.* Chicago: University of Chicago Press.

Grisso, Thomas, Laurence Steinberg, Jennifer Woolard, Elizabeth Cauffman, Elizabeth Scott, Sandra Graham, Fran Lexcen, N. Dickon Reppucci, and Robert Schwartz. 2003. "Juveniles' Competence to Stand Trial: A Comparison of Adolescents' and Adults' Capacities as Trial Defendants." *Law and Human Behavior* 27: 333–63.

Gross, Samuel R., Kristen Jacoby, Daniel J. Matheson, Nicholas Montgomery, and Sujata Patil. 2005. "Exonerations in the United States: 1989 through 2003." *Journal of Criminal Law and Criminology* 95: 523–60.

Grubb, W. Norton, and Marvin Lazerson. 1982. *Broken Promises: How Americans Fail Their Children.* New York: Basic Books.

Gruber, Staci A., and Deborah A. Yurgelun-Todd. 2006. "Neurobiology and the Law: A Role in Juvenile Justice." *Ohio State Journal of Criminal Law* 3: 321–40.

Gudjonsson, Gisli H. 2003. *The Psychology of Interrogations and Confessions: A Handbook.* New York: John Wiley & Sons.

Guevara, Lori, Cassia Spohn, and Denise Herz. 2004. "Race, Legal Representation and Juvenile Justice: Issues and Concerns." *Crime and Delinquency* 50: 344–71.

———. 2008. "Race, Gender, and Legal Counsel: Differential Outcomes in Two Juvenile Courts." *Youth Violence and Juvenile Justice* 6: 83–104.

Guggenheim, Martin, and Randy Hertz. 1998. "Reflections on Judges, Juries, and Justice: Ensuring the Fairness of Juvenile Delinquency Trials." *Wake Forest Law Review* 33: 553–93.

Gun-Free Schools Act 20 U.S.C.A. § 7151 (2012).

Hacker, Andrew. 1992. *Two Nations: Black and White, Separate, Hostile, Unequal.* New York: Ballantine Books.

Haley v. Ohio, 332 U.S. 596 (1948).

Hamparian, Donna, Linda K. Estep, Susan M. Muntean, Ramon R. Priestino, Robert G. Swisher, Paul L. Wallace, and Joseph L. White. 1982. *Youth in Adult Courts:*

Between Two Worlds. Washington, DC: Office of Juvenile Justice and Delinquency Prevention.

Handler, Joel F., and Julie Zatz, eds. 1982. *Neither Angels nor Thieves: Studies in Deinstitutionalization of Status Offenders*. Washington, DC: National Academy Press.

Hanson, Jamie, and Daniel A. Hackman. 2012. "Cognitive Neuroscience and Disparities in Socioeconomic Status." In *Biological Consequences of Socioeconomic Inequalities*, edited by Barbara Wolfe, William Evans, and Teresa E. Seeman, 158–86. New York: Russell Sage Foundation.

Hanson, Jamie, Nicole Hair, Amitabh Chandra, Ed Moss, Jay Bhattacharya, Seth D. Pollak, and Barbara Wolfe. 2012. "Brain Development and Poverty: A First Look." In *Biological Consequences of Socioeconomic Inequalities*, edited by Barbara Wolfe, William Evans, and Teresa E. Seeman, 187–214. New York: Russell Sage Foundation.

Harlow, Caroline Wolf. 2000. *Defense Counsel in Criminal Cases*. Washington, DC: Bureau of Justice Statistics, U.S. Department of Justice.

Harlow v. Fitzgerald, 457 U.S. 800 (1982).

Harmelin v. Michigan, 501 U.S. 957 (1991).

Harris, Donald J. 1994. "Due Process v. Helping Kids in Trouble: Implementing the Right to Appeal from Adjudications of Delinquency in Pennsylvania." *Dickinson Law Review* 98: 209–35.

Harris v. Wright, 93 F.3d 518 (9th Cir. 1996).

Hart, H. L. A. 1968. *Punishment and Responsibility*. New York: Oxford University Press.

Hartney, Chris, and Linh Vuong. 2009. *Created Equal: Racial and Ethnic Disparities in the U.S. Criminal Justice System*. Oakland, CA: National Council on Crime and Delinquency.

Hawes, Joseph. 1971. *Children in Urban Society: Juvenile Delinquency in Nineteenth-Century America*. New York: Oxford University Press.

Hawkins, Darnell F., and Kimberly Kempf-Leonard. 2005. *Our Children, Their Children: Confronting Racial and Ethnic Differences in American Juvenile Justice*. Chicago: University of Chicago Press.

Higham, John. 1988. *Strangers in the Land: Patterns of American Nativism, 1860–1925*. 2nd ed. New Brunswick, NJ: Rutgers University Press.

Hinton, Elizabeth. 2016. *From the War on Poverty to the War on Crime: The Making of Mass Incarceration in America*. Cambridge, MA: Harvard University Press.

Hirschfield, Paul J. 2008. "Preparing for Prison? The Criminalization of School Discipline in the USA." *Theoretical Criminology* 12: 79–101.

Hoeffle, Janet C. 2013. "The Jurisprudence of Death and Youth: Now the Twain Should Meet." *Texas Tech Law Review* 46: 29–69.

Hofstadter, Richard. 1955. *The Age of Reform: From Bryan to F.D.R.* New York: Knopf.

Holland, Paul, and Wallace J. Mlyniec. 1995. "Whatever Happened to the Right to Treatment?: The Modern Quest of a Historical Promise." *Temple Law Review* 68:1791–835.

Holt, Kevin. 2015. "The Inbetweeners: Standardizing Juvenileness and Recognizing Emerging Adulthood for Sentencing Purposes after *Miller.*" *Washington University Law Review* 92: 1393–1420.

Horton v. Goose Creek Ind. School District, 690 F.2d 470 (5th Cir. 1982).

Howe, Scott W. 2001. "The Troubling Influence of Equality in Constitutional Criminal Procedure: From *Brown* to *Miranda, Furman* and *Beyond.*" *Vanderbilt Law Review* 54: 359–450.

Howell, James C. 1996. "Juvenile Transfers to the Criminal Justice System: State-of the Art." *Law and Policy* 18: 17–60.

Howell, James C., Barry C. Feld, and Daniel P. Mears. 2012. "Young Offenders and an Effective Justice System Response." In *From Juvenile Delinquency to Adult Crime: Criminal Careers, Justice Policy, and Prevention*, edited by Rolf Loeber and David P. Farrington, 200–44. New York: Oxford University Press.

Hoyt, Stephanie, and David G. Scherer. 1998. "Female Juvenile Delinquency: Misunderstood by the Juvenile Justice System, Neglected by Social Science." *Law and Human Behavior* 22: 81–107.

Human Rights Watch. 2009. *World Report*. www.hrw.org.

———. 2012. *When I Die . . . They'll Send Me Home: Youth Sentenced to Life in Prison without Parole in California—An Update*. www.hrw.org.

Hurwitz, John, and Mark Peffley. 1997. "Public Perceptions of Race and Crime: The Role of Racial Stereotypes." *American Journal of Political Science* 41: 375–401.

Illinois v. Caballes, 543 U.S. 405 (2005).

Illinois v. Gates, 462 U.S. 213 (1983).

In re Bailey, 782 N.E.2d 1177 (Ohio 2002).

In re BMB, 955 P.2d 1302 (Kan. 1998).

In re Christopher H., 596 S.E.2d 500 (S.C. Ct. App. 2004).

In re D.D.N., 582 N.W.2d 378 (Minn. Ct. Ap. 1998).

In re Dino, 359 So. 2d 586 (La. 1978).

In re D.J., 817 So. 2d 26 (La. 2002).

In re Eric J., 25 Cal. 3d 522, 601 P.2d 549 (1979).

In re F.B., 442 Pa. Super. 216, 658 A.2d 1378 (Pa. 1995).

In re Gault, 387 U.S. 1 (1967).

In re J.F. and G.G., 714 A.2d 467 (Pa. Super. Ct. 1998).

In re K.G., 808 N.E.2d 631 (Ind. 2004).

In re L.M., 186 P.3d 164 (Kan. 2008).

In re Manuel R., 207 A.2d 719 (Conn. 1988).

In re Oliver, 333 U.S. 257 (1948).

In re Seven Minors, 99 Nev. 427, 664 P.2d 947 (Nev. 1983).

In re W.A.F., 573 A.2d 1264 (D.C. App. 1990).

In re Winship, 397 U.S. 358 (1970).

In the Interest of Jerrell C.J., 699 N.W.2d 110 (Wis. 2005).

Israel, Jerold H. 1977. "Criminal Procedure, The Burger Court, and the Legacy of the Warren Court." *Michigan Law Review* 75: 1319–424.

Jackson v. Hobbs, 132 S. Ct. 548 (2012).

Jacobs, James B. 2014. "Juvenile Criminal Record Confidentiality." In *Choosing the Future for American Juvenile Justice*, edited by Franklin E. Zimring and David S. Tanenhaus, 149–68. New York: New York University Press.

Jaggers, Jeremiah, Sarah Young, and Wesley T. Church II. 2014. "Police Work with Juveniles" In *Juvenile Justice Sourcebook*. 2nd ed., edited by Wesley T. Church II, David W. Springer, and Ablert R. Roberts, 149–66. New York: Oxford University Press.

J.A.R. v. State, 689 So. 2d 1242 (Fla. Dist. Ct. App. 1997).

J.D.B. v. North Carolina, 131 S. Ct. 2394 (2011).

Jensen, Eric L., and Linda K. Metsger. 1994. "A Test of the Deterrent Effect of Legislative Waiver on Violent Juvenile Crime." *Crime and Delinquency* 40: 96–104.

Johnson, David R., and Laurie K. Scheuble. 1991. "Gender Bias in the Disposition of Juvenile Court Referrals: The Effects of Time and Location." *Criminology* 29: 677–99.

Johnson, Sara B., Jenna L. Riss, and Kimberly G. Noble. 2016. "State of the Art Review: Poverty and the Developing Brain." *Pediatrics* 137:1–16.

Jones, Judith B. 2004. *Access to Counsel*. Washington, DC: Office of Juvenile Justice and Delinquency Prevention.

Juszkiewicz, Jolanta. 2000. *Youth Crime/Adult Time: Is Justice Served?* Washington, DC: Building Blocks for Youth.

Kaban, Barbara, and Ann E. Tobey. 1999. "When Police Question Children, Are Protections Adequate?" *Journal of the Center for Children and the Courts* 1: 151–60.

Kalven, Harry, and Hans Zeisel. 1966. *The American Jury*. Chicago: University of Chicago Press.

Kang, Jerry. 2005. "Trojan Horses of Race." *Harvard Law Review* 118: 1489–593.

Kassin, Saul. 2005. "On the Psychology of Confessions: Does Innocence Put Innocents at Risk?" *American Psychologist* 60: 215–28.

Kassin, Saul, and Gisli H. Gudjonsson. 2004. "The Psychology of Confessions: A Review of the Literature and Issues." *Psychological Sciences in Public Interest* 5: 33–69.

Kassin, Saul, Steven A. Drizin, Thomas Grisso, Gisli H. Gudjonsson, Richard A. Leo, and Allison D. Redlich. 2010. "Police-Induced Confessions: Risk Factors and Recommendations." *Law and Human Behavior* 34: 49–52.

Katz, Michael B. 1968. *The Irony of Early School Reform: Educational Innovation in Mid-Nineteenth Century Massachusetts*. Boston: Beacon Press.

———. 1986. *In the Shadow of the Poorhouse: A Social History of Welfare in America*. New York: Basic Books.

———. 1989. *The Undeserving Poor: From the War on Poverty to the War on Welfare*. New York: Pantheon Books.

———, ed. 1993. *The "Underclass" Debate: Views from History*. Princeton, NJ: Princeton University Press.

Kazdin, Alan E. 2000. "Adolescent Developmental, Mental Disorders, and Decision Making of Delinquent Youths." In *Youth on Trial: A Developmental Perspective on Juvenile Justice*, edited by Thomas Grisso and Robert Schwartz, 33–66. Chicago: University of Chicago Press.

Kempf-Leonard, Kimberly. 2007. "Minority Youth and Juvenile Justice: Disproportionate Minority Contact after Nearly 20 Years of Reform Efforts." *Youth Violence and Juvenile Justice* 5: 71–87.

Kempf-Leonard, Kimberly, and Pernilla Johansson. 2007. "Gender and Runaways: Risk Factors, Delinquency, and Juvenile Justice Experiences." *Youth Violence and Juvenile Justice* 5: 308–27.

Kempf-Leonard, Kimberly, and Lisa L. Sample. 2000. "Disparity Based on Sex: Is Gender-Specific Treatment Warranted?" *Justice Quarterly* 17: 89–128.

Kennedy, Randall. 1997. *Race, Crime, and the Law*. New York: Vintage Books.

Kennedy v. Louisiana, 554 U.S. 407 (2008).

Kenney v. Mendoza-Martinez, 372 U.S. 144 (1963).

Kent v. United States, 383 U.S. 541 (1966).

Kett, Joseph F. 1977. *Rites of Passage: Adolescence in America 1790 to the Present*. New York: Basic Books.

Kim, Catherine Y., Daniel J. Losen, and Damon T. Hewitt. 2010. *The School-to-Prison Pipeline: Structuring Legal Reform*. New York: New York University Press.

Kinder, Donald R., and Tali Mendelberg. 1995. "Cracks in American Apartheid: The Political Impact of Prejudice among Desegregated Whites." *Journal of Politics* 57: 402–24.

King, Kenneth J. 2006. "Waiving Childhood Goodbye: How Juvenile Courts Fail to Protect Children from Unknowing, Unintelligent, and Involuntary Waivers of Miranda Rights." *Wisconsin Law Review* 2006: 431–78.

Klarman, Michael J. 2000. "The Racial Origins of Modern Criminal Procedure." *Michigan Law Review* 99: 48–97.

———. 2004. *From Jim Crow to Civil Rights: The Supreme Court and the Struggle for Racial Equality*. New York: Oxford University Press.

Kluger, Jeffrey. 2006. "Taming Wild Girls." *Time*, May 1, 54–55.

Kolko, Gabriel. 1963. *The Triumph of Conservatism: A Reinterpretation of American History, 1900–1916*. New York: Free Press.

Kozol, Jonathan. 1991. *Savage Inequalities: Children in America's Schools*. New York: Harper.

———. 2005. *The Shame of the Nation: The Restoration of Apartheid Schooling in America*. New York: Broadway Books.

Krezmien, Michal P., Peter E. Leone, and Michael G. Wilson. 2014. "Marginalized Students, School Exclusion, and the School-to-Prison Pipeline." In *Juvenile Justice Sourcebook*. 2nd ed., edited by Wesley T. Church II, David W. Springer, and Albert R. Roberts, 267–88. New York: Oxford University Press.

Krisberg, Barry. 2012. "Juvenile Corrections: An Overview." In *Oxford Handbook of Juvenile Crime and Juvenile Justice*, edited by Barry C. Feld and Donna M. Bishop, 748–70. New York: Oxford University Press.

Krisberg, Barry, James Austin, and Patricia Steele. 1989. *Working Juvenile Corrections: Evaluating the Massachusetts Department of Youth Services*. San Francisco: National Council on Crime and Delinquency.

———. 1991. *Unlocking Juvenile Corrections*. San Francisco: National Council on Crime and Delinquency.

Kupchik, Aaron. 2006. *Judging Juveniles: Prosecuting Adolescents in Adult and Juvenile Courts*. New York: New York University Press.

———. 2010. *Homeroom Security: School Discipline in an Age of Fear*. New York: New York University Press.

———. 2014. "The School-to-Prison Pipeline: Rhetoric and Reality." In *Choosing the Future For American Juvenile Justice*, edited by Franklin E. Zimring and David S. Tanenhaus, 94–119. New York: New York University Press.

Kupchik, Aaron, Jeffrey Fagan, and Akiva Liberman. 2003. "Punishment, Proportionality, and Jurisdictional Transfer of Adolescent Offenders: A Test of the Leniency Gap Hypothesis." *Stanford Law and Policy Review* 14: 57–83.

Kurlychek, Megan, and Brian D. Johnson. 2004. "The Juvenile Penalty: A Comparison of Juvenile and Young Adult Sentencing Outcomes in Criminal Court." *Criminology* 42: 485–517.

———. 2010. "Juvenility and Punishment: Sentencing Juveniles in Adult Criminal Court." *Criminology* 48: 725–58.

LaBelle, Deborah. 2004. *Second Chances: Juveniles Serving Life without Parole in Michigan Prisons*. American Civil Liberties Union, www.aclu.org.

LaFave, Wayne. 1987. *Search and Seizure: A Treatise on the Fourth Amendment*. St. Paul, MN: West Pub. Co.

LaFave, Wayne, Jerold H. Israel, Nancy J. King, and Orin S. Kerr. 2009. *Criminal Procedure*. 5th ed. St. Paul, MN: Thomson-West.

Lanza-Kaduce, Lonn, Jodi Lane, Donna M. Bishop, and Charles E. Frazier. 2006. "Juvenile Offenders and Adult Felony Recidivism: The Impact of Transfer." *Journal of Crime and Justice* 28: 59–77.

Larson, Kimberly. 2003. "Improving the 'Kangaroo Courts': A Proposal for Reform in Evaluating Juveniles' Waiver of *Miranda*." *Villanova Law Review* 48: 629–68.

Lasch, Christopher. 1977. *Haven in a Heartless World: The Family Besieged*. New York: Basic Books.

Lauritsen, Janet L. 2005. "Racial and Ethnic Differences in Juvenile Offending." In *Our Children, Their Children: Confronting Racial and Ethnic Differences in American Juvenile Justice*, edited by Darnell F. Hawkins and Kimberly Kempf-Leonard, 83–104. Chicago: University of Chicago Press.

Lawrence, Richard. 2007. *School Crime and Juvenile Justice*. 2nd ed. New York: Oxford University Press.

Lefstein, Norman, Vaughan Stapleton, and Lee Teitelbaum. 1969. "In Search of Juvenile Justice: *Gault* and Its Implementation." *Law and Society Review* 3: 491–562.

Leiber, Michael J. 2003. *The Contexts of Juvenile Justice Decision Making: When Race Matters*. Albany: State University of New York Press.

———. 2013. "Race, Pre- and Post-Detention, and Juvenile Justice Decision Making." *Crime and Delinquency* 59: 396–418.

Lemann, Nicholas. 1992. *The Promised Land: The Great Black Migration and How It Changed America*. New York: Vintage Books.

Leo, Richard A. 1996. "Inside the Interrogation Room." *Journal of Criminal Law and Criminology* 86: 266–303.

———. 2008. *Police Interrogation and American Justice*. Cambridge, MA: Harvard University Press.

Leo, Richard A., Steven A. Drizin, Peter J. Neufeld, Bradley R. Hall, and Amy Vatner. 2006. "Bringing Reliability Back In: False Confessions and Legal Safeguards in the Twenty-First Century." *Wisconsin Law Review* 2006: 479–539.

Lerner, Steven. 1986. *Bodily Harm*. Bolinas, CA: Common Knowledge Press

Levin, David J., Patrick A. Langan, and Jodi M. Brown. 1996. *State Court Sentencing of Convicted Felons, 1996*. Washington, DC: U.S. Department of Justice, Bureau of Justice Statistics, Office of Justice Programs.

Levitt, Steven D. 1998. "Juvenile Crime and Punishment." *Journal of Political Economy* 106: 1156–85.

Lichter, Daniel T. 1997. "Poverty and Inequality among Children." *Annual Review of Sociology* 23: 121–45.

Lieberson, Stanley. 1980. *A Piece of the Pie: Black and White Immigrants since 1880*. Berkeley: University of California Press.

Lindsey, Duncan. 2009. *Child Poverty and Inequality: Securing a Better Future for America's Children*. New York: Oxford University Press.

Lipsey, Mark W. 2009. "The Primary Factors That Characterize Effective Interventions with Juvenile Offenders: A Meta-Analytic Overview." *Victims and Offenders* 4: 124–47.

Lockett v. Ohio, 438 U.S. 586 (1978).

Loeber, Rolf, and David P. Farrington. 1998. *Serious and Violent Juvenile Offenders: Risk Factors and Successful Interventions*. Thousand Oaks, CA: Sage Publications.

———. 2012. *From Juvenile Delinquency to Adult Crime: Criminal Careers, Justice Policy, and Prevention*. New York: Oxford University Press.

Loeber, Rolf, David P. Farrington, James C. Howell, and Machteld Hoeve. 2012. "Overview, Conclusions, and Key Recommendations." In *From Juvenile Delinquency to Adult Crime: Criminal Careers, Justice Policy, and Prevention*, edited by Rolf Loeber and David P. Farrington, 315–83. New York: Oxford University Press

Logan, Wayne A. 1998. "Proportionality and Punishment: Imposing Life without Parole on Juveniles." *Wake Forest Law Review* 33: 681–726.

Lopez, Ian Haney. 2014. *Dog Whistle Politics: How Coded Racial Appeals Have Reinvented Racism and Wrecked the Middle Class*. New York: Oxford University Press.

MacArthur Foundation Research Network on Adolescent Development and Juvenile Justice. 2006. *Development and Criminal Blameworthiness*. www.adjj.org.

MacDonald, John M., and Meda Chesney-Lind. 2001. "Gender Bias and Juvenile Justice Revisited: A Multiyear Analysis." *Crime and Delinquency* 47: 173–95.

Mack, Julian W. 1909. "The Juvenile Court." *Harvard Law Review* 23: 104–22.

MacKenzie, Doris Layton, and Rachel Freeland. 2012. "Examining the Effectiveness of Juvenile Residential Programs." In *Oxford Handbook of Juvenile Crime and*

Juvenile Justice, edited by Barry C. Feld and Donna M. Bishop, 771–800. New York: Oxford University Press.

Mahoney, Anne Rankin, and Carol Fenster. 1982. "Female Delinquents in a Suburban Court." In *Judge, Lawyer, Victim, Thief: Women, Gender Roles & Criminal Justice*, edited by Nicole Hahn Rafter and Elizabeth Anne Stanko, 221–36. Boston: Northeastern University Press.

Males, Mike, and Dan Macallair. 2000. *The Color of Justice: An Analysis of Juvenile Court Transfers in California*. Washington, DC: U.S. Department of Justice, Building Blocks for Youth.

Manduley v. Superior Court of San Diego County, 41 P.3d 3 (Cal. Sup. Ct. 2002).

Manfredi, Christopher P. 1998. *The Supreme Court and Juvenile Justice*. Lawrence: University of Kansas Press.

Mapp v. Ohio, 367 U.S. 643 (1961).

Maroney, Terry A. 2009. "The False Promise of Adolescent Brain Science in Juvenile Justice." *Notre Dame Law Review* 85: 89–176.

———. 2011. "Adolescent Brain Science after *Graham v. Florida*." *Notre Dame Law Review* 86: 765–93.

Martarella v. Kelley, 349 F. Supp, 575 (S.D.N.Y. 1972); *enforced* 359 F. Supp. 478 (S.D.N.Y. 1973).

Martinson, Robert. 1974. "What Works? Questions and Answers about Prison Reform." *Public Interest* 35: 22–54.

Massey, Douglas S., and Nancy A. Denton. 1993. *American Apartheid: Segregation and the Making of the Underclass*. Cambridge, MA: Harvard University Press.

Massey, Hillary J. 2006. "Disposing of Children: The Eighth Amendment and Juvenile Life without Parole after Roper." *Boston College Law Review* 47: 1083–118.

Matza, David. 1964. *Delinquency and Drift*. New York: Wiley.

Mauer, Marc. 1999. *Race to Incarcerate*. New York: New Press with the Sentencing Project.

Mauer, Marc, Ryan King, and Malcolm Young. 2004. *The Meaning of "Life": Long Prison Sentences in Context*. Sentencing Project, www.sentencingproject.org.

Maxson, Cheryl L., and Malcolm W. Klein. 1997. *Responding to Troubled Youth*. New York: Oxford University Press.

McKeiver v. Pennsylvania, 403 U.S. 528 (1971).

McNeece, C. Aaron, and Tiffany Ryan. 2014. "Juvenile Justice Policy: Current Trends and 21st-Century Issues." In *Juvenile Justice Sourcebook*. 2nd ed., edited by Wesley T. Church II, David W. Springer, and Albert R. Roberts, 37–60. New York: Oxford University Press.

Mears, Daniel P. 2012. "The Front End of the Juvenile Court: Intake and Informal versus Formal Processing." In *Oxford Handbook of Juvenile Crime and Juvenile Justice*, edited by Barry C. Feld and Donna M. Bishop, 573–605. New York: Oxford University Press.

Mendelberg, Tali. 1997. "Executing Hortons: Racial Crime in the 1988 Presidential Campaign." *Public Opinion Quarterly* 61: 134–57.

———. 2001. *The Race Card: Campaign Strategy, Implicit Messages, and the Norm of Equality*. Princeton, NJ: Princeton University Press.

Mennel, Robert. 1973. *Thorns and Thistles: Juvenile Delinquents in the United States 1825–1940*. Hanover, NH: University Press of New England.

Meyer, Jessica R., and N. Dickon Reppucci. 2007. "Police Practices and Perceptions Regarding Juvenile Interrogation and Interrogative Suggestibility." *Behavioral Sciences and the Law* 25: 727–80.

Mickelson, Roslyn Arlin. 2008. "Twenty-First Century Social Science on School Racial Diversity and Educational Outcomes." *Ohio State Law Journal* 69: 1173–227.

———. 2015. *School Integration and K-12 Educational Outcomes: A Quick Synthesis of Social Science Evidence*. National Coalition on School Diversity, http://school-diversity.org.

Miller, Jerome. 1991. *Last One Over the Wall*. Columbus: Ohio State University Press.

———. 1996. *Search and Destroy: African-American Males in the Criminal Justice System*. Cambridge, UK: Cambridge University Press.

Miller, Susan L. 2005. *Victims as Offenders: The Paradox of Women's Violence in Relationships*. New Brunswick, NJ: Rutgers University Press.

Miller v. Alabama, 132 S. Ct. 2455 (2012).

Milliken v. Bradley, 418 U.S. 717 (1974).

Minnesota Sentencing Guidelines Commission, comment II.B.406 (1980).

Miranda v. Arizona, 384 U.S. 436 (1966).

Missouri v. Seibert, 542 U.S. 600 (2004).

Moffitt, Terri E. 1993. "Adolescence-Limited and Life-Course-Persistent Antisocial Behavior: A Developmental Taxonomy." *Psychological Review* 100: 674–701.

———. 2003. "Life-Course-Persistent and Adolescence-Limited Antisocial Behavior: A 10-Year Research Review and a Research Agenda." In *The Causes of Conduct Disorder and Serious Juvenile Delinquency*, edited by Benjamin Lahey, Terrie Moffitt, and Avshalom Caspi, 49–75. New York: Guilford.

Monahan, Kathryn, Laurence Steinberg, and Alex R. Piquero. 2015. "Juvenile Justice Policy and Practice: A Developmental Perspective." *Crime and Justice* 44: 577–619.

Monell v. N.Y. Department of Social Services, 436 U.S. 658 (1978).

Montgomery v. Louisiana, 136 S. Ct. 718 (2016).

Moore, Michael S. 1997. "Choice, Character, and Excuse." In *Placing Blame*, edited by Michael S. Moore, 548–94. New York: Oxford University Press.

Moore v. Dempsey, 261 U.S. 86 (1923).

Moriearty, Perry L. 2011. "Framing Justice, Media Bias, and Legal Decisionmaking." *Maryland Law Review* 69: 849–909.

———. 2008. "Combating the Color-Coded Confinement of Kids: An Equal Protection Remedy." *New York University Review of Law and Social Change* 32: 285–343.

———. 2015. "*Miller v. Alabama* and the Retroactivity of Proportionality Rules." *University of Pennsylvania Journal of Constitutional Law* 17: 929–90.

Morse, Stephen J. 1998. "Immaturity and Irresponsibility." *Journal of Criminal Law and Criminology* 88: 15–67.

——. 2004. "New Neuroscience, Old Problems." In *Neuroscience and the Law: Brain, Mind, and the Scales of Justice*, edited by Brent Garland, 157–91. New York: Dana Press.

——. 2006. "Brain Overclaim Syndrome and Criminal Responsibility: A Diagnostic Note." *Ohio State Journal of Criminal Law* 3: 397–412.

Moynihan, Daniel P. 1965. *The Negro Family: The Case for National Action*. Washington, DC: U.S. Department of Labor, U.S. Government Printing Office.

Muhammad, Khalil Gibran. 2010. *The Condemnation of Blackness: Race, Crime and the Making of Modern Urban America*. Cambridge, MA: Harvard University Press.

Mulvey, Edward P., and Carol A. Schubert. 2012. "Youth in Prison and Beyond." In *Oxford Handbook on Juvenile Crime and Juvenile Justice*, edited by Barry C. Feld and Donna M. Bishop, 843–70. New York: Oxford University Press.

Murphy v. Waterfront Commission, 378 U.S. 52 (1964).

Murray, Charles. 1984. *Losing Ground: American Social Policy, 1950–1980*. New York: Basic Books.

Myers, David L. 2003. "The Recidivism of Violent Youths in Juvenile and Adult Court: A Consideration of Selection Bias." *Youth Violence and Juvenile Justice* 1: 79–101.

Myers v. State, 839 N.E.2d 1154 (Ind. Sup. Ct. 2005).

Myrdal, Gunnar. 1962. *An American Dilemma: The Negro Problem and Modern Democracy*. 2nd ed. New Brunswick, NJ: Transaction Publishers.

Nagy, Zoltan, Helena Westerberg, and Torkel Klingberg. 2004. "Maturation of White Matter Is Associated with the Development of Cognitive Functions during Childhood." *Journal of Cognitive Neuroscience* 16: 1227–33.

Nance, Jason P. 2013. "Students, Security, and Race." *Emory Law Journal* 63: 1–57.

——. 2014. "School Surveillance and the Fourth Amendment." *Wisconsin Law Review*: 79–137.

——. 2015. "Students, Police, and the School-to-Prison Pipeline." *Washington University Law Review* 93: 1–57.

National Advisory Commission on Civil Disorders. 1968. *Report*. Washington, DC: U.S. Government Printing Office.

National Commission on Children. 1991. *Beyond Rhetoric: A New American Agenda for Children and Families*. Washington, DC: U.S. Government Printing Office.

National Research Council. 1993. *Losing Generations: Adolescents in High-Risk Settings*. Washington, DC: National Academy Press.

——. 2013. *Reforming Juvenile Justice: A Developmental Approach*. Washington, DC: National Academies Press.

——. 2014. *The Growth of Incarceration in the United States: Exploring Causes and Consequences*. Washington, DC: National Academies Press.

National Research Council and Institute of Medicine. 2001. *Juvenile Crime, Juvenile Justice*. Washington, DC: National Academy Press.

——. 2011. *The Science of Adolescent Risk-Taking: Workshop Report*. Washington, DC: National Academies Press.

Nellis, Ashley. 2012. *The Lives of Juvenile Lifers: Findings from a National Survey*. Washington, DC: Sentencing Project.

———. 2016. *A Return to Justice: Rethinking Our Approach to Juveniles in the System*. Lanham, MD: Rowman & Littlefield.

Nellis, Ashley, and Ryan S. King. 2009. *No Exit: The Expanding Use of Life Sentences in America*. Sentencing Project, www.sentencingproject.org.

Nelson v. Heyne, 491 F.2d 352 (7th Cir. 1974).

N.G. v. Connecticut, 382 F.3d 225 (2d Cir. 2004).

Noble, Kimberly G., Suzanne M. Houston, Natalie H. Brito, Hauke Bartsch, Eric Kan, Joshua M. Kuperman, Natacha Akshoomoff, David G. Amaral, Cinnamon S. Bloss, Ondrej Libiger, Nicholas J. Schork, Sarah S. Murray, B. J. Casey, Linda Chang, Thomas M. Ernst, Jean A. Frazier, Jeffrey R. Gruen, David N. Kennedy, Peter Van Zijl, Stewart Mostofsky, Walter E. Kaufmann, Tal Kenet, Anders M. Dale, Terry L. Jernigan, and Elizabeth R. Sowell. 2015. "Family Income, Parental Education and Brain Structure in Children and Adolescents." *Nature Neuroscience* 18: 773–78.

Norris v. Alabama, 294 U.S. 587 (1935).

Note. 1966. "Juvenile Delinquents, the Police, State Courts, and Individualized Justice." *Harvard Law Review* 79: 775–810.

Note. 1988. "Developments in the Law: Race and the Criminal Process." *Harvard Law Review* 101: 1472–641.

Note. 2006. "A Matter of Life and Death: The Effect of Life-without-Parole Statutes on Capital Punishment." *Harvard Law Review* 119: 1838–54.

Oliver, J. Eric, and Tali Mendelberg. 2000. "Reconsidering the Environmental Determinants of White Racial Attitudes." *American Journal of Political Science* 44: 574–89.

Oliver, Mary Beth. 1999. "Caucasian Viewers' Memory of Black and White Suspects in the News." *Journal of Communication* 49: 46–60.

Omi, Michael, and Howard Winant. 1994. *Racial Formation in the United States: From the 1960s to the 1990s*. New York: Routledge.

Orfield, Gary, and Erica Frankenberg. 2008. *The Last Have Become First: Rural and Small Town America Lead the Way on Desegregation*. University of California, Los Angeles, Civil Rights Project, https://civilrightsproject.ucla.edu.

Orfield, Gary, John Kuscera, and Genevieve Siegel-Hawley. 2012. *E Pluribus . . . Separation: Deepening Double Segregation for More Students*. University of California, Los Angeles, Civil Rights Project, https://civilrightsproject.ucla.edu.

Orfield, Myron. 2015. "*Milliken, Meredith*, and Metropolitan Segregation." *University of California Los Angeles Law Review* 62: 364–462.

Ornelas v. United States, 517 U.S. 690 (1996).

Owen-Kostelnik, Jessica, N. Dickon Reppucci, and Jessica R. Meyer. 2006. "Testimony and Interrogation of Minors: Assumptions about Maturity and Morality." *American Psychologist* 61: 286–304.

Packer, Herbert L. 1968. *The Limits of the Criminal Sanction*. Stanford, CA: Stanford University Press.

Parent, Dale G., Valerie Lieter, Stephen Kennedy, Lisa Livens, Daniel Wentworth, and Sarah Wilcox. 1994. *Conditions of Confinement: Juvenile Detention and Corrections Facilities*. Washington, DC: Office of Juvenile Justice and Delinquency Prevention.

Patterson, Gerald R., and Karen Yoerger. 2002. "A Developmental Model for Early- and Late-onset Delinquency." In *Antisocial Behavior in Children and Adolescents: A Developmental Analysis and Model for Intervention*, edited by J. B. Reid, G. R. Paterson, and J. Snyder. Washington, DC: American Psychological Association

Paulsen, Monrad. 1966. "*Kent v. United States*: The Constitutional Context of Juvenile Cases." *Supreme Court Review* 1966: 167–92.

———. 1967. "The Constitutional Domestication of the Juvenile Court." *Supreme Court Review* 1967: 233–66.

Paus, Tomáš, Alex Zijdenbos, Keith Worsley, D. Louis Collins, Jonathan Blumenthal, Jay N. Giedd, Judith L. Rapoport, and Alan C. Evans. 1999. "Structural Maturation of Neural Pathways in Children and Adolescents: In Vivo Study." *Science* 283: 1908–11.

Peffley, Mark, Jon Hurwitz, and Paul Sniderman. 1997. "Racial Stereotypes and Whites' Political Views of Blacks in the Context of Welfare and Crime." *American Journal of Political Science* 41: 30–60.

People v. Caballero, 282 P.3d 291 (Cal. 2012).

People v. Carp, 852 N.W.2d 801 (Mich 2014).

People v. Chavez, 228 Cal. App. 4th, 18, 175 Cal. Rptr. 3d 334 (2014).

People v. Dilworth, 661 N.E.2d 310 (Ill. 1996).

People v. Gutierrez, 324 P.3d 245 (Cal. 2014).

People v. Pruitt, 278 Ill. App.3d 194, 214 Ill. Dec. 974, 662 N.E.2d 540 (Ill. App. 1 Dist. 1996).

Petersilia, Joan. 1981. "Juvenile Record Use in Adult Court Proceedings: A Survey of Prosecutors." *Journal of Criminal Law and Criminology* 72: 1746–71.

Phillips, Kevin P. 1969. *The Emerging Republican Majority*. New York: Arlington House.

Pickett, Robert. 1969. *Houses of Refuge: Origins of Juvenile Reform in New York State, 1815–1857*. Syracuse, NY: Syracuse University Press.

Pinard, Michael. 2003. "From the Classroom to the Courtroom: Reassessing Fourth Amendment Standards in Public School Searches Involving Law Enforcement Authorities." *Arizona Law Review* 45: 1067–124.

Piquero, Alex R. 2008. "Disproportionate Minority Contact." *Future of Children* 18: 59–79.

Piquero, Alex R., J. David Hawkins, and Lila Kazemian. 2012. "Criminal Career Patterns." In *From Juvenile Delinquency to Adult Crime: Criminal Careers, Justice Policy, and Prevention*, edited by Rolf Loeber and David P. Farrington, 14–46. New York: Oxford University Press.

Platt, Anthony. 1977. *The Child Savers: The Invention of Delinquency*. 2nd ed. Chicago: University of Chicago Press.

Plessy v. Ferguson, 163 U.S. 537 (1896).

Podkopacz, Marcy Rasmussen, and Barry C. Feld. 1995. "Judicial Waiver Policy and Practice: Persistence, Seriousness and Race." *Law and Inequality Journal* 14: 73–178.

———. 1996. "The End of the Line: An Empirical Study of Judicial Waiver." *Journal of Criminal Law and Criminology* 86: 449–92.

———. 2001. "The Back-Door to Prison: Waiver Reform, 'Blended Sentencing,' and the Law of Unintended Consequences." *Journal of Criminal Law and Criminology* 91: 997–1071.

Poe-Yamagata, Eileen, and Michael A. Jones. 2000. *And Justice for Some: Differential Treatment of Minority Youth in the Justice System.* Washington, DC: Youth Law Center.

———. 2007. *And Justice for Some.* National Council on Crime and Delinquency, www.nccdglobal.org.

Postman, Neil. 1994. *The Disappearance of Childhood.* New York: Vintage Books.

Poulin, Anne Bowen. 1996. "Female Delinquents: Defining Their Place in the Justice System." *Wisconsin Law Review* 1996: 541–75.

Poulos, Tammy Meredith, and Stan Orchowsky. 1994. "Serious Juvenile Offenders: Predicting the Probability of Transfer to Criminal Court." *Crime and Delinquency* 40: 3–17.

Pound, Roscoe. 1937. Forward to Pauline V. Young, *Social Treatment in Probation and Delinquency.* New York: McGraw Hill.

Powe, Lucas A., Jr. 2000. *The Warren Court and American Politics.* Cambridge, MA: Harvard University Press.

Powell v. Alabama, 287 U.S. 42 (1932).

President's Commission on Law Enforcement and Administration of Justice. 1967a. *The Challenge of Crime in a Free Society.* Washington, DC: U.S. Government Printing Office.

———. 1967b. *Task Force Report: Juvenile Delinquency and Youth Crime.* Washington, DC: U.S. Government Printing Office.

Prison Litigation Reform Act (PLRA). 18 U.S.C.A. §3626 (1999).

Puritz, Patricia, and Kim Brooks. 2002. *Kentucky—Advancing Justice: An Assessment of Access to Counsel and Quality of Representation in Delinquency Proceedings.* Washington, DC: American Bar Association Juvenile Justice Center.

Puritz, Patricia, Mary Ann Scali, and Ilona Picou. 2002. *Virginia: An Assessment of Access to Counsel and Quality of Representation in Delinquency Proceedings.* Washington, DC: American Bar Association Juvenile Justice Center.

Puritz, Patricia, and Wendy Shang. 2000. "Juvenile Indigent Defense: Crisis and Solutions." *Criminal Justice* 15: 22–28.

Putnam, Robert. 2015. *Our Kids: The American Dream in Crisis.* New York: Simon & Schuster.

R. v. D.B., [2008] S.C.C. 25 (Supreme Court of Canada).

Rainville, G. A., and Steven K. Smith. 2003. "Juvenile Felony Defendants in Criminal Courts." Washington, DC: Bureau of Justice Statistics, Office of Justice Programs, U.S. Department of Justice.

Rainwater, Lee, and Timothy M Smeeding. 2005. *Poor Kids in a Rich Country: America's Children in Comparative Perspective.* New York: Russell Sage.

Reba, Stephen M., Randee J. Waldman, and Barbara Bennett Woodhouse. 2011. "'I Want to Talk to My Mom': The Role of Parents in Police Interrogation of Juveniles."

In *Justice for Kids: Keeping Kids out of the Juvenile Justice System*, edited by Nancy E. Dowd, 219–38. New York: New York University Press.

Redding, Richard E. 2008. *Juvenile Transfer Laws: An Effective Deterrent to Delinquency?* Washington, DC: Office of Juvenile Justice and Delinquency Prevention.

Redding, Richard E., and Lynda E. Frost. 2001. "Adjudicative Competence in the Modern Juvenile Court." *Virginia Journal of Social Policy and the Law* 9: 353–409.

Redding, Richard E., and James C. Howell. 2000. "Blended Sentencing in American Juvenile Justice." In *The Changing Borders of Juvenile Justice: Transfer of Adolescents to the Criminal Court*, edited by Jeffrey Fagan and Franklin Zimring, 145–80. Chicago: University of Chicago Press.

Redding, Richard E., and Sarah M. Shalf. 2001. "The Legal Context of School Violence: The Effectiveness of Federal, State, and Local Law Enforcement Efforts to Reduce Gun Violence in Schools." *Law and Policy* 23: 297–343.

Redlich, Allison D., and Steven Drizin. 2007. "Police Interrogation of Youth." In *The Mental Health Needs of Young Offenders: Forging Paths toward Reintegration and Rehabilitation*, edited by Carol L. Kessler and Louis J. Kraus, 61–78. Cambridge, MA: Cambridge University Press.

Redlich, Allison D., Melissa Silverman, Julie Chen, and Hans Steiner. 2004. "The Police Interrogation of Children and Adolescents." In *Interrogations, Confessions, and Entrapment*, edited by G. Daniel Lassiter, 107–26. New York: Kluwer Academic.

Redlich, Allison, Melissa Silverman, and Hans Steiner. 2003. "Pre-Adjudicative and Adjudicative Competence in Juveniles and Young Adults." *Behavioral Sciences and the Law* 21: 393–410.

Rice v. Cooper, 148 F.3d 747 (7th Cir. 1998).

R.L.R. v. State, 487 P.2d 27 (Alaska 1971).

Roberts, Julian V. 1996. "The Role of Criminal Records in the Sentencing Process." *Crime and Justice: A Review of Research* 22: 303–62.

Rodriguez, Nancy. 2010. "The Cumulative Effect of Race and Ethnicity in Juvenile Court Outcomes and Why Pre-Adjudication Detention Matters." *Journal of Research in Crime and Delinquency* 47: 391–413.

Rogers, Richard. 2008. "A Little Knowledge Is a Dangerous Thing . . . Emerging Miranda Research and Professional Roles for Psychologists." *American Psychologist* 63: 776–87.

Rogers, Richard, Kimberly S. Harrison, Daniel W. Schuman, Kenneth W. Sewell, and Lisa L. Hazelwood. 2007. "An Analysis of Miranda Warnings and Waivers: Comprehension and Coverage." *Law and Human Behavior* 31: 177–92.

Rogers, Richard, Lisa L. Hazelwood, Kenneth W. Sewell, Kimberly S. Harrison, and Daniel W. Schuman. [Rogers et al.] 2008a. "The Language of Miranda Warnings in American Jurisdictions: A Replication and Vocabulary Analysis." *Law and Human Behavior* 32: 124–36.

Rogers, Richard, Lisa L. Hazelwood, Kenneth W. Sewell, Daniel W. Schuman, and Hayley L. Blackwood. [Rogers et al.] 2008b. "The Comprehensibility and Content of Juvenile Miranda Warnings." *Psychology, Public Policy and the Law* 14: 63–87.

Roper v. Simmons, 543 U.S. 551 (2005).

Rosenberg, Irene M. 1980. "The Constitutional Rights of Children Charged with Crime: Proposal for a Return to the Not So Distant Past." *University of California at Los Angeles Law Review* 27:656–721.

Rossow, Lawrence F., and Jacqueline A. Stefkovich. 1995. *Search and Seizure in the Public Schools.* 2nd ed. Cleveland: Educational Law Association.

Rothman, David J. 1980. *Conscience and Convenience: The Asylum and Its Alternative in Progressive America.* Boston: Little, Brown.

Roush, David W., Michelle Brazeal, and Wesley T. Church II. 2014. "Juvenile Detention." In *Juvenile Justice Sourcebook.* 2nd ed., edited by Wesley T. Church II, David W. Springer, and Albert R. Roberts, 193–214. New York: Oxford University Press.

Rummel v. Estelle, 445 U.S. 263 (1980).

Ryerson, Ellen. 1978. *The Best-Laid Plans: America's Juvenile Court Experiment.* New York: Hill and Wang.

Safford Unified School District #1 v. Redding, 129 S. Ct. 2633 (2009).

Saks, Michael J. 1997. "What Do Jury Experiments Tell Us about How Juries (Should) Make Decisions?" *Southern California Interdisciplinary Law Journal* 6: 1–53.

Sampson, Robert J., and John H. Laub. 1993. *Crime in the Making: Pathways and Turning Points through Life.* Cambridge, MA: Harvard University Press.

Sampson, Robert J., and Janet L. Lauritsen. 1997. "Racial and Ethnic Disparities in Crime and Criminal Justice in the United States." *Crime and Justice: A Review of Research* 21: 311–74.

Sampson, Robert J., and William Julius Wilson. 1995. "Toward a Theory of Race, Crime, and Urban Inequality." In *Crime and Inequality*, edited by John Hagan and Ruth D. Peterson, 37–54. Stanford, CA: Stanford University Press.

Sanborn, Joseph B., Jr. 1992. "Pleading Guilty in Juvenile Court: Minimal Ado about Something Very Important to Young Defendants." *Justice Quarterly* 9: 127–49.

———. 1993a. "The Right to a Public Jury Trial: A Need for Today's Juvenile Court." *Judicature* 76: 230–38.

———. 1993b. "Philosophical, Legal and Systemic Aspects of Juvenile Court Plea Bargaining." *Crime and Delinquency* 39: 509–27.

———. 1998. "Second-Class Justice, First-Class Punishment: The Use of Juvenile Records in Sentencing Adults." *Judicature* 81: 206–13.

———. 2009. "Juveniles' Competency to Stand Trial: Wading through the Rhetoric and the Evidence." *Journal of Criminal Law and Criminology* 99: 135–213.

Sanders, Jerry. 2005. "How to Defuse 'Girl on Girl' Violence." *Christian Science Monitor*, June 23, www.csmonitor.com.

Santana v. Collazo, 714 F.2d 1172 (1st Cir. 1983).

Scelfo, Julie. 2005. "Bad Girls Go Wild." *Newsweek*, June 12, www.newsweek.com.

Schaffner, Laurie. 1998. "Female Juvenile Delinquency: Sexual Solutions, Gender Bias, and Juvenile Justice." *Hastings Women's Law Journal* 9: 1–25.

Schall v. Martin, 467 U.S. 253 (1984).

Schiraldi, Vincent, and Jason Ziedenberg. 2000. "The Florida Experiment: Transferring Power from Judges to Prosecutors." *Criminal Justice* 15: 46–58.

Schlossman, Steven. 1977. *Love and the American Delinquent: The Theory and Practice of "Progressive" Juvenile Justice*. Chicago: University of Chicago Press.

Schlossman, Steven, and Stephanie Wallach. 1978. "The Crime of Precocious Sexuality: Female Juvenile Delinquency in the Progressive Era." *Harvard Educational Review* 48: 65–94.

Schneider, Anne L. 1984. "Deinstitutionalization of Status Offenders: The Impact on Recidivism and Secure Confinement." *Criminal Justice Abstracts* 16: 410–32.

Schubert, Carol A., Edward P. Mulvey, Thomas A. Loughran, Jeffrey Fagan, Laurie A. Chassin, Alex R. Piquero, Sandra H. Losoya, Laurence Steinberg, and Elizabeth Cauffman. 2010. "Predicting Outcomes for Youth Transferred to Adult Court." *Law and Human Behavior* 34: 460–75.

Scott, Elizabeth S. 1992. "Judgment and Reasoning in Adolescent Decisionmaking." *Villanova Law Review* 37: 1607–69.

———. 2000. "The Legal Construction of Adolescence." *Hofstra Law Review* 29: 547–98.

Scott, Elizabeth S., and Thomas Grisso. 1997. "The Evolution of Adolescence: A Developmental Perspective on Juvenile Justice Reform." *Journal of Criminal Law and Criminology* 88: 137–89.

———. 2005. "Developmental Incompetence, Due Process, and Juvenile Justice Policy." *North Carolina Law Review* 83: 793–846.

Scott, Elizabeth S., Thomas Grisso, Marsha Levick, and Laurence Steinberg. 2015. *The Supreme Court and the Transformation of Juvenile Sentencing*. New York: Columbia University Press.

Scott, Elizabeth S., N. Dickon Reppucci, and Jennifer L. Woolard. 1995. "Evaluating Adolescent Decision Making in Legal Contexts." *Law and Human Behavior* 19: 221–44.

Scott, Elizabeth S., and Laurence Steinberg. 2003. "Blaming Youth." *Texas Law Review* 81: 799–840.

———. 2008. *Rethinking Juvenile Justice*. Cambridge, MA: Harvard University Press.

Schwartz, Ira M. 1989. *(In) Justice for Juveniles: Rethinking the Best Interests of the Child*. Lexington, MA: Lexington Books.

Schwartz, Ira M., Martha W. Steketee, and Victoria W. Schneider. 1990. "Federal Juvenile Justice Policy and the Incarceration of Girls." *Crime and Delinquency* 36: 503–20.

Schwartz, Ira M., Neil Alan Weiner, and Guy Enosh. 1998. "Nine Lives and Then Some: Why the Juvenile Court Does Not Roll Over and Die." *Wake Forest Law Review* 33: 533–52.

Scott v. Illinois, 440 U.S. 367 (1979).

Sentencing Project. 2014. *Slow to Act: State Responses to 2012 Supreme Court Mandate on Life without Parole*. www.sentencingproject.org.

Sheffer, Julianne P. 1995. "Serious and Habitual Juvenile Offender Statutes: Reconciling Punishment and Rehabilitation within the Juvenile Justice System." *Vanderbilt Law Review* 48: 479–512.

Sherman, Lawrence W., and Richard A. Berk. 1984. "The Specific Deterrent Effects of Arrest for Domestic Assault." *American Sociological Review* 49(2): 261–72.

Sickmund, Melissa, and Charles Puzzanchera. 2014. *Juvenile Offenders and Victims: 2014 National Report.* Office of Juvenile Justice and Delinquency Prevention, www.ojjdp.gov.

Sickmund, Melissa, T. J. Sladky, Wei Kang, and Charles Puzzanchera. 2015. *Easy Access to the Census of Juveniles in Residential Placement.* Office of Juvenile Justice and Delinquency Prevention, www.ojjdp.ncjrs.org.

Sickmund, Melissa, A. Sladky, and W. Kang. 2014. *Easy Access to Juvenile Court Statistics: 1985–2011.* Office of Juvenile Justice and Delinquency Prevention, www.ojjdp.gov.

Simon, Jonathan. 2007. *Governing through Crime: How the War on Crime Transformed American Democracy and Created a Culture of Fear.* New York: Oxford University Press.

Singer, Simon I., and David McDowall. 1988. "Criminalizing Delinquency: The Deterrent Effects of the New York Juvenile Offender Law." *Law and Society Review* 22: 521–35.

Singleton, Lacey Cole. 2007. "Say 'Pleas': Juveniles' Competence to Enter Plea Agreements." *Journal of Law and Family Studies* 9: 439–55.

Skiba, Russell J., Robert S. Michael, Abra Carroll Nardo, and Reece L. Peterson. 2002. "The Color of Discipline: Sources of Racial and Gender Disproportionality in School Punishment." *Urban Review* 34: 317–42.

Skiba, Russell, et al. 2006. "Are Zero Tolerance Policies Effective in the Schools? An Evidentiary Review and Recommendations." Zero Tolerance Task Force, American Psychological Association, www.apa.org.

Slobogin, Christopher. 2007. "Lying and Confessing." *Texas Tech Law Review* 39: 1275–92.

Smith v. Daily Mail Publishing Co., 443 U.S. 97 (1978).

Smith v. Doe, 538 U.S. 84 (2003).

Smith v. State, 444 S.W.2d 941 (Tex. Ct. Civ. App. 1969).

Smook v. Minnehaha County Juvenile Detention Center, 457 F.3d 806 (8th Cir. 2006).

Snyder, Howard N. 2012. "Juvenile Delinquents and Juvenile Justice Clientele: Trends and Patterns in Crime and Justice System Responses." In *Oxford Handbook of Juvenile Crime and Juvenile Justice*, edited by Barry C. Feld and Donna M. Bishop, 3–30. New York: Oxford University Press.

Snyder, Howard N., and Melissa Sickmund. 1995. *Juvenile Offenders and Victims: A National Report.* Washington, DC: Office of Juvenile Justice and Delinquency Prevention.

———. 1999. *Juvenile Offenders and Victims: A National Report.* Washington, DC: Office of Juvenile Justice and Delinquency Prevention.

———. 2006. *Juvenile Offenders and Victims: A National Report.* Washington, DC: Office of Juvenile Justice and Delinquency Prevention.

Solem v. Helms, 463 U.S. 277 (1983).

Sowell, Elizabeth R., Paul M. Thompson, Colin J. Holmes, Terry L. Jernigan, and Arthur W. Toga. 1999. "In Vivo Evidence for Post-Adolescent Brain Maturation in Frontal and Striatal Regions." *Nature Neuroscience* 2: 859–61.

Sowell, Elizabeth R., Paul M. Thompson, Kevin D. Tessner and Arthur W. Toga. 2001. "Mapping Continued Brain Growth and Gray Matter Density Reduction in Dorsal Frontal Cortex: Inverse Relationships during Postadolescent Brain Maturation." *Journal of Neuroscience* 21: 8819–29.

Sowell, Elizabeth R., Doris A Trauner, Anthony Gamst, and Terry L Jernigan. 2002. "Development of Cortical and Subcortical Brain Structures in Childhood and Adolescence." *Developmental Medicine and Child Neurology* 44: 4–16.

Spear, L. P. 2000. "The Adolescent Brain and Age-Related Behavioral Manifestations." *Neuroscience and Biobehavioral Reviews* 24: 417–63.

———. 2010. *The Behavioral Neuroscience of Adolescence*. New York: W. W. Norton & Co.

Sridharan, Sanjeev, Lynette Greenfield, and Baron Blakley. 2004. "A Study of Prosecutorial Certification Practice in Virginia." *Criminology and Public Policy* 4: 605–32.

Stanford v. Kentucky, 492 U.S. 361 (1989).

Stapleton, W. Vaughan, and Lee E. Teitelbaum. 1972. *In Defense of Youth: A Study of the Role of Counsel in American Juvenile Courts*. New York: Russell Sage.

State ex rel. D.D.H. v. Dostert, 269 S.E.2d 401 (W. Va. 1980).

State v. Best, 987 A.2d 605 (N.J. 2010).

State v. Brown, 879 So.2d 1276 (La. 2004).

State v. Hezzie R., 580 N.W.2d 660 (Wis. 1998).

State v. Hitt, 42 P.3d 723 (Kan. 2002).

State v. Lawley, 91 Wash. 2d 654, 591 P.2d 772 (1979).

State v. Lyle, 854 N.W.2d 378 (Iowa 2014).

State v. Null, 836 N.W.2d 41(Iowa 2013).

State v. Presha, 163 N.J. 304, 748 A.2d 1108 (N.J. 2000).

State v. Ragland, 836 N.W.2d 107 (Iowa 2013).

State v. Sweet, 879 N.W.2d 811 (Iowa 2016).

State Plans, 42 U.S.C. §5633(a)(16) (2000).

Steffensmeier, Darrell. 1993. "National Trends in Female Arrests, 1960–1990: Assessment and Recommendations for Research." *Journal of Quantitative Criminology* 9: 411–41.

Steffensmeier, Darrell, Jennifer Schwartz, Sara Hua Zhong, and Jeffery Ackerman. 2005. "An Assessment of Recent Trends in Girls' Violence Using Diverse Longitudinal Sources: Is the Gender Gap Closing?" *Criminology* 43: 355–405.

Steinberg, Laurence. 2008. "A Social Neuroscience Perspective on Adolescent Risk-Taking." *Developmental Review* 28: 78–106.

———. 2010. "A Dual Systems Model of Adolescent Risk-Taking." *Developmental Psychobiology* 52: 216–24.

———. 2014. *Age of Opportunity: Lessons from the New Science of Adolescence*. New York: Houghton Mifflin Harcourt.

Steinberg, Laurence, Dustin Albert, Elizabeth Cauffman, Marie Banich, Sandra Graham, and Jennifer Woolard. 2008. "Age Differences in Sensation Seeking and Impulsivity as Indexed by Behavior and Self-Report: Evidence for a Dual Systems Model." *Developmental Psychology* 44: 1764–78.

Steinberg, Laurence, and Elizabeth Cauffman. 1996. "Maturity of Judgment in Adolescence: Psychosocial Factors in Adolescent Decision Making." *Law and Human Behavior* 20: 249–72.

———.1999. "The Elephant in the Courtroom: A Developmental Perspective on the Adjudication of Youthful Offenders." *Virginia Journal of Social Policy and Law* 6: 389–417.

Steinberg, Laurence, and Kathryn C. Monahan. 2007. "Age Differences in Resistance to Peer Influence." *Developmental Psychology* 43: 1531–43.

Steiner, Benjamin. 2005. "Predicting Sentencing Outcomes and Time Served for Juveniles Transferred to Criminal Court in a Rural Northwestern State." *Journal of Criminal Justice* 33: 601–10.

———. 2009. "The Effects of Juvenile Transfer to Criminal Court on Incarceration Decisions." *Justice Quarterly* 26: 77–106.

Steiner, Benjamin, Craig Hemmens, and Valerie Bell. 2006. "Legislative Waiver Reconsidered: General Deterrent Effects of Statutory Exclusion Laws Enacted Post 1979." *Justice Quarterly* 23: 34–59.

Steiner, Benjamin, and Emily Wright. 2006. "Assessing the Relative Effects of State Direct File Waiver Laws on Violent Juvenile Crime: Deterrence or Irrelevance?" *Journal of Criminal Law and Criminology* 96: 1451–77.

Stinneford, John F. 2011. "Rethinking Proportionality under the Cruel and Unusual Punishment Clause." *Virginia Law Review* 97: 899–978.

Streib, Victor L., and Bernadette Schremp. 2007. "Life without Parole for Children." *Criminal Justice* 21: 4–12.

Strom, Kevin J., Tara D. Warner, Lisa Tichavsky, and Margaret A. Zahn. 2014. "Policing Juveniles: Domestic Violence Arrest Policies, Gender, and Police Response to Child-Parent Violence." *Crime and Delinquency* 60: 427–50.

Sullivan, E. Thomas, and Richard S. Frase. 2009. *Proportionality Principles in American Law: Controlling Excessive Government Actions.* New York: Oxford University Press.

Sumner v. Shuman, 483 U.S. 66 (1987).

Sutton, John R. 1988. *Stubborn Children: Controlling Delinquency in the United States.* Berkeley: University of California Press.

Sweeten, Gary, Shawn D. Bushway, and Raymond Paternoster. 2009. "Does Dropping out of School Mean Dropping into Delinquency?" *Criminology* 47: 47–88.

Tanenhaus, David S. 2000. "The Evolution of Transfer out of the Juvenile Court." In *The Changing Borders of Juvenile Justice: Transfer of Adolescents to the Criminal Court,* edited by Jeffrey Fagan and Franklin Zimring, 13–44. Chicago: University of Chicago Press.

———. 2004. *Juvenile Justice in the Making.* New York: Oxford University Press.

————. 2011. *The Constitutional Rights of Children:* In re Gault *and Juvenile Justice.* Lawrence: University of Kansas Press.

————. 2012. "The Elusive Juvenile Court: Its Origins, Practices, and Re-Inventions." In *Oxford Handbook of Juvenile Crime and Juvenile Justice,* edited by Barry C. Feld and Donna M. Bishop, 419–44. New York: Oxford University Press.

Tanenhaus, David S., and Steven A. Drizin. 2003. "Owing to the Extreme Youth of the Accused: The Changing Legal Response to Juvenile Homicide." *Journal of Criminal Law and Criminology* 92: 641–705.

Tappan, Paul W. 1946. "Treatment without Trial." *Social Forces* 24: 306–11.

Tate v. State, 864 So. 2d 44 (Fla. Dist. Ct. App. 2003).

Taylor-Thompson, Kim. 2003. "States of Mind/States of Development." *Stanford Law and Policy Review* 14: 143–73.

Tepfer, Joshua A., Laura H. Nirider, and Lynda M. Tricarico. 2010. "Arresting Development: Convictions of Innocent Youth." *Rutgers Law Review* 62: 887–941.

Terry v. Ohio, 392 U.S. 1 (1968).

Theriot, Matthew T. 2009. "School Resource Officers and the Criminalization of Student Behavior." *Journal of Criminal Justice* 37: 280–87.

Thompson v. Oklahoma, 487 U.S. 815 (1988).

Tiffin, Susan. 1983. *In Whose Best Interest? Child Welfare Reform in the Progressive Era.* Westport, CT: Greenwood Press.

Tinker v. Des Moines Sch. Dist., 393 U.S. 503 (1969).

T.L.O. v. New Jersey, 469 U.S. 325 (1985).

Tonry, Michael. 1995. *Malign Neglect: Race, Crime, and Punishment in America.* New York: Oxford University Press.

————. 1996. *Sentencing Matters.* New York: Oxford University Press.

————. 2004. *Thinking about Crime: Sense and Sensibility in American Penal Culture.* New York: Oxford University Press.

————. 2011. *Punishing Race: A Continuing American Dilemma.* New York: Oxford University Press.

Torbet, Patricia, Richard Gable, Hunter Hurst IV, Imogene Montgomery, Linda Szymanski, and Douglas Thomas. 1996. *State Responses to Serious and Violent Juvenile Crime: Research Report.* Washington, DC: Office of Juvenile Justice and Delinquency Prevention, National Center for Juvenile Justice.

Tracy, Paul E., Marvin E. Wolfgang, and Robert M. Figlio. 1990. *Delinquency Careers in Two Birth Cohorts.* New York: Plenum.

Trattner, Walter. 1970. *Crusade for the Children: A History of the National Child Labor Committee and Child Labor Reform in New York State.* Chicago: Quadrangle Books.

————. 1984. *From Poor Law to Welfare State: A History of Social Welfare in America.* 3rd ed. Westport, CT: Greenwood.

Twentieth Century Fund Task Force. 1976. *Fair and Certain Punishment.* New York: McGraw-Hill.

Twentieth Century Fund Task Force on Sentencing Policy toward Young Offenders. 1978. *Confronting Youth Crime.* New York: Holmes & Meier.

Tyack, David B. 1974. *The One Best System*. Cambridge, MA: Harvard University Press.

United States v. Bland, 472 F.2d 1329 (D.C. Cir. 1972), cert. denied, 412 U.S. 909 (1972).

United States v. Carolene Products, 304 U.S. 144 (1938).

United States v. Cortez, 449 U.S. 411 (1981).

United States v. Davis, 48 F.3d 277 (7th Cir. 1995).

United States v. Johnson, 28 F.3d 151 (D.C. Cir. 1994).

United States v. McDonald, 991 F.2d 866 (D.C. Cir. 1993).

United States v. Smalley, 294 F.2d 1030 (8th Cir. 2002).

United States v. Sokolow, 490 U.S. 1 (1989).

United States v. Tighe, 256 F.3d 1187 (9th Cir. 2001).

United States v. Williams, 891 F.2d 212 (9th Cir. 1989).

U.S. General Accounting Office. 1991. *Noncriminal Juveniles: Detentions Have Been Reduced but Better Monitoring Is Needed*. Washington, DC: U.S. General Accounting Office.

——. 1995a. *Juvenile Justice: Juveniles Processed in Criminal Court and Case Dispositions*. Washington, DC: U.S. General Accounting Office.

——. 1995b. *Juvenile Justice: Representation Rates Varied as Did Counsel's Impact on Court Outcomes*. Washington, DC: U.S. General Accounting Office.

Valentino, Nicholas A. 1999. "Crime News and the Priming of Racial Attitudes during Evaluation of the President." *Public Opinion Quarterly* 63: 293–320.

Viljoen, Jodi L., and Thomas Grisso. 2007. "Prospects for Remediating Juveniles' Adjudicative Incompetence." *Psychology, Public Policy, and Law* 13: 87–114.

Viljoen, Jodi, Jessica Klaver, and Ronald Roesch. 2005. "Legal Decisions of Preadolescent and Adolescent Defendants: Predictors of Confessions, Pleas, Communication with Attorneys, and Appeals." *Law and Human Behavior* 29: 253–78.

Viljoen, Jodi, Erika Penner, and Ronald Roesch. 2012. "Competence and Criminal Responsibility in Adolescent Defendants: The Roles of Mental Illness and Adolescent Development." In *Oxford Handbook of Juvenile Crime and Juvenile Justice*, edited by Barry C. Feld and Donna M. Bishop, 526–48. New York: Oxford University Press.

Viljoen, Jodi, and Ronald Roesch. 2005. "Competence to Waive Interrogation Rights and Adjudicative Competence in Adolescent Defendants: Cognitive Development, Attorney Contact, and Psychological Symptoms." *Law and Human Behavior* 29: 723–42.

Viljoen, Jodi, Patricia Zapf, and Ronald Roesch. 2007. "Adjudicative Competence and Comprehension of Miranda Rights in Adolescent Defendants: A Comparison of Legal Standards." *Behavioral Sciences and the Law* 25: 1–19.

von Hirsch, Andrew. 1976. *Doing Justice*. New York: Hill and Wang.

——. 1985. *Past vs. Future Crimes*. New Brunswick, NJ: Rutgers University Press.

——. 2001. "Proportionate Sentences for Juveniles: How Different than for Adults?" *Punishment and Society* 3: 221–36.

Wacquant, Loïc. 2001. "Deadly Symbiosis: When Ghetto and Prison Meet and Mesh." *Punishment and Society* 3: 95–133.

———. 2008. "Commentary." In *Race, Incarceration, and American Values*, edited by Glen Loury, with Pamela S. Karlan, Tommie Shelby, and Loïc Wacquant, 57–72. Cambridge, MA: MIT Press.

Wald, Johanna, and Daniel F. Losen. 2003. "Defining and Redirecting a School-to-Prison Pipeline." In *Deconstructing the School-to-Prison Pipeline: New Directions for Youth Development*, edited by Johanna Wald and Daniel F. Losen, 9–16. Cambridge, MA: Wiley Periodicals.

Wald, Johanna, and Lisa Thurau. 2001. *First, Do No Harm: How Educators and Police Can Work Together More Effectively to Preserve School Safety and Protect Vulnerable Students*. Policy Brief. Cambridge, MA: Institute for Race and Justice, Harvard University.

Walkover, Andrew. 1984. "The Infancy Defense in the New Juvenile Court." *University California Los Angeles Law Review* 31: 503–62.

Ward, Geoff K. 2009. "The 'Other' Child Savers: Racial Politics of the Parental State." In *The Child Savers: The Invention of Delinquency*, edited by Anthony M. Platt, 225–41. New Brunswick NJ: Rutgers University Press.

———. 2012. *The Black Child-Savers: Racial Democracy and Juvenile Justice*. Chicago: University of Chicago Press.

Weaver, Cynthia, Edward Byrnes, and Wesley T. Church II. 2014. "Mental Health and Youth in the Juvenile Justice System: Current States and Evidence-Informed Future Directions." In *Juvenile Justice Sourcebook*. 2nd ed., edited by Wesley T. Church II, David W. Springer, and Albert R. Roberts, 413–38. New York: Oxford University Press.

Weisselberg, Charles D. 2008. "Mourning Miranda." *California Law Review* 96: 1519–601.

Weissman, James C. 1983. "Toward an Integrated Theory of Delinquency Responsibility." *Denver Law Journal* 60: 485–518.

Weithorn, Lois A. 1988. "Mental Hospitalization of Troublesome Youth: An Analysis of Skyrocketing Admission Rates." *Stanford Law Review* 49: 773–838.

Welsh, Brandon C. 2012. "Delinquency Prevention." In *Oxford Handbook of Juvenile Crime and Juvenile Justice*, edited by Barry C. Feld and Donna M. Bishop, 395–418. New York: Oxford University Press.

Welsh, Brandon C., Mark W. Lipsey, Frederick P. Rivara, J. David Hawkins, Steve Aos, and Meghan E. Hollis-Peel. 2012. "Promoting Change, Changing Lives: Effective Prevention and Intervention to Reduce Serious Offending." In *From Juvenile Delinquency to Adult Crime: Criminal Careers, Justice Policy, and Prevention*, edited by Rolf Loeber and David P. Farrington, 245–77. New York: Oxford University Press.

West Virginia State Board of Education v. Barnette, 319 U.S. 624 (1943).

Western, Bruce. 2006. *Punishment and Inequality in America*. New York: Russell Sage Foundation.

White, Henry George, Charles E. Frazier, Lonn Lanza-Kaduce, and Donna M. Bishop. 1999. "A Socio-Legal History of Florida's Transfer Reforms." *University of Florida Journal of Law and Public Policy* 10: 249–76.

Wiebe, Robert H. 1967. *The Search for Order, 1877–1920*. New York: Hill and Wang.

Wilkerson, Isabel. 2010. *The Warmth of Other Suns: The Epic Story of America's Great Migration*. New York: Vintage Books.

Wilson, James Q. 1975. *Thinking About Crime*. New York: Basic Books.

Wilson, James Q., and George L. Kelling. 1982. "Broken Windows." *Atlantic Monthly*, March, 29–38.

Wilson, John J., and James C. Howell. 1995. "Comprehensive Strategy for Serious, Violent, and Chronic Juvenile Offenders." In *Serious, Violent and Chronic Juvenile Offenders*, edited by James C. Howell, Barrry Krisberg, J. David Hawkins, and John J. Wilson, 36–46. Thousand Oaks, CA: Sage Publications.

Wilson, William J. 1987. *The Truly Disadvantaged*. Chicago: University of Chicago Press.

———. 1996. *When Work Disappears: The World of the New Urban Poor*. New York: Alfred A. Knopf.

———. 2009. *More than Just Race: Being Black and Poor in the Inner City*. New York: W. W. Norton & Co.

Winner, Lawrence, Lonn Lanza-Kaduce, Donna M. Bishop, and Charles E. Frazier. 1997. "The Transfer of Juveniles to Criminal Court: Reexamining Recidivism over the Long Term." *Crime and Delinquency* 43: 548–63.

Wolcott, David B. 2005. *Cops and Kids: Policing Juvenile Delinquency in Urban America, 1890–1940*. Columbus: Ohio State University Press.

Wolfgang, Marvin, Robert Figlio, and Thorsten Sellin. 1972. *Delinquency in a Birth Cohort*. Chicago: University of Chicago Press.

Woodson v. North Carolina, 428 U.S. 280 (1976).

Woolard, Jennifer L. 2012. "Adolescent Development, Delinquency, and Juvenile Justice." In *The Oxford Handbook of Juvenile Crime and Juvenile Justice*, edited by Barry C. Feld and Donna M. Bishop, 107–22. New York: Oxford University Press.

Woolard, Jennifer L., Hayley M. D. Cleary, Samantha A. S. Harvell, and Rusan Chen. 2008. "Examining Adolescents' and Their Parents' Conceptual and Practical Knowledge of Police Interrogation: A Family Dyad Approach." *Journal Youth Adolescence* 37: 685–98.

Yarborough v. Alvarado, 541 U.S. 652 (2004).

Youngberg v. Romeo, 457 U.S. 307 (1982).

Zane, Dale. 1987. "School Searches under the Fourth Amendment: *New Jersey v. T.L.O.*" *Cornell Law Review* 72: 368–96.

Zimring, Franklin E. 1978. "Background Paper." In *Confronting Youth Crime: Report of the Twentieth-Century Fund Task Force on Sentencing Policy toward Young Offenders*, edited by Franklin E. Zimring, 31–104. New York: Holmes and Meier.

———. 1981a. "Notes toward a Jurisprudence of Waiver." In *Major Issues in Juvenile Justice Information and Training: Readings in Public Policy*, edited by John C. Hall, Donna Martin Hamparian, John M. Pettibone, and Joseph L. White, 193–206. Columbus, OH: Academy for Contemporary Problems.

———. 1981b. "Kids, Groups and Crime: Some Implications of a Well-Known Secret." *Journal of Criminal Law and Criminology* 72: 867–902.

———. 1996. "Kids, Guns, and Homicide: Policy Notes on an Age-Specific Epidemic." *Law and Contemporary Problems* 59: 25–37.

———. 1998. *American Youth Violence*. New York: Oxford University Press.

———. 2000a. "The Common Thread: Diversion in Juvenile Justice." *California Law Review* 88: 2477–95.

———. 2000b. "The Punitive Necessity of Waiver." In *The Changing Borders of Juvenile Justice*, edited by Franklin E. Zimring and Jeffrey Fagan, 207–26. Chicago: University of Chicago Press.

———. 2000c. "Penal Proportionality for the Young Offender: Notes on Immaturity, Capacity, and Diminished Responsibility." In *Youth on Trial: A Developmental Perspective on Juvenile Justice*, edited by Thomas Grisso and Robert Schwartz, 271–90. Chicago: University of Chicago Press.

———. 2002. "The Common Thread: Diversion in the Jurisprudence of Juvenile Courts," in *A Century of Juvenile Justice*, edited by Margaret K. Rosenheim, Franklin E. Zimring, David S. Tanenhaus, and Bernardine Dohrn, 142–57. Chicago: University of Chicago Press.

———. 2004. *An American Travesty: Legal Responses to Adolescent Sexual Offending.* Chicago: University of Chicago Press.

———. 2007. *The Great American Crime Decline*. New York: Oxford University Press.

———. 2013. "American Youth Violence: A Cautionary Tale." *Crime and Justice* 42: 265–98.

———. 2014. "Minority Overrepresentation: On Causes and Partial Cures." In *Choosing the Future for American Juvenile Justice*, edited by Franklin E. Zimring and David S. Tanenhaus, 169–86. New York: New York University Press.

Zimring, Franklin E., and Jeffrey Fagan. 2000. "Transfer Policy and Law Reform." In *The Changing Borders of Juvenile Justice*, edited by Franklin E. Zimring and Jeffrey Fagan, 407–24. Chicago: University of Chicago Press.

Zimring, Franklin E., and Gordon Hawkins. 1997. *Crime Is Not the Problem: Lethal Violence in America*. New York: Oxford University Press.

Zimring, Franklin E., and David S. Tanenhaus. 2014. "On Strategy and Tactics for Contemporary Reforms." In *Choosing the Future for American Juvenile Justice*, edited by Franklin E. Zimring and David S. Tanenhaus, 216–34. New York: New York University Press.

INDEX

ABOUT THE AUTHOR

Barry C. Feld is Centennial Professor of Law Emeritus at the University of Minnesota Law School. He is the author or editor of ten previous books, including *Kids, Cops, and Confessions: Inside the Interrogation Room* and *Bad Kids: Race and the Transformation of the Juvenile Court.*